Bureaucratic
Authoritarianism

Bureaucratic Authoritarianism

Argentina, 1966–1973,
in Comparative Perspective

Guillermo O'Donnell

Translated by James McGuire
in collaboration with Rae Flory

UNIVERSITY OF CALIFORNIA PRESS
Berkeley · *Los Angeles* · *London*

University of California Press
Berkeley and Los Angeles, California

University of California Press, Ltd.
London, England

© 1988 by
The Regents of the University of California

Library of Congress Cataloging-in-Publication Data

O'Donnell, Guillermo A.
  Bureaucratic authoritarianism.

  Translation of: El Estado Burocrático
Autoritario. Argentina 1966–1973
  Includes index.
  1. Argentina—Politics and government—1955–1973.
2. Authoritarianism—Argentina. I. Title.
JL2031.03513 1987   982'.063   86–25033
ISBN 0–520–04260–3 (alk. paper)

Printed in the United States of America

1 2 3 4 5 6 7 8 9

Contents

List of Tables and Figures   vii

Preface   xi

1. Theoretical and Historical Background to the Study
   of the Bureaucratic-Authoritarian State   1

2. The Implantation of the Bureaucratic-Authoritarian
   State   39

3. Paternalists, Liberals, and Economic Normalization   72

4. The Normalization Program of 1967–1969   103

5. Economic Successes and Political Problems   145

6. Crisis and Collapse   164

7. Levingston: The "Nationalization" of the
   Bureaucratic-Authoritarian State   197

8. The Garden of the Diverging Paths   227

9. Economic Crisis and Political Violence   264

10. A Curious End to a Sad Story   301

Methodological Appendix   327

Index   331

List of Tables and Figures

Tables

1. Planning According to Size of Industrial Firm   18
2. Domestic Investment (1960–1966)   42
3. Public Finances (1960–1966)   43
4. Gross Domestic Product and Private Consumption (1964–1969)   104
5. Per Capita Gross Domestic Product by Major Economic Activities (1964–1969)   105
6. Volume of Industrial Production (1965–1969)   106
7. Investment (1964–1969)   107
8. Inflation in the Cost of Living for Buenos Aires (1963–1969)   108
9. Net Foreign Exchange Reserves of the Argentine Central Bank (1966–1969)   108
10. Balance of Trade (1964–1969)   109
11. Balance of Payments: Net Capital Movements (1964–1969)   110
12. Interest Rates for the U.S. Dollar on the 30-day Futures Market (1966–1969)   111
13. Budget of the National Government (1965–1969)   112
14. Industrial Wages (1966–1969)   113
15. Nonindustrial Wages (1966–1969)   113
16. Monetary Data (1965–1969)   115
17. Withholding Tax on Exports (1966–1969)   116

18. Tax Revenues of the National Government (1964–1969)   117
19. Origins of Overall Public Investment (1966–1969)   118
20. Investment by the National Government (1965–1969)   119
21. Beef Prices (1964–1969)   121
22. Salaries of Lower-Middle Sectors (1966–1969)   122
23. Salaries of Upper-Middle Sectors (1966–1969)   123
24. Gross Profits of Major Economic Sectors (1964–1969)   124
25. Loans to Industrial Firms According to Size   126
26. Profits of Industrial Subsidiaries of U.S.-based Transnational Corporations (1966–1969)   128
27. Productivity and Exploitation Rates for Economic Sectors (1965–1969)   129
28. Value Added, Productivity, and Exploitation Rates for Subsectors of Argentine Industry and Industrial Subsidiaries of U.S.-based Transnational Corporations (1965–1969)   131
29. Poll on Current Situation, June 1968   137
30. Political Opinions in Argentina, 1971   254
31. Industrial Wages (1966–1972)   265
32. Nonindustrial Wages (1966–1972)   266
33. Salaries of Lower-Middle Sectors (1966–1972)   267
34. Inflation in the Cost of Living for Buenos Aires (1963–1972)   269
35. Relative Prices of Beef, Grain, and Flax (1966–1972)   271
36. Ratio of Minimum Wage of Industrial Workers to Prices of Food and Agricultural Products (1966–1972)   272
37. Disaggregation of the Cost-of-Living Index for Buenos Aires (1966–1972)   273
38. The Budget of the National Government (1966–1972)   274
39. Tax Revenues of the National Government (1964–1972)   275
40. Net Foreign Exchange Reserves of the Argentine Central Bank (1966–1972)   276
41. Balance of Payments: Net Capital Movements (1966–1972)   278
42. Direct Foreign Investment Authorized under the Regime of Industrial Promotion (1960–1972)   279
43. Argentine Foreign Trade (1966–1972)   279
44. Foreign Loans to the Argentine Government and Foreign Debt (1966–1972)   280
45. Investment (1965–1972)   281

46. Gross Domestic Product and Private Consumption (1964–
1972)   282
47. Ratio of Black Market Rate to Official Market Rate for
the U.S. Dollar (1966–1972)   283
48. Interest Rates for the U.S. Dollar on the 30-day Futures
Market (1966–1972)   284
49. Gross Profits of Major Economic Sectors (1966, 1969–
1972)   285
50. Productivity and Exploitation Rates for Economic Sectors
(1966, 1969–1972)   287
51. Value Added, Productivity, and Exploitation Rates for
Subsectors of Argentine Industry (1966, 1969–1972)   288
52. Acts of Protest and Violence (1960–1972)   290
53. Strikes and Work Stoppages (1956–1972)   291
54. Street Demonstrations (1960–1972)   295
55. Acts of Political Violence (Annual Totals) (1960–1972)   296
56. Acts of Political Violence (Monthly Count) (1960–1972) 298
57. Guerrilla Actions: Acts of Armed Political Violence Exclusive of Bombings (1965–1972)   299
58. Attitudes toward Terrorism   309
59. Respondents Who Feel That Terrorism Is Justified   310

Figures

1. Long-term Outlook: Steady Decline   19
2. Long-term Outlook: Fluctuating Decline   20
3. Minimum Wage of Unmarried Industrial Workers (1964–
1972)   268
4. Inflation in the Cost of Living for Greater Buenos Aires
(1963–1972)   270

Preface

This book presents the findings of an empirical investigation into the political and economic processes in Argentina between June 1966 and March 1973. By interpreting these processes through concepts whose theoretical status is made explicit at the outset, and by comparing this case to analogous ones—Brazil after 1964, Uruguay and Chile after 1973, and Argentina (again) after 1976—the book is intended to advance the understanding of what I have termed the bureaucratic-authoritarian (BA) state, and on the basis of this understanding to analyze and critique the characteristics and consequences of this form of rule. In the course of the research that went into this book, it proved necessary to move back and forth across several levels of analysis and data, from the most structural to those related to the perceptions and ideological orientations of some key actors of the period. This shifting back and forth was costly in time and effort but indispensable for tracing a sequence of events that cannot properly be reduced to any single level of analysis.

Behind this book is a personal story. In 1971, as soon as I had finished my first book,* I began the research for the present one, using as a starting point interviews I had conducted between 1966 and 1968. The research was completed in late 1974, and by mid-1975 this book had assumed its present form. During that interval, however, events in

---

Modernización y Autoritarismo (Buenos Aires: Editorial Paidós, 1972). Published in English as *Modernization and Bureaucratic-Authoritarianism* (Berkeley: Institute of International Studies, University of California at Berkeley, 1973; second edition with postscript, 1979).

Argentina, together with the publication of another book* and several articles that I felt responded to more urgent concerns, prevented me from putting the finishing touches on the present work. Shortly thereafter the March 1976 coup, and the extraordinarily repressive regime it inaugurated, made it impossible to publish the book in Argentina. I might have published it in other languages, but it was not until recently, when it became possible again to publish it in Argentina, that I found the motivation to polish the version I had sadly shelved in 1976, update the footnotes, and prepare the present version for publication. This not-too-academic attitude was due in large part, I suspect, to another central motivation—and hope—of this work: that it may serve as an informed argument about the immense costs (not only the ones inflicted on the bodies of those more dreadfully victimized) that we Argentines have exacted from ourselves as a result of the pervasive political violence and the recurrent attempts to establish authoritarian rule that have characterized the past decades. Such tragedies are commonplace in our time. Detailed study of the processes, errors, and passions that generated the one discussed here may be a useful undertaking, if only to demonstrate that at least this one was not unavoidable.

The book I would write today about the 1966–73 period in Argentina would be different from the one I wrote between 1974 and 1976. But it would not necessarily be better, since my current perceptions of that period are perhaps too heavily colored by subsequent events, particularly the extraordinary cruelty of the 1976–83 second Argentine BA. The crises and violence of the 1966–73 period pale in comparison to what unfolded after 1976. The reader, however, must try to view the present text in historical perspective, since that future was not in the minds of those who made the history of the 1966–73 years. What happened during that period, especially after 1969, was perceived as a confluence of crises, hopes, and fears entirely new to Argentine experience. If we ignore this crucial fact, we will not be able to comprehend why political actors behaved as they did before 1973, or especially how, and how much, such behavior contributed to what has occurred since then in Argentina.

This book has benefited from my discussions with many persons, in particular my colleagues and friends Fernando Henrique Cardoso, Marcelo Cavarozzi, David Collier, Shepard Forman, Albert Hirschman,

*Guillermo O'Donnell and Delfina Linck, *Dependencia y Autonomía* (Buenos Aires: Amorrortu Editores, 1973).

Sarah Hirschman, Helio Jaguaribe, Abraham Lowenthal, Cándido Mendes, Oscar Oszlak, Adam Przeworski, Philippe Schmitter, the late Kalman Silvert, and Francisco Weffort. I want to express my special gratitude to David Apter, Robert Dahl, and Alfred Stepan.* I wish also to acknowledge the many valuable contributions I received at the various places through which I wandered as a result of events in my country and in my personal life: the Centro de Estudios de Estado y Sociedad (CEDES) in Buenos Aires, the Institute for Advanced Studies at Princeton, the University of Michigan, the Instituto Universitario de Pesquisas de Rio de Janeiro (IUPERJ) and, most recently, the Helen Kellogg Institute at the University of Notre Dame. At various stages I received financial support from Yale's Office for Advanced Political Studies, the Danforth Foundation, the Council for Scientific and Technological Research in Argentina, the Guggenheim Foundation and the Carnegie Endowment for International Peace, and for the preparation of the present version, from the Helen Kellogg Institute. Support was also provided by CEDES, with funding supplied by institutional subsidies from the Ford Foundation and Sweden's SAREC. I extend my deepest gratitude to the persons and institutions involved.

James McGuire has been much more than the translator of a difficult text by a difficult author; with exceptional dedication and talent, he made me aware of more than a few flaws in the Spanish version. Having struggled with other English translations of my very Hispanic writing, I was very fortunate that Grant Barnes, then of the University of California Press, invited an excellent scholar like McGuire to undertake this one.

To my loves, past and present, my apologies for the more than a few moments that this book stole from us, and my thanks for their support.

One final word. Interviews with many of the most important actors of the period were an indispensable source for this book, since they enabled me to understand the significance of certain episodes and to

---

*This community of colleagues and friends includes William Smith, who arrived in Argentina in 1974 to do research toward his doctoral dissertation at Stanford University. By that time I had basically completed my research and was struggling with the first draft of this book. Since Smith's project focused on the same period as my own, and since our approaches were quite similar, we engaged in frequent and fruitful discussions. When Smith returned to the United States, we agreed to safeguard the identity of each text by refraining from reading the other's until both had been completed. The product of Smith's research is "Crisis of the State and Military-Authoritarian Rule in Argentina, 1966–1973" (Ph.D. diss., Stanford University, 1980). This work is an excellent contribution to the study of Argentina and to the theory of authoritarian forms of rule. In spite of the coincidences, Smith and I gave different emphases to our texts, making them much more complementary than overlapping.

check information whose reliability I could not otherwise assess. To preserve the anonymity of those interviewed, I was compelled at several points to suppress information that would have lent further credibility to some of my arguments. Such decisions were motivated not only by basic research ethics, but also by the fact that many of those I interviewed remained in Argentina during the post-1973 period, when it was dangerous indeed to be recognized as the source of certain opinions or the bearer of the memory of certain events—dangerous to the extent that assassinations have claimed the lives of the vast majority of the persons who have died since I interviewed them. They represent the innumerable victims to whose memory I dedicate this book.

ONE

Theoretical and Historical Background to the Study of the Bureaucratic-Authoritarian State

Argentina between 1966 and 1973 serves in this book as a case study of the implantation, social impact, and collapse of a type of state I have termed bureaucratic-authoritarian (BA). The first section of this chapter introduces some of the basic concepts to be used and elaborated upon as we examine the Argentine BA and compare it with similar cases. The remainder of the chapter outlines the decisive antecedents to the BAs implanted in Argentina and other Latin American countries during the 1960s and 1970s, beginning with the emergence of the popular sector as an important actor during the period that followed the collapse of oligarchic domination. Both the ambiguous relationship of this process to the issues of citizenship and political democracy (section 2) and the largely concomitant process of the transnationalization of Latin American economies and societies (section 3) are analyzed.

The processes of popular activation and social and economic transnationalization gave rise to crises that formed the more immediate antecedent to the BAs. The fourth section contains a general discussion of crises. The fifth section distinguishes among various types of crisis in order to lay the groundwork for analyzing the ones that, at varying levels of intensity, preceded the implantation of the BAs. The sixth section summarizes attributes that define the BA and distinguish it from other forms of authoritarian rule. The seventh consists of a brief excur-

To facilitate the reading, notes have been separated into two categories. Those at the bottom of the page elaborate the arguments and information presented in the text, while those at the end of the chapter refer exclusively to sources.

1

sus defining the social and political actors whose conflicts and alliances constitute a central theme in this study.

1. ON THE CAPITALIST STATE AND RELATED THEMES[1]

The BA is a type of capitalist state, and should therefore be understood in the light of the distinctive attributes of capitalist states in general. The most important characteristics of such states, and of other concepts to be used throughout this book, are delineated in this section.

A. STATE AND STATE APPARATUS

The basic (though not the only) network of social relations in a capitalist society, and the one that characterizes it as capitalist, is the one formed by its relations of production. These relations are established in one of society's basic cells: the workplace and work process. Ordinary consciousness views these relations as exclusively economic, but closer inspection reveals that they are constituted by other aspects as well. One such aspect is the coercive guarantee they contain for their effectiveness and reproduction. The state, according to the view set forth here, is a part, or more precisely an aspect, of these relations: the one that supplies its coercive guarantee. The state, as the guarantor of the capitalist relations of production, is (no less than their economic aspects) a necessary and primordial part of these relations. In addition to guaranteeing their effectiveness and reproduction, the state also organizes the capitalist relations of production by articulating and buffering the relationships among classes and by providing elements necessary to their "normal," unchallenged reproduction.

It is crucial to underscore that the state is the guarantor not of the immediate interests of the bourgeoisie, but of the ensemble of social relations that establish the bourgeoisie as the dominant class. It is a capitalist state, not a state *of* the bourgeoisie. Insofar as it guarantees and organizes capitalist social relations, the capitalist state guarantees and organizes the social classes inherent in them—including the dominated classes, although what the state guarantees in respect to them is their reproduction as such, i.e., as dominated classes.

Some important consequences stem from the fact that the state is the guarantor and organizer of the capitalist relations of production, and not of the immediate interests of the bourgeoisie. It is particularly important to recognize that the state, even in opposition to the concrete demands of the bourgeoisie, may assume a custodial role with respect to the dominated classes. The general interest of the bourgeoisie as a whole—the effectiveness and reproduction of the social relations that ensure its condition as a dominant class—entails the placing of constraints on the microeconomic rationalities of its members. The processes set in motion by such rationalities, if left unchecked, could culminate either in the physical extinction of the working class or in its recognition of the exploitative character of its relationship with the bourgeoisie. The demystification of capitalist exploitation would undermine a fundamental support of ideological domination: the commonsense perception of the relations of production as freely agreed upon, purely economic, and nonexploitative. In turn, the disappearance of this perception would lead to a generalized challenge to these relations and the domination inherent in them.

Up to this point I have discussed the capitalist state on an analytical level upon which one might also situate, for example, the concept of class or of capitalist social relations. Just as one cannot see "the bourgeoisie," one cannot see "the state." But at a concrete (that is, nonanalytical) level, these categories are objectified in social actors, among which are the institutions or apparatuses of the state. I have argued that the capitalist state is primarily and constitutively one aspect (which must be comprehended analytically) of capitalist social relations. The state, in this fundamental sense, is a part of society; society is the more basic and inclusive category. But in terms of the concrete social actors who are the bearers of these (and other) social relations, the state is also an apparatus, or a set of institutions. Just as the commodity is an objectified moment in the global process of the production and circulation of capital, the institutions of the state are an objectified moment in the global process of the production and circulation of power. Like the commodity, these institutions are of great importance and have crucial effects of their own. But it is wrong to confuse them with the whole state and thereby lose sight of the state's foundations at the very heart of society.

Ordinary consciousness reduces the capitalist state to its institutions, just as it isolates the commodity from its origins in the production and circulation of capital. The limitation of commonsense perceptions to the concrete—fetishized—appearance of the state and capital is the principal cloak behind which class domination (and with it the domination of the state) is concealed and protected. More precisely, the fetishized appearance of the state apparatus as the "whole" state underlies the illusion that this apparatus constitutes a "third" social actor, unbiased and external to the relations that link the capitalist to the worker. Actually the state, as we have seen, is a constitutive part of those relations. This appearance of externality is what allows the state to operate as the organizer of capitalist society: because the state seems to stand apart from society, it can proclaim itself, and will usually be perceived, as the unbiased guardian and agent of a general interest. But the state is the agent of an interest that is general but partialized: that of the effectiveness and reproduction of certain—intrinsically unequal—social relations. It is by no means, however, the agent of a general interest that is impartial with respect to the structural positions of the social classes.

B. NATION

The state serves a general interest, which is the general interest of the effectiveness and reproduction of the social relations that constitute both the dominant and the dominated classes. The discourse emitted by the state apparatus claims, however, that it serves an undifferentiated general interest: that of the nation. The nation is the arc of solidarities that postulates a homogeneous "we" that is distinct from the "they" of other nations. The effectiveness of the state's coercive guarantee is based on its control of the means of coercion in a territory whose boundaries mark the limits of the nation's arc of solidarities. It is for these reasons that the state is, or tends to become, a national state: its territorial boundaries delimit the scope of its coercive supremacy, and it is the undifferentiated interest of social actors *qua* members-of-the-nation that the state apparatus claims to serve.

C. *PUEBLO*

The custodial role of the state with respect to the dominated classes can lead to recognition of the *pueblo,* i.e., the least favored members of the nation. *Pueblo* is an inherently ambiguous category.[2] At certain conjunctures the poor and weak who constitute the *pueblo* may channel explosive demands for substantive justice that conflict with the state and the basic social relations, or pact of domination,[3] that it guarantees and organizes. By articulating such demands, these actors may come to identify themselves not just as *pueblo* but as dominated classes who self-consciously challenge the system of social domination. But in other circumstances the identification as *pueblo* may inhibit the formation of class identities, serving instead to define its members as subordinate actors in processes whose main protagonists are dominant class fractions struggling among themselves.*

D. CITIZENSHIP

Just as each social actor appears abstractly free and equal before the market, commodities and money, citizenship embodies another moment of abstract equality. In a political democracy, the state institutions ground their claim to the right to command and coerce on the basis of the free wills of the members of the nation as citizens. The image of a society made up of equal citizens abstracted from their actual positions in society is in various senses false, but, just as the concepts of state, nation and *pueblo* harbor ambiguities, this image of citizenship contains a side of truth as well as one of falsity. On the one hand, the image of a society composed of free and equal citizens usually provides optimal cover for the social domination embodied in the capitalist relations of production. On the other hand, citizens in a political democracy enjoy, on the basis of their abstract equality, the right to organize around goals they are (in principle) free to define, as well as the right to be protected from and compensated for arbitrary acts by the state institutions or other social actors. Moreover, citizenship and political democracy entail mechanisms and entitlements that often permit the dominated classes to carve out social and political spaces from which to articulate demands and realize interests that are both objectively and subjectively important to them. Furthermore, as we shall see, the mechanisms and opportunities associated with political democracy may at certain conjunctures provide the dominated classes institutional channels and resources through which

---

*In order not to overcomplicate this introductory theoretical sketch, I have limited myself to the ideal case of a social formation where capitalist social relations are strongly predominant. Moreover, I have restricted myself to relations of production, with no discussion of other relations of domination—those not directly based on the work process—that the state usually also guarantees and organizes. In the study of social formations where capitalist relations have become predominant over other types of relations of production, it makes sense to start (for reasons of conceptual parsimony) with the ideal type of those relations—which, as we have seen, are not only economic—that articulate and subordinate the rest. As we shall see, this is only a preparatory step for historically specific analysis, which must also introduce those other relations and try to present them in their dynamic interplay with the former.

the foundations of social domination may be shaken and, eventually, destroyed. Thus, as with the other categories already analyzed, the specific implications of citizenship and political democracy cannot be determined a priori; they depend on circumstances that must be recognized and assessed through detailed historical analysis.

E. REGIME AND GOVERNMENT

Two other categories need to be defined: *regime* and *government*. The regime is the set of effectively prevailing patterns (not necessarily legally formalized) that establish the modalities of recruitment and access to government roles and the criteria for representation and the permissible resources that form the basis for expectations of access to such roles.[4] These criteria may be derived from classical democratic theory (citizenship, parties and party membership), from articulations of interests in society (as in the case of corporatist representation), and/or from membership in certain state institutions (such as in highly militarized regimes).* The government is the set of persons who occupy the top positions in the state apparatus in accordance with the rules of a given regime, and who are formally entitled to mobilize the resources controlled by the state apparatus (including those on which the coercive supremacy of that apparatus is based) in support of their directives or prohibitions. In other words, the government is the apex of the state apparatus, and the regime is the network of routes that lead to it.

The concepts outlined in this section will serve to structure and orient the remaining portion of the chapter, in which we shall examine some processes that made a decisive contribution to the implantation of bureaucratic-authoritarian states in Argentina (1966 and 1976), Brazil (1964), Chile (1973), and Uruguay (1973).[5]

---

*Type of regime and type of state usually correspond closely but not exactly. A regime that is democratic or competitive, or, in the terminology of Robert Dahl, "polyarchic" (cf. esp. *Modern Political Analysis* [New York: Prentice-Hall, 1966]), implies universalistic criteria of representation (citizenship) and of patterns of social representation— i.e., patterns that are not determined unilaterally by incumbents of the state institutions. Such a regime is incompatible, for example, with a bureaucratic-authoritarian state (as defined below). On the other hand, an authoritarian state can coexist with a regime made up of a single party, a dominant party (Mexico), two formally authorized parties (Brazil prior to 1979), or no party at all (Chile today), and can impose more or less rigid constraints on corporative representation, with differing biases with respect to the various social classes.

2. *PUEBLO* IN LATIN AMERICA

A. *PUEBLO*

Most populations in Latin America forged their national identities much more as a *pueblo* than as a citizenry. At various times—and not only through the so-called populisms*—sectors that previously were excluded from all forms of political participation (except as subordinated members of clientelistic systems) burst forth as a *pueblo*. They were recognized as members-of-the-nation through demands for substantive justice, which they posed not as dominated, exploited classes but as victims of poverty and governmental indifference. The disadvantaged sectors (*los pobres*) who constituted the *pueblo* saw themselves (and were proclaimed by the political leaders who sought their support) as embodying what was most authentically national, and they contrasted these national orientations and aspirations to the "foreignness" of the ruling oligarchies and their international allies.

Los pobres were not the main protagonists in the process by which they themselves became members-of-the-nation. From Getúlio Vargas's image as the "father of the poor" to the more mobilizing discourse of Eva Perón, the *pueblo* emerged as both a part and a consequence of a broad alliance. This alliance, dominated by the urban middle sectors and that part of the urban bourgeoisie that seemed capable of playing a dynamic role in development, sought to liquidate the oligarchic states. The supposedly archaic character of the oligarchy and the conspicuously foreign character of transnational capital linked to the export of primary products were set in contrast to the newly defined national-popular identity.

*I shall address the issue of populism here only in very general terms, partly because of space limitations and partly because there exist few comparative studies that examine in detail the political transformations that took place in Latin America following the rupture of the oligarchic state. A work that clarifies various aspects of the periods preceding the implantation of the BAs is Marcelo Cavarozzi, "Populismos y 'partidos de clase media' (Notas comparativas)," *Documento CEDES/G.E. CLACSO* 3, Centro de Estudios de Estado y Sociedad (Buenos Aires, 1976). The main contributions to the analysis of Latin American populisms are those of Francisco Weffort; cf. esp. his collected essays in *O populismo na política brasileira* (Rio de Janeiro: Editora Paz e Terra, 1980). For important contributions to the comparative study of the populist periods and the BAs that succeeded them, see David Collier, "The Bureaucratic-Authoritarian Model: Synthesis and Priorities for Future Research," and Robert Kaufman, "Industrial Change and Authoritarian Rule in Latin America: A Concrete Review of the Bureaucratic-Authoritarian Model," both in *The New Authoritarianism in Latin America,* ed. Collier; and Ruth Berins Collier, "Popular Sector Incorporation and Regime Evolution in Brazil and Mexico," in *Brazil and Mexico: Patterns in Late Development,* ed. Sylvia Ann Hewlett and Richard Weinert (Philadelphia: Institute for the Study of Human Issues, 1982).

Why did the previously excluded sectors in most Latin American countries form their collective identities more as a *pueblo* than as a citizenry? First, in such countries the abstract ideas of equality upon which citizenship is based were not well developed, basically owing to the incomplete diffusion of capitalist relations at the time when the national-popular identities began to crystallize.* Even in relatively homogeneous countries like Argentina and Uruguay, the previously excluded became members-of-the-nation at the same time as a great wave of urbanization and industrialization was taking place. The clustering of these great social transformations in most Latin American countries contrasts with the longer, more sequential historical rhythms of the core capitalist countries, where capitalist relations expanded more gradually and came to predominate throughout society prior to the expansion of citizenship by the electoral enfranchisement of the whole (male) population. A second reason why the *pueblo* became the main locus of new national identities in Latin America is that in many cases these identities were formed at the same time as the urban economy was undergoing rapid expansion. This economic growth furnished resources that enabled governments to project an image of concern for, and to some extent to promote, the interests of the popular sector.† During such periods governments, together with key parties and movements, tended to orient their discourses in support of those whom incumbents of the state apparatus and members of the dominant classes had formerly viewed as nothing more than silent masses subject to occasional upheavals. To a degree and for a duration that varied according to the country, it seemed that the state really was a national-popular state. More than a few of those who had come to consider themselves members of the *pueblo* not only experienced improvements in their material conditions, but also took part in the nationalist rituals in which the populist govern-

*During the oligarchic and populist periods, Latin American societies were not as fully articulated by capitalist relations as were the societies of the center countries when mass citizenship came upon the scene. Some consequences of these contrasting experiences are discussed by Marcelo Cavarozzi in "Elementos para una caracterización del capitalismo oligárquico," *Documento CEDES/G.E. CLACSO* 12, Centro de Estudios de Estado y Sociedad (Buenos Aires, 1979). I have borrowed from this work the concept of "cellular domination."

†The appeal to *lo popular* was characteristic of governments established during the interval between the rupture of the oligarchic state and the implantation of the BA, regardless of whether these governments owed their existence to movements that actively promoted such appeals. During this era the discourse of the state apparatus was "popularized," even if on some occasions its popular content had a rather hollow ring.

ments celebrated their "victories" over the oligarchy and transnational capital.*

B. CITIZENSHIP AND POLITICAL DEMOCRACY

In the countries of Latin America, with the partial exception of Chile and Uruguay, citizenship never assumed a preponderant role in the forging of political identities. As noted above, the limited scope of ideas of citizenship in Latin America was due partly to the absence of fully and extensively capitalist societies that foster, and are nurtured by, other levels of abstract equality. Another reason for the secondary role of citizenship is that the periods in which the popular sector burst into the national political arenas were fraught with conflict over restricted and fraudulent forms of oligarchic democracy. Such "democracy" often was—and was perceived as—a sham concocted by conservative forces to stifle popular advances. During the popular irruptions, however, diverse factions of the oligarchy would frequently come out in support of a "democracy" they had seldom practiced in the past. Such democratic posturing was notoriously ambivalent. With the emerging populist alliances convinced that "democracy" was little more than a hoax designed to fetter the advance of the *pueblo,* and with conservatives and oligarchs fearful of the enormous electoral support upon which those who appealed to the *pueblo* could rely, democracy, and the ideas and institutions of citizenship with which it is associated, through the period appealed to very few political actors. With their shallow roots, citizenship and democracy proved unable to withstand the crises out of which the bureaucratic-authoritarian states emerged.

The initial political activation of the popular sector cannot be considered properly a class movement in any of the countries we are studying, since the previously excluded sectors did not recognize themselves as dominated classes and were unable to set their own goals or to determine the general direction of the process. The popular activation was channeled not into overt class struggle, but rather toward a recomposition of the dominant classes. This recomposition consisted on the one hand of the displacement of the agrarian-based oligarchies from their previously

*Such nationalist rituals were of immense symbolic importance. They ranged from expropriations to more moderate decisions, such as the purchase of British-owned railroads by the first Peronist government in Argentina, which was attended by an elaborate ceremony in which it was implied that with this act the state, identified with its *pueblo,* fully constituted the nation.

central position within the dominant classes, and on the other of the emergence as key social and economic actors of the newest and most dynamic appendages of the world capitalist center. In some cases (such as Mexico and Argentina, each in its own way and at its own time) the national-popular emergence had largely subsided when, by the late 1950s and early 1960s, the great surge toward the transnationalization of the urban productive structure took place. Elsewhere (as in Brazil and Chile, again each in its own way) the processes of popular activation and transnationalization largely overlapped. But in all of the cases with which we are here concerned, the popular activation, the displacement of the agrarian-based oligarchies, and the intense transnationalization of the economy and society led to a rapid expansion of capitalist relations. The advance of all of these processes was, however, subject to a key limitation. The democratic (in Chile and Uruguay) or populist (in Brazil and Argentina) "state of compromise"[6] remained viable only so long as the *pueblo*'s demands for substantive justice did not collide with the constraints imposed by the way in which the economy was expanding and becoming extensively transnationalized.

As a result of this clash between popular sector demands and the requirements of the new mode of economic expansion, many actors, including some who had initially supported the popular activation, began to search for ways to drive a wedge between the *pueblo* and the nation and to ground the latter in an alternative referent. Such initiatives, which began well before the adoption of explicitly authoritarian solutions, were put forth in a situation where democracy and citizenship remained weakly rooted and where the *pueblo* had overcome, if only partially and in a subordinate fashion, its earlier political marginalization. The resulting presence and demands of the popular sector, even though they were not expressed in class terms and therefore posed no direct challenge to social domination, were perceived nonetheless as increasingly dangerous. For the dominant classes, new and old alike, this became the Gordian knot that had to be cut.*

---

*My previous research has centered on the processes alluded to in this paragraph, especially on their elective affinities with the emergence of the BAs and—contrapuntally— with the tortuous ways in which Latin American societies have grappled with the problem of political democracy. No discussion of such themes can fail to recognize the contributions made by the analyses of Fernando Henrique Cardoso; cf. (with Enzo Faletto) *Dependencia y Desarrollo en América Latina* (Mexico City: Siglo XXI, 1969), and the postscript in the English edition, *Dependency and Development in Latin America* (Berkeley and Los Angeles: University of California Press, 1979); and his essays collected in *Estado y Sociedad en América Latina* (Buenos Aires: Nueva Visión, 1973), and *Autoritarismo e Democratização* (Rio de Janeiro: Editora Paz e Terra, 1975).

3. DEPENDENCY AND THE
TRANSNATIONALIZATION OF SOCIETY

Existing theories of the state have not adequately considered whether the state's "boundaries" coincide with those of the nation and of society. In the centers of world capitalism, where the state may be viewed on the one hand as the link between the domestic capitalist relations of production and the system of social domination, and on the other as an arc embracing the entire nation, it is taken for granted that state, society, and nation are coterminous. This view has been challenged on the periphery, above all in studies of dependency, which argue that society is not coterminous with the nation.[7] However, this argument is seldom extended to the state–society–nation triad.[8]

Following the Second World War, the mode of linkage between the Latin American countries we are studying and the world market changed considerably. Primary-product export ties to the world capitalist center did not disappear, but they became increasingly subordinated—in terms of the dynamics of capital accumulation and the relative weight of the classes associated with each activity—to the operations of transnational corporations (TNCs). These corporations adapted to the protectionist policies enacted in these countries during the 1930s and 1940s by vaulting over customs and exchange barriers to become direct producers in and for the domestic market.[9] TNC subsidiaries increasingly displaced firms engaged in the production and export of primary goods as the dynamic motor of the transnationalization of capital, and in so doing they accentuated the oligopolistic characteristics of each domestic market. Not only the activities of the TNCs themselves but also the changes their activities stimulated in the world financial and commercial systems promoted this transnationalization. Especially in the countries with the largest domestic markets, TNC subsidiaries, together with some state institutions, predominated in the economic sectors (primarily industry and nontraditional services) that became the new dynamic axis of economic growth. The TNCs remained the major vehicles of the transnationalization of these Latin American economies and societies until the world crisis that began in the mid-1970s gave financial capital a preponderant role.

These processes gave rise to capitalist societies whose attributes define them as historically original. They are dependent capitalisms because in their normal functioning* they assign a decisive role to transnational

*The idea of "normality" in the functioning of a capitalist economy is discussed in section 4 of this chapter.

capital and their circuits of capital accumulation are completed not within the domestic market but in the centers of world capitalism. They are also extensively industrialized societies, owing as much to the relative weight of industry in the economy as to the significance of industry in class formation and articulation. Because of this coexistence of dependency and extensive industrialization, the capitalisms of Latin America are marked by acute imbalances.[10] It is enough to note that (1) they produce few of the capital goods and little of the technology they utilize; (2) they generate locally only a small fraction of the services involving the production, transmission and processing of information; (3) their balance of payments tends to be negative even if their balance of trade is positive; (4) their domestic capital markets are at best embryonic; (5) a large proportion of their largest and fastest-growing private economic entities are TNC subsidiaries; and (6) their distribution of all kinds of resources (not just economic ones) are significantly more unequal than in the center capitalisms, in spite of which (7) available goods and services tend to mirror those found in the core capitalist countries.

To summarize, the productive structures of these societies are complex and differentiated, but at the same time they are unbalanced and incomplete in that their vertical integration is limited by the dearth of internal production of complex capital goods and of technology. The imbalances just described suggest that these economies and some of the problems they confront are not the same as those of the center capitalist countries. On the other hand, the Latin American economies that concern us here differ in important ways from those that conform to the archetypal image of "underdevelopment," in which the domestic productive structure is less complex and industry less extensive.

But transnationalization involves more than the presence of TNC subsidiaries as the most dynamic private economic entities in these societies. The insertion of transnational capital as a direct producer within and for the domestic market is part of a larger process of capitalist expansion involving the subordination and reconstitution of the whole economy and society. Once it had undermined the earlier supremacy of enterprises and classes engaged in the export of primary products, the entry of TNCs into domestic markets led to a profound recomposition of the bourgeoisie. What occurred was less the capture of an already existing productive structure (although this too resulted from the most parasitical forms of transnational expansion) than the creation of new industrial, commercial and service sectors and activities. As a result of these changes, one part of the preexisting urban bourgeoisie, overwhelmingly national in terms of the location of its decision-making centers and the origins of its capital, found itself relegated to the traditional, slowest-growing, least technology- and capital-intensive, and most competitive sectors of the economy. On the other hand, other national firms, most of them newly created, associated themselves with the TNC subsidiaries, either by providing them with inputs or services or by acquiring their products for last-stage processing or for sale.[11] Entrenched as they are in a larger matrix of economic relationships built by and around the TNCs, such firms can be considered national only in a formal sense. Located in power networks (both economic and non-economic) controlled by the TNC subsidiaries, their modalities of capital accumulation tend to remain subordinate to those of the TNCs,* and in no sense are such firms in the hands of an independent bourgeoisie in control of its own accumulation, the technology it utilizes, and the social relations it begets. Even local firms that have expanded outside the network of direct linkages to the TNC subsidiaries are profoundly transnationalized. To succeed, they have had to "modernize" in a dual sense: by imitating the type of product, services, advertising, and marketing characteristic of the TNCs, and by importing equipment, trademarks, technologies, and services that convert them into replicas of those subsidiaries.†

Finally, what is socially deemed a "need" on the periphery is in large measure a function of this very transnationalization, whose dynamic agents foster a pattern of expensive consumption epitomized by an insatiable thirst for new products. This is socially absurd in societies marked by inequalities much more profound than those of the central capitalist countries, and the tensions that result from such patterns of consumption have important political consequences. Some of the demands for substantive justice associated with the self-affirmation of the *pueblo* reflect "needs" induced by this pattern of "development," but such demands, even as they ratify the imitative and transnationalized cast of the productive structure, also strain the limits of this structure by highlighting its relative and absolute inequalities.

---

*Contrary to what is assumed in simplistic conceptualizations of dependency, this subordination does not preclude serious conflicts between the TNCs and the national firms to which they are linked. These conflicts, however, tend to be defined and resolved within the limits imposed by the subordination of the latter to the former. I have developed this theme and related ones—to which we shall return later in this book—in "Notas para el estudio de la burguesía local," CEDES *Estudios Sociales* 12 (Buenos Aires, 1978).

†Or, more precisely, into partial replicas of these subsidiaries. The more limited range of products offered by these firms, coupled with their restricted capacity to introduce innovations, makes it more difficult for them to adapt to domestic economic conditions and to international competition.

Let us return to a crucial point raised in the first paragraph of this section. In the era of primary product exports, the real frontiers of dependent societies were already more blurred than those of the center capitalisms. But once transnational capital began to push its way into the urban productive structure, it became even more evident that these frontiers stretched well beyond the boundaries supposedly demarcated by their respective states. The uppermost ranks of the bourgeoisie in the countries we are studying now contain a number of strategic decision-making centers that lie beyond the territorial limits claimed by the state. Society, or more specifically its most dynamic and economically power-ful elements, has overflowed the nation-state. The state institutions can negotiate some of the terms under which the TNC subsidiaries penetrate the domestic economy, but they are powerless to challenge the role of these subsidiaries as crucial agents of transnationalization. The con-spicuous presence of these extranational centers of decision-making in territories controlled by a state that cannot cease to proclaim itself a national state bears important consequences. In the first section of this chapter, attention was called to the systematic bias of the state (as an aspect of a social relation and as an apparatus) toward the reproduction of society as, fundamentally, an ensemble of social relations that gives rise to a system of class domination. This bias tends to be hidden when the state appears as a state-for-the-nation, but it may become visible when society is recast to incorporate within the upper ranks of its bourgeoisie the above-mentioned segments of transnational capital. With this recasting, the state and the nation encompass neither a sub-stantial part of society's most dynamic actors nor the social relations that make them socially and economically dominant.[12] Accordingly, the state tends to lose credibility as the active synthesis of the nation.

The political activation of the popular sector and the transnationali-zation of society were fundamental antecedents to the BAs. The state that fostered and to some extent embodied the national-popular move-ments was, at the same time, subject to the expansive tendencies of world capitalism that paved the way for the insertion of new segments of transnational capital into the domestic economy and society. With tempos and sequences specific to each case,* the period following the

---

*In certain cases, notably Brazil and Mexico, the dynamic economic expansion of the state apparatus permitted an escape from the dilemmas posed by the combined presence of a highly transnationalized upper bourgeoisie and a weak local bourgeoisie. But as has recently become clear in both countries, this escape was limited and temporary and did not improve the social distribution of resources.

rupture of the oligarchic state saw the growth of the contradiction between, on the one hand, the rise of the *pueblo* as the principal constituent of the nation and, on the other, the limitations imposed by a productive structure that accentuated existing social and economic inequalities while overflowing the boundaries upon which the state founds its claim to be the agent of the national interest.

4. ON ECONOMIC CRISES

The preceding discussion has called attention to some of the ways in which the societies where the BAs have emerged differ from those of the central capitalisms. Nonetheless, both types of societies are supposed to function normally. But what is meant by "normal"? The answer is given on the basis of criteria used to evaluate the functioning of the central capitalisms. The application of such criteria to the societies that concern us here has important political consequences.

A modern capitalist economy is considered to be functioning normally when its dynamic reproduction, or expansion, takes place without major disruptions to capital accumulation, and in particular to the accumulation of its large economic entities. Such "normality" is the perpetual but opaque crisis of an uneven and unequalizing growth whose chief beneficiaries are these large entities and whose capital accumulation subordinates the behavior of other economic actors and the overall distribution of resources in the rest of society. "Normal" economic functioning is measured in terms of indicators that define a "satisfactory" economic situation as one in which there are few impediments to the existing pattern of capital accumulation. Moreover, those who judge whether the economy is functioning normally are usually the ones whose actions and abstentions are most capable of influencing those indicators. A different assessment might well result if indicators usually overlooked were taken into account, or if actors holding other criteria conducted the evaluation. As Alice in Wonderland learned, the degree to which things are going "well" or "poorly" depends on the power wielded by those who evaluate them.

When is a capitalist economy operating in a "satisfactory" manner? Such a judgment seems to be based on the following conditions: (1a) capitalists—particularly those who control large-scale enterprises— enjoy rates of profit they consider satisfactory for their own activities and for the overall performance of the economy; (2a) profits are reinvested in sufficient proportion to stimulate what these actors consider to be a reasonably high and sustained rate of economic growth; and (3a) those same actors expect that the above conditions will be maintained (or improved) in the relevant future, i.e., as far ahead as their time horizons extend.* These conditions can be stated in the negative: the economic situation is abnormal or unsatisfactory when any of the following circumstances exist: (1b) capitalists—particularly those who control large-scale enterprises—receive rates of profit they do not consider satisfactory; or (2b) profits accrue at a satisfactory rate but are not channeled into investments in sufficient amount to generate what they consider a reasonably high and sustained rate of growth; or (3b) conditions (1a) and (2a) are met, but those actors feel that the outlook for the future is unfavorable or unpredictable. Given any of these conditions, the economic situation will be judged unsatisfactory, and actors will adjust their behavior accordingly.

It should be noted that each capitalist, in judging whether the economic situation is satisfactory, assesses the existing situation but also makes a prediction about the future that he or she considers relevant. If the prediction is that in this future the "relevant" variables will behave in a negative or unpredictable fashion, the capitalist will evaluate the situation as unsatisfactory. The most pessimistic prediction, however, is not that these variables will assume still more negative values or that they will become even harder to predict. For the capitalists, the most pessimistic prediction is rather that existing social arrangements will be replaced by others in which they themselves have no place, and in which judgments as to whether the economy is performing in a satisfactory manner are made by other actors, using alternative criteria. For capitalists the most pessimistic prediction is the elimination of capitalism.

The normal functioning of an economy depends in large measure on whether its more influential actors evaluate its situation as satisfactory. However trivial this point may seem, it has a number of implications. First, this appraisal is codified. A code is a partial map of reality that draws attention toward some of its aspects and away from others. A code filters information by distinguishing "relevant" from "irrelevant" data, and by ordering the data considered relevant in hierarchical fashion such that some pieces of information are classified as important, others as secondary, and still others as those, important or not, about

---

*Some assumptions underlying "normality" are of course historically specific: at t_1 they can differ from those at t_n, and in country A they can differ from those in country B. Nonetheless, it seems to this author that in capitalist countries of medium or high complexity they would have to satisfy the general conditions stated in the text.

which nothing can be done. Usually implicit in the ordering process is a putative system of causal connections in which certain consequences are believed to follow regularly from certain situations. Codes, as partial visions of reality, obscure those aspects of a situation that go badly when, or because, those on which they focus are going well. Like ideology, of which it is an explicit and articulated segment, a code may represent with a fair degree of accuracy one aspect of reality even as it neglects or profoundly distorts other aspects, or as it confuses the single aspect with the whole reality.

Whose evaluation of a complex capitalist economy really matters? "Everyone's" matters to some degree, but in a highly oligopolized structure the evaluations of the monopolistic or oligopolistic actors matter the most. These actors have the power to influence greatly, by their actions and abstentions, the current and future condition of many economic and social relations. It happens that the criteria encoded for evaluating the overall economic situation are homologous with those used by the actors who control the largest economic units to evaluate their own situation. On the whole, things are "going well" for the economy when, and because, things are going well for its large mono/oligopolistic units. Whether things are going well for the latter depends in turn largely on whether those who control such units consider the situation on their own plane of activity to be satisfactory. But what is the meaning of "going well" at the level of these large, complex, and bureaucratized organizations? To answer this question it is sufficient to summarize some themes set forth in the extensive literature on the topic.[13] Such organizations (1) use highly routinized guidelines to conduct and evaluate their activities; (2) use similarly routinized criteria to determine what constitutes the "satisfactory" attainment of the goals they have set for themselves (typically, a certain ratio of profit to capital and/or sales, and a certain share of the market); (3) try to absorb and control the areas of uncertainty that they have learned may have a negative impact on their performance; and (4) contain internal coalitions with specialized activities and entrenched routines that make it difficult to change the behavior they have learned. Furthermore, in comparison to other actors these organizations have a long-term outlook, owing to their internal complexity, the nature of their investments, and the scope of their activities, which are typically specialized and not easily learned or unlearned. The short- and medium-term bases on which most small commercial and industrial firms operate—rational for entrepreneurs whose limited resource base re-

TABLE I   PLANNING ACCORDING TO SIZE OF INDUSTRIAL FIRM

	Time Horizon of Plan		
	1 Year	*2 to 3 Years*	*4 or More Years*
Investment Plans			
Large firms	93 %	78 %	52 %
Medium-sized firms	83 %	53 %	23 %
Small firms	58 %	8 %	2 %
Sales Plans			
Large firms	93 %	63 %	40 %
Medium-sized firms	74 %	35 %	21 %
Small firms	37 %	2 %	0 %
Production Plans			
Large firms	91 %	61 %	38 %
Medium-sized firms	70 %	32 %	18 %
Small firms	33 %	0 %	0 %

SOURCE: Fundación de Investigaciones Económicas Latinoamericanas (FIEL), "El Planeamiento en las empresas," Buenos Aires, 1973 (mimeo).

stricts their capacity to process information—is unsuitable for those large organizations.

The Argentine case, as the data in Table 1 indicate, provides evidence that large industrial firms have significantly longer planning horizons than smaller ones.* Every firm's evaluation of its situation contains a prediction of the future as well as an assessment of current conditions, but the future dimension is especially important for larger enterprises. Suppose that the actual state of the world is that depicted in Figure 1, where t_1 is the current year and t_2 . . . t_7 are the following years. Suppose also that a value (of, say, expected profits) within the 70–80 range on the vertical axis allows for the judgment that the economic situation is satisfactory and that a value in the 30 range or below produces the opposite assessment. Given a predicted value of 90 for year t_2, actor A, whose time horizon is one year, will judge the situation to be very

*These figures are still more significant if we take into account that the firms surveyed are stock corporations (*sociedades anónimas*). This means that the sample excludes the numerous small and medium-sized firms that are individually owned or that adopt other forms of association.

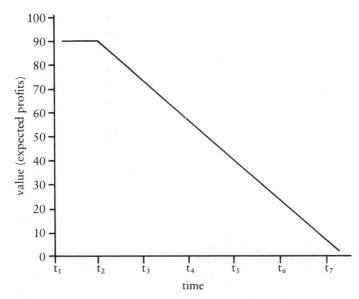

Figure 1.   Long-term Outlook: Steady Decline

satisfactory. But for actor B, an oligopolist whose time horizon extends for several years, the situation will be considered far from satisfactory, since the predicted values decline steadily after t_2. Actor B will therefore begin immediately to act in such a way as to minimize the risks apparent in this negative long-term forecast.

Now let us suppose that the situation is as depicted in Figure 2, which registers the same values as Figure 1 for the first and last years. Actor A's evaluation, which remains limited to a one-year horizon, is even more optimistic (note the predicted improvement during the first year). But actor B's assessment not only terminates, as in Figure 1, at an unsatisfactory point; it also forecasts, in contrast to Figure 1, considerable fluctuation, which will make it more difficult to plan ahead and to adjust decisions accordingly. Hence actor B's evaluation will be even more pessimistic.

These examples suggest that when the medium- and long-term outlook approaches either of the situations discussed, the rational response is to maximize gains in the short term and minimize the losses and risks predicted for the future. The tendency to respond in this way is accentuated when fluctuations are predicted, as in Figure 2.

In the Latin American countries where BAs were eventually implanted, the codified indicators by which the overall situation was evalu-

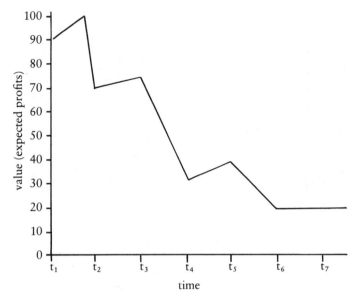

Figure 2.   Long-term Outlook: Fluctuating Decline

ated were both deteriorating and performing erratically. These trends generated evaluations that were even more negative than those of actor B in Figure 2. The real actors could foresee further deterioration and fluctuations, but (unlike the omniscient forecaster in the example) they could not predict, except in the very short run, the timing and intensity of the fluctuations.

A situation in which economic conditions are deteriorating and in which it is almost impossible to predict medium-term fluctuations (except to say that they will occur along a negative trend) creates an especially perverse type of economy. The only rational behavior in such an economy is to engage in plunder, i.e., to restrict the actor's operations to activities with satisfactory short-term outlooks while leaving as little as possible at stake for the time when the situation is predicted to deteriorate further. It is especially irrational to risk capital in investments that will mature in the medium or long term. The aggregate result of this micro-rational behavior is widespread financial speculation and capital flight, the effects of which are worsened by the suspension, also owing to predictions of deterioration and uncertainty, of capital inflow from abroad. Still, the situation does not lead to complete disinvestment because, apart from the various institutional rigidities that make this difficult, it makes sense to maintain a minimum of capital on hand to participate in successive rounds of plunder. As the process continues, financial speculation intensifies and tends more and more to eclipse other activities, further dislocating the productive structure and subverting the normal patterns of capital accumulation.

It is worth analyzing some consequences of this kind of situation. First, the circumstances just outlined do not prevent firms from realizing high profits—the fruit of their maximization of short-term gains. But high profits do not give rise to optimism; on the contrary, they reinforce the very pessimism that inspired the strategy whereby the high profits were generated. Thus an apparently paradoxical situation emerges in which capitalists are acutely dissatisfied with circumstances in which most of them may be reaping inordinately high profits. Second, plunder is rational for everyone. As capitalists disinvest and speculate, it makes no sense for workers to heed injunctions to "moderate their demands" to aid an economy that, in any case, will continue to deteriorate. For everyone the only meaningful gains are those that can be realized immediately. Third, the plunderers know that they live in a world of pillage. This awareness results in the relaxation of institutional and ideological controls, which become increasingly irrelevant with the evaporation of the predictability and stability that they support and presuppose. Each *ego* assumes that every *alter* will maximize short-term gains, resulting in a situation where everyone contributes to a world of high uncertainty. Ultimately, the situation approaches what David Apter has called the "randomization" of behavior.[14]

In understanding how this micro-rational behavior contributed to the economic crises that precipitated the BAs, the following elements are crucial. First, as judgments about current and future economic conditions prompt decisions that make such evaluations self-fulfilling prophecies, a point is reached at which the aggregate effect of rational micro-level decisions becomes profoundly irrational in terms of the capitalist code to which the most powerful economic actors (among others) subscribe. Second, while an economy of plunder can yield high profits, its incompatibility with medium- and long-range planning undercuts the advantages that the largest economic units enjoy over other actors. This ensures that the largest enterprises will remain intensely dissatisfied, even if they profit from speculative plunder. Finally, as a result of this process, the economy becomes progressively incapable of reproducing the conditions for its own functioning, normal or not.

Since it is the contextually rational behavior of individual units that drives a process so at odds with the logic of the prevailing capitalist code, it is evident that this process can be halted only by someone outside these actors' microeconomic and short-term rationality. Such intervention could come from actors who subscribe to a different code—i.e., from a revolution. But another possibility is that someone who adheres to the same capitalist code, but is not similarly subject to microeconomic rationality, could step in to restore conditions under which the aggregate outcome of the behaviors of individual capitalists might once again be perceived as normal and satisfactory.

This discussion has remained at a relatively high level of abstraction and has included a minimum of factors. Even so, the state institutions have entered the picture as that "someone" who can transcend the microeconomic rationality on the basis of which even the largest economic units act, and who may be capable of restoring the general conditions for the normal functioning of society *qua* capitalist. Implicit throughout our discussion was a state that was failing to guarantee such conditions. Moreover, in a crisis triggered by an economy of plunder that has gone "too far," the foundations of the class structure and the domination implicit within it are unavoidably shaken. At this point the crisis engulfs the whole state, which, far from being the foundation of order, is caught up in, and aggravates, the crisis. This gives rise to efforts to restore the state to its role of effective guarantor and organizer of social domination and "normal" patterns of capital accumulation.

We can now turn our attention to more concrete matters.

5. POLITICAL AND ECONOMIC CRISES: CONVERGENCES

Prior to the emergence of their respective BAs, Argentina, Brazil, Chile, and Uruguay did not meet the general conditions for the normal functioning of a capitalist economy. Rather, to varying degrees their economies were characterized by (1) pronounced fluctuations in the growth of the economy and its principal sectors; (2) large intersectoral transfers of income; (3) a high and rising rate of inflation, also subject to strong fluctuations; (4) recurrent balance-of-payments crises; (5) suspension of direct investment and long-term credit from abroad, exacerbated by captial outflows; (6) declining private investment; and (7) sizeable fiscal deficits. From the standpoint of the codified criteria discussed in the previous section, these economies were seen as performing very unsatisfactorily and doomed to continue deteriorating toward the point at which the very survival of capitalism would be at stake.

These troubles were alarming enough, but they were made worse because they did not occur in a political vacuum: the economic crisis was interlaced with a no less profound political crisis. The emergence of the *pueblo* involved the expansion of an urban-based popular sector,* one component of which was a working class that had grown rapidly and had become geographically concentrated as a result of the rate and type of industrialization taking place at the time. This urban popular sector intervened, with a growing voice and weight of its own, in a political arena in which conflicts over the allocation of resources had become increasingly acute. These conflicts strengthened the political activation† of the popular sector at the same time that they amplified the fluctuations of the economy. The resulting political turmoil is well described by the concept of "mass praetorianism,"[15] which describes a situation in which a growing number of political actors are embroiled in conflicts barely, and decreasingly, regulated by institutional and normative controls. This situation tends to correspond on the one hand to an increasing randomization of social relations and, on the other, to a worsening of the economic crisis.

From the standpoint of the dominant classes, both domestic and external, the economic and social crisis in the countries in which the BAs emerged involved more than the absence of the general conditions for normal economic functioning. It also raised the possibility (more or less imminently, depending on the case) that capitalism itself would be eliminated. This perceived danger—the most pessimistic of predictions—was a key factor in the decisions that led to the implantation of the BAs. Praetorianism, the randomization of social behavior, uncertainty, and negative expectations combined to narrow even further the limits imposed by the economic crisis and the transnationalization of society. These troubles were compounded by the demands of an increasingly activated popular sector and its leadership, which became more difficult to satisfy as the economic crisis worsened and which eroded the vertical—corporatizing[16]—controls previously imposed on the popular sector's organizations. The state apparatus, for its part, displaying an

---

*By urban popular sector I mean the ensemble formed by the working class and the unionized segments of the middle sectors.

†By the political activation of the popular sector I mean its ongoing presence in national political conflicts and alliances, a presence that obliges other actors (including state institutions) to respond to the interests and demands voiced by this sector (one such response may be repression). The political activation of the popular sector entails its control of organizational and informational resources that allow it to maintain a fairly continuous presence in the political arena.

extremely low level of autonomy with respect to all sectors and classes, had become a battleground for social forces whose micro-rationalities it could not reconcile with the normal functioning of the economy. Moreover, with its enormous deficits and seldom-implemented policies, the state apparatus made its own contribution to the uncertainties, fluctuations, and conflicts of the time. Democratic or not, the praetorian state was representative—too representative—of classes, sectors, and groups that viewed its resources and institutions as part of the booty in each round of plunder and conflict.

6. ON CRISES

The term *crisis* is too general. Since the social and/or political dimensions of a crisis can attain very different levels of intensity, it is useful to distinguish among several kinds of crises.

(1) *Crisis of Government.* The first type of crisis is characterized by political instability, and calls to mind a parade of high officials, including presidents, prematurely forced from office. This type of crisis has important consequences, since it is usually accompanied by erratic changes in public policies and by a widespread feeling that no public power can possibly establish itself. The state apparatus under these conditions tends to appear before society bereft of its majestic façade of authority, revealing itself to be little more than a site of struggles among rival groups.

(2) *Crisis of Regime.* In the second type of crisis, groups not only expel each other from the government, but also seek to establish new channels of access to governmental roles and new criteria for political representation. This type of crisis is also significant in that it reveals potentially explosive disagreements among competing groups. But unaccompanied by yet more severe levels of crisis, crises of regime and government float upon the surface of society. Latin America abounds with examples of "political instability" and regime transformation that have had little or no effect on economic performance or on social domination.

(3) *Expansion of the Political Arena.* During such a crisis groups, parties, movements, or government personnel appeal to classes or social sectors on the basis of collective identities that conflict with those of the established participants in the political arena. Successful* appeals to *lo*

---

*By successful I mean that such appeals evoke responses that lead to the emergence of new collective actors in the political arena. See Landi, "Sobre lenguajes, identidades y ciudadanías políticas," Laclau, *Politics and Ideology in Marxist Theory,* and Norbert Lechner, "Postfacio," in *La crisis del estado en América Latina,* ed. Lechner.

popular, or to wage-earners as a class, introduce political forces and collective identities that the existing regime cannot absorb without undergoing important transformations. But even if they are successful, such appeals do not necessarily produce parallel transformations at the level of social domination, nor do they necessarily entail the collapse of the existing regime or government. Nonetheless, this crisis is always a matter of grave concern for the dominant classes, who would prefer that the political arena remain confined to discourses and appeals under their own control.

(4) *Crisis of Accumulation.* A fourth type of crisis is produced when subordinate classes take actions that recurrently impede what the dominant classes view as the normal functioning of the economy. As we shall see in examining the Argentine situation prior to 1966, a crisis of accumulation does not necessarily imply a challenge to social domination: the popular sector and those who represent it in the political arena may have no intention of attacking the fundamental (capitalist) parameters of society. But such a crisis may touch interests perceived as more crucial than those affected by the crises we have sketched thus far. A diagnosis of persistent impediments to capital accumulation suggests to the dominant classes that the demands of the popular sector are dangerously exceeding the limits of the economy and society. These classes tend therefore to define the situation as one in which the capitalist parameters of society will sooner or later be threatened, regardless of whether the popular sector or their political representatives seek to pose such a threat. The situation so defined, the dominant classes conclude that in some way—ranging from cooptation to coercion—the dominated classes must be put "in their place." Often perceived as a necessary condition for achieving this goal is the severance of the bonds that link the popular sector to political personnel who are judged to be making "excessive" or "irresponsible" demands on its behalf. Thus, although a crisis of accumulation initially manifests itself as an economic problem, its diagnosis and the remedies prescribed for it tend to make it a central political conflict.

(5) *Social (or Cellular) Domination.* This principal and most profound crisis affects the very foundation of capitalist society: the social relations that constitute and articulate its social classes. This crisis is marked by the appearance among the dominated classes of behaviors and abstentions that are not consistent with the reproduction of the social relations central to a capitalist society. "Rebelliousness," "subversion," "disorder," and "lack of discipline" are labels affixed to situa-

tions that threaten the continuity of what previously were assumed to be the natural attitudes and practices of the dominated classes. Such situations manifest themselves in daily life in "improper" attitudes toward social "superiors," in unusual forms of interpersonal relations among socially "unequal" persons, in the questioning of traditional patterns of authority in such settings as the family, the school, and even the street, and—specifically characterizing this crisis—in the challenging of the bourgeoisie's claim* to the right to organize the work process and to appropriate and allocate the capital it generates. Such a challenge may involve anything from "excessive" demands concerning the organization and operation of the work process, to the seizure of productive units, to open challenges to the social role of the capitalist as owner and to the entrepreneur as possessor of the means of production.

Crises of social domination pose a crucial threat to the existing order. They reveal that ideological controls have deteriorated sharply and that coercion is failing to eliminate "disorder"—i.e., that the state is failing to guarantee the reproduction of basic social relations and, with them, of the system of social domination. Such a crisis is therefore at the same time the supreme political crisis: a crisis of the state not only, nor so much, as an apparatus, but in its primary aspect as guarantor and organizer of social domination. A crisis of social domination is a crisis of the state *in* society. Of course, this crisis has deep repercussions within the state institutions, but it can be fully understood only from a perspective that recognizes the state first and foremost as an indispensable support of domination *within* society.

None of the other crises examined is as directly and radically threatening as a crisis of social domination, in which the actions and intentions of (at least) the most active and vocal segments of the dominated classes point toward what is most worrisome to the bourgeoisie and to the capitalist state: the abolition of the bourgeoisie as a class, and therefore of the existing system of social domination. By itself, however, a crisis of social domination is limited to the cellular, micro levels of society. But it is usually combined with crises of government, regime, and expansion of the political arena, and obviously also with a crisis of accumulation. The two situations we turn to now are variants that may accompany, and intensify, a crisis of social domination.

(6) In the first variant, political parties and/or government person-

---

*Or, in the case of bureaucratic socialism, of similar claims on the part of state officials.

nel, echoing and accentuating the tremors raised by the crisis of social domination, attempt to found a new social order.

(7) The second variant, which may or may not arise jointly with the preceding one, is brought on by armed attempts to divest the state apparatus of coercive supremacy over its territory. Such attempts may take place in the absence of any or all of the crises discussed earlier, but their chances of success increase when they coexist with other crises, especially with a crisis of social domination.

Each kind of crisis may be combined in various ways with others. The crisis of government (type 1) has constituted the "normal" history of Latin America. Crises of regime (type 2) and of expansion of the political arena (type 3) together marked the liquidation of the oligarchic state and the recomposition of a social order based on bourgeois domination. Type 2 and type 3 crises have appeared profoundly subversive (and as such have been harshly repressed) when they have involved the peasantry, since such involvement could not but subvert the prevailing (noncapitalist or barely capitalist) patterns of social domination in the rural areas. A type 3 crisis characterized the Chilean political democracy during the 1960s; it was not until the period just prior to the implantation of the bureaucratic-authoritarian state in 1973 that the system of social domination was challenged. A crisis of accumulation (type 4), together with crises of government and regime, existed in Argentina just before the inauguration of the 1966 BA. A crisis of social domination was barely visible in pre-1966 Argentina, and only slightly more so in pre-1964 Brazil, where the implantation of the BA was precipitated by crises of government, regime, and expansion of the political arena. By contrast to the preceding cases, a crisis of social domination was the decisive element in the implantation of BAs in Argentina, Chile, and Uruguay during the 1970s. The Chilean situation prior to 1973 approximated a type 6 crisis, while circumstances in Argentina and Uruguay during the 1970s (where armed organizations disputing the state's coercive supremacy over the national territory, not political parties or government personnel seeking a fundamental change in the social order, were decisive in precipitating the countries' respective BAs) conformed closely to a type 7 crisis.

The dominant classes may perceive type 1, type 2, and even type 3 crises as abnormalities it would be advisable—but not essential—to correct. Type 4 crises, in which the dominant classes confront what they view as "excessive" demands by the popular sector for economic benefits or organizational autonomy, likewise fall short of challenging the capitalist parameters of society. But type 5, type 6, and type 7 crises, by contrast, are always seen by the dominant classes as fundamental threats to their social position.* Argentina experienced prior to 1966 the convergence of an accumulation crisis with crises of regime and government. But at that time no political party attempted to alter the capitalist parameters of society (as in pre-1973 Chile); no armed organizations disputed the coercive supremacy of the state (as in Argentina and Uruguay during the 1970s); and no government personnel sought either to expand the political arena to incorporate previously marginalized classes and sectors (as in pre-1964 Brazil) or to challenge cellular domination (as in pre-1973 Chile). By comparison, then, the crisis that preceded the 1966 Argentine BA was quite mild, even if, as we shall see, it was by no means insignificant.

Each type of crisis, in addition to combining with other types, can vary in intensity. Comparative analysis of these combinations and degrees of intensity helps us account for the varied reactions of the dominant classes (as well as of the armed forces and of more than a few middle sectors) that lead to the implantation of BAs, and for variations in the repression that is subsequently applied. The period preceding the 1964 coup in Brazil combined elements of crisis that by comparison also seem rather mild. However, the rapid pace of political activation of segments of the popular sector (including parts of the peasantry) at the time seemed to many to pose a serious threat. This perception was reinforced by the fact that it was largely government personnel, including President Goulart, who seemed responsible for the crisis of expansion of the political arena and for incipient signals of a crisis of social domination. But even as the participation of government personnel heightened the perception of a threat, it underscored the weakness of a challenge that had only shallow roots in the dominated classes. The Brazilian case thus suggests that another pertinent factor is the location of the dynamic axis of each crisis. If, as in Brazil, the axis runs through the state apparatus, the process, though it tends to appear very threatening, may be extirpated with relative ease. From this standpoint, the case of pre-1966 Argentina is at the opposite pole, since there it was neither

---

*For an initial discussion of threat as a crucial factor in the implantation of the BA, see Guillermo O'Donnell, "Reflections on the Patterns of Change in the Bureaucratic-Authoritarian State," *Latin American Research Review* 12, no. 1 (Winter 1978): 3–38. In the present context I am trying to disaggregate this concept and to refine it for comparative use.

political parties nor the government, but forces that arose within society, that fostered the crisis of accumulation and first hints of a crisis of domination. But in view of the comparative mildness of the crises preceding their respective coups, the Argentine and Brazilian cases resemble one another more than their counterparts of the seventies, which emerged out of crises of social domination.

In Chile prior to 1973, the impetus for the crisis of social domination came from government personnel and political parties proclaiming socialist goals, as well as from direct challenges to capitalism at the cellular level. Both the perception and the reality of the threat during this period in Chile were much more profound and imminent than in pre-1964 Brazil or pre-1966 Argentina. The other cases of the 1970s—Uruguay and pre-1976 Argentina—also approached this situation of grave and imminent threat. Each of these countries also experienced a crisis of social domination, but one propelled, to a far greater degree than in Chile, by armed organizations that disputed the coercive supremacy of the state. The challenges posed by these armed organizations were of sufficient gravity to produce a perception of a threat perhaps less imminent, but probably no less intense, than in Chile. The greater magnitude of the perceived threat prior to the implantation of each of the three 1970s BAs generated subsequent levels of repression far in excess of anything experienced in Argentina between 1966 and 1973 or in Brazil after 1964. It was also decisive in accelerating the respective economic crises toward extremes unmatched during the sixties;* the key factor promoting the full fruition of a plunder economy prior to each of the 1970s BAs was the fear and uncertainty that the crises of social domination generated among the bourgeoisie and many middle sectors.

The foregoing allows us to clarify the concept of hegemonic crisis. Crises of types 1, 2, and 3 are best viewed as involving tensions that prevent the state from functioning, on certain institutional levels, in a manner consistent with the majestic and stable appearance that helps make it the guarantor and organizer of existing social relations. But these types of crisis do not threaten the basic supports of social domination; they are compatible with a high degree of ideological control and with the continued effectiveness of the coercive guarantee that the state supplies to the capitalist relations of production. Similarly, a crisis of

---

*It should suffice to say that the annual rates of inflation in Chile in September 1973, and in Argentina during March 1976, easily surpassed 500 percent, far in excess of the rates registered before the 1964 Brazilian coup or the Argentine coup of 1966.

accumulation (type 4) falls short of challenging the capitalist parameters of society.

Since crises of types 1, 2, 3, and 4 do not involve a direct challenge to the fundamental parameters of society *qua* capitalist, they do not in themselves expose the constitutive and fundamental reality of the state. By contrast, a crisis of social domination (type 5), whether or not it merges with a crisis of type 6 or 7, is properly considered a crisis of hegemony. A crisis of social domination involves more than the widespread malfunctioning of the patterns by which society is reproduced from day to day. It also involves—and this is what defines it as a crisis of hegemony—the emergence of widespread denials that the existing relations of domination are, as they once seemed, natural or equitable. A crisis of hegemony also involves, consequently, the calling into question of the right of capitalists to appropriate the economic surplus and to direct the work process.

A crisis of hegemony shakes class relations so severely that the bourgeoisie realize that their existence as a class is in more or less immediate jeopardy. Class struggles thus emerge, both objectively and subjectively, as a crucial component of the situation. It cannot be too strongly emphasized that a crisis of hegemony is also a crisis of the state, but not solely or primarily as a set of institutions. Rather, it is a crisis of the state in its original and fundamental aspect: a crisis of the state *in* society. A crisis of hegemony involves the abandonment by the state of its role as guarantor and organizer of the fundamental social relations of a capitalist society. A crisis of social domination, of cellular domination, of hegemony, and of the state *in* society are thus equivalent terms. This equivalence underscores the links between the state, society, and the social relations that constitute the capitalist character of each.*

Despite the absence of a crisis of hegemony in pre-1966 Argentina, the situation preceding the implantation of the BA had crossed a threshold at which the dominant classes felt endangered enough to adopt or

---

*This discussion stops short of resolving the specific question of when, and under what actual circumstances, a society can be said to be undergoing a hegemonic crisis. It is obviously unnecessary for the entire popular sector or working class to pose a challenge to hegemony; on the other hand, it is not sufficient to identify isolated pockets of society in which the fundamental social relations of capitalism are being questioned. The crucial point would seem to be where the crisis of hegemony has extended beyond these isolated and probably ephemeral pockets. At this point the crisis may not involve the entire range of dominated classes, but it becomes a political problem of the first order and captures the attention of all political actors. Perhaps the best barometer would be the fears experienced by the bourgeoisie. The impact of these fears is as great in the political sphere as it is in the economic realm, where they generate a rush by the members of this class to salvage their immediate interests in the face of what they believe is an imminent social catastrophe.

support drastic measures to eliminate the perceived sources of the threat. But the effects of the crisis are not limited to the bourgeoisie. High and erratic inflation, sudden transfers of income, widespread unpredictability, feelings of increasing social and economic disorder, and the eventual emergence of radical discourses deeply disturb a broad spectrum of middle sectors and institutional groups. The response of these actors is to follow their most defensive proclivities: they call for the restoration of "order," issue moral condemnations of the plunder economy, and long for the appearance of leaders endowed with sufficient "authority" to restore the state apparatus to the role of a stable and benevolent tutor. When the defensive reactions of these middle sectors converge with the fears of the bourgeoisie, an alliance is forged around a common desire for "order" and "authority."

The specificity of the BA in relation to other, past and present, authoritarian states in Latin America lies in this defensive reaction by the dominant classes and their allies to crises involving a popular sector that has been politically activated and is increasingly autonomous with respect to the dominant classes and the state apparatus. This reaction includes an agreement among those who implant and support the BA that its main tasks should be the subordination and strict control of the popular sector, a sharp reversal of the tendency toward autonomy of its class organizations, and the elimination of its capacity to express itself in the political arena.

Now we can proceed to delineate the characteristics of the bureaucratic-authoritarian state.

7. THE BUREAUCRATIC-AUTHORITARIAN STATE

The BA is a type of authoritarian state whose principal characteristics are:

(1) It is, primarily and fundamentally, the aspect of global society that guarantees and organizes the domination exercised through a class structure subordinated to the upper fractions of a highly oligopolized and transnationalized bourgeoisie. In other words, the principal social base of the BA is this upper bourgeoisie.

(2) On the institutional level, it is a set of organizations in which specialists in coercion have decisive weight, as do those who seek to "normalize" the economy. The crucial role played by these actors is the institutional expression of the main tasks that the BA undertakes: the

restoration of "order" by means of the political deactivation of the popular sector, on the one hand, and the "normalization" of the economy, on the other.

(3) It is a system of political exclusion of a previously activated popular sector, which is subjected to strict controls designed to eliminate its earlier presence in the political arena. This is achieved by coercion, as well as by the destruction or strict governmental control of the resources (especially those embodied in class organizations and political parties or movements) that sustained this activation. Such exclusion is guided by the determination to impose "order" on society and to ensure its future viability.

(4) This exclusion brings with it the suppression of citizenship and political democracy. It also involves prohibiting (and enforcing this prohibition with coercion) any appeals to the population as *pueblo* and, of course, as class. The suppression of the institutional roles and channels of access to the government characteristic of political democracy is aimed at the elimination of the roles and organizations (political parties among them) that once served as channels for appeals for substantive justice. These channels are considered incompatible with the reimposition of order and with the normalization of the economy. The BA is thus based on the suppression of two fundamental mediations between state and society: citizenship and *pueblo*.

(5) It is also a system of economic exclusion of the popular sector, inasmuch as it promotes a pattern of capital accumulation strongly biased in favor of large, oligopolistic units of private capital and some state institutions. Preexisting inequalities are thus increased.

(6) Through its institutions it endeavors to "depoliticize" the handling of social issues, which are entrusted to those who deal with them according to the supposedly neutral and objective criteria of technical rationality. This is the obverse side of the prohibition against raising issues linked to *pueblo* or class.

(7) Its regime—which, while usually not formalized, is clearly identifiable—involves closing the democratic channels of access to the government. More generally, it involves closing the channels for the representation of popular and working-class interests. Access is limited to those who stand at the apex of large organizations (both state and private), especially the armed forces, large enterprises, and certain segments of the state's civil bureaucracy.

The features just enumerated permit us to distinguish the BA from other authoritarian states. This is not just any authoritarianism, but one marked by characteristics that signal the historical specificity I have sketched in the preceding pages.*

8. A CONCEPTUAL AND METHODOLOGICAL EXCURSUS

It seems advisable at this point to anticipate the empirical referents of some terms that will be used frequently throughout this book.

(1) The *upper bourgeoisie* is composed of the larger and more powerful (monopolistic or oligopolistic) fractions of urban private capital, both national and transnational.

(2) *Transnational capital* refers to the TNC subsidiaries established in the domestic market (which usually are the most dynamic component of the upper bourgeoisie) and/or, depending on the context, to large enterprises based abroad, including the headquarters of those subsidiaries and private financial institutions.

(3) The *local bourgeoisie* includes the small and medium-sized fractions of national capital, *not* the monopolized or oligopolized segments of national capital, which form part of the upper bourgeoisie.

(4) The *Pampean bourgeoisie* consists of the fraction of the agrarian bourgeoisie that exploits Argentina's pampean region.

(5) The *bourgeoisie* is the ensemble formed by the preceding four categories. On the other hand,

(6) *organizations of the upper bourgeoisie* are those organizations that, during the period studied here, expressed the interests of various fractions of the upper bourgeoisie: the Unión Industrial Argentina (UIA), the Cámara Argentina de Comercio (CAC), and the Bolsa de Comercio de Buenos Aires (Buenos Aires Stock Exchange), as well as

---

*The BA can hardly be confused with any variant of political democracy. But it is worthwhile to specify certain features that set it apart from other authoritarianisms. It is possible to distinguish the BA from (1) Latin America's traditional forms of authoritarian rule, in which an oligarchy and segments of transnational capital engaged in the export of primary products dominate subordinate classes that have undergone little or no political activation and whose working-class component is small; (2) the more or less authoritarian variants of populism, in which expansionist economic policies promote the formation of a coalition consisting of nationalist and anti-oligarchic groups involved in new industries, fractions of transnational capital producing for the domestic market, various middle sectors, and a recently activated and politically incorporated popular sector; and (3) fascism, which is based on a more genuinely national bourgeoisie and led by a party, or movement, and leadership with characteristics that differ markedly from those of the political actor that brings about the implantation of the BA and occupies its highest governmental posts: the armed forces. For a comparison of the BA and fascism, see Atilio Borón, "El fascismo como categoría histórica: en torno al problema de las dictaduras en América Latina," *Revista Mexicana de Sociología* 2 (1977).

the principal organizations of the Pampean bourgeoisie, the Sociedad Rural Argentina (SRA) and the Coordinadora de Asociaciones Rurales de Buenos Aires y la Pampa (CARBAP). The same term applies to the association that claimed to represent all of those organizations, the Asociación Coordinadora de Instituciones Empresarias Libres (ACIEL). Where appropriate, these organizations will be referred to individually.

(7) *Associations of the local bourgeoisie* include the Confederación General Económica (CGE) and the Confederación General de la Industria (CGI). Henceforth, these organizations will be identified by their acronyms.

Finally, (8) the *leading periodicals* consist of certain daily newspapers (*La Prensa, La Nación, La Razón, Economic Survey*) that regularly express the viewpoints of the upper bourgeoisie and/or the Pampean bourgeoisie. I have also utilized other periodicals (particularly the dailies *Clarín* and, after 1971, *La Opinión,* as well as the weeklies *Análisis, Primera Plana, Panorama,* and *Confirmado*) whose viewpoints are more ambiguous, and more variable over the course of the period to be examined. The periodicals in this latter group will be identified by name. I use the term *media* to refer to the ensemble formed by all the publications mentioned above and the television and radio stations.

Let us now tackle a methodological point. It is assumed throughout the book that it is reasonably correct to attribute authentic representation to the various organizations of the bourgeoisie, i.e., that the views and demands such organizations presented basically corresponded to those of the actors for whom they claimed to speak. The problematic character of this assumption derives from the question of whether, and to what degree, it is valid to say that the views expressed by leaders, ranging from those of a small group to those of a nation, basically correspond to the opinions and attitudes of those whom they claim to represent. The degree and character of this correspondence is, of course, an empirical question. The following discussion is an attempt to show that this assumption is not too problematic for the organizations of the bourgeoisie during the period of Argentine history studied in this book.

The CGE was founded in 1953, during Perón's second presidency, as part of a corporatist scheme to "complement" the Confederación General de Trabajo (CGT). The CGE was designed to absorb the obstinately anti-Peronist organizations of the upper bourgeoisie, subsuming under a single entity the representative associations of agrarian, commercial, financial, and industrial capital. This attempt was partially successful only with respect to industrialists. Industrial capital was represented through the CGI, which dominated the CGE to such an extent that in the vernacular of politics and journalism it was usually confused with the latter. Despite its claim to be "the" representative of Argentine industry, the CGE–CGI after Perón's ouster in 1955 basically represented small and medium-sized firms, mostly owned by Argentine nationals and located in the interior of the country. In 1960 the organizations of the upper bourgeoisie formed a superordinate body, ACIEL, at the same level as was originally projected for the CGE. ACIEL included the UIA, the CAC and the SRA (among others) and like its constituents expressed active hostility toward the CGE–CGI. Since industrial firms predominated in the CGE–CGI, many of the resulting conflicts pitted the CGE against the UIA. There emerged from these conflicts a widespread perception that the UIA expressed the interests of the oligopolistic and transnationalized sectors of industry (or, according to the term I have proposed, the upper bourgeoisie), while the CGE–CGI bore a similar relationship to the small and medium fractions of national industrial capital (or, in my terminology, the local bourgeoisie). This perception emerged in spite of the fact that each institution claimed to represent industry as a whole. The UIA supported its claim to overall representativeness by pointing out that its affiliated enterprises generated a substantial part of industrial value added, while the CGE–CGI backed its similar claim by arguing that its affiliated enterprises greatly exceeded in number those of the UIA. These claims, both of which are accurate, together constitute an interesting synopsis of the structure of Argentine industry. But perhaps the most important indication that the split between the ACIEL–UIA on the one hand and the CGE–CGI on the other expressed a fundamental cleavage within the industrial sector is that the leaders of those associations, as well as political actors and observers of the time, *believed* that it expressed such a cleavage and the divergent interests that stemmed from it.

The cleavage between the ACIEL–UIA and the CGE–CGI had important political correlates. From the standpoint of the UIA and, in general, of the leading periodicals and the organizations of the upper bourgeoisie, the CGE–CGI was a remnant of Peronism's "totalitarian" leanings. Its leaders (including José B. Gelbard, who headed the organization from its inception until 1973) were viewed as suspiciously close to those origins and as supportive of the demagogic policies associated with Peronism. The leaders of the CGE–CGI, for their part, viewed the UIA and in general the ACIEL and its associates as expressions of monopolistic and foreign-oriented interests that blocked off the expansion of the domestic market and militated against economic development led by the "national entrepreneurs." Although there exist no studies that would allow us to determine conclusively that owners and managers of enterprises affiliated with the UIA and the CGE–CGI shared the perceptions of their respective leaderships regarding the other organization's social bases and political orientation, there was clearly a consensus among practically all actors and observers that such perceptions were close to the mark.* On the other hand, it is important to note that many of the top leaders of the CGE–CGI came not from the type of firm most characteristic of that organization but from enterprises that, although generally medium-sized, had been created relatively recently, used modern technology, and were linked to TNC subsidiaries and/or to the state apparatus. However, the issue of the social origins of the CGE leaders (to which I shall return) is not the same as that of whether the public stands taken by those leaders really represented the opinions of the CGE membership.

NOTES

1. The arguments presented in this section are developed in Guillermo O'Donnell, "Apuntes para una teoría del estado," *Documento CEDES/G.E. CLACSO* 9, Centro de Estudios de Estado y Sociedad (Buenos Aires, 1977); also published in *Revista Mexicana de Sociología* 1 (1979): 1157–99.
2. The reflections on the *pueblo* set forth here and in the following section draw on the contributions of Ernesto Laclau, *Politics and Ideology in Marxist Theory* (London: New Left Books, 1977) and Oscar Landi, "Sobre lenguajes, identidades y ciudadanías políticas" in *Estado y política en América Latina,* ed. Norbert Lechner (Mexico City: Siglo XXI, 1981).
3. The state as a pact of domination is discussed in Fernando Henrique Cardoso, "Estado Capitalista e Marxismo," *Estudos CEBRAP* 21 (1977).
4. For a similar definition, which also underscores the distinction between state and regime, see David Collier, ed., *The New Authoritarianism in Latin America* (Princeton: Princeton University Press, 1979), 402–403.
5. The implantation of the 1966 Argentine BA is analyzed in more detail in O'Donnell, *Modernization and Bureaucratic-Authoritarianism,* and in Guillermo O'Donnell, "Modernization and Military Coups: Theory, Practice, and

---

*It should be added that my interviews with leaders of the CGE–CGI and the UIA corroborate these perceptions, as does another study based on interviews with leaders of these organizations: John Freels, *El sector industrial en la política nacional* (Buenos Aires: EUDEBA, 1970), and "Industrialists and Politics in Argentina: An Opinion Survey of Trade Association Leaders," *Journal of Inter-American Studies and World Affairs* 12, no. 3 (July 1970). See also Jorge Niosi, *Los empresarios y el estado argentino (1955–1969)* (Buenos Aires: Siglo XXI, 1974), and Dardo Cúneo, *Crisis y comportamiento de la clase empresaria* (Buenos Aires: Pleamar, 1967).

the Argentine Case" in *Armies and Politics in Latin America,* ed. Abraham F. Lowenthal and J. Samuel Fitch (New York: Holmes & Meier Publishers, 1978).

6. This concept is taken from Weffort, *O populismo na política brasileira.*

7. Cf. esp. the pioneering and still unsurpassed work of Cardoso and Faletto, *Dependencia y Desarrollo en América Latina.*

8. One suggestive effort along these lines is Norbert Lechner, ed., *La crisis del estado en América Latina* (Buenos Aires: El Cid Editores, 1977). The world capitalist center's view of itself is also open to question; Nicos Poulantzas undertook an interesting analysis of this problem in "La internacionalización de las relaciones capitalistas de producción y el estado nacional" in *Las clases sociales en el capitalismo de hoy* (Mexico City: Siglo XXI, 1975).

9. On the worldwide expansion of TNCs, see Myra Wilkins, *The Making of Multinational Enterprise: American Business Abroad from 1914 to 1970* (Cambridge: Harvard University Press, 1974). There are also several good studies of TNC expansion in specific Latin American countries. On Brazil, Carlos von Dellinger and Leonardo Cavalcanti, *Empresas multinacionais na industria brasileira* (Rio de Janeiro: IPEA, 1975), and Fernando Fajnzlber, *Estrategia industrial e empresas internacionais: posição relativa de América Latina e do Brasil* (Rio de Janeiro: IPEA/INPES, 1971). On Mexico, Fernando Fajnzlber and Trinidad Martínez Tarragó, *Las empresas transnacionales: Expansión a nivel mundial y proyección en la industria mexicana* (Mexico City: Fondo de Cultura Económica, 1976). On Argentina, Juan V. Sourrouille, *El impacto de las empresas transnacionales sobre el empleo y los ingresos: el caso de la Argentina* (Geneva: International Labor Office, World Employment Program, 1976), and "La presencia y el comportamiento de las empresas extranjeras en el sector industrial argentino," *Estudios CEDES* 1, no. 2 (1978), and the data compiled in O'Donnell and Linck, *Dependencia y Autonomía,* ch. 3.

10. The most comprehensive study of the characteristics of Latin American industrialization is Juan Ayza, Gerard Fichet and Norberto González, *América Latina: Integración económica y sustitución de importaciones* (Mexico City: ECLA, Fondo de Cultura Económica, 1976). Two interesting attempts to conceptualize the specificities of industrialization in Argentina are Richard D. Mallon and Juan V. Sourrouille, *Economic Policy-Making in a Conflict Society: The Argentine Case* (Cambridge: Harvard University Press, 1975), and Marcelo Diamand, *Doctrinas económicas, desarrollo e independencia* (Buenos Aires: Editorial Paidós, 1973).

11. See Albert O. Hirschman, *The Strategy of Economic Development* (New Haven: Yale University Press, 1957), and "The Political Economy of Import-substituting Industrialization in Latin America," in *A Bias for Hope* (New Haven: Yale University Press, 1971).

12. On this and related points, see Lechner, ed., *La crisis del estado en América Latina.*

13. Within the literature on this topic, see James March and Herbert Simon, *Organizations* (New York: John Wiley & Sons, 1958); Richard Cyert and James March, *A Behavioral Theory of the Firm* (Englewood Cliffs, N.J.: Prentice-Hall, 1963); and the pertinent articles in *Handbook of Organizations,* ed. James March (Chicago: Rand McNally, 1965).

14. David Apter, *Choice and the Politics of Allocation* (New Haven: Yale University Press, 1971).

15. Samuel P. Huntington, *Political Order in Changing Societies* (New Haven: Yale University Press, 1968).

16. On corporatism, see Philippe Schmitter, "Still the Century of Corporatism?" in *The New Corporatism,* ed. Frederick Pike and Thomas Stritch (Notre Dame: University of Notre Dame Press, 1974); also Guillermo O'Donnell, "On 'Corporatism' and the Question of the State," in James Malloy, ed., *Authoritarianism and Corporatism in Latin America* (Pittsburgh: Pittsburgh University Press, 1977), 47–88.

TWO

The Implantation of the Bureaucratic-Authoritarian State

1. THE BACKGROUND TO THE 1966 COUP

The June 1966 coup in Argentina had been discussed and promoted openly for at least the preceding year.* On June 28, the commanders in chief of the army, navy, and air force decided to act, and General Julio Alsogaray and his escort forced President Illia to leave the House of Government. There was almost no opposition to the coup within the armed forces, and there was practically no civilian attempt to prevent it. It became clear in the following days that, except for the unseated Radical party, some minor parties and a substantial part of the university community, the coup had the approval of most of the population† and of nearly all social organizations.

---

*As *La Nación* put it: "The coup is discussed with familiarity, as if it were inevitable. The only uncertainty is its likely date, for which there exists a wide range of possibilities" (June 5, 1966). Among the sources worth consulting for open discussion (and promotion) of the coup are the weeklies *Primera Plana*, *Confirmado*, *Panorama*, and *Análisis*, beginning about a year prior to June 1966. Important dailies such as *La Prensa*, *Clarín*, and *La Razón* contain references that are only slightly more veiled. For an account of the conspiracy and the events of the day of the coup, see *Extra*, "Lo que nunca se contó," June 1979. Not a single news publication of more than minimal circulation came out in support of the Radical government.

†A poll taken in Greater Buenos Aires soon after Illia was ousted revealed that 66% of those questioned approved the coup while only 6% opposed it. Furthermore, 73% felt that the national situation would improve, 17% believed it would stay the same, and only 9% thought it would deteriorate ("A y C Investigación," July 4, 1966, mimeo). Because of the small sample and incomplete information about the methodology employed, these figures should be viewed with caution. According to another survey, 77% of the respondents in Greater Buenos Aires responded affirmatively to the question: "Do you believe

This reveals an important difference between the Argentine case and its Brazilian and Chilean counterparts: the 1966 coup had the support, or at least the acquiescence, of a considerable part of the popular sector, and was endorsed by a majority of political and union leaders. Moreover, it had the backing of the Peronists and of Perón himself.* To these and other actors, the coup seemed to be a necessary move against an ineffectual and unrepresentative government that had become the passive accomplice to widespread disorder, not an attack on the popular sector, its organizations, and its channels of political expression.

Since I have analyzed the background of the 1966 coup in other works,[1] the present discussion of the topic will be limited to those antecedent factors that continued to shape the situation once the new government was installed. In comparative perspective, one such factor stands out: the relative mildness of the crisis and the proportionately reduced threat to the prevailing social order at the time when the BA (bureaucratic-authoritarian state) was implanted. The moderate character of this crisis and threat did not prevent the emergence of public policies, social and economic consequences, and patterns of opposition typical of all BAs. It did, however, permit the early appearance of tensions and conflicts, and certain economic successes, which appeared later or not at all where the BA was implanted in the context of a more extreme crisis and threat.

To get a better picture of the conditions under which the 1966 Argen-

---

that the revolution of June 28 was necessary?" (*Correo de la Tarde,* July 6–12, 1967, pp. 1, 12; sample of 1,000 persons interviewed in the federal capital, methodology unknown). In addition, all of the media applauded the coup, and influential political journalists were lyrical in their enthusiasm. Mariano Grondona, for example, wrote: "The nation and the caudillo go forth among a thousand crises in their search to be united until, for better or worse, they celebrate their mysterious matrimony" (*Primera Plana,* June 30, 1966, p. 3); and Bernardo Neustadt declaimed: "After Onganía there is nothingness. The void, the ultimate abyss. . . . Onganía has recently proved his effectiveness. His authority. His leadership. If he imparted order to a fading army, why not to a country? He can and he should. He will" (*Extra,* August 1966, p. 4).

*Among those who issued statements in support of the coup were Francisco Prado (secretary-general of the CGT) and the major union leaders; cf. *La Nación,* June 30, p. 8, July 1, p. 7, and July 2, p. 14, 1966. Some of these statements, such as the one made on June 30 by the CGT (text in Santiago Senén González, *El sindicalismo después de Perón* [Buenos Aires: Editorial Galerna, 1971], 95–99), were cast in terms as vitriolic in their condemnation of the previous government as they were optimistic with respect to the one just implanted: "The chaotic social, political, and economic situation gave rise to the failure of constituted power, the lack of authority, and the total bankruptcy of [the government's] representativeness. Once again the chaos has engulfed those responsible for it. Once again a government has fallen victim to its own ideas." For Perón's initial reactions to the coup, which were laudatory but more cautious, *La Nación,* June 29, 1966, p. 11.

tine BA was implanted, let us examine the economic situation prior to the 1966 coup. During 1964 and 1965, the only complete years of Radical government, the GNP grew by an impressive 10.3% and 9.1%, while per capita consumption increased by 10.0% in 1964 and 7.4% in 1965. These 1964 and 1965 growth rates, which should be viewed in the light of the depressed baseline of 1962 and 1963 (when GNP changed ⁻3.1% and ⁻3.9% respectively), were not sustained into the first half of 1966, when GNP recorded a practically zero rate of growth. However, the impressiveness of economic growth under the Radical government indicates that it is not in this area that its downfall can be accounted for.* But the performance of other economic variables shows that the general situation was not as bright as these growth rates suggested. As can be seen in Table 2, gross domestic investment as a percentage of GDP decreased markedly during Illia's term. Public investment as a percentage of GNP underwent a similar decline, especially the productive investments that appear in national accounts statistics as destined for "economic sectors." Movements of international capital also registered a negative trend: the net balance of long-term loans (measured in current United States dollars) totaled $2 million in 1964, $4 million in 1965, and ⁻$105 million in 1966 (most of it before the coup), while the net balance of short-term capital flows was ⁻$39 million in 1964, ⁻$177 million in 1965, and ⁻$76 million in 1966.†

Turning from these overall indicators to the state's economic institutions, it is clear from Table 3 that a large fiscal deficit was still present even after the post-1964 recovery of current income and tax revenues.

Despite the impressive GNP growth, the data just examined show clear signs that the economy was faltering.‡ By the first half of 1966 it

*Inflation was quite high under the Radical government (1963: 24.0%; 1964: 22.1%; 1965: 28.6%; 1966: 31.9%). However, this did not represent a substantial change from the earlier years of the decade (1960: 27.1%; 1961: 13.7%; 1962: 28.1%), and in 1959 inflation had reached a peak of 113.9% (Ministerio de Economía [or Hacienda—the name changes], *Boletín Trimestral de Estadística*, various issues).

†Likewise, direct foreign investment, after reaching rather high levels in the preceding years (US$209 million in 1959, $112 million in 1960, $133 million in 1961, and $86 million in 1962), came virtually to a standstill under the Radical government (US$35 million in 1963, $34 million in 1964, $6 million in 1965, and $2 million in 1966) (Ministerio de Economía, *Informe Económico 1970*, IV Trimestre [Buenos Aires, 1971], and FIEL, *Indicadores de Coyuntura*, various issues).

‡Furthermore, the reserves of the Central Bank in the month preceding the coup amounted to US$209 million, less than the imports of two months. The foreign reserves held at the end of the preceding years were US$558 million in 1961, $222 million in 1962, $375 million in 1963, $272 million in 1964, and $301 million in 1965. It should be pointed out that the relative stability of this variable under the Radical government was achieved through a sharp decline in capital goods imports (BCRA, *Boletín Estadístico*, various issues).

TABLE 2   DOMESTIC INVESTMENT

	Gross Domestic Investment as % of Gross Domestic Product	Total Public Investment (in 1960 pesos) (index 1960=100.0)	Public Investment in Productive Activities (in 1960 pesos) (index 1960=100.0)
1960	19.6	100.0	100.0
1961	19.1	96.5	93.1
1962	18.1	85.3	82.7
1963	13.1	84.9	85.3
1964	15.2	75.5	75.4
1965	16.1	82.1	80.4
1966	14.1	63.0	59.7

SOURCES: Column 1: BCRA, *Sistema de cuentas de producto e ingreso de la Argentina*, vol. 2, *Cuadros estadísticos* p. 187. Columns 2 and 3: calculated from Consejo Nacional de Desarrollo, *Plan Nacional de Desarrollo y Seguridad*, vol. 2, p. 26 (Buenos Aires, 1970).
NOTE: Data deflated by the index of national wholesale prices.

was definitely on a recessive path. But as was suggested above, trends in these economic variables do not go far in accounting for the 1966 coup. The emergence of this BA is best understood from the standpoint of the crises of government, regime, and accumulation that gathered momentum after the 1955 overthrow of President Juan Perón. The military government that was consolidated after the 1955 coup implemented vindictive policies against Perón and Peronism (or Justicialism, as Perón's movement was also called). As a result of these policies, the economic situation of most of the popular sector declined. Unions (most of them controlled by Peronists) were subjected to recurrent harassment and to unsuccessful attempts to divide them or to deliver them into the hands of non-Peronist unionists. Laws were passed prohibiting Peronists from running candidates and from conducting party activities. In 1963, after a coup terminated the civilian government of Arturo Frondizi and rival military factions had engaged in a series of armed confrontations, the Radical government of Dr. Illia was elected with a mere twenty-five percent of the vote cast, as massive numbers of Peronists abstained or cast blank ballots. Immediately thereafter, nearly all organizations of the urban and Pampean bourgeoisies mounted a strong attack against the new government, which just as quickly found itself at loggerheads with the unions and the Peronists.

TABLE 3   PUBLIC FINANCES

	Tax Revenues as % of Gross Domestic Product	Current Income of National Government (in 1960 pesos) (index 1960=100.0)	Deficit of National Government (in millions of 1960 pesos)	Savings* of National Government (in millions of 1960 pesos)
1960	9.1	100.0	147.0	235.8
1961	9.4	121.2	54.5	325.5
1962	7.5	131.8	227.2	−134.6
1963	7.8	88.7	258.3	10.3
1964	5.7	89.4	575.0	−79.0
1965	7.2	106.5	247.3	63.4
1966	9.1	118.9	394.9	−7.0

SOURCES: Column 1: Dirección General Impositiva, *Boletín Informativo*, 12 (Buenos Aires, 1976). Columns 2 and 3: BCRA, *Gobierno General. Cuenta de ingresos y gastos corrientes*, vol. 4 (Buenos Aires, 1976): 18–24. Column 4: FIEL, *Indicadores de coyuntura*, various issues.

*"Savings" is current income minus current expenditures.

NOTE: Data deflated by the index of nonagrarian wholesale prices.

At no time after 1955 did the Argentine regime succeed in absorbing Peronism's electoral strength, which amounted to at least the first plurality of the vote. As was demonstrated by Frondizi's ouster, even the possibility that Peronism might win an election—including a non-Presidential one—was sufficient to provoke a coup. The electoral proscription of Peronism, given its enormous influence within the popular sector, badly corroded the legitimacy of the regime and the authority of the elected governments of the 1955–66 period. But the regime's inability to absorb Peronism had deeper causes.

Electoral proscription left the unions as the main organizational bulwark of Peronism and reinforced the weight of the working class within the movement.* Once closely tied to the state apparatus, the unions, still under Peronist leadership, had attained by 1958 considerable autonomy from it—despite, and partly because of, three years of government attempts to weaken or capture them. The electoral pact between Perón and Frondizi which allowed the latter to win the 1958 presidential election marked the point at which this autonomy was consolidated. As

*White-collar unions and their middle-sector constituents were not incorporated (or reincorporated) into Peronism until the late 1960s and early 1970s. The unions' acquisition of decisive weight within the Peronist movement occurred in the great urban centers.

president, however, Frondizi failed to comply with many terms of the pact, and in 1959 the unions launched a great wave of strikes. These strikes, and the repression with which they were met, were key aspects of a turbulent period that culminated in 1962 and 1963 in the overthrow of Frondizi and in combat between rival factions of the armed forces. By this time the unions and their national-level organization (the CGT) had become important political actors in their own right. In the context of a nearly stagnant economy* and a succession of ineffectual governments operating under the constant threat of a military coup, the unions gave powerful voice to the demands of the popular sector. Strikes, street demonstrations, and strident manifestos were the main vehicles of those demands, though union leaders also displayed considerable skill—and we shall return repeatedly to this crucial point—at pragmatic negotiation.[2] These union actions resulted in economic benefits for the rank and file, but gains won by the workers were canceled by inflation and unfavorable government policies, perpetuating a cycle that led, again and again, to massive mobilizations in support of the union leaders' demands.[3] A more enduring consequence of this turbulent cycle of activity was that union leaders were able to gain control of important resources for their increasingly complex and bureaucratized organizations (and, in more than a few cases, of personal benefits for themselves). The actions of these leaders, together with the high preexisting activation of the popular sector, gave rise during the 1955–66 period to dramatic confrontations between the unions and successive governments, exacerbating the economic fluctuations and the political troubles of the period.[†]

*During 1959, 1962, and 1963 the GNP actually declined.

†Several years later, a union leader formerly affiliated with Vandorism (a union alignment we shall examine in due course) described these tactics in the following terms: "Actually, there could not have been an organ better suited [than the union] to a working class guided by its defensive mentality, since the ultimate goal [of the union] is negotiation. Certainly, in the light of the economic crisis and political instability in which the country found itself, there was no reason why this negotiation had to be institutional: the union can resort to the strike, but also to financing political parties, and to factory occupations. This transition [from] its own means—the strike—to less familiar ones—the political struggle—to still others, such as factory takeovers, which imply subverting the capitalist order, should not be misunderstood. It [was] the correlation of forces, the conjuncture, that [determined] the specific tactic to be used in pursuit of an unchanging goal: the defense of the gains made under Peronism. If there is one attribute by which this zig-zag movement can be characterized, it is realism: a narrow realism, if you will, serving the interests of a political pressure group, but in no way a 'utopian' view that [would have led the unions to break their ties to] institutions and social forces and adopt a position of extreme intransigence" (Miguel Gazzera, *Los Libros* 9 [July 1970]: 4). See also Miguel Gazzera and Norberto Ceresole, *Peronismo, autocrítica y perspectivas* (Buenos Aires: Editorial Descartes, 1970).

Union leaders forged a complex relationship with Perón, who had been in exile since 1955, as they became what he often called "the backbone of the Movement." Though each was dependent on what the other contributed to the movement's popular support and vitality, both Perón and the union leaders attempted throughout the 1955–66 period to subordinate and even eliminate the role of the other. Despite these conflicts, however, union leaders and most of the rank and file shared with Perón an ideology that proposed a "more just" and socially balanced version of capitalist development. Perón, the fitful Peronist party, and the union leaders stood as firmly against "communism" as they did against "liberal," laissez-faire, and antistatist ideas. Likewise, their main social base did not articulate anticapitalist goals. The main hope of most of the popular sector lay in a Peronist government that would put the country back on the capitalist, nationalist, and statist path that had been cut short by the 1955 coup. The fundamentally economistic stance of most leaders and members of the Peronist unions promoted recurrent alliances with various fractions of the bourgeoisie; this goes a long way toward explaining why the 1966 Argentine BA was implanted in the context of a relatively low-level threat.

But if the ideology and goals of the popular sector and its leaders made for a comparatively mild threat, the situation also contained a number of elements that were deeply disturbing to the bourgeoisie and its allies. To begin with, the unions were quite effective in translating their frequent and often disruptive demands into economic advantages for their social bases and their own organizations. Efforts to "normalize" the economy (to which we shall return) repeatedly met strong resistance from the popular sector—articulated mainly through the unions—which forged alliances with regional and bourgeois sectors also adversely affected by those attempts. These efforts at economic normalization and the resistance they provoked contributed greatly to an epileptic pattern of economic growth.[4]

The capacity of the unions to press effectively for their demands was regarded by many as the fundamental obstacle to economic stabilization and development. Accordingly, the bourgeoisie and most of its organizations demanded, with increasing urgency after 1955, that successive governments "depoliticize" the unions (i.e., isolate them from the popular support they enjoyed through their affiliation with Peronism) and deprive them of their considerable resources. The bourgeoisie felt that the only way to guarantee their key class interest of preserving satisfactory conditions of capital accumulation was to thoroughly "domesticate" the unions.

However—and this was the second matter of grave concern—the demands of the bourgeoisie and their allies fell upon very weak governments. Attempts to normalize the economy through recessionary policies aimed at lowering inflation and alleviating balance-of-payments crises were countered by great waves of strikes and popular mobilizations. Apparently overwhelmed by widespread "disorder," the civilian governments of the 1958–66 period found themselves perpetually on the verge of a coup. In the short run (and the always imminent coup made the long run irrelevant), the only way to eliminate this disorder was to satisfy a significant part of the demands that generated it. But this implied "demagogically" canceling normalization policies, ensuring a return to severe fluctuations in the major economic variables. One important consequence of this pattern of recurrent, massive, and often successful popular mobilizations was that, although popular sector leaders remained explicitly committed to capitalism, the popular sector itself was viewed by the bourgeoisie and its allies with increasing trepidation.

A third matter of concern for the dominant classes was that the governments of 1955–66, born with the original sin of the electoral proscription of Peronism and obliged repeatedly to attempt economic normalization, could not but antagonize the popular sector. But when elections approached and Peronist votes could not be ignored (since, even if Peronism was banned, Perón and/or the union leaders could deliver their votes to other parties), and when concessions had to be made to dampen social disorder, those same governments could not but antagonize the bourgeoisie. This is one of the main reasons why many called with increasing insistency for the installation of a new state and regime—not just a new government—that would be strong enough to subordinate or atomize the popular sector and the unions, and at the same time independent of the mechanisms that raised the unsolved enigma of the electoral strength of Peronism. The amorphous movement made up of Perón's leadership, the unions, the intermittent Peronist party, and the popular sector (which together, in the words of the Peronist leader John W. Cooke, constituted the "curse of bourgeois Argentina") had to be, once and for all, "put in its place."

To understand the factors that precipitated the 1966 coup and that continued to have an effect thereafter, it is important to examine the policies with which the Radical government attempted to weaken and

eventually divide Peronism.* The Radical government's attempts to su-
pervise (and in some cases manipulate) electoral procedures within the
unions, as well as to control the use of their funds, drew sharp criticism
from union leaders. Moreover, despite the Radicals' promises that
Peronism would be allowed to present candidates in future elections, it
was clear that the high command of the armed forces was not prepared
to allow the Peronists to gain access to important government posts.†
Too, very much alive in the army and the air force were old populist
illusions of a "union of the *pueblo* and the armed forces" that would
promote many social and economic policies dear to the Peronists. These
illusions represented an attractive possibility to the Peronist leaders
(especially unionists), who were engaged in serious conflicts with the
Radical government and who knew that the electoral route to government remained closed for them. Such considerations encouraged these
leaders to place themselves in the vanguard of the opposition to the
Radical government, and to participate actively in promoting the 1966
coup.‡

Partly because of these factors, and partly because the weakness of
the Radical government encouraged aggressive demands, the unions
increased their strike activity during Illia's presidency. Street demonstrations were also called frequently, but most threatening of all was the
Plan de Lucha (battle plan) launched by the CGT with a wave of
workplace occupations in July and August of 1964. The newspapers
reported a total of 1,436 occupations during these two months,§ and in

---

*The attempt to weaken the Peronists was vital for the Radicals since they faced the
typical dilemma of the period: if they banned Peronism, their government would lose all
legitimation and would be placed at the mercy of the armed forces (whose motivations the
Radicals had every reason to suspect). But if they did not proscribe Peronism, there was a
strong likelihood that the Peronists would win elections and—as had happened with
Frondizi—that a coup would bring down their government.

†The military faction defeated in 1962–63 was avowedly anti-Peronist. But it soon
became clear, as we shall see, that anti-Peronism was not the exclusive domain of that
faction, and that the victorious group was far from united on this issue as well as on
others.

‡For accounts of such participation see, for example, *Primera Plana*, March 22, 1966;
and, on the eve of the coup, "Quienes sí/no están con el golpe?" *Primera Plana*, June 28,
1966, p. 6. The active role of many union leaders in promoting the coup was widely
discussed in reasonably well-informed circles.

§See the Methodological Appendix for additional information on these data. Since the
daily newspapers lacked space to give an account of every episode, the figures clearly
underestimate the total number of occupations. Raúl H. Bisio and Héctor Cordone, in
"La Segunda Etapa del Plan de Lucha de la CGT. Un episodio singular en la relación
sindicatos-estado en la Argentina" (Buenos Aires: CEIL, 1980, mimeo), note that the
CGT estimates of the number of occupations that took place in successive waves between
May 21 and July 24, 1964, differ substantially from those of the government, but in both
cases the figures are impressive. According to the CGT, 11,000 occupations involving a

quite a few instances workers held hostage executives of the firms they took over.

The demands of the CGT, though they displayed the economistic features already noted, were aimed at creating a climate of disorder that would help bring about a coup. Despite rather obvious connivances between union leaders and the armed forces, several aspects of the 1964 actions were cause for serious concern among the bourgeoisie and the leading periodicals. First, by taking control, in a massive and coordinated stroke, of most of the country's industrial plant, the working class had demonstrated a formidable capacity for action. Second, such actions could be interpreted as a revolutionary exercise that might be restaged in pursuit of goals very different from those expressed by the CGT. Third, and no less threatening, was the spontaneity with which the rank and file frequently went beyond the instructions of national union leaders, as was demonstrated by the taking of hostages and by instances where the workers for brief periods kept the factories they occupied in operation. Together, these aspects of the 1964 actions seemed to demonstrate that the situation could easily evolve toward something far worse than the existing impediments to capital accumulation.

The Radical government ignored the calls of the bourgeoisie and most of the media for the use of all-out repression to regain control of the factories. It opted instead for the slow procedure of asking for court injunctions to clear the plants. This choice was influenced by Illia's firm belief in due process of law. But it also reflected his awareness that by ordering a military evacuation of the factories he might precipitate a coup or at least make his government the captive of armed forces less interested in sustaining it than in finding the right moment to remove it. But in choosing this option the Radical government lent further credence to arguments that it could not guarantee the most fundamental aspects of public order.

The concerns of the bourgeoisie were expressed in several ways. Negative expectations and uncertainty concerning the timing of the coup and the policy orientations that might emerge from it were reflected in various forms of speculative behavior. Such behavior was manifested in a sharp rise in quotations for the dollar on the futures

---

total of 3,913,000 workers occurred during this period, while the government, which made no estimate of the numbers of workers participating, came up with a figure of 2,361 occupations. It should be noted that an undetermined number of plants were taken more than once.

market and on the black market.* The figures cited earlier for the movements of international capital also manifest this surge of speculative activity.† The thirty-day interest rate for U.S. dollars on the futures market is seen in the following monthly averages:[5]

1965	Jun	3.6	1966	Jan	5.9
	Jul	14.0		Feb	4.7
	Aug	6.9		Mar	15.4
	Sep	6.8		Apr	30.2
	Oct	11.6		May	47.9
	Nov	31.8			
	Dec	10.8			

Most of the media and the organizations of the upper bourgeoisie reiterated tirelessly that the government, although it could not itself be accused of subversive aims, was, through its passivity, lack of authority and inefficacy, the unwilling but effective promoter of dangers that went far beyond mere disorder. The Radical government and, more generally, the various regimes and governments that had existed since 1955, having shown themselves incapable of absorbing the electoral weight of Peronism and of keeping the unions and the popular sector in line, seemed condemned to foment "subversion."‡

Although the massive actions of 1964 were not repeated in 1965 and 1966, numerous incidents continued to take place, some of which again

---

*The extraordinary increases in these quotations during the months immediately prior to the June 1966 coup provide an eloquent testimony to the feeling (at least among those segments of the upper bourgeoisie and financial speculators who have easy access to this market) that the end was near. For discussion of these premonitions and their relation to the turmoil in the foreign exchange market, see *Economic Survey*, June 7, 14, and 21, 1966.

†It should be stressed that this is not a study of the Radical government and cannot, therefore, provide an evaluation of its policies. Considering the hostile environment created from the beginning by the armed forces, the bourgeoisie and the unions, and the no less hostile stances of important political forces (such as *Desarrollismo*, inspired by ex-President Frondizi, and a large part of Peronism), the Radical government achieved some notable successes, both in several areas of economic policies and in its efforts to restore democratic rights and guarantees. However, its capacity to make and implement policy was overwhelmed by the enormous constellation of forces that converged to promote the 1966 coup.

‡The entrepreneurs with whom I talked at the time or interviewed later considered the participation of union leaders in promoting the 1966 coup as the epitome of how absurd and dangerous the situation had become. It seemed to them imperative to put an end to the Radical government, and even more important to halt the series of "weak" and "demagogic" governments which had been endured for too long. But these goals required a coup, and the contacts between union leaders and some currents within the armed forces provoked serious concern among those entrepreneurs about the direction the coup might take.

culminated in the occupation of factories.* On top of these incidents came some violent clashes in various regions of the country, particularly in the province of Tucumán.† In an effort to appease the unions and gain a foothold within the popular sector, the government enacted legislation providing for automatic monthly cost-of-living adjustments for wages and salaries. It also tried to gain congressional approval of a law that would have greatly increased job security. Decried by the leading periodicals and the upper bourgeoisie as the ultimate example of demagoguery, the latter legislation was debated inconclusively by Congress in sessions fraught with incidents that did little to enhance the already low prestige of that institution and of politicians in general. The introduction of price controls further antagonized the bourgeoisie, while a number of nationalistic policies (involving restrictions on the expatriation of capital, foreign exchange controls, and some decisions affecting oil-producing activities‡) provoked the hostility of transnational capital and of the domestic sectors linked to it.

As if this were not enough, provincial elections in 1965 showed that Radicalism remained incapable of competing electorally with Peronism, even if—as was the case in the province of Mendoza—the Peronist vote was divided between two slates of candidates, one backed by union leaders and the other by Perón. The results of the 1965 elections seemed

*Partly as a reaction to these events, the organizations of the upper bourgeoisie in the first half of 1966 sharpened their criticism of the alleged "unrestrained statism" in the Radical government's economic policies and the government's "passivity" in the face of the "wave of subversion." See the statements of the ACIEL, the UIA, the SRA, the CAC, and the Buenos Aires Stock Exchange in *La Nación*, April 16 and 23, May 6, 10, 11, 13, and 14, and June 5, 1966. The CGT chimed in with its own criticisms of the government (*La Nación*, April 1, 1966, p. 14) and a June 6, 1966, national work stoppage on the heels of numerous strikes involving such crucial occupational sectors as judicial employees, municipal employees, public transportation, airline, postal, telecommunications and railroad workers, and teachers and professors.

†In response to these events, the upper bourgeoisie and the leading periodicals expressed fear and hostility. After asserting that "general disorder" prevailed in the country, *La Prensa* remarked that "there is practically no constituted authority that functions to safeguard public tranquility and individual security. Threat is the rule, and is easily converted to violence . . . . Industrial plants, business offices, schools, and public offices are regularly transformed into garrisons or fortresses by rebellious groups protesting delays in the payment of wages and salaries one day, and disagreeing with an administrative decision or expressing solidarity with the perpetrators of earlier outrages the next" (June 6, 1966, p. 8). On the presumed subversive implications of this situation see *La Nación*, January 13, March 17 and 24, April 21, and June 2, 11, 19 and 26, 1966; *Primera Plana*, January 10 and 17, March 31, and June 17, 1966; *Confirmado*, January 6, March 10 and 24, May 26, and June 2 and 23, 1966; and *Economic Survey*, February 1 and 15, March 22, and June 7, 1966. These and other publications unequivocally promoted the coup.

‡The major decision involving the oil sector was the cancellation of contracts concluded during Frondizi's presidency with United States oil companies.

to indicate that unless the Peronists were again banished from the electoral arena, the future of Radicalism would be to prepare the way for a Peronist presidency—precisely when the principal social base of Peronism had begun to raise, through the *Plan de Lucha* and its offshoots, the spectre of a crisis of social domination. A Peronist victory, moreover, would assure a pivotal role to Perón himself, who remained totally unacceptable to a substantial part of the dominant classes and to the armed forces.

A brief recapitulation is in order. The threat existing prior to the 1966 coup was undoubtedly perceived as much greater than it actually was. This perception was exaggerated still further by those who manipulated public opinion in order to promote the coup. Nonetheless, we must reconstruct the events from the point of view of those who experienced them. By 1966 much of Argentine society perceived the events we have discussed as expressions of a crisis that—beyond its government, regime, and accumulation dimensions—had begun to show a dangerous potential for the "subversion" of social domination. These impressions were accentuated by a government that appeared unable to contain the popular activation that was gathering momentum as Peronists, unions, and much of the popular sector expressed their hostility not just toward the Radical government but toward a regime that denied them access to government through the electoral process. The support these actors gave to the 1966 coup expressed not only their rejection of that regime but also their hope that the new state would be based on an alliance in which the economic and corporate interests of at least the unions would play a larger and more consistent role.

The relatively low intensity of the threat that precipitated the 1966 coup, together with the widespread support the coup received, seemed to offer a golden opportunity for a national reconciliation. Its only requirement seemed to be that the little that remained of an ill-fated semidemocracy be retired from the scene. Winners and losers alike believed that they had won.

2. CURRENTS WITHIN THE ARMED FORCES

The way in which the Argentine armed forces intervened on June 28, 1966, must be understood in the light of their own history following the overthrow of Perón. Between 1955 and 1963, factionalization paved the way for repeated coups and internal *putsches* and provoked a marked relaxation in military discipline. This factionalization gave rise around 1962 to a "professionalist" reaction aimed at restoring the armed forces' cohesion, increasing its operational capacity, and equipping its officers to approach social problems from the standpoint of the national security doctrines newly in vogue on the continent. These aims reflected the view that dissension within the armed forces stemmed from repeated interventions into national politics, from alliances with political parties and civilian groups, and from the choice of goals subordinated to those established by civilians. To remedy this situation, the professionalists proposed that the armed forces place themselves above politics, intervening only when circumstances (which they reserved the right to define) posed an "imminent danger to national security."* This "return to the barracks" implied, in the turbulent period that followed the overthrow of President Frondizi, that the electoral system would be allowed to survive, albeit constrained by the ban on Peronism. The professionalist reaction against the most politicized officers culminated in the armed conflicts of 1962 and 1963, which resulted in a decisive victory for the former. Because their position implied a break with the *golpismo* of the defeated faction (which was intent on immediately eliminating the regime of parties and elections), the professionalists came to be known as "legalists"— a term whose irony became apparent soon afterward. The victory of the professionalists paved the way for new elections in 1963, which brought the Radicals to government after a Peronist abstention.

The army, in which Commander in Chief Lt. General Juan Carlos Onganía had achieved undisputed leadership, emerged from the armed clashes of 1962–63 clearly dominant over the navy and the air force. Under Onganía's command, the armed forces largely achieved the professionalists' organizational goals and temporarily suspended the pattern of frequent interventions and plots against the government. But if in so doing the armed forces declared themselves above politics, they by no means placed themselves outside of politics. The ongoing political crisis and the Radical government's lack of social support kept alive the possibility of a coup. But now that the armed forces were reasonably reunified and committed to the doctrine of national security, any future coup would be decided upon and executed through formal lines of command. The armed forces retained a vivid memory of the costs and uncertainties brought on by their previous factionalization. This mem-

---

*The consummate expression of this position is the speech by Lt. General Juan C. Onganía made in, of all places, West Point, New York (*La Nación*, August 6, 1964, p. 1).

ory was expressed in a commitment to avoid situations that might again dissolve the lines of command and precipitate armed confrontations. Onganía was known to be a firm adherent of this view: jeopardizing the hard-won unity and discipline of the armed forces could mean the collapse of the one institution that had managed to "organize itself" in the midst of the factionalism, turmoil, and "hierarchical disintegration" prevailing in society and in the civilian state apparatus.* We shall hear echoes of these themes in the chapters that follow.

The experience of the armed forces in the years prior to the 1966 coup had other consequences that influenced the direction of subsequent events. First, if their factionalization had resulted from direct interference in party politics and in the daily conduct of government, then similar risks seemed to be entailed by intervening once again, dismantling the constitutional system and delaying its restoration indefinitely. The government installed by the 1966 coup sought to prevent this by appointing civilians to the highest levels of government, including all of the national ministries and secretariats, and (together with retired military officers) to top positions in the provinces and state enterprises. The idea was that the armed forces would be the "backbone of the revolution," but would "neither govern nor co-govern." Their participation was formally limited to certain nonexecutive organizations of which only the commanders in chief and a few especially designated officers were members.† Officers on active duty were prohibited from exercising any executive function of government‡ and from interfering in the daily conduct of government affairs.§ For Onganía, such policies had the desirable effect of increasing his autonomy from the armed forces, but the main reason this military government was so little militarized had to do with the interpretation that Onganía and many of

---

*The concern with avoiding new factionalization played a key role in the timing of the coup. Important elections, scheduled for 1967, would once again pose the dilemma of whether or not to proscribe the Peronists; the June 1966 coup sought to head off this dilemma and the divisive effects it would have had within the armed forces; cf. O'Donnell, "Modernization and Military Coups."

†These organizations were the National Council on Development (CONADE), the National Security Council (CONASE), the National Council on Science and Technology (CONACYT), the Armed Forces General Staff, the Secretariat of Information (SIDE), and the military junta. None of these organizations was formally part of the executive branch.

‡An exception was made with regard to the railroads. It was believed—mistakenly—that a team of officers on active duty would be efficient enough to ameliorate the railroads' catastrophic deficit.

§The ministers and secretaries I interviewed stated that they were under orders from Onganía to report to him any pressure or personal request from active-duty members of the armed forces.

his fellow officers placed on the recent history of the armed forces. We shall see, however, that the resulting isolation of General Onganía from his colleagues generated increasing dissatisfaction among the latter, particularly after 1969 when the armed forces had to suppress spectacular popular uprisings in Rosario and Córdoba.

A second consequence of the recent experience of the armed forces was that many of its officers saw what they regarded as their successful reorganization as a model for orienting the new government's goals and criteria. They believed they had eliminated their own factionalism, first, because they had reestablished an institutional order based on hierarchically defined lines of authority; second, because each component of the armed forces confined itself to its area of specialization; and third, because all members shared general views and goals which, when attained, would fully satisfy, with no genuine reason for conflict, the interests of everyone, irrespective of the position and function that each occupied in the whole. This self-image scarcely corresponded to reality; but the important point is that it was generalized to society as a whole, in the statements of Onganía and in various important military documents of the period, as we shall see. To ward off the collapse the armed forces had narrowly averted, it was now the nation that had to be saved from factionalism and conflict, from "politicization," and from its own "crisis of authority."

But a third consequence of what took place in the armed forces during the early 1960s involves the continuity within its ranks of discrepant ideological tendencies. The officers who triumphed in 1963 agreed on a "return to the barracks" in order to preserve their institution, but this did not rule out important disagreements regarding a number of issues that could not be avoided after the 1966 coup. To understand this point we must turn to an examination of the main currents existing within the professionalist military of 1966.*

What I shall henceforth term the paternalist current was prominently represented by Onganía and was highly influential in his entourage, in the Ministry of the Interior (the ministry in charge of political affairs), and among an unknown but certainly important proportion of the mem-

_____

*Since this discussion is based on public statements and on my interviews with high-ranking officers, it is difficult to determine the support for these currents among the lower ranks. All evidence suggests that the younger the officers the more likely they were to support the paternalists or nationalists rather than the liberals (currents that are discussed below). But the preferences of the younger officers did not prevent the liberals, in the period being studied, from by and large controlling the armed forces, with the exception of the air force which remained a stronghold of the nationalists.

bers of the armed forces. Admirers of Francisco Franco, close to traditionalist currents within the Catholic Church, and for the most part of
middle-class provincial origin, the members of this current held views
that corresponded closely to the "authoritarian mentality" described by
Juan Linz.[6] Although their corporatist outlook was shot through with
organicist metaphors, it fell short of a fascist ideology thanks to a
conservatism impregnated with hostility to all forms of political mobilization and to the dream of restoring the social integration of a mythical
patriarchal past. Conservatives or, better, traditionalists, their ideal society would be as alien to mass politics as to big business. Reluctant to
accept capitalism, profit, and big corporations, they believed that in the
long run these could be superseded by a less prosaic and selfish social
system. Meanwhile the *pueblo*, the ultimate beneficiary of their efforts,
would have to wait, confident and disciplined, until their tutors had
created the conditions under which such a new system might emerge.
The paternalists, advocates of "order," "authority" and depolitici-
zation, wore a modern stripe in their fascination with *técnicos* (techno-
crats) who, they felt, would take care of one of the more urgent but, in
the paternalists' view, ultimately not too important sides of the government: the economy. These *técnicos* seemed to be the bearers of a cool
rationality that apparently supported (and this was the source of the
paternalists' fascination with them) the paternalists' denial of the inherently conflictual character of most social issues.

A second, "nationalist"* current within the armed forces resembled
the first in many respects, but it is important not to confuse the two.
Both were authoritarian and corporatist, but while the paternalists favored an "apolitical" and "demobilized" society, the nationalists hoped
to achieve their goals by building and manipulating mass movements.
The nationalists nurtured dreams of a union between the *pueblo* and the
armed forces, viewing the former as an atomized mass incapable of
generating its own leaders and ready to be mobilized behind an ideology
affirming the "genuinely national" in its sharp rejection of "communism" as well as of "liberal," "individualistic," and internationalist
patterns of capitalist growth. The nation they wished to construct required a strong state apparatus, more active economically than the one
envisioned by the paternalists and better disposed to repress in good
conscience. The size and predominantly foreign character of big busi-

---

*I use the terms *nationalists* and *liberals* (the latter for the current discussed below)
with some misgivings, as both have connotations that are not consistent with their usage
in this book. I trust that the reader will be careful to note the meanings I give them here.

ness evoked the hostility of the nationalists, who saw in the "national entrepreneurs" the political and economic base for a nationalist version of capitalism. Moreover, the nationalists hoped—with clearly fascist overtones—to combine corporatism and the authoritarian mobilization of the *pueblo,* by means of a movement, not a party, that they would control from the government. The proponents of this late and decidedly authoritarian flowering of populism were to discover that the *pueblo* was unwilling to mobilize within the limits they wished to impose, and that the local bourgeoisie, too weak in some of its fractions and too penetrated by transnational capital in others, was unwilling to play the crucial role they had assigned it in the "national revolution."

The "liberals" comprised a third current within the armed forces. I ignore the social origins of the non-leadership members of this current, but it should be noted that, unlike their nationalist and paternalist peers, those who led this current during the period we are studying— General Julio Alsogaray, General Alejandro Lanusse, and many of their close associates—came from the urban upper class. The liberals, in contrast to the nationalists and paternalists, were not provincial in their origins and outlook. Their friends and social connections were likely to be oriented toward the upper bourgeoisie and its entourage of lawyers, economists, publishers, and intellectuals. They considered themselves true democrats and were skeptical of the pronouncements of allegiance to democracy that from time to time their nationalist and paternalist colleagues felt obliged to make. From the liberals' point of view, the imposition of an authoritarian state was a lamentable necessity that did not rule out the ultimate restoration of political democracy, albeit in a form insulated from the "demagogic" irruptions that had characterized the pre-1966 period. Unlike the paternalists and nationalists, the liberals were unreservedly pro-capitalist and had a much better grasp than the other currents of the workings of a capitalist economy. They had nothing against big business; to the contrary, it formed part of their civilian milieu. The military liberals and the upper bourgeoisie cultivated their mutual relationship with a keen awareness of its importance to both of them. Not surprisingly, the liberals were, as we shall see, the only secure source of military support for those who took charge of the economic policies of the BA.

A fourth current, probably with more participants than the others, remained in the background. It consisted of careerist military unaffiliated with the above-mentioned currents. While hardly congenial to the liberals' outlook, those who belonged to this group were always alert to, and prepared to follow, the changing distribution of power within the armed forces.

This sketch of ideologies and tendencies within the armed forces will come into sharper focus as we examine the ways in which they interacted with other factors during the 1966–73 period. One peculiarity of the Argentine case is that during this period each of the three major military currents occupied the presidency: the paternalists with Onganía in 1966–70, the nationalists with Levingston in 1970–71, and the liberals with Lanusse in 1971–73. These currents converged to put an end to the semidemocracy prevailing from 1955 to 1966 and to inaugurate a new state and regime aimed at achieving, in an unspecified period of time, a broad set of goals that included restoring "international respect" to Argentina, "modernizing" the country, "assuring national unity," "promoting the general welfare," and "redirecting the nation on its road to greatness."[7]

Onganía, who held great prestige in the armed forces and projected an image of authority and sobriety that seemed especially suited to the times, was the obvious choice to lead this undertaking. His appointment to the presidency attested to his skills as a military leader, but the decision to exclude the armed forces from direct participation in the government prevented him from exercising this military leadership. In fact, the elevation of the most prominent representative of the paternalists to the highest governmental position enabled the liberals to achieve significant control within the armed forces. Of the members of the liberal current, General Julio Alsogaray and his brother Álvaro* played a particularly active role in promoting the coup and in shaping the decisions made immediately thereafter. The influence of liberals was apparent in the "Acts of the Argentine Revolution," particularly in the sections (in Appendix 3) devoted to "Economic Policy" and "Labor Policy."[8] The content and language of these texts, in spite of some ambiguities, reflected their liberal origins, especially in their emphasis on free enterprise and private initiative and in their affirmation of constitutional democracy as the ultimate goal of the authoritarian interlude.[9] The contrasts between these documents and those authored later by Onganía and his associates underscore the ideological distance separating the liberals from the paternalists.

---

*Álvaro Alsogaray had served as Economy Minister during the presidencies of Frondizi and Guido (1958–63). The short-lived and largely unsuccessful economic policies he implemented under each government provoked deep recessions and sharp declines in wages and salaries and did little to establish his popularity.

The commander in chief of the army at the time of the coup was General Pascual Pistarini, an officer with little influence. He was replaced in December 1966 by Julio Alsogaray, who was later relieved of command after a series of conflicts with Onganía. In terms of military prestige and civilian support, the obvious choice to succeed Alsogaray as commander in chief was another liberal, General Alejandro Lanusse. Lanusse played a central role in the overthrow of Onganía and in the selection and subsequent removal of Onganía's successor, General Marcelo Levingston. Lanusse himself served as president during the last phase of the "Argentine Revolution," which was marked by the search for a negotiated agreement with the political and social forces that the 1966 coup had sought to exclude.

The conflicts among these military currents added momentum to the problems faced by this BA. They also provide insight, by way of the contrast between the paternalism of Onganía and the liberalism of Castelo Branco and his group,[10] into important differences between the Argentine and Brazilian cases. But it is important to emphasize here (and to substantiate in the following chapters) the relationship between the comparative mildness of the threat that preceded the implantation of the 1966 Argentine BA and the early emergence of sharp conflicts among the major currents in the armed forces. One advantage of studying the Argentine case of 1966 is that it enables us to examine these conflicts and the ideological differences that underlie them. In cases of high previous threat, though, those conflicts and differences still exist. Following the initial period of the BA, which is characterized by efforts to impose order and to normalize the economy, such differences surface once again, regardless of whether the process culminates in the collapse of the BA or in the achievement of what its supporters view as important successes.[11] But the later and less pronounced emergence of internal conflicts in cases implanted under more extreme conditions of crisis and threat provides a good comparative benchmark against which to assess how and to what degree such conflicts determine political processes after the BA is installed.

3. PATERNALISTS AND LIBERALS

The "Argentine Revolution" began with the announcement that it would persist for as long as it took to "modernize" the country, to "reunite Argentina with its destiny," and to eradicate the evils of the 1955–66 period, which were said to include inflation, sluggish economic growth, acute social conflict, corruption, "sectoral egoism," "subversion," "lack of faith" and the absence of "spiritual cohesion" among Argentines, and the "inorganic," "unrepresentative" character of civilian organizations. Society had to be integrated and "amalgamated" with a state apparatus that would be transformed into an "effective" set of institutions. To this end, it was necessary to begin by imposing "order." Once achieved, this "order," bursting with the fruits of economic growth, would allow for an equitable distribution of goods and opportunities. Still later, once a stable and legitimated system was in place, it would permit the restoration of "political activity." The workings of this new order would be nurtured by the "genuine representativeness" of the "basic organizations of the community."[12]

These goals were to be achieved in three stages. The first, "economic" stage would be devoted to imposing order and repairing the worst of the damage that the previous period of "chaos and irresponsible demagoguery" had produced in the economy and the state apparatus. That period would be succeeded by a "social stage" which, on the basis of the achievements of the first one, would promote distributive justice and "structural transformations." The third and final stage was the "political" one, which would produce the harmonious "amalgamation" of the new state and the "genuinely representative organizations of the community," all imbued with the value of solidarity.*

These three stages corresponded to the ideology of Onganía and the paternalists. This ideology revealed a fundamental bias in its conception of politics as synonymous with disorder, fragmented interests, and demagogic promises leading to premature expectations. Politics was seen as a realm of manipulation and opportunism, offensive to the moralistic code of the paternalists. Whereas one of the paternalists' goals was to secure the stability necessary to initiate "profound" (social and economic) transformations, "politics" meant sacrificing long-term solutions. Politics was equated with the "division of the Argentines."†

---

*See also Onganía's statements on the goal of promoting "participation" through the "basic organizations of the community" once such organizations had been "ordered" and "made truly representative" (*La Nación*, October 30, 1966, p. 1). Minister of the Interior Enrique Martínez Paz made similar remarks (*La Nación*, November 9, p. 8; November 11, p. 1; November 27, p. 1, 1966).

†To his denunciations of social factionalization and "disintegration" Onganía added, "One day political parties will have to be replaced by other organizations, equally political, based on a revitalized community, based on ideals rather than biases, and loyal to the Nation before the group" (*La Nación*, December 31, 1966, p. 8). Martínez Paz added that "old-style politics have definitively ended" because "political parties encouraged the division of the people and, comfortable in the pretense of a purely formal and sterile legality, established [polarized] choices as a system," aggravated by the parties' own "lack of true

The paternalists envisioned a new order in which social and spiritual integration would reign, eliminating all genuine cause for conflict. State and society would form an organic whole in which each individual member, and each of the sectors into which these members were to be integrated, would perform functions contributing to the well-being of everyone, including the less favored, to whom the rulers would dispense justice when the economic situation permitted. Only those who stooped to unjustifiable egoism could oppose this vision, and the paternalists' policies could be tough when it came to removing the obstacles to the social integration they envisaged. Such expressions of "disorder" and "lack of cohesion" as elections, political parties, and strikes would have to be suppressed in order to achieve the overriding goal of "spiritual cohesion." This task required a strong state which, from the standpoint of this hierarchical, integrationist and corporatist ideology, was the only perspective from which to discern the general interest.

The antipolitical bias inherent in the paternalist ideology would persist even after the utopia of the "organized community" had been achieved. Political parties might eventually exist, but they would represent integrative conceptions of the common good rather than sectoral interests. Moreover, they would form but one aspect, and by no means the most important, of participation, which would center on commissions and councils composed of the functionally specialized basic organizations of the community—great bodies of workers, entrepreneurs, and professionals—that would be organically linked to the highest levels of the state apparatus. In this scheme, participation would consist of relaying information (technical in character and, owing to the diffusion throughout society of values of solidarity, transcending particularized interests) to better equip the government for decision-making.

This vision corresponded to more than a few members of the armed forces and to various groups within the Catholic Church, particularly in its upper strata. Its law-and-order implications held some potential appeal for the middle sectors, but its moralism tended to alienate this highly secularized and politically cynical sector.* Neither the agro-

---

representativeness, their inauthenticity, their egoism." Argentina's political parties, according to Martínez Paz, were "the expression of special interests that did not coincide with the national interest . . . and constituted a struggle among factions artificially crystallized around ideological banners" (*La Prensa*, November 27, 1966, pp. 1, 7).

*The new authorities undertook "morality campaigns" and censored various publications and public events for "obscenity." Their popular appeal was not increased by the baroque protocol that surrounded their public appearances or by the closing of publications that satirized their attitudes.

exporters, with their strongly antistatist orientation, nor the local and international factions of the upper bourgeoisie, whose outlook was neither parochial nor traditionalist, were likely to be drawn to the paternalist ideology. The paternalist outlook was explicitly antiliberal, not only in its stated rejection of "formal democracy" but also in its vision of a tutelary, corporatizing state aimed at preserving a "just equilibrium" among social classes. On the other hand, the tutelary state of the paternalists was not the entrepreneurial state of the nationalists. Moreover, the paternalists tried to distance themselves from the dominant classes, aware that they had to gain their support but convinced that these classes had to be tightly controlled in order to achieve a society more balanced and more concerned with distributive justice than any the dominant classes were willing to tolerate.*

The ideology of the liberals also deserves attention. While the paternalists had to compensate for their weak social bases by entrenching themselves in the state apparatus, the liberals in the armed forces reached out to the dominant classes and to society's most powerful organizations. Transnational capital, the organizations of the upper bourgeoisie, the oligopolistic fractions of urban capital, and the leading periodicals all found themselves speaking the same language as the military liberals and provided the points of departure and return for the civilian liberal *técnicos* who took control of the principal economic levers of the BA. This current was not hostile toward the growth of the state apparatus (a position that distinguished it from the laissez-faire ideology of some of its more traditional, agrarian-based allies), provided that such enlargement supported the expansion of the oligopolistic productive structure controlled by their main social allies. These views were at odds with both the equilibrating state envisioned by the paternalists and the entrepreneurial statism of the nationalists.

Notwithstanding these differences, there were important convergences at the beginning of this BA among paternalists, nationalists, and liberals. All saw the first task of the BA as imposing "order," and all were anxious that the BA be regarded as capable of projecting its domination for an extended period of time. These points of agreement enabled the three currents to ally in executing the coup that implanted the BA.

---

*The paternalists I interviewed clearly felt that they did not belong to the world of big business and that their goals would require the imposition of controls that the upper bourgeoisie would not accept with good grace.

4. INDECISION AND CONFUSION

I have indicated that the 1966 coup took place with widespread acquiescence. This was also true for Onganía's designation as president by the junta of commanders in chief. Onganía seemed to be an introverted and unspectacular leader, projecting the image of a future in which order and calm would prevail. The initial statements of Onganía and the Junta,[13] which concerned order, reconciliation, and the serious and efficient management of public affairs, evoked favorable responses.* It therefore came as no surprise that the first step taken by the "Argentine Revolution" (apart from baptizing itself as such) was to suppress the institutions that the new authority considered to be the main causes of the frustrations of the past. Congress and political parties were disbanded, political activity was prohibited, and, with the intention of putting it to good use, party property was diverted to public education.[14] Nothing was said as to whether political parties would exist in the future, but even the liberals applauded the elimination of *these* parties.† Furthermore, since the BA had been implanted to eradicate disorder and subversion, a "National System of Planning and Action for National Security"[15] was instituted, resulting in the creation of the National Security Council (CONASE).

With the bourgeoisie enthused,‡ union leaders expressing their support, Perón blessing the coup, various ex-political parties offering their personnel to the new government, and the Radicals bereft of any capacity to oppose the coup, the "disorder" of the previous period seemed to have been dispelled by the image of authority that the new government assiduously projected. The universities, "politicized and plagued by leftists," were seen as the only remaining bastions of conflict. Many approved when the universities were "intervened"—the legally elected officers replaced by government appointees—on July 29, 1966, although there were some objections to the brutalities committed in the process.[16]

---

*An example of the initial euphoria of some intellectual sectors is the collective volume entitled *La "Revolución Argentina." Análisis y prospectiva* (Buenos Aires: Ediciones Depalma, 1966). A more concrete indication of optimism about the future was the sharp rise in quotations on the Buenos Aires Stock Exchange in the week after the coup. *Economic Survey* reported these gains to be the highest on record (July 5, 1966, p. 58).

†See the enthusiastic statements of all the media during the week of July 3–10, 1966, on the "definitive" elimination of these agents of "demagoguery" and "ineffectiveness" or even of "totalitarianism."

‡For expressions of support from all of the organizations of the upper bourgeoisie, see *La Nación*, July 14, 1966. The CGT was also happy with the new government; see *La Nación*, August 24, 1966, p. 5.

But they were deceived who waited for the torrent of decisions out of which would arise a "revolutionary mystique." The first cabinet was composed of self-proclaimed "moderate nationalists" who shared the president's paternalist orientation. Military liberals, like General Alsogaray, returned to their divisional commands, while prominent liberal civilians (like his brother Álvaro, who was appointed ambassador to the United States) were removed from the day-to-day conduct of government affairs. One of the most visible paternalists in the new cabinet was Interior Minister Enrique Martínez Paz. In addition to generating some qualms over the way he managed the closing-down of the universities, Martínez Paz obviously enjoyed proclaiming the "end of politics" in Argentina and denouncing the infinite evils for which he blamed the political parties. He also condemned democracy unequivocally.[17] Another paternalist, Secretary of Government Mario Díaz Colodrero, made similar statements, although he was more cautious in his denunciations of formal democracy. For his part, Onganía insisted that the initial, economic stage of the Argentine Revolution focus on two tasks in addition to economic normalization: the implantation of "order and authority" in society and the reorganization of the state apparatus. The latter was to be made more efficient by cutting personnel, "rationalizing" the central administration and public enterprises, improving tax collection, and implementing ambitious projects to expand the physical infrastructure.* Since public works projects took considerable start-up time and since the only visible fruits of "rationalization" were mountains of charts and regulations, the task attended to most rapidly was the dismissal of numerous public employees.[18]

The prospect of a streamlined state apparatus that would focus on assuring favorable conditions for the expansion of private capital was well received by the upper bourgeoisie.† But it clashed head-on with the public employees' unions and with the port workers, who began an extended strike when the "modernization" of the port of Buenos Aires

---

*The goal of reorganizing the state apparatus was stressed repeatedly by Onganía: "It is necessary to give preference to the organization of the state . . . to place a high priority on organizing the state such that this takes precedence over the other one that must also be organized, which is the community" (*La Nación*, October 30, 1966, p. 1). Cf. also his speech in *La Nación*, November 8, 1966, p. 4, and *Planeamiento y desarrollo de la acción de gobierno-directiva*.

†The presidents of the UIA and the CAC responded enthusiastically to the announcement that the state apparatus was to be rationalized (*La Nación*, August 19, 1966, p. 1 and August 23, 1966, p. 7). Other organizations of the upper bourgeoisie also voiced their support (*La Nación*, November 9, 1966, p. 8). It is also worth noting that quotations on the Buenos Aires Stock Exchange rose sharply immediately following this announcement.

commenced with massive layoffs and changes in the work process.[19] Similarly, the effort to overcome the sugar monoculture of Tucumán Province, which was defined as another major modernization task, began with a series of mill closings, aggravating the poor employment situation of that region and generating numerous strikes and violent protests.[20] The government did not take this heavy-handed approach, however, in dealing with workers in other sectors dominated by private capital. In August 1966 two important unions—the metal workers and the textile workers—began the renegotiation of their collective agreements by denouncing the "selfishness" of their employers and threatening to strike.[21] In these cases the government intervened to achieve a "just solution" that left employers protesting that the workers had made fundamental gains at their expense.*

Government officials also turned a deaf ear to demands for the repeal of the Law of Professional Associations (which was seen as the main mechanism underlying the "excessive power" of the unions) and for the establishment of "free unions."† They opted instead for policies aimed at shifting control of the CGT to union leaders who were expected to be responsive to the paternalists. This decision was an early indication of a problem that would surface repeatedly throughout the period: the paternalists did not want to atomize the unions, as the liberals and the upper bourgeoisie demanded, but to unify them under their own control.

As the CGT struggled with the ambiguities resulting from the government's differing policies toward its member unions,‡ the bourgeoisie was heartened by episodes that began to reveal that, in spite of the "equili-

---

*Onganía was in attendance when, with great ceremony, the metal workers signed their Collective Work Agreement. The UIA complained that the government had exerted pressure on behalf of the workers in arranging both this agreement and the one signed by the textile workers. These protests cost the Undersecretary of Labor his job (*La Nación*, October 5, 1966, p. 1, and UIA, *Memoria Anual, 1966–1967* [Buenos Aires, 1967], p. 59).

†The leading periodicals were the first to raise the issue of "free unions," arguing that if political parties were disbanded, "reasons of equity" demanded that a similar policy should be applied to the CGT, since it was the main organizational base of Peronism. They also asserted that existing laws that denied workers the freedom to decide whether or not to join a union and that prevented the emergence of a plurality of unions were obviously "totalitarian" vestiges of the past which would be intolerable in the era of liberty that had just been inaugurated. See *La Nación*, August 25, p. 6, and December 15, p. 6, 1966, and February 16, 1967; *La Prensa*, December 18, 1966, p. 6 and January 25, 1967, p. 6; and *Economic Survey*, July 19, 1966, p. 605.

‡In October 1966 Francisco Prado was reelected secretary general of the CGT. He and other CGT leaders immediately announced their desire to "carry on a dialogue with the government and with business" (*La Nación*, October 27, 1966, p. 20), and encouraged participation in the "Argentine Revolution" (*La Nación*, August 26, p. 11 and November 2, p. 1, 1966).

brating" designs of the paternalists, the working class and various middle sectors were among the losers under the BA. One such episode was a speech by Onganía in which he reiterated commonplaces dear to the upper and Pampean bourgeoisies.* Another, more important, signal was the sanctioning of the Law of Mandatory Arbitration, which prohibited strikes or work stoppages until the issues in conflict had been submitted to government arbitration.† The paternalists viewed this law as necessary in the short run for halting the strikes that had begun to shatter the peace of the first days of the BA, and in the long run for eliminating activities incompatible with their utopia of an "organized community." Closer to the mark were the perceptions of the upper bourgeoisie and the leading periodicals, as well as of some union leaders, who realized that the Law of Mandatory Arbitration, given the already effected suppression of the electoral system, deprived the popular sector of its only remaining institutionalized means for articulating its demands. It was also quite clear that this law weakened the popular sector not only in its dealings with the state apparatus but also in its direct relations with the bourgeoisie.‡

The attempts to manipulate the CGT, the sanctions imposed on

*La Nación, November 8, 1966, p. 1. Besides announcing a frontal attack on inflation and the fiscal deficit, Onganía stated that "it is the intention of this government that industry remain in the hands of industrialists, and not in those of the state," whose activities would be limited to energy and steel and to "resolving problems of infrastructure." Onganía also criticized "foreign exchange differentials detrimental to exportation" and "a system of taxation that [undermines] the security of the [agricultural and livestock] producer," raising the hopes of the Pampean bourgeoisie—which soon would be disappointed—for favorable directions in economic policy. Onganía's speech nevertheless displayed paternalist overtones in referring to "the technical capability and responsibility of the Argentine worker, which are amply demonstrated in the environment of a well-organized enterprise whose proper functioning is assured by a balanced sense of authority and reciprocal loyalty."

†Law 16,936 of August 27, 1966. As in a Collective Work Agreement, the settlement arbitrated by the government would be binding for all workers and enterprises in a specified economic activity.

‡In spite of these implications, the leadership of the CGT (which remained determined to "carry on a dialogue") issued a mild and ambiguous commentary on this law; see the press release reprinted in Santiago Senén González, El sindicalismo después de Perón (Buenos Aires: Editorial Galerna, 1971), 101–102. More critical responses came from unions excluded from the CGT leadership. The UIA responded to the Law of Mandatory Arbitration by applauding "the advances made in the rectification of norms and customs in labor and union relations" (UIA, Memoria Anual, 1966–1967, p. 57). Later, in commenting on this law and on the subsequent freeze on salaries, the UIA remarked chastely that, although it had always defended "freedom from state intervention" in relations between employers and workers and unions (as well as in other areas), "it is appropriate to recognize that in special situations and emergencies it is legitimate to adopt measures to assure public order . . . in such a way as to ensure harmony with the ends pursued [through economic policy]" (UIA, Memoria Anual, 1967–1968 [Buenos Aires, 1968], pp. 33–34).

public-sector unions, the pro-labor decisions taken with regard to the contracts negotiated in the metallurgical and textile sectors, and the Law of Mandatory Arbitration were all ostensibly the work of the Ministry of Economy and Labor, headed by Jorge Salimei. Salimei was a self-made man from the food industry with no direct ties to transnational capital, and a socially conscious "Catholic entrepreneur" both in his public stands and in the paternalist approach he took to managing his own enterprises. Salimei found himself directing a heterogeneous team that included other "Catholic entrepreneurs," some liberals, and some Christian Democratic *técnicos* who were well to the left of their colleagues. When Ambassador Alsogaray publicized his view that Argentina should sign a Guarantee of Investments Agreement with the United States in order to attract U.S. capital, both Salimei and Onganía took the position that, despite the indispensability of foreign capital, the abdication of Argentine sovereignty entailed by the ambassador's proposition was out of the question.* If this nationalist gesture did little to arouse the enthusiasm of the upper bourgeoisie, it was equally unsuccessful in helping Salimei resolve the conflicts internal to his team† or discover some way out of his obvious confusion as to what to do about the economy. The year 1966 closed with zero economic growth‡ and a decline in the rate of investment.§ Furthermore, a devaluation had improved neither the precarious balance-of-payments situation‖ nor the inflation inherited from the previous record.# Still worse in the eyes of the bourgeoisie was that, in the wake of union complaints about price increases,[22] price controls were imposed and sanctions enacted against

---

*Alsogaray even announced the signing of such an agreement (*La Nación*, July 26, 1966). By contrast, Onganía stated that while foreign capital would be welcomed, a Guarantee of Investments Agreement was unnecessary.

†Before the end of the year, Salimei forced the resignations of the Christian Democratic *técnicos*, including the president of the Central Bank.

‡During 1966 GNP rose only 0.7% above its 1965 level, equivalent to a per capita drop of ⁻0.4% (BCRA, *Sistema de cuentas de producto e ingreso de la Argentina*, vol. 2, *Cuadros estadísticos* [Buenos Aires, 1975]).

§In 1966 gross fixed domestic investment fell 7.7% below its 1965 level. The net balances of short-term capital movements, long-term capital movements, and direct foreign investment were, respectively, ⁻$105 million, ⁻$76 million, and $2.6 million (figures in then-current U.S. dollars). See tables 7, 11, and 42 for these figures and their sources.

‖At the close of 1966 the net reserves of the BCRA were US$176.9 million, less than the $208.9 million held in the month preceding the coup (see Table 9).

#The average monthly cost-of-living increase in Greater Buenos Aires in the second half of 1966 was 3.5%, which represented no improvement over either the second half of 1964 or the second half of 1965, when the monthly cost of living increase averaged 3.0% (see Table 8).

the "unscrupulous businessmen" who disregarded them.* The "state interventionism" of the preceding years, which had "penalized business" while ignoring that the "real" sources of inflation and sluggish economic growth were excessive wages and salaries and the fiscal deficit, had reared its head once again.[23]

Another notable feature of the second half of 1966 was a growing wave of student protest.[24] Its momentum increased after a student participating in a street demonstration in Córdoba was killed by the police, an action that made a major impact in a country as yet unaccustomed to episodes of this sort.

To the bourgeoisie, certain aspects of the situation seemed satisfactory. But there were others—too many others—that did not. Above all, the government was plainly uncertain about the overall direction of its policies. It seemed as if the great opportunity provided by the June coup was on the verge of being wasted. What had been unthinkable in June was taking place four months later: rumors of military unrest were circulating, and the possibility that discontent within the armed forces might lead to another coup could not be brushed aside.† Onganía could not easily be dispensed with, but the same did not hold for his collaborators. Martínez Paz and Salimei became the main targets of criticism‡ and, apparently to eliminate dead weight, Onganía requested their resignations. On December 30, 1966, Onganía named Guillermo Borda Minister of the Interior and Adalbert Krieger Vasena Minister of Economy. Similar pressures within the army had already led to the removal of Pistarini as commander in chief and to his replacement by Julio Alsogaray.

In the meantime, the paternalists had failed in their efforts to engineer the emergence of a CGT leadership favorable to them. Economic and

---

*For the announcement that price control legislation (passed before the coup) would be put into effect, see La Nación, August 4, 1966, p. 1. Also, a "Regulation of Supply" law (n. 17,017) was enacted on November 18, 1966, increasing the government's capacity to control prices and raising the penalties for infractions.

†See, for example, reports about the "unusual proliferation" of tense military meetings, in La Nación, October 9, p. 6, and December 8, p. 6, 1966. "Military unrest" was also discussed in an article entitled "Behind the Crisis" in La Nación, December 11, 1966, p. 8, and in Primera Plana, December 6, pp. 8, 12 and December 13, pp. 14, 17, 1966. My interviews with military officers confirmed these tensions.

‡The "corporatism" of the Minister of the Interior and his staff was criticized in La Nación, October 6, p. 6 and November 13, p. 6, 1966; Primera Plana, October 25, 1966, p. 12; and Economic Survey, January 10, 1967, p. 1. Liberals such as Roberto Alemann, José A. Martínez de Hoz, Álvaro Alsogaray, and Adalbert Krieger Vasena were proposed as candidates for Minister of Economy; cf. La Nación as early as August 14, 1966, p. 6, and Primera Plana, November 22, 1966, p. 18.

social policy in the months that followed the coup had irritated everyone. Moreover, it was evident that the government was going to push ahead with its goal of "rationalizing" the state apparatus. This plan, together with the Law of Mandatory Arbitration, drove into opposition the current that Salimei and his team had counted on as their principal ally within the unions: the 62 *Organizaciones de Pie*, headed by José Alonso, which in October 1966 was defeated in a bid for the top positions in the CGT. It was assumed that the unions in this current were loyal to Perón, who, wasting no time in reversing his initial position, was now sending messages urging opposition to the government.* The paternalists' overtures to the 62 *de Pie*, despite their lack of success, pushed into opposition the latter's main rival, the 62 *Organizations* (or Vandorists), led by Augusto Vandor. Accordingly, it was not long before all the principal union currents were publicizing their disillusionment with the "antipopular" policies adopted, no longer by the "Argentine Revolution," but by "the government that emerged from the June coup." The Vandorists, the 62 *de Pie*, and the Independents (who were at the time the other major union alignment) all came out against the above-mentioned November speech in which Onganía sought to reassure the bourgeoisie. With this convergence the union leadership, which until recently had been fraught with divisions, now seemed to have pulled itself together in opposition to a government that seemed, to the upper bourgeoisie, committed to folly: not only had it thrown away an excellent opportunity to complete the divisions within the union leadership, it had actually helped to heal them and, in so doing, had made itself the target of the newfound unity. On December 1, 1966, the CGT, even as it insisted that it was disposed to engage in "dialogue" with the government, declared a national work stoppage, under pressure from public employees' unions chafing from the effects of "rationalization," from the 62 *de Pie*, from Perón's exhortations to oppose the government, and from the growing unreceptiveness of many Vandorist unions to the negotiated settlements still advocated by Vandor and his associates.†

---

*On Perón's change of position, *Primera Plana*, April 11, 1967, p. 17. Perón ordered a public demonstration to take place on Peronism's commemorative day, October 17. The demonstration was forbidden by the government and gave rise to clashes in the streets that added another element of déjà vu to the "Revolution" inaugurated with so much fanfare in June (*La Nación*, October 18, 1966, p. 4).

†The CGT combined criticism of economic policy stressing unemployment, the cost of living, low wages, and "laissez-faire minorities" with offers for "dialogue" and "participation" (*La Nación*, December 9, p. 1, December 18, pp. 1–18, and December 29, p. 9, 1966).

Meanwhile, most nationalist civilian groups* had by this stage distanced themselves from what seemed to them to be a purely administrative government which, far from spearheading the "National Revolution," had adopted a "liberal" economic policy and had retained at its core persons as notoriously associated with this tendency as Ambassador Alsogaray—who, for his part, never missed a chance to criticize the economic and labor policies of his government. Less than six months after the coup, the government seemed to be cut off from society and sustained precariously by armed forces that showed unmistakable signs of unrest.

With the cabinet changes at the end of December, Onganía's government (defined in terms of whether its top positions were occupied by officials close to his person and orientations) had ended. July to December 1966 is properly viewed as an interim period, characterized principally by the confusion of many of the relevant actors as to who had actually won and lost the June 28 coup. When this period ended, the real work of the BA began.

NOTES

1. For an overview of this period see my *Modernization and Bureaucratic-Authoritarianism* and "Modernization and Military Coups." The basic work on the armed forces of Argentina is Alain Rouguié, *Pouvoir militaire et société politique en republique argentine* (Paris: Presses de la Fondation Nationale des Sciences Politiques, 1978). Cf. also Carlos A. Fayt, *El político armado: dinámica del proceso político Argentino (1960–1971)* (Buenos Aires: Pannedille, 1971) and Robert Potash, *El ejército y la política en la Argentina, 1945–1962: De Perón a Frondizi* (Buenos Aires: Editorial Sudamericana, 1981).

2. On these patterns of behavior and related themes, see Marcelo Cavarozzi, "Sindicatos y política en Argentina, 1955–1958," *Estudios CEDES* 1, 1982. See also Rubén Zorrilla, *Estructura y dinámica del sindicalismo argentino* (Buenos Aires: Editorial La Pléyade, 1974).

3. On this cycle see my *Modernization and Bureaucratic-Authoritarianism*, 115–63.

4. The ways in which these shifting sociopolitical alliances evolved between 1955 and 1966 are analyzed in my "State and Alliances in Argentina, 1956–1976," *Journal of Development Studies* 15, no. 1 (October 1978): 3–33.

5. Calculated from FIEL, *Indicadores de coyuntura*, various issues.

*For expressions of initial support by nationalist groups, see *Azul y Blanco*, July and August 1966. Not long thereafter, when this publication became critical of the government's "vacillations" and "mediocrity" in carrying out the "National Revolution," it ceased publication.

6. Juan Linz, "An Authoritarian Regime: Spain," in *Mass Politics*, ed. Eric Allardt and Stein Rokkan (New York: Free Press, 1970), 251–83.

7. *Mensaje de la Junta Revolucionaria al Pueblo Argentino* and *Acta de la Revolución Argentina*, anexo 3: *Políticas del Gobierno Nacional*, Secretaría de Prensa de la Presidencia de la Nación, Buenos Aires, June 28, 1966.

8. *Mensaje de la Junta Revolucionaria.*

9. *Mensaje de la Junta Revolucionaria.*

10. On the liberal, internationalist and pro-capitalist ideology of Castelo Branco and his group, see Alfred Stepan, *The Military in Politics: Changing Patterns in Brazil* (Princeton: Princeton University Press, 1971), and Luis Viana Filho, *O Governo Castelo Branco* (Rio de Janeiro: Livraría José Olympo Editora, 1975).

11. For discussion of these divergences in the paths of the BAs, see O'Donnell, "Reflections on the Patterns of Change," and "Tensions in the Bureaucratic-Authoritarian State and the Question of Democracy," in *The New Authoritarianism in Latin America*, ed. David Collier (Princeton: Princeton University Press, 1979). A more detailed, and updated, discussion of these and related themes is Guillermo O'Donnell and Philippe Schmitter, "Tentative Conclusions about Uncertain Transitions," in *Transitions from Authoritarian Rule: Southern Europe and Latin America*, ed. Guillermo O'Donnell, Philippe Schmitter, and Laurence Whitehead (Baltimore: The Johns Hopkins University Press, 1986).

12. Statements along these and similar lines can be found in *Planeamiento y desarrollo de la acción de gobierno-directiva* (Buenos Aires: Secretaría de Prensa de la Presidencia de la Nación, 1966), and in the speech by Onganía published in *La Prensa*, September 15, 1966, p. 1.

13. See *Mensaje de la Junta Revolucionaria al Pueblo Argentino* and *Mensaje del Teniente General Onganía al Pueblo de la República con motivo de asumir la Presidencia de la Nación* (Buenos Aires: Secretaría de Prensa de la Presidencia de la Nación, June 30, 1966).

14. Law 16,894, July 3, 1966.

15. Law 16,940, October 8, 1966. See also the subsequent Law 17,401 on the "Repression of Communism." For a commentary on this legislation from the perspective of national security doctrines, see the book by the first Secretary of CONASE, General Osiris Villegas, *Políticas y estrategias para el desarrollo y la seguridad nacional* (Buenos Aires: Editorial Pleamar, 1969).

16. For a description of this intervention and of the violence with which university buildings were cleared, see "Crónica de un conflicto," *Revista Latinoamericana de Sociología* 2/3 (1966): 84–96.

17. See *La Nación*, October 26, 1966, p. 1.

18. On the first mass layoffs in the central administration, see *La Nación*, September 1, 1966, p. 1. On the "Railroad Restructuring Plan," see *La Nación*, December 3, 1966, p. 1.

19. On the "rationalization" of the port facilities (which resulted in a notable improvement in operations), see *La Nación*, October 8, 1966, p. 1. On the strike, see *La Nación*, October 19, 1966, p. 1.

20. For the announcement of the *Plan Tucumán* and the strikes and field burnings it provoked, see *La Nación*, August 22, p. 1, and August 28, p. 1, 1966.

21. *La Nación*, August 27, 1966, p. 1.

22. See the statements of the CGT in *La Nación*, August 13, p. 16, October 4, p. 4, November 14, p. 1, and December 9, p. 1, 1966.

23. For complaints about the reimposition of price controls and the allegedly resurgent statism, see statements by the UIA (*La Nación*, September 3, p. 1, and November 1, p. 1, 1966); the ACIEL (*La Nación*, November 5, 1966, pp. 1–18); and the CAC (*La Nación*, December 10, 1966, p. 1).

24. On university students' strikes and demonstrations, see *La Nación*, August 20, p. 16 (Córdoba); August 23, p. 4 (Buenos Aires); August 24, p. 18 (Córdoba); September 8, p. 4 (national strike); September 10, p. 18 (Córdoba); September 12, p. 1 (Tucumán); October 2, p. 16 (Tucumán); October 6, p. 4 (Córdoba); and October 6, p. 20 (Rosario), all in 1966.

THREE

Paternalists, Liberals, and Economic Normalization

1. NEW ACCOMMODATIONS BETWEEN PATERNALISTS AND LIBERALS

It was clear by the beginning of 1967 that Onganía, if his government was to survive, would have to respond with significant concessions to the complaints of the bourgeoisie, the liberals, and the media. His choice of Adalbert Krieger Vasena to replace Salimei as Minister of Economy and Labor represented one such concession. Few persons could have presented upper bourgeoisie credentials as impeccable as those of Krieger Vasena.[1] In addition to having been a high-ranking official during the presidency of General Pedro Aramburu (1955–58), Krieger Vasena had served as an adviser to and member of the boards of directors of several large corporations, including TNC subsidiaries, and was well connected with international organizations and banks. His appointment, which was supported by a virtual plebiscite of the upper bourgeoisie and the media,[2] marked the point at which crucial segments of the state apparatus were placed under the direction of a team with close ties to the most dynamic and transnationalized factions of the dominant classes. For their part, paternalists I interviewed contrasted Krieger Vasena's reputation for pragmatic liberalism with the more dogmatic stances of earlier "candidates" for the Economy Ministry*

---

*According to my interviews, Nicanor Costa Méndez, the Minister of Foreign Relations, played a crucial role in the selection of Krieger Vasena, presenting his "candidacy" to Onganía and assuring the president and other influential paternalists that Krieger Vasena was not a "dogmatic liberal."

(including Álvaro Alsogaray, José A. Martínez de Hoz, and Roberto Alemann) and hoped that his appointment would allow them to make the best of a bad situation.

Krieger Vasena presided over an empire that comprised the Ministry of Labor as well as the Economy and Finance ministries.[3] Rubens San Sebastian, a civil servant with an acknowledged talent for manipulating unions, was appointed Labor Secretary. The other top posts in the ministry were assigned to persons with backgrounds similar to Krieger Vasena's: of thirty or so occupants of such positions, with the possible exception of four about whose careers I could not obtain information, all had served as advisers to or members of the boards of directors of large corporations, many of which were TNC subsidiaries or private international lending organizations. Young *técnicos,* often with backgrounds as middle-ranking executives or consultants to large corporations, were prominent among undersecretaries and in advisory positions.

The domain of the Krieger Vasena team extended to the Ministry of Foreign Relations, headed by Nicanor Costa Méndez, who despite his nationalist past is best described as a liberal in view of his ideology, his personal contacts, and the enterprises with which he was connected. This domain also embraced the Ministry of Public Works, which was staffed by officials with backgrounds similar to those of the personnel in the Ministry of Economy and Labor and was dependent on that ministry for funding. However, the domain of the Krieger Vasena team stopped short of the Ministry of Social Welfare, which comprised, in addition to the secretariats of Social Security, Health, and Housing, a newly created "Secretariat of Community Assistance and Development," which was entrusted to a series of Onganía's intimates, none of whom was able to determine what this Secretariat was supposed to do. Several Social Welfare ministers were appointed in succession on the basis of the middle-of-the-road positions they occupied between the liberals and the paternalists, which did nothing to enhance their influence on public policies.

The paternalists remained in control of the Interior Ministry and of Onganía's presidential staff. Guillermo Borda, the newly appointed Interior Minister, held opinions that were not much different from those of his predecessor, Martínez Paz, although they were enunciated in a more sophisticated tone. The orientation of the Secretariat of Education and Culture, which came under the jurisdiction of the Interior Ministry, remained unchanged. Díaz Colodrero stayed on as Secretary of Government, and it was not long before he and Borda were again condemning the "disorder," "lack of authority," and "sectoralization" that the country had suffered during the period that ended with the 1966 coup[4] and insisting on the need to construct a "strong state" to eradicate these problems once and for all.* If any doubt remained that Onganía was thinking along similar lines, it was dispelled by statements and speeches in which he returned to the themes that earlier had aroused concern over his "corporatism."†

Despite these rhetorical continuities, the paternalists now added an important nuance to their approach to governing. While they claimed to concentrate on achieving order and solidarity in the country, they now left the liberals in charge of decision making on economic and most social issues. This division of labor opened the door for a rather precarious understanding between the paternalists and the liberal *técnicos*. The paternalists, as was noted earlier, viewed politics as synonymous with factionalism, confusion, and disorder, as a hindrance to the "social integration and harmony" so dear to their ideology. Politics, accordingly, would have no place in the "Argentine Revolution." A "political solution" was out of the question until a day far in the future when parties, if they still existed, had been integrated into "a community structured around the Councils and Commissions of the basic organizations of the community." Until that time, the "politics of the Revolution" would consist of following Ortega y Gasset's advice: "Argentines: to facts, to facts."‡ The goal of such politics was, in its first

*Díaz Colodrero insisted that "a fundamental assumption of the revolutionary process is order founded on authority" and that "few objectives are as pressing as that of ordering the state, proportioning and rationalizing it according to modern criteria so that it can meet its commitments effectively" (*La Razón*, May 16, 1968, p. 1).

†Cf., esp., Secretaría de Difusión y Turismo, *Discurso del Presidente de la Nación en la Comida de Camaradería de las Fuerzas Armadas*, July 6, 1967 (Buenos Aires, 1967), and *Mensaje al País del Presidente de la Nación Teniente General Juan Carlos Onganía*, December 29, 1967 (Buenos Aires, 1967). In the latter Onganía stated: "The Revolution dissolved political parties but refrained from intervening in other organs of the community, in the belief that [such organs] would find internally the strength to recommit themselves to the service of the country. Business as well as labor organizations must exert themselves so that we may achieve our goal of bringing the government close to the community and governing with it. It is our hope that the organs of the community will be restructured . . . with men representative of the new era the country seeks to enter, and that the basic organs of the community will acquire a weight and strength they lack today. . . . No group or sector shall abuse the whole" (p. 6). For concern in the leading periodicals over these expressions of the president's corporatism, see *La Prensa*, July 2, p. 1; August 9, p. 8; and October 11, p. 5, 1967.

‡Speech by Díaz Colodrero in *La Razón*, May 16, 1968, p. 1. According to Borda, "The government is reproached for lacking a political plan. What is not noticed is that this

phase, to establish "order" and initiate economic transformations by achieving social peace and economic stability, undertaking vast infrastructural projects "for the modernization and physical integration of the country," "rationalizing" public administration, improving provincial finances, and laying the foundations for "spiritual integration" and "respect for authority." This first, economic phase would be succeeded by a social phase, characterized by "structural changes" and the just distribution of the fruits of development. Later still, the revolution would enter a third stage, the political phase, which would culminate in the "organic amalgamation of the state with the organized community."*

For the moment, the primary task was to implement the revolution's economic phase. To this end, technical expertise was accorded top priority. What mattered to the paternalists was not who directed these undertakings but that they were promptly and effectively carried out.† Achieving the goals of the economic phase would, however, demand sacrifices of a society which, lacking the "solidarity" that was to emerge only with the "social phase," was unprepared to make them spontaneously. The paternalists felt that the politicization of the unions and of other organizations prevented them from recognizing the "intrinsically technical"

---

plan in its first phase exists and has yielded good fruit. It has consisted up until now of something very simple, yet at the same time very complex and difficult to achieve: the unification and pacification of the nation, the restoration of order, and the restitution of governmental authority. . . . Ours is a politics of deeds" (*La Razón*, June 27, 1967, p. 1). According to Onganía, "We know what politics consists of: a party platform and an electoral agenda, after which everything goes on as before, with the lie of long-unpracticed democracy. . . . Democracy should not be confused with the mechanical and obligatory act of voting, nor with the now dissolved political parties" (*La Nación*, July 6, 1967, p. 9). For Onganía, politics was destructive of what was most important, i.e. the "spiritual process of reconstructing the unity of the Nation, [which requires that] conflict between interests and sectors be subordinated to a common ideal, the ideal we all share" (*La Nación*, July 6, 1967, p. 11).

*Thus, "Nothing could be further from the thinking of the Revolution than the search for political solutions" (*Discurso del Presidente*, p. 20). Onganía stated in a press conference that "analysis of the theme of electoral politics must necessarily be postponed. If the government were to proceed at this time in any other way, the goals already achieved would be undermined, and the future of the Nation would be jeopardized, as in the recent past, by the disruption of the spiritual and material stability necessary to the Republic." Onganía believed it was necessary first to achieve "functionally organic participation" in the town governments—the "most suitable environment" for social integration—and from there to proceed until the "full amalgamation" of the "basic organizations of the community with the State" was achieved (*La Nación*, April 1, 1968, p. 1).

†Nearly all the paternalists I interviewed expressed a firm belief in the neutrality of technical expertise.

nature of the tasks at hand, and that this was the main obstacle to the success of the economic phase. Such organizations would therefore have to be tightly controlled until "social integration and solidarity" had been achieved.

The paternalists' intransigent bias against politics and their new division of labor with the liberals resulted in the reduction of their actual role to not much more than the conservation of "order." Such order was deemed indispensable for the completion of the economic phase, the actual content of which the liberals were granted high autonomy to determine. Thus it was left to the paternalists to apply repression, to make the unions "genuinely representative," and to "hierarchize" education—as well as to persist in a corporatist rhetoric that kept alive the concerns of the liberals.

It also seemed necessary to Onganía to guard his government against the influence of sectoral interests. To this end a secretariat was created in the presidency to screen the laws Onganía was requested to sign. This represented an attempt by Onganía and the paternalists to accord themselves a veto power over all proposed government policies, and it created much friction with the Krieger Vasena team,* even though the latter retained all initiative in formulating the economic policies that became the Argentine Revolution's center of gravity.

Can ideology and political incompetence explain the paternalists' willingness to bear the political costs of the economic phase while yielding so much power to the civilian liberals? Partly, but there were other reasons. One is that, as we shall see, the BA is not viable without economic normalization, which assigns a preeminent role to the upper fractions of local and transnational capital for whom the only acceptable government interlocutors are the liberal military and the liberal civilian *técnicos*. In situations of high previous threat, the depth of the economic crisis and the paternalists' and nationalists' obsession with imposing order usually leave little doubt that the liberals must be given ample control of social and economic policy. In cases such as post-1966 Argentina, where the BA is implanted in the context of a milder crisis

---

*The staff of this secretariat kept growing and expanding its duties. Its disagreements with the liberals generated conflicts and a mutual animosity that was confirmed in my interviews. For commentary on this situation and complaints about the alleged obstructionism by the Office of the Presidency, see *Primera Plana*, July 11, 1967, p. 13, and *La Nación*, July 27, 1967, p. 6, which, in its usual cryptic style, alluded to "rumored problems of communication" between Onganía and Krieger Vasena. See also Roberto Roth, *Los años de Onganía* (Buenos Aires: Ediciones La Campana, 1980). The author of this book—the highest-ranking civilian in the Office of the Presidency—provides an interesting perspective on these conflicts.

and threat and where it is less clear which sectors have really won and lost, there is more room for ambiguity and delay in determining what actors will take command of the main levers of public policy. But even in such cases of milder crisis and threat, the paternalists have at best an ambiguous relationship with the upper bourgeoisie, and the harsh imposition of order deprives them of any support they might have hoped to win from the popular sector and some middle sectors. Given their narrow social base, the most the paternalists can hope for, if they retain significant support in the armed forces, is to entrench themselves in some parts of the state apparatus while surrendering to the liberals the most important levers of social and economic policy.

In Brazil after the 1964 coup this problem was less acute, since a liberal, Castelo Branco, was president. Later, presidents Costa e Silva and Garraztazu Medici, with their nationalist (as defined in the previous chapter) leanings, coexisted with Delfim Neto and his economic policies, which were as favorable to transnationalization and the upper bourgeoisie as were those of Castelo Branco's economic team, although less orthodox. In post-1973 Chile, paternalists and nationalists have held high government posts but have achieved little influence over social and economic policy, which has been made primarily by liberal *técnicos* whose record since 1975 has been one of paradigmatic orthodoxy.[5] In Argentina between 1966 and 1970, by contrast, the paternalists occupied far more space in the institutional system of the state than was the case in the other BAs and, even after relinquishing much of it, maintained an uneasy coexistence, punctuated by conflicts, with the upper bourgeoisie and the civilian liberals who controlled most of the levers of social and economic decision making. The resulting tensions between paternalists and liberals constituted, as we shall see, one of the shoals upon which this BA foundered.

Because of their archaic ideology and because they lack any real social support, the paternalists have no alternative but to implement—clumsily—many of the economic policies dear to the upper bourgeoisie. An alternative in this context does not mean an abstract possibility, but a choice objectively available to the paternalists in a situation characterized by two vectors: one, the recent implantation of a state based on the exclusion of the popular sector, and the other, the existence of an extensively industrialized, dependent, and unbalanced capitalist society of the type in which, as we saw in chapter 1, the BA tends to emerge when certain crises unfold. The problems that precipitate such crises—conflicts that increasingly reveal their class content, the difficulties of indiscriminately continuing import substitution, the decline in domestic and foreign investment, the need to relieve mounting pressure on the balance of payments, the inability of the pre-coup governments to implement policies and to control the activities of their allies and adversaries—are deeply rooted, and the ambiguous solutions attempted by the paternalists can do little to eliminate them.[6] By contrast, there is little ambiguity to the solution advocated by the liberals, which consists of implementing orthodox economic policies. Such policies are consistently capitalist in a dual sense: first, they are congruent with the reproduction of these dependent, industrialized, and unbalanced capitalisms; second, they are supported, and usually designed and enacted, by persons very close to the most concentrated and transnationalized segments of the bourgeoisie.

The paternalists (and the nationalists) are, in various senses, more anti-leftist than the upper bourgeoisie and the civilian *técnicos*. However, their aim of superseding both "materialist communism" and "internationalistic capitalism" does little to improve their relations with an upper bourgeoisie upon which, like it or not, they depend during the BA. It also produces a diluted and truly inefficient version of capitalist social and economic policies. Even as the paternalists affirm that private property is sacred (although it must also serve a social function), and that transnational capital is welcome so long as it conforms to national policies and priorities, the policies they enact are shadows of those the liberals apply better and with greater support. Moreover, the paternalists' view of the state apparatus as responsible for controlling "excessive profits" and "sectoral egoism" is, to the upper bourgeoisie, evidence of their inability to accept the logic of capital accumulation. Rhetoric about the "spiritual content" of development and detailed inventories of its ultimate beneficiaries once the era of "sacrifices" has ended only reinforce this view. Seeking support, the paternalists direct their discourse (of which I quote some typical, recurrent terms) to the bulk of the population, including the popular sector—but they listen briefly (if at all) before acting on their perceptions of more tangible realities. As we shall see when we turn to the Levingston presidency, paternalists and nationalists can impose their social and economic policies only at the Pyrrhic price of foundering along with the BA. If the paternalists and nationalists are to preserve any presence within the institutional system of the BA—in certain public enterprises, in provincial governments, in embassies, and in the thousand crevices of a state apparatus that has navigated so many seas—they must relinquish to the liberals, as the main governmental interlocutors for the upper bourgeoisie, the public-policy levers of capital accumulation: wage, credit, investment, trade, and monetary policy, and decisions involving the country's relationship with the world capitalist system. What remains in the hands of paternalists and nationalists is the tribute that the liberals must pay to the relation of power embodied in the coercive institutions that are equally vital to the BA.

2. A DEFEAT FOR THE UNIONS

We have seen that the unions, after being disabused of their initial illusions, were driven into opposition. By the end of 1966, the CGT was condemning layoffs of public employees and protesting the decline in real wages brought on by state policies and continued inflation.* In February 1967, the CGT launched a *Plan de Acción* (Plan of Action) with statements demanding wage and salary increases and participation in government decision-making, but which closed rather modestly with calls for an unspecified change in economic policy and hints that most of its demands were negotiable. The Plan of Action called for "educative campaigns" and "mobilizations" to be followed by nationwide strikes culminating in factory occupations similar to those of 1964.[7] Prior to 1966 a similar combination of fundamentally moderate demands and massive mobilizations had proved effective in wresting concessions from governments that knew that disorder could trigger a military coup. But in the conditions prevailing in the early months of 1967, the Plan of Action was doomed to precipitate a major union defeat.

The government responded swiftly. The CGT was accused of resorting to subversive tactics, and the National Security Council (CONASE) was convened. It concluded that "communist groups" had influenced the Plan and that the CGT's "efforts to subvert internal order and threaten social peace" had "national security implications." With "all forms of dialogue interrupted," military and police agencies were instructed to "initiate adoption of the proposed measures in the degree

*See the statements of the CGT in *La Nación,* December 9, 1966, pp. 1, 14. After criticizing the "international monopolies," unemployment, wage levels, and the cost of living, the CGT attacked the "free trade minorities . . . [that] introduce division among the Argentines, set social groups against one another, obscure what unifies us, and exalt conflicting interests." The CGT leadership did affirm, however, its intent to "carry on a dialogue" with the government and with bourgeois organizations; see also the CGT in *La Nación,* December 29, 1966, p. 9. Public sector employees, who were direct victims of state "rationalization," adopted more combative language, as did the *62 de Pie* union current which, as was mentioned above, had been barred from the CGT leadership. See *Crónica,* November 30, 1966, p. 17, and February 28, 1967, p. 15.

and order of priority called for."[8] Simultaneously, the government froze the funds of several unions and notified state employees that participation in the strikes would be grounds for dismissal without compensation.[9] The unions were also warned that if they persisted in their present course their "legal personality"* would be suspended or revoked.[10] This would mean, among other things, that union leaders would be removed from their positions and that unions would lose their main economic resource—the funds they received from government-mandated employer withholdings of a percentage of wages and salaries paid.

After considerable debate and agonizing doubts, union leaders decided to proceed with the strikes scheduled for February and March.† But the strikes failed to generate high levels of absenteeism; the CGT had mistaken the government's rapid loss of popularity for popular willingness to engage in active opposition. For the moment Argentines were not disposed to participate in the kind of political agitation whose apparent end they had applauded in June 1966. An attempt by the CGT to convene the organizations of the bourgeoisie to "analyze the situation" likewise met with little success. Except for the CGE, which cautiously agreed to a "dialogue" and exhorted the CGT to find "constructive solutions," the rest of the bourgeois organizations refused to meet with an organization that had placed itself "outside the law."[11] Instead, they seized the opportunity to reiterate what they had emphasized since the coup: that the CGT, as the political arm of a "totalitarian" movement—Peronism—was itself a totalitarian organization. The CGT, argued the leaders of the organizations of the bourgeoisie, by taking advantage of the Law of Professional Associations‡ had

*One of the corporatist legacies of the 1946–55 Peronist era was that a union, before being recognized as the exclusive representative of the workers in a given branch of economic activity, had to be granted *personeria legal* (legal personality) by the government.

†According to *La Nación* (February 26, 1967, p. 2), the Vandorists moved initially to cancel the *Plan de Acción* but were outvoted by the remaining union currents. This turn of events was confirmed in my interviews, where I also learned that many union leaders—not only Vandorists—were anxious to reach an accord with the government that would allow them to retire gracefully from the situation. However, both paternalists and liberals (although, as we shall see, with different ends in mind) saw the Plan of Action as a golden opportunity to defeat the unions and rejected all overtures from the CGT leadership. It is interesting that the CGT, while engaged in a confrontation with the government and at a time when the organizations of the upper bourgeoisie were demanding more repression, declared that "the methods of struggle associated with the *Plan de Acción* are clearly and finally not directed against the business sector" (*La Razón*, February 28, 1967, p. 9).

‡The Law of Professional Associations, enacted in 1945, repealed in 1955, and partially reenacted in 1959, established most of the "privileges" enjoyed by the CGT and the unions to which the liberals, the upper bourgeoisie, and most of the media objected. Such "privileges" included the granting of "legal personality" to one and only one "representative" union in each economic sector, the mandatory affiliation with that union of all

made itself into a brazen obstacle to the freedom of association of which their own organizations were, of course, a salutary example. The upper bourgeoisie, after years of enduring governments too weak to shackle the CGT and its affiliated unions, now saw a golden opportunity to realize one of their major goals: to atomize the representation of workers and employees. The best way to achieve this goal was, in their view, first to destroy the CGT and then to grant the "freedom" to organize any number of unions and confederations and to join and contribute to any of them. The upper bourgeoisie felt that in the absence of such reforms, "union power" would continue to disrupt the "social peace" and the extended period of capital accumulation without which there could be no "real solutions" for Argentina.*

Faced with a popular sector reluctant to follow its Plan of Action, vigorously attacked by opposing class interests, and threatened by a government that could rely on ample support for its efforts to "tame" the unions, the CGT had to choose between pursuing its present course, which could only lead to harsher repression, or submitting to what was nothing less than unconditional surrender. Meanwhile, the government imposed new repressive measures† that resulted in mass dismissals of public employees,[12] and reports were leaked to the press that the CGT was about to be dissolved.[13] Simultaneously the government suspended or revoked the legal personalities of the textile, sugar, chemical, metallurgical, and telephone workers' unions. Together with the unions that were "intervened"—whose elected leaders were replaced by government appointees—during 1966 (representing port workers, loggers, typographers, newspaper vendors, telephone employees, workers in the tobacco and fishing industries, and various types of public employees),[14] the sanctioned unions, which included most of the largest and wealthi-

---

workers in the sector wishing to organize, and the compulsory withholding by employers of a percentage of wages and salaries (including those of workers or employees who were not members of the union) for direct deposit into the union's bank account. The law further allowed the government, under a variety of circumstances, to suspend or cancel the union's "legal personality" or to "intervene" the union, replacing its statutorily elected leadership with a government-appointed "intervenor."

*See the *Memorias anuales* (Buenos Aires, 1967) of the SRA, CAC, and UIA. The leading periodicals, which had been making an issue of "union power" since June 1966, insisted on these new union "freedoms"; see, for example, *La Nación*, February 16, 1967, p. 6; and *La Prensa*, December 18, 1966, p. 6, and January 25, 1967, p. 6.

†Especially the "Civil Defense Law," Law 17,192 of March 4, 1967, which allowed the government, "in the interest of national security," to place civilians—including, of course, strikers—under military jurisdiction, making them subject to military discipline and penalties for "desertion" (from the workplace).

est, comprised some 930,000 members, or approximately 45 percent of Argentina's unionized workers and employees.*

The suspension or withdrawal of legal personality deprived the leaders of the penalized unions of control over their organizations, and allowed employers to cease making the payroll deductions that had formerly financed these unions' activities. These sanctions, together with the government's evident willingness to employ additional coercion against "rebellious" unions, meant that any further action along the lines of the Plan of Action would have to be taken clandestinely and without resources that had previously been available. Very few union leaders were prepared to go underground or to accept the radicalization to which clandestine activity quite certainly would have led. These constraints persuaded the CGT directorate to suspend activities connected with the Plan of Action and to convene the organization's supreme authority, the Central Committee of the Confederation, "to undertake a thoroughgoing analysis of the problem."[15] The committee met promptly, as the government was imposing new penalties against public employees—including the firing of more than 100,000 railroad workers—which, like those imposed earlier, furnished a welcome opportunity for "administrative rationalization." Despite the abstention of most Vandorists and the opposition of the typographers (whose union was soon to assume a crucial militant role) and other sanctioned unions, the committee voted to call off the remaining items on the agenda of the Plan of Action, including general strikes scheduled for March 21 and 22.[16]

The defeat of the CGT was complete, not only because the committee's decision meant unconditional surrender, but also because of the infighting that immediately emerged as recriminations flew between those who complained of having been irresponsibly forced to follow a losing strategy (a reproach aimed also at Perón, who had ordered a combative stance)[17] and those who leveled charges of treason at the many lukewarm supporters of the Plan of Action. Internal divisions also stemmed from the ingratiating tactics that many penalized unions soon adopted to try to convince the government to "regularize" them, and from the influence gained within the CGT by the less combative unions that had been exempted from governmental sanctions. The CGT leader-

*Calculations based on union membership data for 1963 in Documentación e Información Laboral (DIL), *Nucleamientos sindicales*, Serie Documentos (Buenos Aires, July 1982). These must be considered rough approximations; see Juan Carlos Torre, "La tasa de sindicalización en la Argentina," *Desarrollo Económico*, no. 48 (January–March, 1973): 78–93. There can be no doubt, however, that these measures decapitated the CGT, since they affected most unions capable of mobilizing substantial resources.

ship, lacking strong support from their rank and file, unwilling to call new strikes, and internally fragmented, thus suffered a defeat that was shared by the popular sector as a whole as soon as Krieger Vasena's policies were made explicit. The defeat of the CGT and the unions cleared the way for the liberals and the upper bourgeoisie to launch their offensive, embodied in the new economic team's policies.

For Onganía and the paternalists the surrender of the CGT was a major and very necessary victory. It revealed that the popular sector was unprepared to follow the previously well established tactics of the union leaders. More important, it seemed to demonstrate that there existed, at last, a government willing and able to impose order. With their appointment of the new economic team and their role in defeating the unions, the paternalists won a respite during which they could continue to share with the liberals the apex of the state apparatus—but at the cost of burning their bridges with the popular sector.

But no sooner had the CGT been defeated than the paternalists were once again at odds with the liberals, the upper bourgeoisie and the leading periodicals over the "union issue." On several occasions in 1967, the Labor Secretary and Onganía himself announced that the Law of Professional Associations was "under review." Moreover, the government sent auditors to examine the handling of union funds (previously a closely guarded secret), and announced that in the future union leaders would be elected directly by the membership at large, using the secret ballot and voter lists purged of improper entries.[18] As they asserted repeatedly, Onganía and his current saw these revisions as first steps toward creating an authentically representative unionism that, after being depoliticized and restricted to its specific functions, would be inserted into the comprehensive corporatist system they envisioned. The outcome would be unified unionism administered by apolitical leaders, mindful of labor's specific contribution to the common good of a socially integrated country.* Such an outcome, however, was very different from what the upper bourgeoisie, the leading periodicals, and the liberals had in mind. If a characteristic dimension of statizing corporat-

---

*The paternalists' sincerity in their efforts to achieve a "just social equilibrium" was matched only by their lack of political skill. On the defeat of the CGT's Plan of Action, Borda felt obliged to declare: "In this episode the government has made explicit its firm commitment to maintaining the principle of authority. It does not flaunt itself as the victor, nor does it propose that any sector should bear the weight of its victory. It simply insists on fulfilling its political and economic plans, and will resist any pressure that stands in the way of its adopting the measures required by the common good, regardless of the social sector from which such pressures might arise" (La Razón, March 16, 1967, p. 1). The paternalists tried hard to deny the great class victory they had won for the bourgeoisie.

ism is the conquest and control of unions by the state apparatus,[19] these actors were no less corporatist than the paternalists. But they, unlike the paternalists, wanted this control exercised over an atomized unionism, a difference that would acquire important ramifications as Krieger Vasena's economic program registered its initial successes.

The year 1967 marked the appearance within unionism of the "New Current of Opinion," made up of *dialoguista,* or participationist, unions that once again applauded the Argentine Revolution and claimed to reject all forms of politicization, opening the way to "participation" as defined by the paternalists.* Widely regarded as exemplars of corrupt and submissive unionism, these unions could offer certain advantages to their own members† but little or nothing to workers as a class. Although the low weight and prestige of the "New Current" among the workers was not congruent with the "authentic representativeness" that the paternalists sought, the latter believed that this sector of unionism could reunify the CGT and, having done so, bring to fruition the "organic and technical participation of the workers."‡

By the middle of 1967, then, the following union currents revolved around the CGT: (1) the participationists, prevented by their opportunism from formulating any consistent strategy; (2) the Vandorists, licking their wounds and proposing a "dialogue" with the government but aware that the kind of participation offered by the paternalists was the kiss of death;§ (3) some leaders of the intervened unions, who were legally barred from the CGT directorate but whose insistence on retaining their posts strengthened the government's resolve to refrain from

---

*The first to align themselves with this current were the construction, electrical, and petroleum workers' unions (*La Nación,* May 29, 1967, p. 6).

†Especially non-wage benefits. The construction workers' union, whose members also benefitted from the 1968–70 construction boom, was especially well rewarded; it was widely rumored, moreover, that its leaders received substantial personal benefits.

‡In the hope of hastening the participationists' takeover of the CGT, the paternalists turned a deaf ear to the conciliatory overtures of the Vandorists and of what remained of the 62 de Pie (*La Nación,* July 10, p. 6 and August 28, p. 6, 1967). (This information was also confirmed in my interviews.) The CGT leadership, following the collapse of the Plan of Action, resigned in May 1967. A predominantly Vandorist Delegates' Commission was appointed to succeed it and was charged with convening a general Congress of the CGT, which would meet in early 1968 (with results we shall consider). The traditional holidays of May 1 and October 17 passed almost unnoticed in 1967, and toward the end of the year the leading periodicals commented gleefully on the CGT's "virtual hibernation" (*La Nación,* December 26, 1967, p. 6).

§Unlike the participationists, the Vandorists kept their distance from the government even as they tried to negotiate with it. These contrasting approaches further separated the two union currents and strengthened Onganía's resolve to keep the CGT "dormant" until the participationists could achieve control of the organization (my interviews).

negotiating with "illegally constituted bodies";* and (4) various still small groups that were beginning to echo calls for more radical struggles. In the midst of such fragmentation, the participationists could hardly be expected to reunify the CGT in a manner consistent with the "authentic representation" appropriate to the "organized community." The upper bourgeoisie, critical of the paternalists for wasting a golden opportunity to atomize the popular sector, was momentarily mollified by their failure to use the participationists to achieve this goal. With the attention of the main actors in the BA focused on the question of whether to integrate or atomize the unions, few noticed that new goals and methods of struggle, much more threatening than those of the ultimately moderate and accommodationist CGT, were beginning to emerge within the popular sector.

3. THE NORMALIZATION PROGRAM

A few days after being appointed Minister of Economy and Labor Krieger Vasena departed for the United States, where the Interamerican Committee of the Alliance for Progress approved his plans for the Argentine economy—which were not yet public knowledge in Argentina.[20] Since the confrontations between the CGT and the government were monopolizing media attention at the time, there was little news coverage of the activities of the new economic team. But immediately after the CGT surrendered, Krieger Vasena took center stage. In a speech of March 13, 1967, he announced some far-reaching decisions: (1) a devaluation of the peso to a rate of 350 to the U.S. dollar (a 40% drop); (2) a "fiscal compensation" for the devaluation, in the form of a tax on foreign exchange holdings and a withholding tax on agricultural and livestock exports, which meant that for both exporters and meat and cereals producers the effective exchange rate remained, as before, at 245 pesos per U.S. dollar; (3) a significant reduction of import duties; (4) "liberalization" of the foreign currency market; and (5) various measures designed to "streamline" public spending. Equally important was the tone of the speech, which introduced the new policies as the first steps of a broad program designed to reduce inflation rapidly (but without recessionary effects) while promoting competition, "efficiency," and foreign investment. The program, it was asserted, would lay the foundations for stable

*See, for example, the Social Welfare Minister's refusal to receive a CGT delegation because it included leaders of unions that the government had intervened (*La Nación*, April 19, 1967, p. 4).

economic development.[21] Other policies adopted in rapid succession included: (6) the suspension of collective bargaining and the granting of an average pay increase of 15 percent for workers in the private sector; shortly after a similar raise was granted to state employees, after which wages were frozen for the next twenty-one months;[22] (7) the termination of automatic extensions of leases of rural property (which had been established during the Peronist era and, to the perpetual protest of the landowners, had not been abolished by the 1955–66 governments);[23] (8) the conclusion of a voluntary price agreement with representatives of eighty-five leading industrial firms who agreed to freeze prices for six months in exchange for special access to bank credit and state contracts;[24] (9) tax write-offs for the purchase of agricultural and industrial machinery;[25] (10) a change in the method of valuation of corporate assets, which significantly decreased corporations' tax liability;[26] (11) a 50 percent tax reduction on housing investments;[27] and (12) the establishment of special credit lines for the financing of durable consumer goods purchases and housing improvements.[28] Other steps were taken whose impact was less direct but which offered transnational capital further proof of the government's commitment to economic orthodoxy.*

These policies were applauded by the upper bourgeoisie and its organizations.† Foreign actors were also quick to express their approval: no sooner had the March 13 speech ended than the wire services relayed news of the "confidence" it had awakened in Europe and the United States.[29] This approval was confirmed days later by the IMF's announce-

---

*Particularly the Hydrocarbons Law of June 24, 1967 (no. 17,318) and the prompt and full satisfaction of claims by transnational oil companies for compensation for the cancellations of exploration and exploitation rights. These cancellations had been decided by the Illia government (*La Nación,* April 17, 1967, p. 1).

†For the reaction of the UIA, see *La Nación,* March 15, p. 1 (although this organization protested the reduction of import duties), April 7, p. 1 and September 2, p. 16, 1967; of the CAC, *La Nación,* March 15, p. 1, March 23, p. 7 and May 3, p. 6, 1967 (telegram to Krieger Vasena congratulating him on the "external support" won by the program), and August 2, 1967, p. 1; of the ACIEL, *La Nación,* March 18, 1967, p. 3 (although requesting that the government tighten the screws further in matters of "labor policy" and fiscal deficit); of the Buenos Aires Stock Exchange, *La Nación,* April 20, 1967, p. 6. For the reactions of leading periodicals see, for example, the editorials in *La Nación,* March 16, p. 6, May 2, p. 6, and July 15, p. 6, 1967, and *Economic Survey,* issues of March and April 1967. The CGE and the CGI adopted a cautious attitude, expressing only their "concern" with the cost increases they assumed would accompany devaluation and their distress over the government's "inexplicable failure to consult" with them before adopting these measures (*La Nación,* March 18, 1967, p. 3). The organizations of the Pampa bourgeoisie (SRA and CARBAP in particular) registered their opposition to the withholding tax on exports in a lukewarm manner, and they expressed their enthusiastic support for remaining policies, especially the law concerning rural leases (*La Nación,* May 4, 1967, p. 18). For more details on the reactions of these organizations see their respective *Memorias* for the period we are studying.

ment that it had granted Argentina a standby loan of $125 million,[30] which opened the way for new credits from a consortium of European banks (US$100 million), United States banks (US$100 million), and the United States Treasury (US$75 million).[31] Finally, the U.S. Department of State—which had publicly criticized the 1966 coup—declared its support for Krieger Vasena's program, saying it "had modified [United States] policy with respect to the granting of aid to Argentina."[32]

Krieger Vasena's March 13 speech marked the beginning of an offensive by the upper bourgeoisie, based on the defeat of the unions and on the control exercised over economic policy by a team intimately linked to the most powerful fractions of the dominant classes. The major short-term goal of this offensive was to eradicate inflation and relieve pressure on the balance of payments. It was assumed that once this goal had been achieved and reinforced by inducements to domestic and foreign investors (and by the favorable "business climate" that all of this would generate), stable growth would soon follow.*

Prior to Krieger Vasena's ministry, Argentine stabilization programs had been based on the premise that excessive demand was the main cause of balance-of-payments deficits and inflation. The remedies that followed from this diagnosis were recessionary: cutbacks on credit and public spending, restrictions of the money supply, deliberate reductions in real salaries and wages, and sharp devaluations of the peso. Such decisions temporarily improved the balance of payments by reducing domestic economic activity, which diminished the demand for imports and increased the surpluses available for export. However, since devaluation meant higher domestic prices for imports and exportable goods, and since credit and monetary restrictions meant higher interest rates, inflation, instead of abating, increased.[33]

The innovation of the program inaugurated in March 1967 was its diagnosis that the main causes of inflation were to be found on the side of costs and in the psychological factors involved in expectations of high inflation. It followed from this assumption that the cure for inflation would lie not in restrictive management of monetary variables but in reversing expectations and stabilizing factor costs. This diagnosis helps explain why the new economic team tried to control a number of crucial prices, including those of (1) labor, in the form of a mandatory wage freeze that was to last almost two years; (2) industrial products, the

---

*The emphasis on reducing inflation and gaining internal and external confidence is evident in speeches by Krieger Vasena reprinted in *Política económica Argentina*, Ministerio de Economía y Trabajo.

prices of which were controlled at the wholesale level through a voluntary price agreement supported by a growing number of industrial
firms; (3) exportable commodities (mostly foods) sold on the domestic
market, whose export value in pesos was held constant by the above-
mentioned withholding tax; (4) fuel and public services, which, after
being increased sharply during the first months of the program, were
subsidized with revenues accruing to the Treasury as a result of the
withholding tax on exports; and (5) foreign exchange, in that another
formal* devaluation was ruled out for the foreseeable future.

A second innovation of the March 1967 program was the withholding tax on exports to compensate for the effects of the devaluation. In
the past, devaluations led to windfall profits for exporters and Pampean
producers of agricultural and livestock goods, and to sharp rises in the
prices of meat and grain sold on the domestic market. These changes
resulted in often enormous (if quite rapidly reversed) transfers of income from the urban sector to exporters, to the financial sector, and to
the Pampa bourgeoisie. The withholding tax that accompanied the
March 1967 devaluation gave the state apparatus a large amount of
new revenue, demonstrating that Krieger Vasena, his team, and their
principal social base were neither "oligarchs" nor "anti-statists."

4. NORMALIZATION AND BUREAUCRATIC AUTHORITARIANISM

The policies enacted by Krieger Vasena's economic team were designed to achieve what I have termed *economic normalization*. In this
section we shall examine some general aspects of the relation between
normalization and the BA. Having done so, we shall be better equipped
to analyze in chapter 4 the data pertaining to the Argentine program of
1967–69.

In the period immediately following its implantation, the BA con-
fronts two basic and intimately related problems. One is the imposition
of "order," which involves the coercive suppression of the threat posed
by the preceding crises. Attempts are made to deactivate the popular
sector, to control its organizations, to prohibit its expression through
political parties or movements, and to seal off the channels of access to
government that were available to this sector under the previous regime.

---

*The qualifier *formal* is used because the Krieger Vasena ministry, by gradually reducing the withholding tax originally established on the dollars earned by Pampean exports,
actually devalued the peso in relation to this major component of total exports.

If successful, these efforts result in the political exclusion of the popular sector—the obverse side of "order," or "social peace," under the BA. After the praetorian period that precedes the BA, this exclusion appears as a requisite for restoring internal and external confidence in the future of the economy, i.e. for reversing the negative expectations generated by the preceding crisis. But if the imposition of "order" is important in restoring confidence and reversing expectations, another key factor is the existence of a credible guarantee that the BA will be able to sustain this order well into the future. The achievement of such a guarantee is connected to the second great task of the BA, economic normalization.

Fundamentally, economic normalization involves (1) diminishing the sharp fluctuations characteristic of most economic variables during the pre-BA period; (2) reversing the negative trends in these variables; (3) transforming, in ways consistent with points (1) and (2), the expectations of the (oligopolistic) actors with the greatest capacity to shape the economic situation; (4) eliminating, as a requisite for reestablishing "normal" (i.e. unequal and transnationalizing) patterns of economic growth, the economy of plunder characteristic of the previous period; (5) subordinating the economy (and the class structure, although the engineers of normalization do not speak in these terms) to the patterns of expansion of its oligopolized units and, eventually, of some segments of the state apparatus; and (6) repairing the links between the domestic economy and the centers of capitalism.

What does it mean to normalize the economy? How is normalization achieved? When is it possible to say that normalization has been achieved? Whose answers to these questions really count? Let us begin to answer these questions by making some general observations based on the discussion in chapter 1. Normality, for economies such as those in which the BA may emerge, is a situation in which capital accumulation primarily and regularly benefits oligopolized and transnationalized economic units, in conditions that assure them high and reasonably stable rates of profit and growth. In such a situation, the patterns of expansion displayed by these units tend to subordinate those of the rest of the economy to a greater degree than in the more integrated and diversified economies of the capitalist centers.

In the period immediately preceding the implantation of the Brazilian, Argentine, Uruguayan, and Chilean BAs, the dynamic impulse for the economy (until it was choked off by balance-of-payments difficulties) came not so much from large private corporations as from the state apparatus, increases in wages and salaries, mass consumption, and the

opportunities available under these circumstances to the weaker fractions of the bourgeoisie. As those periods drew to a close, mounting
inflation, a growing perception of popular-sector threat, and the weakening of these dynamic economic impulses had two major consequences: (1) the dislocation of the productive structure, due largely to
rapidly increasing inflation and to the defensive strategies adopted by
most economic actors (ranging from disinvestment and voracious speculation to outright flight from the national market); and (2) an increasing
disjunction between these productive structures and the world capitalist
centers, except for the channels that allowed for accelerated extraction
of capital and for the participation of some external actors in successive
rounds of plunder in the domestic economy. As a result of these processes, the supremacy of the oligopolized and transnationalized economic units was interrupted, in the sense that they no longer set the
rhythms of the economy or regularly subordinated the behavior of other
units, even if they were able to reap inordinately high profits during
successive rounds of plunder.

Superficially, normalization involves only policies designed to combat inflation and to improve the balance of payments. But normalization has at least two other dimensions. The first involves the restitution
of the economic supremacy of the oligopolized and transnationalized
units in such a way that they regain heavy influence over the performance of the economy's main variables. The second dimension of normalization consists of the restoration of close links between the local
economy and the world capitalist system, in ways that involve, in contrast to the pre-BA period, capital movements away from as well as
toward the capitalist centers.

Following the implantation of the BA, the major problem for the
victors—apart from imposing "order"—is to induce the upper bourgeoisie and transnational capital to fulfill once again its "normal" role in the
economy. The difficulty of achieving this goal is in direct proportion to
the depth of the prior crisis. The deeper the crisis—and therefore the
more severe the prior threat—the greater the dislocation of the economy
and of its upper stratum of oligopolized and transnationalized units.
Greater too are the balance-of-payment difficulties, inflation, disinvestment, and the degree to which the state apparatus has abandoned its
role of promoting the reproduction of an economy subordinated to the
upper bourgeoisie. Greater too is the exodus of transnational capital
and local capitalists, and more stringent are the safeguards they demand

for returning to a society that has recently displayed such an explosive potential. Moreover, the deeper the previous threat and crisis, the more pronounced the diversion of capital to financial speculation. This diversion leads, both before and after the implantation of the BA, to the disproportionate growth of financial corporations and banks, as well as of numerous institutional inventions set up for participating in an economy of plunder. Eventually the plunder approaches its limit: the metamorphosis of much of the economy's productive capital into financial capital. These processes imply that the deeper the prior crisis (especially when the crisis is one of social domination, as was the case prior to the coups of the 1970s), the longer and steeper the climb to restore anything resembling normal economic functioning, regardless of how successful the BA may have been in its task of imposing "order."

The implantation of the BA typically coincides with acute balance-of-payments deficits and high inflation. At this point few of the economy's dynamic impulses do not aggravate one or both of these problems. How can such a situation be ameliorated? Above all, how can expectations be changed so as to stimulate an influx of foreign capital and promote investments in productive sectors? These are not easy tasks. Let us begin by examining inflation, perhaps the major symbol and synthesis of the economic troubles preceding the BA. A necessary condition for medium- and long-term economic calculations is the reduction of inflation to "reasonable" levels and the generation of expectations that these levels will continue to decline, or at least remain stable. "Controlled" inflation is a crucial component of normalization. Inflation is only superficially an increase in the general level of prices; it results from the aggregation of a succession of fluctuations in the structure of relative prices. In such conditions, particularly when inflation is high, whatever economic gains each actor may achieve tend to be short-lived, since they generate reactions from other actors who, in attempting to improve or recover their relative positions, produce both new changes in relative prices and new impulses toward higher inflation.*

The higher inflation becomes, the farther behind lag the incomes and prices of sectors that do not have sufficient power to participate in this race. Typically among the hardest hit are the most poorly organized segments of the popular sector, pensioners, some regions, and the state

---

*Since the 1940s the Argentine economy has been characterized not only by high and erratic inflation but also by abrupt changes in the structure of relative prices (see de Pablo, "Precios relativos," and Mallon and Sourrouille, *Economic Policy-Making*).

apparatus as a whole.* However, the best organized segments of the popular sector, in a democratic or praetorian context, sometimes come out ahead in this shifting kaleidoscope of relative prices. More than the overall rate of inflation, these disaggregated fluctuations are inimical to the normal functioning of the economy. Relative price shifts are usually more violent and unpredictable than are changes in the general inflation rate, and they operate at a level more directly relevant for determining the economic performance of each actor. They do not, as we have seen, preclude high profits for individual economic actors, but relative price fluctuations increase the uncertainty of medium- and long-term forecasts—a problem, as noted in chapter 1, that generates particularly vexing problems for bigger and more complex enterprises.†

I have argued that the normal functioning of minimally complex economies is incompatible with a high and fluctuating rate of inflation. The preceding discussion allows a more precise statement of this argument: the normal functioning of such economies, including those in which the BA tends to emerge, is incompatible with a rate of inflation that is the aggregate and largely unpredictable outcome of pressures exerted by a broad range of social actors. The reproduction of these capitalisms does not require a zero or even a low rate of inflation. The Brazilian case during the years of the "miracle" (1968–73) shows a rather high but reasonably stable and predictable rate of inflation, generated by stimuli that do not interfere with important, consistent, and predictable capital accumulation.

Once the BA is implanted and controls have been established on wages and salaries, inflationary impulses (discounting exogenous stimuli with which any country must contend) emerge basically from two camps: (1) the bourgeoisie, especially its upper fraction, whose market power is euphemistically expressed in its "price leadership," and (2) a state apparatus that tends to adapt its decisions and nondecisions to a codified "rationality" that is consistent with a highly oligopolized and transnationalized economic structure.

---

*For data and an analysis that show the Argentine state apparatus to have been one of the big losers in this race, due to the failure of the prices of its services and taxes to keep pace with the overall rate of inflation, see Carlos Díaz Alejandro, *Essays on the Economic History of the Argentine Republic* (New Haven: Yale University Press, 1970); Mallon and Sourrouille, *Economic Policy-Making;* and Óscar Oszlak, "Inflación y política fiscal en la Argentina: el impuesto a los réditos en el período 1955–1965," Centro de Investigationes en Administración Pública, Instituto Torcuato Di Tella, Buenos Aires, 1970.

†These forecasting problems are exacerbated by a high level of threat, when the more oligopolistic and transnationalized firms are, or consider themselves, preferred targets for expropriation.

To the upper bourgeoisie, an annual inflation rate of, say, 30 percent may be intolerable if it is unforeseen or if it is due largely to wage increases or government policies it considers demagogic. By contrast, the same rate may be perfectly acceptable—well within the peculiar "normality" of these capitalisms—if it has been foreseen and largely stimulated by the upper bourgeoisie itself. The same level of inflation, in short, may have very different economic and political implications, depending on which social actors are responsible for generating it. Inflation, its fluctuations, and the factors that give rise to it are far from being exclusively economic problems; they express alliances, triumphs, and defeats within a changing array of social forces. One expression of the exclusion of the popular sector under the BA is its inability to act as a co-contributor to inflation. This exclusion, of course, leaves room for conflicts over which state activities and fractions of the bourgeoisie will continue to stimulate, and to benefit from, the inflation that remains. For the moment, however, this is not our concern.

After inflation the second major economic problem initially facing the BA involves the balance of payments. At the outset, the foreign exchange situation is grim: reserves are depleted and access to international credit is virtually nonexistent. Transnational capital, moreover, seeking redress for nationalizing or socializing decisions often made by the governments of the preceding period, places heavy pressure on the scarce resources remaining. How, then, can the country obtain the foreign capital it urgently needs to sustain internal economic activity, if only at the recessionary levels imposed by orthodox economic policies? During the first stages of normalization, the answer to this question depends fundamentally on the behavior of financial capital, especially its transnational segments.* Immediate—and costly—efforts are required to gain the confidence of such capital; "freedom" is restored to international capital movements, and accounts left over from the previous period are generously settled by the government of the BA. These actions, it is hoped, will be the first steps toward "normalizing" the dependent relation of these economies with the world capitalist system.

I argued in chapter 1 that the assessment of these economies that matters the most is that of their largest and most dynamic economic units. In the first stages of normalization, it should now be added, the

---

*Transnational financial capital is mainly concerned with the likelihood that the country will honor its foreign debt. By contrast, the conditions under which transnational industrial and commercial capital will again decide to take medium- and long-term risks are, as we shall see, more rigorously defined.

judgments of financial capital are particularly important. If a normaliza-tion program is not deemed rational and adequate by the largest eco-nomic units and by national and transnational financial capital, it has very little chance of success. There may be any number of policies capable of leading to normalization. Given the relation of social forces that crystallizes under the BA, however, the only viable ones are those acceptable to these actors. This subset of policies is very limited and is subject to some of the most rigid and explicitly codified criteria of economic "rationality."

Economic policy in a BA is typically in the hands of officials who apply a code of economic orthodoxy. What does it mean to be ortho-dox? This is what is codified. Given a situation combining high inflation with a balance-of-payments crisis, orthodoxy prescribes (1) a drastic reduction in the fiscal deficit; (2) strict wage and salary controls; (3) careful control of credit and the money supply; (4) elimination of subsi-dies for mass consumption; (5) improved economic efficiency, to be achieved basically by cutbacks on the effective protection of domestic production; (6) free movements of capital in and out of the country; and (7) avoidance of sharp and unforeseen currency devaluations. These prescriptions do not derive from some ontological truth. They are crite-ria formulated by transnational capital, the upper bourgeoisie, and an "economic science" spawned by a complex network of institutions, "gurus," and popularizers. At least until very recently (and certainly during the period we are studying), it was enough to read the recommen-dations of the IMF to recognize the extent to which its judgments de-pend on whether or not it had been persuaded that a government had the will and capacity to apply the orthodox code. The IMF is the certi-fier of the rationality of normalization programs. As the recognized custodian of this rationality, its assessments are crucial for the decisions of other transnational financial institutions, public and private alike. Indeed, a favorable judgment by the IMF is usually less significant for the sums directly involved than for the role it plays in certifying to other financial actors that a given county is worthy of new loans or repayment moratoria.[34]

The judgments of the upper bourgeoisie and, particularly in the first period of the BA, of transnational capital would not be so decisive were it not for two circumstances already pointed out: the profound transna-tionalization of these productive structures and the need to decrease inflation and to ameliorate the balance-of-payments squeeze inherited from the period previous to the BA. This combination of circumstances means that the large domestic and transnational economic actors who evaluate the normalization program are at the same time those whose actions and omissions exercise decisive influence over the success or failure of the stated goals of that program. These actors' criteria about what is rational and acceptable are codified on the basis of the normal functioning of the center capitalisms. Such criteria express—and advance—the dominant position of these actors, both locally and in the world capitalist system. "Freedom of initiative," the "free" movement of capital, "efficiency" unhampered by the "sentimentality" of protecting "marginal" producers, fiscal and wage "discipline"—these are some of the axioms of orthodoxy whose consequences are particularly beneficial to the largest and most dynamic economic units.

One consequence of this codification is that the BA's officials have little leeway in choosing the direction and main content of policies with which to pursue normalization. In other words, orthodoxy is a necessary condition for gaining the approval of crucial domestic and transnational economic actors and for modifying their expectations. The approval and confidence of these actors are, in turn, conditions for normalization under the BA.

On closer observation, however, the success (in its own terms) of a normalization program depends on other factors as well. Control of economic policy making in the BA by liberal *técnicos* who adhere to the orthodox code is not sufficient to win the approval and change the expectations of the key economic players. Nor is it sufficient if these *técnicos* present impeccable credentials, go out of their way to proclaim their orthodoxy, and adopt policies that carefully conform to the canon. Such conditions, after all, prevailed during the repeated normalization programs enacted during the praetorian or democratic periods preceding the BA. The problem was that often they prevailed just long enough for disgruntled classes and groups to form a broad alliance to expel those *técnicos* and for those barely implemented programs to add significantly to the fluctuations characteristic of the period. If the reappearance of orthodox *técnicos* is to alter expectations, two more requisites—which reveal that the problem is by no means purely economic—must be satisfied. First, it must be believed that normalization policies will continue to be decided upon, implemented, and sustained for as long as it takes them to yield results. If the weightier domestic and transnational economic actors predict that orthodoxy will be ephemeral, their expectations will continue to be negative, making normalization impossible or much longer and more painful to achieve. Second, the decision to maintain orthodoxy is not made in a social vacuum. If negative expectations are to be reversed, the government must be able to provide a credible guarantee that the weak democratic or praetorian state has been replaced by a state endowed with the will and capacity to prevent, and if necessary to destroy, opposition capable of challenging orthodox policies. This guarantee involves more than a change from democracy to dictatorship; it entails the emergence of a state linked to a social base very different from that of its predecessor. Before the implantation of the BA, public policy danced to the tune of shifting alliances among all reasonably organized sectors of society. The BA presents an entirely different picture: it is characterized by the exclusion of the popular sector, the control of the unions, and the suppression of the political organizations and channels of representation through which these actors previously had been able to express their demands. It is the sustained exclusion of these actors, backed by coercion and, even more important, by the perceived willingness of the government to use coercion whenever "necessary," that is one of the political guarantees of normalization under the BA.

The BA buttresses its policies not only by excluding the popular sector but also by erecting barriers against other classes and sectors. In exchange for the support of the upper bourgeoisie and transnational capital,* the top officials in the BA must also extend a credible guarantee of their will and capacity to resist the temptations of "sentimentality" and "easy roads." This side of the guarantee is aimed not so much against the popular sector—few question that *its* forced exclusion will be maintained—as it is against certain middle sectors and fractions of the local bourgeoisie, most of which are among the initial supporters of the BA. These actors, as we shall see, must also make important sacrifices during the period in which the restoration of the peculiar normality of these capitalisms is attempted. State employees, small merchants, whole regions, and more than a few firms are among those who are not long in discovering that along with the BA has been implanted an efficientist logic that is no less damaging to their economic interests than

---

*Such support by no means excludes friction between segments of the upper bourgeoisie and transnational capital, on one side, and the liberal *técnicos,* on the other. Not infrequently (as we shall see in even the least orthodox program among the various BAs, that of Krieger Vasena), such friction stems from what appears to some of those segments as the excessive orthodoxy of the government. For example, firms already established in the domestic market (including TNC subsidiaries) may protest the consequences of implementing the hallowed principle of opening the economy and making it efficient at the international level.

were the fluctuations of the preceding period. Another central issue is therefore whether the BA can extend a credible guarantee that orthodoxy will be maintained in spite of the grumblings not only of the popular sector but also of a significant part—the more so the stricter the orthodoxy—of the middle sectors and of the local dominant classes. The confidence of the upper bourgeoisie and transnational capital also depends on the answer to this question. Actually, the great test of the government's commitment to orthodoxy during the initial period of the BA is less its willingness to enforce the exclusion of the popular sector than its capacity to remain impassive to the outcries of a significant— and increasing—part of the rest of society.

Krieger Vasena's normalization program was less orthodox than that of Campos and Bulhões in 1964–1967 Brazil, and much less so than the ones implemented in post-1973 Chile and post-1976 Argentina. Was this due to personal idiosyncrasies, or to the different economic schools that to varying degrees influenced these cases? Perhaps, but these factors were less important than two others. The degree of orthodoxy depends first on differences in the international economic conjuncture that attends the implementation of the normalization program. Second, and more important, it depends on the depth of the crisis that precedes the implantation of the BA. The more severe this crisis, the greater the BA's subsequent dependence on financial capital and, therefore, the greater the likelihood that its government will adopt more orthodox policies, even when such orthodoxy poses important obstacles to normalization itself. Let us examine why.

The preceding crisis interrupts, or diverts toward the economy of plunder, the flow of resources between these societies and the capitalist world system. By the time the BA emerges, the confidence of the upper bourgeoisie and transnational capital has been profoundly shaken. The liberal *técnicos* do their best to rebuild this confidence, conforming to the code, but much of the capital needed to revitalize the productive sectors of the economy has fled the threat and uncertainties of the previous crisis. In its efforts to make the country again attractive to foreign capital and to domestic actors deciding whether to repatriate what they have deposited abroad, the government of the BA must compete with other markets around the world. To succeed in this competition, the government, as we have seen, must adopt socially and economically "rational" policies and, equally important, issue a credible guarantee that such policies will be sustained into the future. A crucial component of this guarantee is the "rationalization" of the state apparatus, which involves increasing its capacity to control the excluded classes and sectors, improving its ability to operate the instruments of economic policy, and providing support for future investments by undertaking communications and physical infrastructure projects.

The wait for foreign and domestic investment is neither easy nor brief. Even if the government of the BA enacts orthodox policies and convinces major investors that it is willing and able to maintain them into the future, important investments will not be forthcoming until it is evident that most sectors of the economy are likely to experience reasonable growth. Short of an export bonanza or a major expansion of the economic activities of the state apparatus, however, such growth cannot be achieved without the strong participation of the upper bourgeoisie and transnational capital—precisely those actors who are unwilling to assume this leading role owing to the caution with which they are still evaluating the situation. To make matters worse, the recessionary impact of the policies prescribed by the orthodox code reinforces the underutilization of installed capacity, making it irrational in many sectors of the economy to invest in new plant and equipment. Provided that the balance-of-payments situation has improved, transnational financial capital remains as the only actor willing to operate under these unstable and recessionary economic conditions. But this capital operates in the short term and stands ready to extricate itself as soon as the balance of payments deteriorates or the government enacts unorthodox policies. What, then, can provide the impetus needed in the short run to avoid too deep a recession, and in the longer run to begin generating some economic growth? Obviously, but hardly in accordance with orthodox prescriptions: the state apparatus.

This is another original aspect of these cases. On the one hand, orthodoxy demands a rationalization of the state apparatus involving, among other things, the elimination of excess personnel, a sharp reduction of the fiscal deficit, and the return to private initiative of productive activities appropriated by the state during previous periods. The BA in its initial phase is captive to these requirements, which are crucial tests of commitment to orthodoxy. But, on the other hand, the recessive impact of normalization policies and the continuing lethargy of private (domestic and foreign) investment make the state apparatus, almost by default, the only short-term source of economic stimuli. To provide these stimuli, however, more public spending and investment are required at a time when orthodoxy demands important reductions of the fiscal deficit and the tax base has been diminished by the recession.

To summarize, the orthodox code demands macroeconomic surgery as proof of the "rationality" that the BA must observe, but the impact of orthodox economic policies and the repercussions of the previous crisis lead the microeconomic orientations of the upper bourgeoisie and transnational capital toward an attitude of expectant caution. This attitude stands in the way of the upsurge of private economic activity which, according to the code, is necessary for an optimistic evaluation of the economy's future by these prospective investors. On the other hand, with its tax base at best frozen by negative or zero economic growth, where will the government find the genuine resources needed to stimulate growth? Partly from reductions in the numbers and salaries of public employees, which antagonize the middle sectors that in significant numbers supported the implantation of the BA; partly from various mechanisms which, in the only unquestionable success typically achieved by orthodox policies, improve the foreign exchange situation and facilitate access to short-term international credit;* and partly from improved tax collection procedures. But the new resources generated by these policies fall short of the enormous increase in revenues that is required if the state apparatus is to furnish the main impetus for economic growth without violating the sacred precept of drastically reducing the fiscal deficit. Since any attempt to make up the difference by siphoning resources from the upper bourgeoisie would violate the code and "discourage" this fraction, the end result of these contradictory attempts to "rationalize" the state apparatus while making it an engine of economic growth is typically to worsen income distribution and to increase the penury of the disadvantaged sectors of society.

Having discussed some tensions associated with normalization programs in general, let us turn to the 1967–69 program enacted in Argentina. After examining the specificities of this program, we shall be ready to return to some comparisons.

NOTES

1. See *Primera Plana*, November 22, 1966, p. 18. For information on Krieger Vasena's extensive connections with large national and transnational corporations, as well as with ADELA and other agencies of transnational capital, see Rogelio García Lupo, *Mercenarios y monopolios en la Argentina, de*

---

*Orthodox policies may also generate balance-of-trade surpluses, owing to the combined effect of increased exports and a reduction in the demand for imports deriving from the domestic recession.

Onganía a Lanusse: 1966–1973 (Buenos Aires: Editora Achával Solo, 1973), 116–21; and Gregorio Selser, *El Onganiato: la espada y el hisopo,* vol. 1 (Buenos Aires: Carlos Samonta Editor, 1973), 283–91.

2. See, for example, *Primera Plana,* November 22, 1966, p. 18.

3. Law 19,656 of September 24, 1966.

4. *La Razón,* March 15, p. 1, and June 27, p. 1, 1967 (Borda), and *La Nación,* June 24, 1967, p. 1 (Díaz Colodrero). See also the collective volume *Cinco discursos y una Revolución,* Movimiento Humanista de Derecho, Buenos Aires, 1968.

5. These references to economic policy in Brazil and Chile after their respective coups are based mainly on the following sources. For Brazil, Thomas Skidmore, "The Years between the Harvests: The Economics of the Castelo Branco Presidency, 1964–1967," *Luso-Brazilian Review* 15, no. 2 (Winter 1978): 4–42; Edmar Bacha, *Os mitos de uma década* (Rio de Janeiro: Paz e Terra, 1976); Albert Fishlow, "Some Reflections on Post-1964 Brazilian Economic Policy," in *Authoritarian Brazil: Origins, Policies and Future,* ed. Alfred Stepan (New Haven: Yale University Press, 1973), 69–113; Paulo Singer, *A crise do Milagre* (Rio de Janeiro: Paz e Terra, 1976); André Lara Resende, "A política Brasileira de estabilização: 1967–1968," PUC-IRI (Rio de Janeiro, 1980); Francisco de Oliveira, *A economía da dependencia imperfeita* (Rio de Janeiro: Graal, 1977); Maria de Conceição Tavares, "Acumulação de capital e industrialização no Brazil," Tesis de Livre Docencia, Universidade Federal de Rio de Janeiro, 1978; and José Serra, "O crecimento económico brasileiro (1967–1980) e seus principais problemas," CEPAL–CEBRAP (São Paulo, 1981), mimeo. For Chile, Tomás Moulián and Pilar Vergara, "Políticas de estabilización y comportamientos sociales, 1973–1978," CIEPLAN (Santiago de Chile, 1979); Alejandro Foxley, "Hacia una economía de libre mercado: Chile, 1974–1979," CIEPLAN (Santiago de Chile, 1980), mimeo; and Joseph Ramos, "Inflación persistente, inflación reprimida e hiperinflación: lecciones de inflación y estabilización en Chile," *Cuadernos de Economía,* no. 43 (December 1977): 2–46. Interesting comparative studies include Carlos Díaz Alejandro, "Southern Cone Stabilization Plans," PUC-IRI (Rio de Janeiro, 1980), mimeo; Alejandro Foxley, "Inflación: Brazil y Chile," Estudios CIEPLAN, no. 1 (1979); and, for a broader perspective, Thomas Skidmore, "Toward a Comparative Analysis of the Link between Politics and Economic Development in Argentina and Brazil," University of Wisconsin, 1980, mimeo.

6. On these problems and their implications for economic policy in Argentina, and for references to the extensive literature on this theme, see Adolfo Canitrot, "La experiencia populista de distribución de ingresos," *Desarrollo Económico* 59 (October–December 1975): 331–52. For a more sociologically oriented treatment of this theme, covering a broader period, see O'Donnell, "State and Alliances in Argentina, 1956–1976," *Journal of Development Studies* 15, no. 1 (October 1978): 3–33.

7. On the adoption of the Plan of Action and the hardening of the rhetoric, but not of the demands formulated, see *La Razón,* February 19, 1967, p. 15.

8. Statement by CONASE in *La Nación,* February 15, 1967, p. 1.

9. Statement by CONASE in *La Nación,* February 11, p. 1, and February 25, p. 1, 1967.

10. Statement by CONASE in *La Nación,* February 19, 1967, pp. 1, 16.

11. *La Nación,* February 21, 1967, p. 12, and CGE, *Memoria anual* (Buenos Aires, 1967).

12. *La Nación,* March 6, p. 1; March 7, p. 1; March 9, p. 1; and March 10, p. 1, 1967.

13. See, for example, *Confirmado,* March 14, 1967, p. 14.

14. *Crónica,* June 15, 1967, p. 6.

15. *La Nación,* March 8, 1967, p. 1.

16. *La Nación,* March 11, 1967, p. 1.

17. *Primera Plana,* April 11, 1967, p. 18.

18. *La Nación,* March 17, 1967, p. 18; statements to this effect by Krieger Vasena in *La Nación,* March 23, 1967, p. 6; and communiqués from the Labor Secretary in *La Nación,* March 4, p. 1; March 14, p. 1; and August 21, p. 1, 1967.

19. For a valuable comparative analysis of various dimensions of corporatism, see Ruth Berins Collier and David Collier, "Inducements vs. Constraints: Disaggregating 'Corporatism,'" *American Political Science Review* 73, no. 4 (December 1979): 1046–62.

20. *La Nación,* January 18, 1967, p. 1.

21. For the text of this speech, see Ministerio de Economía y Trabajo, *Política económica argentina—discursos del Ministro de Economía y Trabajo,* vol. 1 (Buenos Aires, 1968), 25–36.

22. Law 17,224 of March 31, 1967.

23. Law 17,253 of April 27, 1967.

24. *La Nación,* May 16, 1967, p. 1. For the terms of this agreement, see Ministerio de Economía y Trabajo, *Política económica Argentina,* 49–50.

25. Law 17,330 of July 5, 1967. Shortly after this law took effect, import duties on capital goods were reduced significantly; *La Nación,* June 11, 1967, pp. 1, 18.

26. Law 17,335 of July 10, 1967.

27. *La Nación,* July 28, 1967, p. 1.

28. *La Nación,* August 5, 1967, pp. 1, 12.

29. See the AP and UPI cables in *La Nación,* March 21, 1967, p. 1.

30. *La Nación,* March 23, 1967, p. 1. Portions of the IMF agreement with the Argentine government are reprinted in *Economic Survey,* May 3, 1967, pp. 9, 18.

31. *La Nación,* April 18, p. 1; May 2, p. 1; and May 3, p. 1, 1967.

32. *La Nación,* April 10, 1967, p. 1.

33. For an expanded treatment of this theme and related ones, see Roberto Frenkel and Guillermo O'Donnell, "The 'Stabilization Programs' of the International Monetary Fund and Their Internal Impacts," in *Capitalism and the State in US–Latin American Relations,* ed. Richard Fagen (Stanford: Stanford University Press, 1979), and the bibliography cited therein. For other studies of the Argentine case, see Juan de Pablo, "Precios relativos, distribución de ingreso y

planes de estabilización: la experiencia Argentina durante 1967–1970," *Desarrollo Económico* 57 (April–June 1975): 247–72, and *Política antiinflacionaria en la Argentina, 1967–1970* (Buenos Aires: Amorrortu Editores, 1972); Mallon and Sourrouille, *Economic Policy-Making;* Mario Brodersohn, "Política económica de corto plazo, crecimiento e inflación en la Argentina," in Jornadas de Economía, *Problemas económicos argentinos. Diagnóstico y política* (Buenos Aires: Ediciones Macchi, 1974), 3–64; and Marcelo Diamand, *Doctrinas económicas, desarrollo e independencia* (Buenos Aires: Editorial Paidós, 1973).

34. This theme is discussed in Frenkel and O'Donnell, "The 'Stabilization Programs' of the International Monetary Fund."

FOUR

The Normalization
Program of 1967–1969

1. SUCCESSES

In contrast to the normalization policies of other BAs, the program launched in Argentina in March 1967 rapidly achieved success, at least from the perspective of its executors and supporters. As we shall see, this result was due principally to the relative mildness of the crisis that preceded the 1966 coup and to certain characteristics of the Argentine economy and society. Let us begin our examination of this program by reviewing its most successful aspects. We shall turn subsequently to other data that show the overall balance of this program to have been substantially more complex.

In 1967 Krieger Vasena's economic program generated modest per capita economic growth. Accelerated growth followed in 1968, and by 1969 the economy was growing at a rate substantially above its mean for previous decades (see Table 4).*

This growth contrasts with the acute and prolonged recessions in Brazil (1964–67), Chile (1973–79), and Argentina (1976–82). Nonetheless, some branches of the Argentine economy fared better than others during Krieger Vasena's term. Table 5 shows that the construction

*In May 1969, after urban riots that had major repercussions for the country's economic situation, Krieger Vasena and his team were obliged to abandon the Economy Ministry. The year 1969 therefore cannot be considered entirely representative of the normalization program on which this chapter focuses. The timing of the Krieger Vasena team's departure should be borne in mind when examining the annual data presented in this table and in subsequent ones. I shall make the appropriate modifications to annual figures wherever monthly or quarterly data are available.

TABLE 4   GROSS DOMESTIC PRODUCT AND PRIVATE CONSUMPTION
(at constant prices)

	Per Capita Gross Domestic Product (in 1966 pesos) (index 1966=100)	% Annual Growth Rate	Per Capita Private Consumption (in 1966 pesos) (index 1966=100)	% Annual Growth Rate
1964	93.6	8.8	94.2	10.0
1965	100.7	7.6	101.1	7.4
1966	100.0	−0.7	100.0	−1.1
1967	101.2	1.2	101.2	1.2
1968	104.2	2.9	103.8	2.5
1969	111.5	7.1	108.9	4.9

SOURCE: BCRA, *Sistema de cuentas de producto e ingreso,* vol. 2, p. 124 ff.
NOTES: Data deflated by the index of national wholesale prices.
These data assume a 1.3% annual rate of population growth.

and mining sectors experienced pronounced growth while the agriculture and livestock sector stagnated. Industry grew little in 1967 but expanded strongly in 1968 and 1969.

Not all industrial subsectors fared equally well when the sector as a whole expanded. Table 6 shows that between 1966 and 1969 the mean overall growth in the industrial subsectors usually considered dynamic was 27.1 percent, while the corresponding mean for the traditional ones was 8.1 percent.

High rates of investment (particularly after 1967) propelled this uneven economic growth. Table 7 illustrates the evolution of investment in various economic sectors and highlights a theme to which we shall return: the extraordinary growth of public investment in construction.

Putting aside for the moment the figures for economic growth, let us examine the performance of the normalization program in meeting two of its major goals: control of inflation and improvement of the balance of payments. The data in Table 8 give eloquent testimony to the program's success in the former endeavor: in early 1968, barely a year after the program was launched, inflation was already on the downswing; by the second half of 1968 and the first half of 1969 it had dropped well below Argentina's historical mean.

The improvement in the balance of payments was no less spectacular.

TABLE 5   PER CAPITA GROSS DOMESTIC PRODUCT BY MAJOR ECONOMIC ACTIVITIES
(in 1966 pesos) (index 1966=100.0)

	Agriculture, Livestock, Hunting and Fishing	Mining and Quarrying	Industry	Electricity and Water	Construction	Commerce	Transport, Storage, and Communications	Finance, Insurance, and Real Estate	Personal and Commercial Services
1964	98.1	91.1	87.3	80.6	90.7	91.2	91.6	93.7	92.8
1965	103.9	94.6	99.3	93.0	94.3	100.6	100.0	97.2	96.2
1966	100.0	100.0	100.0	100.0	100.0	100.0	100.0	100.0	100.0
1967	104.3	111.9	101.5	107.5	112.9	101.0	101.0	102.6	102.8
1968	98.6	126.2	108.1	116.3	133.5	106.4	106.4	107.3	105.6
1969	104.1	138.1	119.8	126.4	159.0	117.4	113.8	112.9	108.3

SOURCE: BCRA, *Sistema de cuentas de producto e ingreso*, vol. 2, p. 124 ff.
NOTE: Data deflated by the index of national wholesale prices.

TABLE 6   VOLUME OF INDUSTRIAL PRODUCTION
(index 1966=100.0)

	1965	1966	1967	1968	1969
(1) Food and beverages	94.1	100.0	104.3	107.5	111.3
(2) Textiles	103.2	100.0	99.3	104.6	106.5
(3) Wood	94.9	100.0	92.3	98.7	106.4
(4) Paper	95.0	100.0	95.5	102.2	110.0
(5) Chemical products	98.1	100.0	101.5	110.1	128.0
(6) Non-metallic minerals	93.4	100.0	104.2	121.1	133.7
(7) Metals	113.8	100.0	106.4	121.8	139.9
(8) Metal products, machines and equipment	101.1	100.0	100.7	107.0	124.1
(9) Other industries	100.6	100.0	105.3	105.9	120.0
Total for industry	99.3	100.0	101.5	108.1	119.8
Average for dynamic industrial sectors (4, 5, 6, 7, and 8)	100.3	100.0	101.7	112.4	127.1
Average for traditional industrial sectors (1, 2, and 3)	97.4	100.0	98.6	109.6	108.1

SOURCE: BCRA, *Sistema de cuentas de producto e ingreso*, vol. 2.

TABLE 7   INVESTMENT
(1966 pesos) (index 1966 = 100.0)

	Gross Fixed Domestic Investment	Investment in Construction		Investment in Equipment		Change in Inventories
		Private	Public	Transport Equipment	Machinery	
1964	104.4	83.1	109.4	95.5	92.5	191.4
1965	107.7	91.8	100.6	108.9	91.9	1,425.9
1966	100.0	100.0	100.0	100.0	100.0	100.0
1967	104.5	102.8	120.9	102.8	102.5	46.5
1968	115.6	115.8	149.3	107.9	115.2	−176.2
1969	140.4	132.9	196.1	122.9	140.9	−5.4

SOURCE: BCRA, *Sistema de cuentas de producto e ingreso*, vol. 2, p. 168 ff.
NOTE: Data deflated by the index of national wholesale prices.

TABLE 8   INFLATION IN THE COST OF LIVING FOR BUENOS
AIRES (% change for each month with respect to the same
month of the preceding year)

	1963	1964	1965	1966	1967	1968	1969
January	30.8	28.5	14.3	40.2	26.7	29.0	8.2
February	24.5	26.4	20.7	36.7	26.6	27.6	5.7
March	35.3	20.3	24.0	36.4	26.7	24.0	7.7
April	32.6	23.0	20.7	37.8	25.6	22.0	8.2
May	24.5	23.2	23.1	36.3	25.5	21.0	6.6
June	23.1	23.5	26.3	32.1	29.9	16.4	
July	18.9	22.1	31.1	28.6	34.2	10.8	
August	16.2	21.0	34.9	27.3	33.1	10.6	
September	15.6	20.4	35.4	27.3	31.7	11.6	
October	17.6	21.4	33.7	28.1	31.3	10.6	
November	21.9	19.7	36.9	26.5	31.2	8.5	
December	27.6	18.1	38.2	29.9	27.3	9.6	

SOURCE: Dirección Nacional de Estadística y Censos, *Boletín estadístico trimestral e
indice de precios al consumidor—Capital Federal,* various issues.

TABLE 9   NET FOREIGN EXCHANGE RESERVES OF THE
ARGENTINE CENTRAL BANK
(in millions of current U.S. dollars)

	1966	1967	1968	1969
January	145.8	155.6	486.7	613.8
February	146.9	151.7	476.8	657.0
March	182.4	203.5	490.9	672.2
April	188.8	292.5	517.5	694.3
May	208.9	395.5	525.3	665.0
June	224.2	465.9	539.8	
July	199.8	494.0	537.0	
August	219.8	497.6	535.7	
September	197.0	494.7	562.2	
October	177.3	481.6	553.4	
November	161.3	482.2	590.0	
December	176.9	500.9	593.3	

SOURCE: BCRA, *Boletín estadístico,* various issues.

TABLE 10   BALANCE OF TRADE
(in millions of current U.S. dollars)

	Public Credits to the National Government and Central Bank	Exports	Imports	Balance of Trade	Net Foreign Exchange Reserves of the Central Bank (% of annual imports)
1964	74	1,410	1,077	331	25%
1965	44	1,488	1,195	293	25%
1966	129	1,593	1,124	468	26%
1967	253	1,464	1,095	369	71%
1968	108	1,367	1,169	198	71%
1969	107	1,612	1,576	36	36%

SOURCE: BCRA, *Boletín estadístico,* and Ministerio de Economía y Trabajo, *Informe Económico,* various issues.

The foreign exchange reserves of the Central Bank were low at the time of the coup and declined still further under Salimei's ministry. But in April 1967 these holdings began a period of rapid growth that peaked in April 1969, the last complete month in office for Krieger Vasena's economic team. The figures are given in Table 9.

This increase in foreign exchange holdings was due in part to an IMF standby loan and to other loans from nonprivate international sources, as well as the positive trade balances of 1967 and 1968 (see Table 10).

An influx of foreign loans from private sources made the largest contribution to improving the foreign exchange situation. Nothing better indicates the confidence of transnational capital than these inflows. Yet nothing better indicates the limits of this confidence: an overwhelming proportion of this capital, as Table 11 shows, came in the form of short-term loans. By comparison, new direct investment and private long-term loans were very scarce. Owing to the large differential between local and international interest rates and to the government's commitment to maintaining a stable peso-dollar exchange rate, Argentina had become an attractive market for financial capital. However, the insignificant balance of long-term capital shows that transnational capital was not yet willing to bet on the long-term prospects of the Argentine economy.

All of these indicators reflect a significant departure from the instabil-

TABLE II   BALANCE OF PAYMENTS: NET CAPITAL MOVEMENTS
(in millions of current U.S. dollars)

	Net Balance of Long-term Capital	Net Balance of Short-term Capital	Change in the International Reserves of the Central Bank
1964	2	−39	−111
1965	4	−177	16
1966	−105	−76	−5
1967: 1st quarter	n.d.	n.d.	5
2nd quarter	n.d.	n.d.	425
3rd quarter	n.d.	n.d.	11
4th quarter	n.d.	n.d.	13
1967 Balance	4	268	480
1968: 1st quarter	1	−15	−2
2nd quarter	−10	0	78
3rd quarter	0	67	40
4th quarter	7	76	44
1968 Balance	27	150	57
1969: 1st quarter	−1	69	77
2nd quarter	13	−44	−82
3rd quarter	29	−66	−83
4th quarter	30	−37	−171
1969 Balance	57	−57	−260

SOURCE: BCRA, *Boletín estadístico,* various issues.
NOTE: "n.d." means no data available.

ity and the negative trends that prevailed before March 1967. Reduced
inflation and new expectations of short-term economic stability were
accompanied by similar signals in other financial indicators. Table 12
shows that quotations for the U.S. dollar on the futures market (which,
as we saw in chapter 2, had proved remarkably sensitive to the final
crisis of the Radical government) plummeted as soon as the March 1967
program was launched.*

*Tables in chapter 9 complete through 1972 the monthly series for these quotations
and for other monthly data presented in this section.

TABLE 12   INTEREST RATES FOR THE U.S. DOLLAR ON THE
30-DAY FUTURES MARKET
(% above the cash quotation) (monthly averages)

	1966	1967	1968	1969
January	5.9	9.5	6.4	1.6
February	4.7	19.2	5.8	1.2
March	15.4	3.6	4.0	1.2
April	30.2	0.0	4.4	1.6
May	47.9	0.6	4.0	2.9
June	13.3	2.0	3.0	
July	28.2	3.2	5.7	
August	16.6	4.8	5.4	
September	21.1	7.2	3.9	
October	30.5	4.9	2.4	
November	14.9	1.2	0.6	
December	7.9	6.2	0.8	

SOURCE: BCRA, *Boletín estadístico*, and FIEL, *Indicadores de coyuntura*, various issues.

We turn now to the fiscal situation. Table 13 shows that the effort to streamline public finances achieved no less remarkable successes. The central government's revenues expanded rapidly in real terms while its expenditures increased very little. By reducing its current expenditures (largely through the layoffs and salary reductions affecting public employees) the government reduced the fiscal deficit even as it increased its capital outlays considerably.

This symphony of successes was unblemished by the sour note that has accompanied the normalization programs of other BAs: a severe drop in wages. Although each indicator in Table 14 has reliability problems, their homogeneous variation over time suffices to show that the industrial working class suffered only a slight wage decline.*

The data covering nonindustrial fractions of the working class (Table 15) show a pattern similar to the one just observed, although wages declined somewhat more for these workers than for their counterparts in the industrial sector.

*It should be noted that the recovery in wages shown in the 1969 data was due entirely to wage hikes granted in the second half of that year, after Krieger Vasena and his team had left office.

TABLE 13 BUDGET OF THE NATIONAL GOVERNMENT
(in 1966 pesos) (index 1966=100.0)

	Total Revenue	Total Expenditures	Current Expenditures	Capital Expenditures	Deficit	Deficit as % of Total Expenditures	Deficit as % of Gross Domestic Product
1965	99.3	88.4	80.7	84.2	62.7	21.2	1.4
1966	100.0	100.0	100.0	100.0	100.0	29.9	3.0
1967	124.8	104.9	95.1	153.0	57.9	16.5	1.7
1968	134.7	102.4	90.9	166.4	26.5	7.7	0.7
1969	144.5	108.5	97.9	170.1	23.9	6.6	0.6

SOURCES: Ministerio de Economía and Ministerio de Hacienda, *Boletín Mensual,* various issues; and Ministerio de Hacienda, Department of the Treasury, unpublished worksheets used in preparing various yearly budgets of the national government.
NOTE: Figures deflated by the index of national wholesale prices.

TABLE 14   INDUSTRIAL WAGES
(in 1966 pesos) (index 1966=100.0)

	Average Annual Industrial Wage (according to the Instituto Nacional de Estadísticas y Censos [INDEC])	Average Hourly Industrial Wage (according to INDEC)	Average Annual Industrial Wage (BCRA data)	Legal Minimum Annual Industrial Wage (weighted average of unmarried workers and married workers with two children)
1966	100.0	100.0	100.0	100.0
1967	99.7	99.1	98.1	98.6
1968	94.4	93.2	90.3	94.9
1969	99.4	96.8	98.3	98.5

SOURCES: INDEC, *Boletín Estadístico Trimestral,* various issues; unpublished worksheets of the BCRA, Department of National Accounts; and Juan de Pablo, "Políticas de estabilización en una economía inflacionaria: un comentario," *Desarrollo Económico 50* (July–September 1973), 401–407.
NOTE: Data deflated by the cost-of-living index for Buenos Aires.

TABLE 15   NONINDUSTRIAL WAGES
(in 1966 pesos)
(index 1966=100.0)

	Minimum Wage for Construction Workers	Minimum Wage for Mine and Quarry Workers	Minimum Wage for Workers in Agriculture and Livestock
1966	100.0	100.0	100.0
1967	100.9	104.7	101.6
1968	92.8	92.0	92.2
1969	94.7	92.7	96.6

SOURCE: Unpublished worksheets of the Consejo Nacional de Desarrollo.
NOTE: Data deflated by the cost-of-living index for Buenos Aires.

To summarize: under the normalization program launched in March 1967 the economy returned rapidly to a fairly high rate of growth; inflation was reduced considerably; the foreign exchange situation took a favorable turn; transnational capital signaled its approval but refrained from long-term commitments; the fiscal situation of the state improved markedly; and the relatively small decline in wages maintained a level of general consumption that lagged behind economic growth but, in comparison with other normalization programs, cannot be considered unsatisfactory. From these points of view the success of the program was as rapid as it was remarkable.* A somewhat different story is told by the data presented in the third section of this chapter, which show that the successes summarized here were by no means achieved without costs and tensions. However, the characteristics and impacts of this program cannot be adequately understood without first examining the ways in which it deviated from a strictly orthodox path.

2. HETERODOXIES

As noted in the preceding chapter, a major innovation of Krieger Vasena's program was that it identified factor costs and the expectations of economic actors as the main causes of inflation. This diagnosis was accepted by the IMF and formed the basis for policies designed to freeze certain crucial prices over the short and medium terms. Among these policies were the wage and salary freeze imposed until the end of 1968, the voluntary price agreement between the government and the largest industrial firms, a pledge to maintain indefinitely the value of the peso against the U.S. dollar, and a commitment not to raise the prices of public services again after increasing them at the start of the program.† Given these price freezes and (equally important) plausible indications that most of them would be maintained for the foreseeable future, the principal economic actors might reasonably be expected to adjust their behavior to a forecast of lowered inflation.

Attributing inflation to costs and expectations rather than to excess demand enabled the economic team to avoid the recessionary policies associated with the latter diagnosis. Accordingly, the agreement with the IMF lacked its usual components of reducing bank credit and the money supply. As is evident from Table 16, both grew significantly during Krieger Vasena's term in office.

*A survey conducted in 1967–68 by John Freels, Jr. shows that the upper bourgeoisie (as represented by leaders of UIA) shared this view of the normalization program. John Freels, Jr., "Industrialists and Politics in Argentina."

†Reflecting these initial increases, the index for the mean real prices charged by state enterprises rose from 100.0 in 1966 to 116.6 in 1967. It subsequently fell to 114.1 in 1968 and 108.1 in 1969. Cf. Horacio Nuñez Miñana and Horacio Porto, "Análisis de la evolución de precios de empresas públicas en la Argentina. Respuesta," *Desarrollo Económico,* no. 66 (July–September 1967): 348.

TABLE 16   MONETARY DATA
(in 1966 pesos) (index 1966 = 100.0)

	Money Supply (at the end of each year)	Coefficient of Liquidity of the Economy	Bank Credit (at the end of each year)
1965	92.3	25	95.0
1966	100.0	26	100.0
1967	114.6	28	109.3
1968	137.7	32	144.1
1969	142.4	30	166.4

SOURCE: BCRA, *Boletín Estadístico*, and FIEL, *Indicadores de coyuntura*, various issues.
NOTE: Data deflated by the index of overall wholesale prices.

While the expansion of the money supply and the loosening of credit* were important in reactivating the economy, other significant impulses came from the opening of new credit lines for housing purchases and personal consumption. Of course the benefits of these new lines of credit went almost exclusively to members of the upper and upper-middle income sectors, since others had little chance of meeting the solvency requirements imposed by the banks. The great increase in private investment in construction (Table 7) was due largely to the increased incomes of these sectors and to their easier access to credit.

Orthodoxy, however, continued to show itself in certain aspects of the economic program and in the IMF agreement even though, as Juan de Pablo has pointed out,[1] the orthodox policies that were implemented were clearly inconsistent with a diagnosis that targeted costs and expectations as the main causes of inflation. Most notably, economic policy adhered to orthodoxy's cherished precept of reducing the fiscal deficit. To achieve this goal, Krieger Vasena and his team came up with the (economically) simple solution referred to earlier: a withholding tax on agricultural and livestock exports, which primarily affected Pampean production. This tax was an expedient mechanism by which to capture part of the differential rent accruing to the Pampean bourgeoisie. As

*The increase in bank credit was supplemented by the growth of financial societies (credit corporations prohibited from operating checking accounts), nearly all of which were linked to banks and/or large economic groups. The participation of these societies in the total flows of the financial system grew from 7.5 percent in 1967 to 11.6 percent in 1969. Data from Agapito Villavicencia, "Flujo global de fondos del sistema financiero institucionalizado argentino. Período 1967–1971," Simposio Latinoamericano para el Desarrollo de Mercados de Capital, Buenos Aires, March 1972.

TABLE 17   WITHHOLDING TAX ON EXPORTS

	(1) National Government Revenue from With- holding Tax on Exports (in millions of 1966 pesos)	(2) Index of (1) (1966=100.0)	(3) Column (1) as % of To- tal National Government Revenue	(4) National Government Revenue from Import Duties (in millions of 1966 pesos)	(5) Index of (4) (1966=100.0)
1966	72	100.0	2.5	576	100.0
1967	500	694.4	13.1	552	95.8
1968	372	516.7	10.1	487	84.5
1969	262	363.9	7.6	654	113.5

SOURCE: Calculated from Ministerio de Hacienda, *Informe Económico*, 4th quarter (Buenos Aires, 1972).
NOTE: Data deflated by the national wholesale price index.

Table 17 shows, the income it generated more than compensated for the decrease in revenues from import duties—which, in another signal of orthodoxy, were lowered.

Several other factors helped reduce the fiscal deficit: a drop in current expenditures (see Table 13), improvements in the efficiency of tax collection, and a rise in indirect taxes that outweighed the 1968–69 decrease in revenue from direct taxes (see Table 18), probably with regressive effects on income distribution.

The data in tables 17 and 18 show that of all sources of state revenue, income derived from the withholding tax on Pampean exports registered by far the largest increase in relation to the years prior to Krieger Vasena's economic program.* The beneficiary of these new funds was the state's central administration. Table 19 shows that the share of total public investment emanating from the central administration increased significantly between 1966 and 1969, while the shares of provincial and local governments and of public enterprises declined. The relatively

*The significance of the funds derived from this withholding tax is evident not only from their sevenfold increase between 1966 and 1967, but also from the fact that these revenues represented about 50 percent of the national government's savings in the year of the launching of the normalization program (1967), and approximately 35 percent in 1968.

TABLE 18   TAX REVENUES OF THE NATIONAL GOVERNMENT
(in 1966 pesos) (index 1966=100.0)

	(1) Revenue from Indirect Taxes	(2) Indirect Taxes as % of Gross Domestic Product	(3) Revenue from Direct Taxes	(4) Direct Taxes as % of Gross Domestic Product	(5) Tax Pressure: (2) + (4) + Contributions to Social Security, as % of Gross Domestic Product
1964		8.9		1.5	14.8
1965	84.9	9.3	80.8	2.4	16.3
1966	100.0	10.6	100.0	2.6	18.0
1967	180.3	12.4	113.7	2.7	20.9
1968	134.3	12.7	87.8	2.2	20.4
1969	141.9	12.0	86.1	2.1	19.1

SOURCE: BCRA, *Sistema de cuentas de producto e ingreso*, vol. 2, p. 268.
NOTE: Data deflated by the national wholesale price index.

passive role of public enterprises in Argentina during this period sets this BA apart from others, especially that of Brazil.

Let us examine how these funds were used. Columns 1 through 4 of Table 20 show that between 1966 and 1969 the national government's capital outlays rose considerably, that outlays destined for investments grew even more, and that investments channeled into public works (primarily roads and communications) increased most of all. Columns 5 and 6 of this table show that, in contrast to previous years, much of this investment was financed with genuine resources from the public treasury. Columns 6 and 7, reflecting these changes, indicate a sharp rise in public investment as a share of both total domestic investment and gross domestic product.

The statements issued by the Economy Ministry during 1967 and 1968 trumpeted the achievements of the economic program and insistently urged foreign and domestic capital to take advantage of the newly achieved order and economic stability by substantially increasing their investments. Krieger Vasena and his team expected that their program would bring a rapid and substantial influx of domestic investment, long-term loans, and direct foreign investment, making foreign capital and the

TABLE 19   ORIGINS OF OVERALL PUBLIC INVESTMENT

	1966	1967	1968	1969
National government (central administration) (%)	18.7	28.4	31.4	32.7
State and joint state/private enterprises and *sociedades anónimas* (%)	49.4	43.4	38.4	38.1
Provincial governments and municipal government of Buenos Aires (%)	30.5	27.2	29.5	28.8
Others (%)	1.4	1.0	0.7	0.4
Total	100.0	100.0	100.0	100.0

SOURCE: Leonardo Anídjar, "El sector público y el mercado de capitales argentinos," Programa Latinoamericano para el desarrollo de mercados de capital (Buenos Aires, 1972), mimeo.

more concentrated segments of the domestic private sector the driving forces in the economy.* As we have seen, however, long-term foreign capital inflows were practically nil in 1967 and 1968. Moreover, domestic and foreign private investment was discouraged by the significant underutilization of installed productive capacity at the time the program was launched. The growth of (mostly private) investment in machinery and transport equipment (Table 7) was much lower than that of public investment (Table 20), and the growth of private consumption (Table 4) was even less impressive, despite the increased demand in the upper-income sectors. Public investment, especially in physical infrastructure, was therefore a critical—but not too orthodox—factor in sustaining the level of economic activity through 1967 and in stimulating economic growth in 1968 and 1969.[†] Given the importance to public revenue of the withholding tax on Pampean exports, it is no exaggeration to conclude

*This expectation is explicit in speeches by members of the economic team. See, for example, Krieger Vasena in *Política económica*, vols. 1 and 2. See also de Pablo, *Política antiinflacionaria en la Argentina*, 118.

†The data in table 7 show that the increase in public construction was heavily responsible for the substantial growth in the construction sector as a whole. It is interesting to note that the growth of public investment did not imply an invasion by the state of directly productive areas, and therefore presented no obstacle (or what might have been perceived as an obstacle) to private capital accumulation. The impression that public and private investment were intended to be "noncompetitive" in this sense is further supported by data showing that public investment in industrial projects declined as a share of total public investment from 11.1 percent for the 1960–66 period to 10.0 percent in 1967, 4.8 percent in 1968, and 2.5 percent in 1969. Figures from Presidencia de la Nación, *Plan trienal para la reconstrucción nacional*, Buenos Aires, 1974.

TABLE 20   INVESTMENT BY THE NATIONAL GOVERNMENT

	(1)	(2)	(3)	(4)	(5)	(6)	(7)
	Capital Expenditures (index 1966=100.0)	Investments (index 1966=100.0)	Investments in Physical Infrastructure and Communications (in millions 1966 pesos)	Index 1966=100.0 of Figures in Column 3	Savings of National Government (in millions 1966 pesos)	Public Investment as % of Gross Domestic Investment	Public Investment as % of Gross Domestic Product
1965	84.2	n.d.	439	96.6	−146	n.d.	n.d.
1966	100.0	100.0	455	100.0	−501	30.5	5.8
1967	153.0	189.7	1,177	258.9	836	35.2	7.1
1968	166.4	233.2	1,061	233.2	653	35.6	7.5
1969	170.1	279.5	1,307	287.3	486	36.6	8.0

SOURCE: Ministerio de Hacienda or Ministerio de Economía y Trabajo, *Informe Económico*, various issues, and unpublished worksheets of the Secretaria de Hacienda, collected and kindly furnished to me by William Smith.

NOTE: Data deflated by the wholesale index price for non-agrarian products.

that the dynamic economic role that the state apparatus played during this period was largely financed by the Pampean bourgeoisie. But we shall see in the next section that this class was not alone in bearing the costs of the normalization program.

3. COSTS AND TENSIONS

The organizations of the Pampean bourgeoisie received with mixed feelings the initial components of Krieger Vasena's economic program. They counted on the positive side a generous scheme of tax reductions on agrarian investments and, above all, the satisfaction of their long-standing claim against the laws freezing the price of rural rents and providing for the automatic extension of tenancy contracts. On the negative side was the withholding tax on exports. This tax, together with low (by then) international prices, worked against the increase in the domestic price of exportable goods—especially beef—that would otherwise have accompanied the March 1967 devaluation. Lower prices for beef, in turn, meant lower prices for its potential substitutes.[2] By thus maintaining relatively low prices for many of the foods important in popular consumption, the withholding tax on Pampean exports helped to moderate the impact of the wage and salary freeze.

Data showing the evolution of beef prices, which suggest reasons for the complaints of the Pampean bourgeoisie, are presented in Table 21. Observe, moreover, that the year chosen as the base for these data (1966) already registers a marked decline from the preceding years.

Although prices for other Pampean products such as cereals and vegetable oils evolved more favorably, the Pampean bourgeoisie had another cause for complaint: evidence that the liberals in charge of economic policy were preparing to enact a tax on potential land rent.* This tax, aimed at forcing the agrarian bourgeoisie to make new capital investments and technological improvements, was seen by the Krieger Vasena team as a way to increase exports and thus lift the ceiling imposed on economic growth by the balance of payments. The prospect of a "confiscatory" and "collectivizing" tax intensified the protests of

---

*This tax would have penalized landholdings with yields below the mean for the ecological area on the basis of which the potential rent was estimated. For an analysis of this project and its implications, see Guillermo Flichman, *La renta del suelo y el desarrollo agrario argentino* (Mexico City: Siglo XXI, 1977); and Nidia Margenat, "Las organizaciones corporativas del sector agrario," Consejo Federal de Inversiones, Buenos Aires (n.d.).

TABLE 21   BEEF PRICES
(in 1966 pesos)
(index 1966=100.0)

	Wholesale Beef Prices	Retail Beef Prices in Buenos Aires
1964	126.4	126.5
1965	120.8	120.9
1966	100.0	100.0
1967	99.2	99.0
1968	94.1	94.2
1969 (1st half)	92.6	93.4

SOURCES: Wholesale prices calculated from FIEL, *Indicadores de coyuntura*, various issues. Retail prices calculated from Lucio Reca and Eduardo Gaba, "Poder adquisitivo, veda y sustitutos: un examen de la demanda de carne vacuna en la Argentina, 1950–1972," *Desarrollo Económico* 50 (July–September 1973).
NOTE: Data deflated by the wholesale price index for non-agrarian products.

the organizations of the Pampean bourgeoisie, already upset over the discouraging prices they were receiving.*

Underlying the policies of the Krieger Vasena team was nothing less than an attempt by the upper bourgeoisie to subordinate to its own patterns of accumulation not just the popular sector but also an agrarian bourgeoisie endowed with enormous economic centrality and with political and ideological power resources which, if less formidable than in the past, still had to be reckoned with. On the other hand, by helping to maintain relatively low prices for food and other wage goods, the withholding tax encouraged governmental hopes that the workers, whose incomes had fallen relatively little, could be appeased or co-opted.

But if Krieger Vasena's program of 1967–69 differed from the normalization policies of other BAs in producing only a mild decline in workers' wages, it was typical in its impact on other social sectors. Table 22 shows that various categories of employees (which together comprised a large proportion of the middle sectors and approximately 40 percent of the economically active population)[†] registered income losses more severe than those of the workers.

*Exacerbating the problems of the Pampean bourgeoisie was the unfavorable international economic conjuncture for Pampean exports, due in large measure to a ban imposed by the European Economic Community on meat imports from Argentina.

†State employees alone accounted for 30 percent of Argentina's economically active population. See José Calvar et al., "Resultados preliminares de una investigación del sector público argentino," BCRA, Buenos Aires, 1976, mimeo.

TABLE 22   SALARIES OF LOWER-MIDDLE SECTORS
(in 1966 pesos) (1966=100.0)

	(1) Basic Salary of Lower-level Employee in the Central Government	(2) Basic Salary of Primary School Teacher	(3) Basic Salary of Commercial Employee	(4) Basic Salary of Lower-level Bank Employee	(5) Basic Salary of Driver of Public Transport Vehicles	(6) Basic Salary of Lower-level Telephone Employee	(7) Basic Salary of Lower-level Employee of the National Institute of Agricultural and Livestock Technology
1966	100.0	100.0	100.0	100.0	100.0	100.0	100.0
1967	92.5	89.0	97.1	99.4	102.9	94.4	78.1
1968	84.4	76.6	86.7	89.6	88.6	87.3	73.2
1969	85.5	85.0	88.7	91.7	90.3	89.2	79.6

SOURCES: Column 1 calculated from unpublished internal documents of the Secretaria de Hacienda. Columns 2–6 calculated from unpublished internal documents of the ex-Consejo Nacional de Desarrollo and the Ministerio (or in some periods Secretaria) de Trabajo, *Boletín de estadísticas sociales*, various issues. Column 7: Centro de Investigaciones en Administracion Publica, Instituto Torcuato di Tella, "Determinación de objectivos y asignación de recursos en el INTA: un análisis crítico" (Buenos Aires, 1971).

NOTES: Data deflated by the cost of living index for Buenos Aires.
"Basic salary" refers to the salary received by an employee with no dependents.

TABLE 23   SALARIES OF UPPER-MIDDLE SECTORS
(in 1966 pesos) (1966=100.0)

	Minister and Subsecretary of the National Government	Department Head or General Coordinator in the Central Government[a]
1966	100.0	100.0
1967	162.5	96.5
1968	139.9	139.5
1969	175.8	176.3

SOURCE: Calculated from unpublished data of the Secretaría de Hacienda kindly furnished by William Smith.
NOTE: Data deflated by the cost of living index for the Federal Capital.
[a]Level 3 of the central public administration

The data in Table 22 correspond to employees in the lower categories. Although direct information on the upper middle sectors is difficult to obtain, the figures in Table 23 suggest that persons in these categories, unlike the great majority of employees, increased their incomes considerably. It was thus as much through their increased salaries as through their easier access to credit that the upper strata of the middle sectors benefited from the economic program.

The traditional petty bourgeoisie, especially small merchants, must also be counted among those penalized by the policies of the 1967–69 period. Owing partly to the sudden "liberation" of urban commercial rents, partly to advances in mass marketing systems, and partly to the persecution of the credit cooperatives (to which I shall return shortly), more than a few segments of the petty bourgeoisie suffered serious income losses and were confronted with evidence that the coup they had initially applauded had produced a government that showed little concern for their interests.

It is harder to generalize about the situation of the local bourgeoisie engaged in medium- and large-scale activities. On the one hand, Table 24 shows that both the financial and the construction sectors showed extraordinary rises in their gross profit rates during 1968 and 1969.*

*The gross profit rate for each sector was calculated by subtracting from the total value of its production outlays for inputs, indirect taxes, and wages and salaries. The gross profit rate is not usually a reliable indicator of effectively realized profits. Nonetheless it is safe to assume that for the years studied here the *change* in the gross profit rate for a given sector is an adequate approximation of the *change* in the effective rate of profit in *that* sector.

TABLE 24   GROSS PROFITS OF MAJOR ECONOMIC SECTORS
(in 1966 pesos) (1966 = 100.0)

	All Economic Activities	Industry	Finance, Insurance, and Real Estate	Construction	Commerce	Agriculture, Livestock, Hunting and Fishing
1964	94.4	93.3	108.2	82.2	93.2	125.3
1965	104.1	106.9	108.5	80.9	104.6	114.5
1966	100.0	100.0	100.0	100.0	100.0	100.0
1967	98.7	91.7	101.0	105.3	101.4	90.9
1968	104.4	96.3	144.2	124.5	100.9	94.0
1969	117.5	109.3	159.9	156.7	113.5	98.0

SOURCE: BCRA, *Sistema de cuentas de producto e ingreso*, vol. 2.
NOTES: Gross profits are calculated by deducting from the gross value of production intermediate consumption, indirect taxes (minus subsidies), and expenditures for wages and salaries.
Data deflated by the respective wholesale price indices.

The upsurge in the construction sector was due to the flood of state investment into public works projects and to increased private construction. The rise in the gross profit rates enjoyed by financial capital had much to do with the substantial expansion of bank credit and with the increase in real interest rates brought on by the decline of inflation.[3] On the other hand, we see that conditions in the agricultural and livestock sector were far from satisfactory, and that the mean gross profit rate in industry as a whole was lower during the 1967–69 period than it had been in 1966, in spite of a strong recovery in 1969.

Since these figures are highly aggregated, they are incapable of indicating whether, within a given sector, some types of firms improved their profit rates while others did not. Table 25 gives some evidence that such variation occurred: the cheapest credits, and those with the longest repayment periods, were extended much more readily to large firms than to small and medium-sized ones.

The fate of credit cooperatives also suggests a deterioration in the economic conditions of the smaller local firms during the 1966–69 period. Prior to 1966 credit cooperatives had been the major source of financing for small and medium-sized commercial and industrial enterprises. Partly because of allegations that these cooperatives were controlled by communists, but much more because they had become stiff competition for the banks and financial corporations, they were subjected after the 1966 coup to various forms of governmental control and harassment. The result of this persecution was that their numbers dropped from 1016 in 1966 to approximately 350 in mid-1969.* The CGE, which had close ties to these organizations, repeatedly protested this blow to the weakest segments of the local bourgeoisie.

Why did the CGE come to the defense of these segments of the local bourgeoisie? After all, the credit problems plaguing the smaller local firms did not affect the firms from which most of the CGE directorate came, which were typically located in the dynamic sectors of the economy. The leaders of the CGE did not begin to voice their opposition to Krieger Vasena and his policies because their immediate economic interests had been damaged. It was rather that the CGE could maintain itself as an important political actor only insofar as its claim to represent the small and medium entrepreneurs remained believable to those entrepre-

---

*The credit cooperatives' participation in the overall flow of financial resources decreased even more than their numbers. See *Economic Survey*, no. 1560 (February 3, 1977):1–3. Prior to the government campaign against them, the credit cooperatives had accounted for nearly 50 percent of the total of loans made by commercial banks. See Mallon and Sourrouille, *Economic Policy-Making*, 128.

TABLE 25   LOANS TO INDUSTRIAL FIRMS ACCORDING TO SIZE
(average, 1967–69)

	Loans from Each Source as % of Firms' Total Funds		
	Large Firms	Medium-sized Firms	Small Firms
1. Bank loans	20.8	13.1	10.4
2. Loans from financial societies	12.3	10.2	7.7
3. Long-term loans	15.8	8.6	8.8

SOURCE: Mario Brodersohn, "Financiamiento de empresas privadas y mercados de capital," Programa Latinoamericano para el desarrollo de mercados de capital (Buenos Aires, 1972).

neurs, as well as to government personnel, other fractions of the bourgeoisie, and the unions. The need to defend the credibility of their claim to represent the weaker fractions of the bourgeoisie gave the CGE directorate a powerful motive to voice the demands and grievances of those fractions.*

A second reason for the CGE's opposition to the government's economic policy was that the new economic team had not seen fit to appoint to the positions that most directly concerned the local bourgeoisie persons receptive to arguments favoring state tutelage of local capital in the face of foreign competition. To the contrary, Krieger Vasena et al. adhered to another orthodox precept: the elimination of "discrimination" against transnational capital. For the sake of efficiency, each economic interest was to be treated "on an equal footing," regardless of the origins of its capital.† The CGE and the unions responded to this posi-

*The issues raised here are rooted in the complex theme of representation. (I referred to some aspects of this theme in the last section of chapter 1.) The social origins and immediate economic interests of the leaders of a given institution constitute only one, and not the most important, of the aspects necessary to understand the issue of representation. More important is the question of the social bases that the leadership purports to represent, and the dialectic established between the way those social bases perceive their own interests and the way their leadership expresses them.

†It is interesting that even the UIA protested what its leaders viewed as excessively orthodox aspects of the Krieger Vasena program, particularly the lowering of import duties and the failure of officials in the Economy Ministry to consult with the UIA when promoting or approving new foreign investments. In addition to the oligopolized fractions of local capital, the branches of transnational capital already embedded in the local market were very influential within the UIA. Each of these fractions was prepared to sacrifice its orthodox canons (as it had done with the government's freezing of wages and salaries) when it came to protecting its foothold in the domestic market against new intrusions of transnational capital. See UIA, *Memoria y balance anual,* 1967–68 and 1968–69.

tion by accusing the economic team of willfully auctioning off the national productive structure to transnational capital.* From the CGE's perspective, the immediate costs imposed by the normalization program were bad enough, but the crucial issue was whether the government would continue its anxious pursuit of transnational capital. Fearing the complete disappearance of state tutelage—which indeed would also have harmed the larger and more dynamic enterprises controlled by the CGE's top leadership—the fractions of the local bourgeoisie represented by the CGE made "denationalization of the economy" and "suffocation of the small and medium entrepreneur" the principal themes of their opposition to the normalization program.

To summarize, the data examined in this section show that the Pampean bourgeoisie, various middle sectors, and a substantial proportion of the lower and middle (and most definitively national) segments of the urban bourgeoisie had few reasons to share the government's enthusiasm over the normalization program.

4. PROFITS, ACCUMULATION, AND EXPLOITATION

Implicit in the data thus far examined are complex issues involving the economic surplus appropriated by various fractions of the bourgeoisie. Official statistics are not designed to capture such phenomena, and the scarce data available at the sectoral and firm levels are of doubtful reliability. But since such issues are crucial to understanding the interplay between politics and economics, a series of approximations will be made, using available indicators, to the patterns of profits that took place during the normalization program of 1967–69.

Since these indicators are indirect and based on methodologies too heterogeneous to allow for strict comparisons, they should be interpreted with caution. Only when the changes such indicators record are of considerable magnitude, and when other indicators of the same phenomena move in the same direction to a similar degree, can we feel reasonably confident that they are valid approximations to actual processes.

The national accounts data on gross profit rates in the major sectors of the Argentine economy (Table 24) showed that industry as a whole was *not* among the net winners of the period. But as suggested earlier, it

*The CGE also complained about the "lack of recognition" it was accorded by the economic team. See its *Memoria anual* for 1967–69 and Jorge Niosi, *Los empresarios y el estado argentino.*

is likely that some firms did much better than these figures suggest, while others did much worse. This guess is supported by comparing trends in the gross profits of industrial subsidiaries of U.S.-based TNCs (Table 26) with trends in profit rates for industry as a whole (recall Table 24). Although these figures are not strictly comparable, they suggest that between 1966 and 1969 the performance of the TNC industrial subsidiaries was much better than that of industry in general.

Despite problems of data comparability and reliability, it is difficult to doubt that at least some segments of the upper industrial bourgeoisie made high profits during Krieger Vasena's term in office, even if they did not achieve the extraordinary ones realized by financial and construction firms. Conversely, if we take into account that industrial subsidiaries of transnational corporations generated approximately 50 percent of industrial value added,[4] and assuming the profits of European and Japanese TNC subsidiaries were not significantly different from those of United States subsidiaries, then the data in Table 24 (showing low profit rates for industry as a whole) imply a significant drop in profitability for smaller, weaker enterprises. This inference suggests that the CGE did not exaggerate when complaining that the normalization program was detrimental to the national entrepreneurs.

Unpublished BCRA data allow us to estimate productivity and exploitation rates for various sectors of the Argentine economy. Productivity for each sector in a given year was calculated by dividing the value added in that sector in that year by the number of persons that sector employed. The rate of labor exploitation in each sector for a given year was calculated by dividing value added by the total amount

TABLE 26   PROFITS OF INDUSTRIAL SUBSIDIARIES OF
U.S.-BASED TRANSNATIONAL CORPORATIONS

	Declared Profits Index (in 1966 pesos) (1966=100.0)	Declared Profits as % of Annual Sales
1966	100.0	14.9
1967	129.9	17.6
1968	142.1	17.6
1969	124.5	13.3

SOURCE: FIEL, *Las empresas extranjeras en la Argentina* (Buenos Aires, 1971).
NOTE: Data deflated by wholesale price index for non-agrarian products.

TABLE 27   PRODUCTIVITY AND EXPLOITATION RATES FOR
ECONOMIC SECTORS
(index 1966=100.0)

	Industry	Finance	Commerce	Construction
Productivity				
1965	99.9	102.5	103.4	90.4
1966	100.0	100.0	100.0	100.0
1967	102.9	103.8	102.0	102.9
1968	110.9	125.1	101.8	101.3
1969	117.3	141.0	112.1	105.1
Exploitation				
1965	101.7	99.0	104.5	89.9
1966	100.0	100.0	100.0	100.0
1967	103.4	104.4	105.0	101.9
1968	121.1	139.6	117.3	109.1
1969	125.2	151.5	126.9	111.0

SOURCE: BCRA, *Sistema de cuentas de producto e ingreso,* vol. 2, p. 220 ff., and unpublished working papers of the BCRA.

NOTES: Value added data deflated by the price indices for the respective products of each sector.

Wage and salary figures deflated by the cost-of-living index for Buenos Aires.

The agricultural and livestock sector has been excluded due to the scarcity and unreliability of wage data.

paid out in the form of wages and salaries to workers or employees in that sector.* Productivity and exploitation data for four major sectors of the Argentine economy are presented in Table 27.

Table 27 shows that between 1966 and 1969 there occurred in all major sectors of the economy (except in the labor-intensive construction sector) a significant rise in productivity. But a still greater rise in the rate of exploitation took place, reflecting the joint effect of the increase in value added and the general though uneven fall in wages and salaries. It is significant in this respect that 1968 (the first complete year of the normalization program) was the year of the sharpest rise in productivity

---

*The data on which these calculations are based (BCRA, unpublished worksheets) distinguish between wages and salaries only for industry (where the figures for wages have been used), not for the other major economic sectors. It is safe to assume that wage remuneration predominates in construction, while salaries are the predominant form of payment in the financial and commercial sectors.

for the industrial and financial sectors; it was also, in every sector, the year of the greatest increase in the exploitation rate. After the resignation of Krieger Vasena and his team in mid-1969, the government raised salaries and wages as part of a strategy of "social pacification" that we shall study in subsequent chapters. It is reasonable to suppose that had this policy reversal not occurred, the 1969 increase in the rate of exploitation would have been even higher than it actually was, especially in view of the strong gains in productivity and value added registered in 1969 by nearly all sectors of the economy. It was not without reason, then, that the organizations of the upper bourgeoisie fought relentlessly for the preservation of the program launched in 1967.

Value added, employment, and wage data from unpublished BCRA documents permit a more precise evaluation of the situation in the industrial sector. These data have been disaggregated into the following industrial subsectors: (1) nondurable consumer goods (primarily for mass consumption), (2) consumer durables, (3) intermediate goods, and (4) capital goods. The consumer nondurables subsector tends to be highly competitive and is composed of many labor-intensive, domestically owned, and small and medium-sized firms. By contrast, the remaining subsectors (referred to jointly as the dynamic ones) tend to be highly oligopolized and are composed of many capital-intensive firms.[5] Productivity and exploitation rates for each of these subsectors and for industrial subsidiaries of U.S.-based TNCs* were calculated in the manner explained above. The results are given in Table 28.

Here again is evidence of the heterogeneity of the processes we seek to uncover. In the nondurable consumer goods subsector, value added rose faster than productivity and exploitation. Productivity and exploitation seem to have risen quite slowly not only because of the labor-intensive character of the consumer nondurables industries but also because of the mildness of the wage losses suffered by the worst-paid workers (employed mainly in this sector) in comparison to their better-paid counterparts. Value added, productivity, and exploitation rates varied similarly in each of the three dynamic subsectors. These varia-

---

*The data for the four industrial subsectors are based on value added, while those for the TNC subsidiaries are based on the total value of production, measured by sales receipts. Since there are indications that in the Argentine economy the ratio of value added to total value of production increased during the 1966–69 period, it is likely that the indexed productivity and exploitation figures for the TNC subsidiaries are below what they would have been had they been based on value added. However, the patterns of change in the data for the TNC subsidiaries are remarkably similar to those for the industrial subsectors in which these subsidiaries (together with TNC subsidiaries of non-U.S. origins and the main locally controlled oligopolistic firms) tend to operate.

TABLE 28   VALUE ADDED, PRODUCTIVITY, AND
EXPLOITATION RATES FOR SUBSECTORS OF ARGENTINE
INDUSTRY AND INDUSTRIAL SUBSIDIARIES OF U.S.-BASED
TRANSNATIONAL CORPORATIONS
(in 1966 pesos) (index 1966=100.0)

	Nondurable Consumer Goods	Durable Consumer Goods	Intermediate Goods	Capital Goods	TNC Subsidiaries
Value added					
1965	96.7	105.2	100.1	99.3	92.9
1966	100.0	100.0	100.0	100.0	100.0
1967	102.9	100.6	101.5	98.5	105.7
1968	107.9	104.5	109.2	104.1	113.3
1969	112.9	125.5	123.2	120.0	133.9
Productivity					
1965	98.2	106.8	100.5	98.4	92.9
1966	100.0	100.0	100.0	100.0	100.0
1967	101.9	110.6	102.7	101.7	102.1
1968	104.2	117.1	115.0	113.2	110.3
1969	104.0	126.9	124.1	124.1	123.1
Exploitation					
1965	98.9	107.8	103.3	101.0	89.8
1966	100.0	100.0	100.0	100.0	100.0
1967	101.2	109.4	104.4	101.7	104.1
1968	111.5	125.3	126.0	124.4	122.2
1969	109.2	131.6	132.2	134.4	131.9

SOURCES: First four columns calculated from unpublished working papers of the BCRA. TNC subsidiaries data from FIEL, *Las empresas extranjeras*.

NOTES: Value added data deflated by the price indices for the respective products of each sector.

Wage data deflated by the cost-of-living index for Buenos Aires.

For TNC subsidiaries: total value of production measured by annual sales according to balance sheet; profits measured as declared on balance sheet before payment of indirect taxes.

tions were very similar to those of the U.S.-based TNC subsidiaries but differed markedly from those of the nondurable consumer goods industries. Between 1966 and 1969 productivity and exploitation rates rose respectively three and six times as much in the dynamic subsectors as in the consumer nondurables subsector. Moreover, the 1969 downturn in the rate of exploitation in the nondurables subsector contrasts with the continued (though attenuated) rise in the exploitation rate in the three dynamic subsectors. This divergence surely reflects that the wage increases granted in the second half of 1969 had a greater impact on the consumer nondurables subsector than on the dynamic subsectors.*

For a more complete picture of the patterns of capital accumulation during the normalization program we should recall that the state apparatus increased its revenues substantially while all wages, some salaries, and many Pampean prices fell. The increase in state revenue led to a strong expansion of public investment that went mainly to projects for improving the physical infrastructure. These projects, in addition to not competing with the activities of the bourgeoisie, furnished forward and backward linkages that further allowed the upper fractions of this class to emerge as the prime beneficiary of the normalization program. We have also seen that the spectacular growth of financial capital and private construction contrasted with the depression of the agricultural and livestock sector and with the moderate growth of industry as a whole. However, the data suggest that while most of the industrial bourgeoisie must have fared rather poorly, the dynamic industrial subsectors performed impressively well.

Data such as those used in this disaggregation of the industrial sector are not available for commerce. But considering that a large proportion of the small commercial firms were hurt by the persecution of the credit cooperatives and by the "liberation" of urban rents, it seems reasonable to assume that the mediocre performance of the commercial sector as a whole was, as in industry, the product of two opposing movements whereby the larger firms fared well while others did poorly.

Thus on one plane the distribution of the period's benefits pitted the urban against the Pampean bourgeoisie. But on a second plane—within the urban bourgeoisie—the financial and construction sectors, the up-

---

*Nondurable consumer goods enterprises and, in general, firms in the less dynamic and more labor-intensive industries are entangled in a dilemma to which we shall return. On the one hand, the relatively low productivity and higher wage and salary costs in such industries mean that their constituent firms must bear higher costs when wage and salary increases are granted. On the other hand, these firms are mostly oriented toward domestic mass consumption and therefore have a strong interest in an expanding domestic market, which tends to occur with wage and salary increases. This orientation toward mass consumption causes such firms special hardships in recessive situations. Although political conjunctures determine expansion or recession, these fractions of industry have frequently allied themselves with the unions (an alliance mediated above all through the CGE) in pursuit of policies, including wage and salary increases, likely to expand the domestic market. For a more detailed discussion of these themes, see O'Donnell, "State and Alliances" and "Notas para el estudio."

per industrial bourgeoisie, and (presumably) the upper segments of commercial capital fared very well indeed. The economically less powerful fractions of the bourgeoisie, which were numerically the most important and far from inert politically, were not as fortunate. The mild income losses of wage earners, and the heavier losses of various categories of salary recipients, further contributed to what appeared increasingly as the solitary feast of the upper bourgeoisie.

5. SIGNIFICANCE OF THE NORMALIZATION PROGRAM OF 1967–69

The data we have examined leave little room for doubt that Krieger Vasena's economic program, beyond its seemingly neutral goals of controlling inflation, improving the balance of payments, and restoring a respectable rate of economic growth, embodied a major offensive by the upper bourgeoisie. The basis for this assertion is not merely that most members of this team came from, and would later return to, transnational financial organizations, or to the largest and transnationalized corporations operating in Argentina—although this is not a trivial consideration. It is also that the policies of the 1967–69 period received the explicit and sustained support of the organizations of the upper bourgeoisie.* Even more important is that the content of the normalization program, and the type of economic growth it generated, consistently reinforced the economic dominance of the upper bourgeoisie.

It is not surprising that a BA's economic normalization program generates losses for the lower middle sectors and the weakest fractions of the bourgeoisie, nor that it severely harms regions outside the main circuits of capital accumulation. Such consequences are implicit in the peculiar normality that these programs seek to impose. The specificity of the 1967–69 program in Argentina consisted in the attempt by the Krieger Vasena team, with the explicit support of the upper bourgeoisie, to subordinate to the patterns of capital accumulation of the largest and most dynamic fractions of urban capital those of an agrarian class as

---

*Among these organizations was the Consejo Empresario Argentino, a group consisting of thirty leaders of the major local and transnational firms. The Consejo was created in 1967 with the help of Krieger Vasena and counted as one of its first presidents José A. Martínez de Hoz, Economy Minister during the second Argentine BA (1976–81). This council acted as a transmission belt between the Economy Ministry and the powerful interests these enterprises embodied. For a discussion of these and related themes, see Jorge Schvarzer, "Estrategia industrial y grandes empresas. El caso argentino" (*Desarrollo Económico*, no. 40, 1978).

powerful and economically central as the Pampean bourgeoisie. The displacement of dominant agrarian classes, or the subordination of their circuits of accumulation to those of an upper bourgeoisie intimately linked to transnational capital and the state apparatus, is no rarity in Latin America; it has occurred under various political forms and in the context of diverse efforts at capitalistic modernization. But in no other Latin American country, except Uruguay, has a dominant agrarian class been endowed with as much homogeneity, economic centrality, and political and ideological weight as the Pampean bourgeoisie.

The withholding tax on Pampean exports was crucial in generating the rapid and substantial increase in state revenues that allowed this normalization program to evade many of the enigmas that other such programs must face.* Moreover, by contributing to the maintenance of low domestic prices for wage goods, the withholding tax helped reduce inflation and cushion the drop in salaries and wages. By 1968, as the liberals (and the paternalists, who congratulated themselves on selecting *técnicos* capable of executing the tasks of the "first phase of the Argentine Revolution") repeated time and again, Krieger Vasena's program could present a panoply of successes without having demanded too many sacrifices of the population at large. On the other hand, some crucial goals had yet to be achieved. It still remained to raise the levels of private domestic investment,[†] to create a capital market, and to increase the flexibility of the interindustrial price structure (which would imply discontinuing the price agreements and thus bestowing even greater rewards on efficient producers).[‡] Wage and salary increases could also be considered, but

---

*By contrast, a withholding tax on exports with crucial influence on public finances was not a workable option for other BAs. In Chile, low international prices for the main export, copper, ruled out this possibility. In Brazil, such appropriations were not feasible because the Brazilian agrarian export products that enjoy stronger comparative advantages in international trade are less important in terms of both total exports and total state finances than Argentina's Pampean exports. The case of Uruguay, on the other hand, shows that the relationships asserted here must not be understood mechanistically. Uruguay's agrarian bourgeoisie is even weightier in relation to other classes than is Argentina's. It was precisely this factor that made Krieger Vasena's solution for Argentina impossible for Uruguay: the urban bourgeoisie in Uruguay is neither politically nor economically strong enough to try to divert to itself a significant part of the differential rent enjoyed by the country's agrarian bourgeoisie.

†Domestic private investment, after remaining at low levels during 1967 and 1968, showed a strong resurgence in 1969 but plummeted in the wake of the urban riots of May of that year. See, in addition to the data presented earlier, de Pablo, *Política antiinflacionaria en la Argentina*.

‡Just before his resignation as Economy Minister, Krieger Vasena proposed dismantling the "price accords" (Krieger Vasena, *Política económica*, vol. 2). Significantly, the successes achieved by the normalization program led in 1969 to attempts to step up, not diminish, orthodoxy. Economic policy for 1969 envisioned not only an end to the freezing

silence was maintained as to whether they would be pegged to improvements in productivity. The economic team and the organizations of the upper bourgeoisie, aware that such goals (which together constituted what I shall call its maximum program) could not be realized overnight, warned repeatedly that grave consequences would arise from any attempt to depart from the course begun in March 1967.

But from the perspective of many other actors, the normalization program had gone too far in channeling the economic surplus toward the upper bourgeoisie, the state apparatus, and the upper strata of the middle sectors. The reasons for the grievances of the lower middle sectors and the traditional petty bourgeoisie should be clear from the data already examined. The picture is more varied and complex for the local bourgeoisie, but it seems clear that domestic capital had few reasons to support many aspects of economic policy and fewer still to evaluate sympathetically the program's promise of a future increasingly open to transnational capital and oriented by the criteria of efficiency defined by the Krieger Vasena team.

The working class suffered only a slight income loss, even though the rate of exploitation increased considerably. However, it was as clear from the paternalists' corporatist designs as from the liberals' goal of atomizing the popular sector that a major decline in the political and economic weight of the unions was in the making. The working class as a whole, as well as the numerous unionized lower middle sectors (predominantly state employees) thus found themselves in danger of losing a resource they had learned to value highly: the capacity for pressure and negotiation provided by powerful unions. Moreover, wage data do not reflect other changes with a negative impact on the popular sector as a whole: the right to strike was effectively revoked, labor authorities made no move to halt arbitrary dismissals and other sanctions against workers, and, most important of all, strict discipline was restored to the workplace, backed by a state apparatus no longer reluctant to employ coercion. Thus, although influential government officials* and some

---

of industrial relative prices but also a greatly reduced role for public investment. It was expected that private investment would rise sharply (as it actually did in the first half of 1969) above the levels of the previous years, thus making (unorthodox) public investment unnecessary. Moreover, it was foreseen that the effective protection of industry against imports would continue to be lowered.

*Commenting on the riots of May 1969, Krieger Vasena expressed his surprise at the participation of workers who were among the most highly paid in the country (cited in Francisco Delich, *Crisis y protesta social,* 2d ed. [Buenos Aires: El Cid Editores, 1976], 236). Equally revealing is that many of the paternalists I interviewed stressed that their

union leaders thought otherwise, the relatively slight decline in wages (and the sharper decline in many salaries) had little chance of pacifying the popular sector or of co-opting the unions—much less of allying the popular sector with the upper bourgeoisie.

A survey taken in mid-1968 provides evidence that the biases of the economic program against the popular sector did not pass unnoticed.* Table 29 underscores the wide disparities in the ways in which various layers of Argentine society perceived economic policy and the BA itself. While the data suggest that in June 1968 the middle sectors (although far from wholly satisfied) had barely begun to mobilize themselves against the BA, they indicate how overwhelmingly the popular sector opposed the existing state of affairs.†

To summarize: the outstanding feature of the 1967–69 period was the attempt by the liberal *técnicos* and the upper bourgeoisie to subordinate not only the popular sector and the weakest fractions of the urban bourgeoisie but also an agrarian class endowed with formidable political and economic centrality. By attempting to recast the apex of the dominant classes at the same time that it endeavored to reinforce its domination over the usual victims of the BAs, the upper bourgeoisie antagonized virtually all other sectors of society.

That the upper bourgeoisie bit off more than it could chew in launch-

---

policies had not been hostile to the popular sector, a claim they based on the assertion that real wages had not declined during their tenure in office. This crude economism remains a curious (though typical) aspect of the perceptions of actors who espoused such a "spiritualist" conception of development.

*Since the source does not explain the methodology used in this survey, these data must be viewed with caution. But even granting an ample margin of error, the differences among the various categories of respondents in the survey are striking enough.

†Other survey data from this period, congruent with the ones presented above, may be found in Tilman Evers, *Militarregierung in Argentinien. Das politische System der "Argentinischen Revolution"* (Hamburg: Institut für Iberoamerika-Kunde, 1973), 146 passim, and in Frederick Turner, "The Study of Argentine Politics through Survey Research," *Latin American Research Review* 10, no. 2 (1975): 73–94. Turner presents data from a survey taken in Buenos Aires in February 1968 (n = 250 men) which show that (at least at that time) opinions about other political issues also were strongly influenced by social position. Regrouping the data presented in Turner's article on attitudes toward U.S. intervention in Viet Nam, we obtain results congruent with and as spectacular as those obtained in response to questions about national affairs (see Table 29).

	Social Position of Respondent		
	High	Middle	Low
(1) Favorable responses toward U.S intervention in Viet Nam	79%	40%	21%
(2) Unfavorable responses toward U.S. intervention in Viet Nam	19%	60%	77%
(3) Don't know, no answer	2%	—	2%

TABLE 29   POLL ON CURRENT SITUATION, JUNE 1968
(Selected Questions)

	Stratums		

Comparing the present government with that of Illia, would you say that Onganía's is better than, the same as, or worse than the previous one?	Upper	Middle	Lower
Better	60%	37%	11%
Same	15	34	34
Worse	25	28	51
Don't know, no answer		1	4
Total	100%	100%	100%

What is the best thing that the government has done in the past two years? (multiple responses allowed)	Upper	Middle	Lower
Social and political stability, image abroad	37%	12%	3%
Economic stability	67	33	8
Rents, housing, pensions	8	22	9
"Rectification" of the university	6	1	
Nothing good	14	41	80

Are you satisfied with the current economic situation?	Upper	Middle	Lower
Yes	42%	16%	13%
No	54	80	86
Don't know, no answer	4	4	1
Total	100%	100%	100%

For those who said "no": Whose fault is it? (multiple responses allowed)	Upper	Middle	Lower
The government's plan	61%	59%	83%
Companies in general	12	15	21
Foreign monopolies	37	26	55
Unions		10	6
Others	10	16	3
Don't know, no answer		10	8

SOURCE: *Primera Plana*, June 25, 1968, p. 21.
NOTES: N=400 in Buenos Aires.
Sampling method not reported.

ing its offensive on all fronts at once is all the more evident considering that the liberals were far from controlling all the top posts in the state apparatus. The problem was not simply that Onganía and his current cherished medium-term hopes that differed in important ways from those of the liberals and the upper bourgeoisie, though this divergence was an obstacle to the achievement of the long-term confidence necessary to build on existing successes. More important, the paternalists' presence in the state apparatus (along with the still-embryonic influence of the nationalists) signified the distribution of influence within the armed forces, the main coercive guarantee of the newly established order: although the liberals controlled many of the top military posts, the paternalists and nationalists retained enough weight within the armed forces to make them a crucial chamber of resonance for the protests of the middle sectors, the local bourgeoisie, and the Pampean bourgeoisie.

The social and economic conditions were therefore ripening for the fusion of a strong oppositional alliance and, within the state apparatus, for the breakdown of the precarious cohesion among the liberals, paternalists, and nationalists. Yet political struggles, both within and outside of the state apparatus, would determine whether this possibility would be realized. But let us defer the examination of such conflicts to chapter 5.

6. CRISIS, THREAT, AND ECONOMIC "SUCCESSES"

While the relative mildness of the crisis in Argentina of 1966 was crucial to the rapid success of this BA in restoring order and achieving many of its economic goals, it was equally important in contributing to the articulation of forces that precipitated its no less rapid collapse. Let us examine the reasons that underlie this apparent paradox.

The 1966 Argentine BA emerged in the context of an accumulation crisis which, unlike those preceding the BAs of the 1970s, involved neither dramatic dislocations in the productive structure nor the redirection of a considerable proportion of commercial and industrial capital toward speculative financial ventures (although, as we saw in chapter 2, there were eloquent indications that confidence was evaporating and that a plunder economy was underway). This accumulation crisis unfolded without a concomitant crisis of social domination and was attended by a relatively low level of threat, which partly accounts, as we shall see, for the armed forces' reluctance to apply the high degree of coercion that the upper bourgeoisie demanded when the continuity of the normalization program was seriously challenged.

The absence of a serious threat to capitalism and its associated patterns of social domination was crucial in creating political and ideological space for an alternative to the normalization program: what many envisioned as a socially just, nationalist, and balanced version of capitalism in which everyone would have a place in the sun—even transnational capital, although its expansion would be closely controlled by the government. Belief in the feasibility of this alternative was to form the ideological cement for a broad-based oppositional alliance whose common denominator was a critique of the "efficientist and transnationalizing" orientations of Krieger Vasena's policies. Likely to participate in such an alliance, in addition to the popular sector, were numerous middle sectors, the members of the local bourgeoisie that voiced their grievances through the CGE, various currents in the armed forces, most union leaders, and the political parties, including Radicals and Peronists.* Ironically, a similar vision was shared by more than a few of the major actors at the apex of the state apparatus, including Onganía and the paternalists. They, however, were prepared to pursue this other form of development only later on, when the economic phase of the Argentine Revolution had come to fruition.

Two major consequences stemmed from the conflict between paternalists and liberals over which style of capitalist development was appropriate for Argentina. First, despite the initial successes of the normalization program, there could be no long-term political guarantee of the future continuity of existing economic policies until a solution was found to the problem of power at the apex of the state apparatus. The uncertainty that the struggle between paternalists and liberals generated among the major domestic and transnational economic actors is suggested by the dearth of direct foreign investment and long-term loans to Argentina between 1967 and 1969. Argentina's failure to attract foreign capital during this period is all the more noteworthy since the 1967–69 years were precisely those in which the Brazilian BA, which had received better marks on the test of its long-term political reliability, began to receive a massive influx

---

*Greatly facilitating the emergence of redistributive goals among certain segments of the bourgeoisie and of the armed forces, and thus promoting the formation of this broad oppositional alliance, was the perception that the crisis of accumulation had been resolved and that no crisis of social domination would erupt in the foreseeable future.

of such resources. The second consequence involved a paradox. So long as the paternalists (and nationalists, although they as yet did not seem too dangerous) remained entrenched in the armed forces and in the highest reaches of the state's civil apparatus, the continuation of the normalization program could be jeopardized by its very achievements. If, as the paternalists and liberals could agree, the program had realized such rapid and important successes—if monetary and exchange rate stability seemed assured, and if economic growth had spurted to impressive levels—then, the paternalists asked, why not begin a period of greater "social sensitivity"? In the first stage of normalization, certain sacrifices had been necessary; these had been exacted efficiently by the liberal *técnicos*. But now that these sacrifices had served their purpose, why not grant significant wage and salary increases and renew efforts to strengthen national enterprises? For the paternalists, a shift toward policies more favorable to the popular sector and the local bourgeoisie would be not only an act of justice desirable per se, it would also further their goal of co-opting the unions and most of the organizations of the bourgeoisie. The paternalists hoped that success in these endeavors would provide them with bases of support they could use to counterbalance what they saw as the excessive weight of the big corporations, not only in society but in the heart of their own government.[6] To achieve this goal the paternalists would have to replace Krieger Vasena et al. in the not too distant future with an economic team whose orientations were closer to theirs.*

The many similarities between the case we are examining and the other BAs must not be allowed to obscure differences that are basic to understanding the dynamics of each one. The method used in this book is to sketch, at a rather high level of abstraction, what all the BAs have in common, as a first step toward discovering, and emphasizing, what is distinctive about each one. To understand the specificity of the case on which this book focuses, it is necessary to take into account some specific features of the general context in which the normalization program of 1967–69 was launched. One such feature was the popular sector's relatively high degree of autonomy with respect to both the state apparatus and the dominant classes. This autonomy derived from a high level of political activation and organizational capacity. But it was also linked to ideological orientations that, as expressed through the unions

---

*Those whom I interviewed both at the time and later explicitly confirmed that the paternalists contemplated replacing Krieger Vasena and his team as soon as the economic phase was over. Further confirmation may be found in Roth, *Los años de Onganía*.

and Peronism, posed no fundamental challenge to social domination and capitalism. These orientations had important consequences both before and after the implantation of the BA. Prior to the 1966 coup, they kept the threat level relatively low. After the coup, once the impacts of the normalization program had created the conditions for a broad-based opposition, these relatively moderate orientations raised the possibility of an alliance between the popular sector, the local bourgeoisie, and various middle sectors. By contrast, the more radical, anticapitalist goals expressed by the popular sectors and their representatives prior to the implantation of other BAs have prevented, or greatly delayed, the formation of a multiclass oppositional alliance capable of posing an effective challenge to the BA. Radicalized popular sector ideologies work against such an alliance because the local bourgeoisie and the numerous middle sectors who might otherwise adhere to it (especially since the normalization programs initiated when the BA is implanted under high-threat conditions tend to have especially harsh consequences for these segments of society) feel that enduring these consequences is a lesser evil than allying themselves with a popular sector that has recently raised, and may raise again, the specter of "communism."

The second distinctive feature of the 1967–69 Argentine normalization program was the use it made of the enormous importance of Pampean production to Argentine exports (and to the whole economy). This importance provided the opportunity to impose the withholding tax that facilitated the quick successes of the program but at the same time gave the Pampean bourgeoisie a strong motive to oppose the BA. Other BAs, by contrast, have faced a complex map of *several* agrarian bourgeoisies and oligarchies with a broad and often conflicting array of interests. In countries like Brazil and Chile, where the dominant agrarian classes are much more fragmented than in Argentina, the production of each fraction is much less important to exports and to the economy as a whole than is that of Argentina's Pampean bourgeoisie. Accordingly, attempts by such fractions to resist policies aimed at modernizing their land tenure patterns and production techniques have tended to be politically isolated and incapable of generating extremely serious problems for the national economy. Argentina, by contrast, ecologically blessed with the fertility of the Pampean region, has been historically cursed by the capacity of those who have appropriated it to resist such attempts at modernization.

The characteristics of Argentina's class structure thus facilitated the opening of two fronts of resistance, which tended to converge, against the offensive launched by the upper bourgeoisie: one that consisted of the popular sector allied to the local urban bourgeoisie, and another that comprised a powerful and homogeneous agrarian bourgeoisie. But it is important to note that the specificities of a class structure operate through political, ideological and economic struggles that are not determined unequivocally by that structure, and in which the history of prior struggles plays an important part. Argentina provides a case in point. The crisis that preceded the June 1966 coup was much less severe than the one that preceded the coup of March 1976. The latter was preceded by a crisis of social domination and by serious challenges to the coercive supremacy of the state apparatus. These challenges, for reasons discussed in chapter 1, also brought with them an economic crisis far more profound than the one that accompanied the implantation of the 1966 Argentine BA. Since the axis of the crisis that preceded the 1976 coup passed through the very heart of social domination and generated very high levels of threat, and since the popular sector was among the perceived agents of this crisis, it took more time, and a humiliating military defeat, before a multiclass political alliance (such as the one that began to take shape in 1968) emerged, in spite of the fact that the normalization program launched in 1976 had far harsher consequences for the popular sector, most middle sectors and the local bourgeoisie than did the program we have studied in this chapter. No less important in explaining why an oppositional alliance took so long to form after 1976 is a second difference, closely related to the one just examined, between the two Argentine BAs: in post-1976 Argentina the upper bourgeoisie did not overextend itself attempting to subordinate the Pampean bourgeoisie. On the contrary, both participated in a tacit alliance under more equal conditions than those the upper bourgeoisie sought to impose during the 1967–69 period. Financial capital moreover played a much more central role after 1976, as might have been expected in view of the higher level of previous threat and, consequently, the more extended economy of plunder that emerged both before and after the implantation of this BA. But the price for eliminating the antagonism between the upper and Pampean bourgeoisies that had plagued the previous Argentine BA was that a tax on Pampean exports could not be used to reduce the fiscal deficit. The failure to reduce the deficit reinforced other repercussions of the more acute previous crisis and helped situate the post-1976 Argentine BA among the cases in which economic policy could not produce successes even faintly resembling those of the 1967–69 period.

The Argentine experience of 1967–69 suggests that the lower the previous threat and crisis the greater, faster, and more conspicuous will be the success of the normalization program. But the very success of this program makes it more likely that forces will emerge capable of pressing for social and economic policies that tend to undermine its continuity. On the other hand, the deeper the previous crisis, the less likely it is (or the longer it takes) for the normalization program to succeed, even in terms of its own premises and stated goals. A deeper previous crisis, by generating greater difficulties for the subsequent normalization program, pushes economic policy toward still greater orthodoxy and increases the likelihood that such orthodoxy will persist over a sustained period of time. In such cases, the permanence in office of the *técnicos* who implement these orthodox policies is assured much more by their failures than by their successes.

Why? First, because in a situation of recession, speculation, high inflation, and hypertrophy of financial capital—all of which are more severe the deeper the previous crisis—redistributive proposals, such as those inspired by the success of Krieger Vasena's program, do not present themselves as viable alternatives. Second, because the continued reverberations of the profound crisis preceding the BA, in addition to discouraging direct private investment from domestic and transnational sources, make it very difficult, if not impossible, for the state apparatus to gather sufficient resources to substitute for those that private investors are not providing. The BA under these circumstances is rendered more dependent on domestic and (especially) transnational financial capital as virtually the only remaining potential supplier of the resources needed to reactivate the economy. As long as the balance of payments seems sufficient to guarantee loan repayments, and insofar as the existence of large differentials between domestic and international interest rates creates the expectation that high profits will be made on those loans, financial capital is largely uninterested in the misfortunes of the domestic economy (and, for that matter, in the domestic success of normalization). Given this lack of interest, it is not surprising that the only concrete achievement observable under BAs that have been forced to fall back on financial capital is an improvement in the balance of payments—often generated by the drop in demand for imports resulting from a domestic recession produced, in turn, by the orthodox economic policies upon which financial capital insists.

Let us recapitulate. The deeper the preceding crisis, the longer and the more tightly financial capital is able to hold the BA (and the country) in its grasp. Under these circumstances, any deviation from what financial capital considers "rational"—i.e. strict application of the canon of orthodoxy—may provoke a particularly severe crash. In such a situation the BA's economic team is left with little choice but to keep applying orthodox policies, hoping that "efficiency" and "productivity" will somehow appear on the horizon. Meanwhile, and largely because of this dearth of options, nothing is done about the huge social and economic costs that such super-orthodox policies generate, even if these costs are regrettable from the point of view of many of the BA's principal actors and supporters. Thus the economy of plunder continues, but, in contrast to the period preceding the BA, few can participate in it while many must bear its costs. By contrast, BAs inaugurated under less extreme circumstances (Argentina in 1966 and Brazil in 1964) have better chances of achieving some significant successes. But under certain circumstances (which we have examined for the Argentine case and will later on contrast with the Brazilian BA), those very successes tend to generate expectations and political alliances that undermine the continuity of the normalization program. In spite of its impressive façade of power, the BA, in both its successful and its unsuccessful variants, offers no easy road—not even to the winners.

NOTES

1. Juan de Pablo, *Política antiinflacionaria en Argentina, 1967–1970* (Buenos Aires: Amorrortu Editores, 1971).
2. See esp. Lucio Reca and Ernesto Gaba, "Poder adquisitivo, veda y substitutos: un reexamen de la demanda interna de carne vacuna en la Argentina, 1950–1972," *Desarrollo Económico,* no. 50 (July–September 1973): 333–346.
3. See Frenkel and O'Donnell, "Stabilization Programs."
4. Juan Sourrouille, *El impacto de las empresas transnacionales sobre el empleo y los ingresos: el caso de la Argentina* (Geneva: International Labor Office, 1976); and "La presencia y el comportamiento de las empresas extranjeras en el sector industrial argentino," *Estudios CEDES,* no. 2, Buenos Aires, 1978.
5. Sourrouille, *El impacto de las empresas transnacionales* and "La presencia y el comportamiento."
6. My interviews.

FIVE

Economic Successes and Political Problems

1. POLITICAL PROBLEMS DURING NORMALIZATION

Having outlined the economic program implemented in March 1967, let us turn to the political situation. On March 5, 1968—at the beginning of the program's triumphant year—Onganía called a meeting of the higher officials in his government to convey to them publicly what the press labeled "the great reprimand." After exhorting them to be "more than ordinary men," he assigned them duties that, in the best military style, had fixed dates for completion. The tone of Onganía's speech clearly expressed its premises: that his leadership alone would determine the course of events and that he had every right to demand that the assembled officials, whom he viewed as his temporary collaborators, recognize his exclusive leadership and raise themselves to the height of the "Revolution."* The episode led to several resignations and to rumblings in the leading periodicals, which reminded their readers that leadership of the Revolution was the responsibility of the armed forces, not of Onganía. Most of the media also began to criticize Onganía and his group for their "corporatist tendencies," their "lack of political definition," and their feeble attempts to define the "democ-

---

*Onganía's address was motivated by his dissatisfaction with the slow pace of policy implementation and administrative rationalization. Declaring that "the current functioning of the state is chaotic," he informed his audience that it was "necessary to begin immediately to give [the state] the modern functioning that the country requires" (*La Nación*, March 6, 1968).

racy" they claimed to espouse.* While continuing to show contempt for the old political parties,† the media increased their coverage of active-duty military liberals, such as generals Alsogaray and Lanusse, as well as of the retired general Eugenio Aramburu (president of Argentina from 1955 to 1958), who was hinting at his willingness to be the candidate of a "civil-military" coalition of "democratic inspiration."

Meanwhile, Krieger Vasena's economic program was recording the important successes noted in the preceding chapter, and "order" seemed assured throughout society. Everything was going so well that the contending currents in the BA, taking advantage of what the paternalists called the tacit consensus of a society still brooding over its dissatisfaction, turned their attention to the struggle for full control of the apex of the state apparatus. As General Alsogaray stepped up his efforts to establish complete liberal command over the army, the paternalists began to press openly for their own program. The paternalists, comfortable in their belief that the liberals were close to completing the "technical" function of normalizing the economy and trumpeting their success at "restoring order" and "reestablishing authority,"‡ announced that although the political phase was still a long way off,§ the Revolution was nearing the beginning of its social phase. What the social phase would involve was not easy to infer from their statements about structural change and integration, but there was little doubt that it would

---

*See, for example, La Nación, March 8, 1968, p. 6, and April 7, 1968, p. 6, and La Prensa, March 10, 1968, p. 8. Characteristically, the paternalists responded to these criticisms by issuing statements that did little more than add to the complaints of their critics. See Onganía's speech in La Nación, March 17, 1968, p. 6, to the effect that "we must accustom ourselves to the thought that the revolutionary regime may last for ten years." Similar statements may be found in Onganía's address to provincial governors in La Nación, April 2, 1968, p. 1. See also Borda's remarks in La Nación, April 26, 1968, p. 1, concerning the "corporations" and the "crisis of liberal philosophy." Borda's comments provoked caustic reactions from La Nación, April 28, 1969, p. 6, and from the ACIEL in La Nación, April 27, 1968, p. 16.

†Although the Peronists, the Radicals, and other political parties had begun in 1967 to talk about forming a civic front to oppose the BA, it was not until the great social convulsions of 1969–70 that the media began to treat them less condescendingly.

‡See, in addition to the statements cited in the preceding chapter, Onganía's remark on television following the assassination of Robert Kennedy: "Let us give thanks to God for the peace that prevails in our country" (La Razón, June 29, 1968, p. 1). See also Onganía's speech to the armed forces in La Nación, August 6, 1968, p. 1.

§See Onganía's August 1968 speech to the armed forces (La Nación, August 6, 1968, pp. 1, 6): "Nothing could be further from the thought of the Revolution than the search for political ways out. The dissolution of the political parties is an irrevocable act." The commander in chief of the air force added that "there exist neither political plans nor the intention to call for elections" (La Nación, August 10, 1968, p. 1). Díaz Colodrero remarked that "what has been called the political phase [of the Argentine Revolution] is still a long way off" (La Nación, August 9, 1968, p. 1).

include two of the goals most worrisome to the upper bourgeoisie. The first of these goals involved the creation and "amalgamation with the state" of "authentically representative organizations of the community." This goal was the clearest expression of the paternalists' aggressive corporatism; it implied the unification not only of the unions (a prospect that the upper bourgeoisie, as we have seen, viewed with apprehension) but also of the organizations of the dominant classes (a prospect that the upper bourgeoisie viewed as intolerable). The second worrisome aspect of the social phase was that it portended the state's dispensation of social justice, using what the upper bourgeoisie and the liberals viewed as premature redistributive policies to compensate the *pueblo* for its sacrifices under the normalization program. Moreover, it was clear that once the social phase had begun, the liberal *técnicos*, having accomplished their mission, would be replaced by officials endowed with greater "social sensitivity" and "national feeling."*

The upper bourgeoisie saw no reason to abandon their own program.[1] Among the main objectives of this program were the continued compression of wages, the dissolution of the CGT, and the passing of legislation guaranteeing workers the freedom to decide whether and in what ways to unionize. The program also called for the privatization of profitable state enterprises and of the social security system and for the termination of the 1967 price agreements so as to increase competition and "bestow greater rewards" on the "most efficient" economic actors.†

The onset of the social phase and the paternalists' efforts to co-opt the unions did not bode well for the maximum program of the upper bourgeoisie. Was it not time, then, to replace Onganía with an officer less prone to corporatist and redistributionist illusions and better able to settle the military situation to the liberals' benefit? Dissatisfaction with Onganía had already been exacerbated by the politically less than astute statements made by his political team, the conflict between the president and General Julio Alsogaray,‡ some of the paternalists' nationalist

---

*See Onganía in *La Nación*, August 6, 1968, p. 1, where he added that the great task of the future social phase would be "integration," guided by the "basic, governing principle of solidarity." See also his statements in *La Nación*, September 8, 1968, p. 1.

†As was noted in chapter 4, Krieger Vasena, in accordance with these aspirations, announced in 1969 an effort to improve efficiency by relaxing constraints on the interindustrial price structure. He also gave notice that the public budget for 1969 assumed a substantial increase in private investment, which did in fact occur during the first half of that year.

‡The conflicts between Alsogaray and the president's press secretary were particularly visible and gave the former a chance to declare publicly that economic policy should stem not from personal preferences but from the program of the Argentine Revolution as expressed through the documents issued by the revolutionary junta.

whims,* and the widely rumored lack of communication between the economic team and the president. But even more worrisome for the upper bourgeoisie and the liberals was the way Onganía and the paternalists were handling the unions and the mounting evidence that the paternalists would not be traveling much farther along the path of the normalization program.

We left the CGT in 1967 in the same condition as we find it in 1968: divided and weakened. The basic difference is that in 1968 the participationists, already dubbed collaborationists, had increased their strength. Yet even as the growth of the participationist current improved its chances of gaining control of the national union apparatus, it induced other currents to converge in Vandorism. It also helped make way, particularly at the regional level, for new alignments which, going well beyond the Vandorists, espoused anti-capitalist goals. These radicalized alignments ranged from classist tendencies (mostly Marxist groups that rejected the ideology of class integration of Peronism) to those upholding "Christian left" views associated with the Theology of Liberation.† The emergence of these alignments was an important development in a unionism previously aligned with (and divided within) Peronism.

In March 1968, the CGT convened a "Normalizing Congress" to elect an executive board to replace the one decapitated by government sanctions twelve months earlier. The Vandorists, flanked to the left by the new radicalized tendencies and to the right by the participationists, were unable to control the congress. The post of secretary-general went to Raimundo Ongaro, a typography worker from the Christian Left who received the support of various left-wing currents and leaders of

---

*Such as reserving for the government the new international satellite communications system that ITT wanted for itself (a decision which, according to my interviews, was made against the wishes of the economic team and the commander in chief of the army). Plans were also made to purchase new military equipment exclusively from European suppliers, and to provide for the local production of some equipment.

†In Argentina, the emergence of the Theology of Liberation was associated with rapid radicalization within the Catholic Church. In March 1968, a group of clergy created the "Movement of Third World Priests." In December the movement launched hunger strikes in the cities of Reconquista and Buenos Aires, and on Christmas Day it picketed the Casa Rosada (where the president conducts official business) to protest the government's economic policy. Similar actions continued, and conflicts emerged between participants in the movement and various bishops. Theology of Liberation and its practitioners were later to have a diffuse but important influence on the "Peronist Left." For a discussion of these new streams of thought and practice within the Catholic Church, see Michael Dodson, "The Christian Left in Latin American Politics" and "Prophetic Politics and Political Theory in Latin America," papers presented at the Seminar on Religion and Politics in Latin America, Woodrow Wilson Center for International Scholars, Washington, D.C., 1978. The journal *Cristianismo y Revolución* was the most comprehensive expression of the movement's ideology.

unions that the government had intervened. Foreseeing that the new leadership would take them in directions more radical than they were prepared to accept (and consequently toward government sanctions that would deprive them of control over their unions), the Vandorists used tenuous legalistic arguments to deny the validity of Ongaro's election. They convened a second congress, and by April 1968 there were two CGTs: the CGT de los Argentinos, led by Ongaro and his sector, and the CGT–Calle Azopardo, with a Vandorist majority.* Each claimed to represent unionism as a whole, but neither was recognized by the government, partly because neither was close to organizing the workers in the way envisioned by the paternalists and partly because the Vandorists—even though the paternalists for obvious reasons preferred them to the current led by Ongaro—were not the apolitical labor bosses that the paternalists wished as representatives of the workers.

Soon after the division of the CGT, the CGT de los Argentinos launched what it called a "frontal assault on the regime."† This campaign consisted of strikes and demonstrations which at first had considerable impact but later were extinguished by repression and the defection of many unions to the less turbulent waters of Vandorism.[2] More important was the eruption in the interior, especially in Córdoba, of numerous factory-level conflicts involving workers in plant-level unions and other ad hoc organizations, many of which held classist ideologies.‡

The division of the CGT, the participationists' inability to control even one of its factions, and the emergence of more radicalized workers' movements—all at a time when the economic program was recording important successes—seemed to the upper bourgeoisie to provide an

---

*The participationist-controlled unions chose to stay in the CGT–Azopardo, but when it became clear that the Vandorists would control it those unions did not participate in its leadership. The participationists and Vandorists collaborated with each other and with the government against the CGT de los Argentinos, but only preliminary to deciding among themselves who would speak for the organized working class.

†See the March 1, 1968, statement in Senén González, El sindicalismo después de Perón, 118–28. The CGT de los Argentinos, which was inspired by left-leaning "Christian social doctrine," distinguished itself from the classist unions by referring to the "social function of property" and by making friendly references to the "national entrepreneurs." See also this current's short-lived journal, CGT (first issued May 1, 1968), and Raimundo Ongaro, Sólo el pueblo salvará al pueblo (Buenos Aires: Editorial Las Bases, 1970).

‡On the first conflicts in the city of Córdoba, many of which took place in automobile factories, see La Nación, May 31, p. 5, and August 14, p. 1, 1968. Also important was a prolonged strike of petroleum workers in several provinces. This strike continued even after it met opposition from the participationist leaders of the petroleum workers' national union; La Nación, September 27, p. 4; October 10, p. 1; and October 30, p. 1, 1968. On the resurgence of student activism, see La Nación, June 14, p. 2; June 15, p. 1; July 2, p. 10; August 5, p. 7; and September 9, p. 4, 1968.

excellent opportunity to dispense with the "old totalitarian law" of professional associations, and to atomize the unions through legal reforms and doses of repression.* To the paternalists, on the contrary, division in the labor movement and symptoms of its radicalization confirmed that "pathological" tendencies had emerged due to the absence of a unified, "authentically representative," and fully depoliticized workers' federation.

Rogelio Coria, the top participationist leader, was anxious to help the paternalists achieve the arrangement they envisioned. His position was distilled in an April 1968 speech in which he appealed explicitly for the comprehensive corporatism favored by the paternalists.† The Vandorist leadership, challenged by the CGT de los Argentinos and anxious to avoid government sanctions, issued a statement in which it not only distanced itself from the more militant wings of the labor movement but also extolled the government as "the apex of the [future] covenant" that would solve the country's problems.[3] Yet even as they extended their hands toward the government, both the Vandorists and the participationists criticized Krieger Vasena's team and its policies from a redistributionist standpoint—although they refrained from criticizing the government as a whole.‡ They were joined in their protests by the CGE, which from its perspective of capitalism with nationalism focused its criticism on the transnationalizing effects of the economic program.§ On

*The upper bourgeoisie issued repeated and strident demands for these actions. It is worth noting in this regard the increasingly urgent tone of La Nación and La Prensa after March 1968. The phrase "old totalitarian law" is taken from a headline in La Nación, December 23, 1968, p. 6.

†On Coria's speech see La Nación, April 14, 1968, p. 4. See also the statements in Crónica (July 5, p. 9, and June 12, p. 6, 1968) by the Construction Workers' Union, which proposed a unified CGT devoted to the cause of "social integration" and denounced Vandorism, along with the radicalized sectors, for being "politicized." For similar statements by other important unions aligned with participationism, see the Textile Workers' Association in La Nación, June 2, 1968, p. 7, and the Light and Power Workers' Association in La Nación, June 9, 1968, p. 11.

‡See the May 1 statement by the Vandorist CGT (Senén González, El sindicalismo después de Perón, 125–26), which criticized wage cuts, the suppression of collective bargaining, the "contraction of the internal market," the "suffocation" of the national bourgeoisie, and the "denationalization" of the productive structure. It also called for "all sectors of the community—workers, entrepreneurs, intellectuals, the Armed Forces, and the Church—to oppose the advance of foreign interests . . . [so as to] formulate a program which in unity with all Argentines will assure the integral development of the national economy." For another statement by the Vandorist CGT protesting "economic policy" but judiciously stopping short of criticizing the "government," see La Nación, June 1, 1968, p. 15.

§The CGE found Krieger Vasena's ministry extremely reluctant to hear its demands and even to recognize it as a representative organization. As was revealed in my interviews, the CGE's difficulties in these areas contrasted with the easy access to the economic team enjoyed by the upper bourgeoisie and their institutions. By 1968, the CGE was

the other side, the upper bourgeoisie and the leading periodicals sharp-ened their distinction between the "nationalist-corporatists" and the "liberal democrats" in the BA, approving only the economic policies carried out by the latter. For the time being, then, each of these actors for its own reasons confined its comments to the Economy Ministry, cautiously avoiding the presidency. Only the Pampean bourgeoisie aligned themselves against the government in its entirety, which had offended them through both the effects of its economic policy and its corporatist political goals.*

Shortly after constituting its authorities, the *CGT-Azopardo* re-quested an audience with Onganía. Vandorism saw in the government's fragmentation a chance to begin negotiations aimed at saving the unions, with their bureaucratic and ideological limitations, from the quite radical path marked out by the *CGT de los Argentinos*. Onganía, showing as al-ways admirable evenhandedness but poor political judgment, rejected this request in a public statement declaring that the authorities of the *CGT-Azopardo* "have not yet been properly recognized [as authentically representative] by the Labor Secretariat."[4] The *CGT-Azopardo* re-sponded by protesting that the government had no desire for a "dialogue with the workers."[5] But despite Onganía's refusal to talk with the Vandorists, he held secret meetings with participationist leaders. News of these meetings, when leaked to the press, provoked the unanimous dis-gust of the liberals, the upper bourgeoisie, and the Vandorists.

The upper bourgeoisie and the liberals were alarmed, especially after Onganía, amid rumors and symptoms of military unrest,† consummated

---

calling attention to such problems as mounting bankruptcies and "denationalization" (*La Nación*, August 13, 1968, p. 1; CGE, *Memoria Anual, 1967–1968* and *1968–1969*). In early 1969 the CGE convened an "Entrepreneurs' Assembly" with the obvious intention of promoting the replacement of the economic team and a reorientation of social and economic policy (*La Nación*, March 12, 1969, p. 4).

*As already noted, the statements of the organizations of the Pampean bourgeoisie acquired a more aggressive tone after the government began seriously to consider impos-ing a tax on potential land rent. See the statements in *La Nación*, May 9, pp. 1, 20 (SRA), November 9, p. 1 (SRA and CRA), November 17, p. 1 (SRA), and December 4, p. 1, 1968; and SRA, *Memoria Anual, 1967–1968* and *1968–1969*. See also the appearance of the Coordinating Council of Agricultural Entities (*La Nación*, October 23, 1968, p. 1), with which various agricultural producers' organizations were affiliated but in which the Pampean bourgeoisie held decisive sway.

†After March 1968 there were widespread rumors that the confrontation between Onganía and Alsogaray would end with the removal of one or the other. On these rumors and on meetings between the high command and both Onganía and Alsogaray, see *La Nación*, March 21, p. 1; May 9, p. 4; May 12, p. 6; May 23, p. 1 (statements by Alsogaray reaffirming the "eminently democratic meaning of the Argentine Revolution"); May 26, p. 6; May 28, pp. 1, 18; and June 5, p. 1, 1968.

his dispute with General Alsogaray by removing him as commander in chief of the army (the commanders in chief of the navy and air force were also forced to step down). Onganía's choice to succeed him was General Alejandro Lanusse, who in terms of weight and prestige within the army was Alsogaray's natural successor. Though a liberal, Lanusse at the time maintained warm personal relations with Onganía.* Alsogaray's subsequent statements did little to calm things down. In his view Onganía, by forcing the retirements of the commanders in chief, had lost his legitimacy within the armed forces and had assumed the most serious responsibility of "personalizing the leadership of the Revolution." Worse still, Alsogaray added, "persons and positions not precisely linked to the democratic spirit and foundation of the Revolution" were responsible for his own removal. Yet another problem was Onganía's "reluctance to engage in constructive dialogues . . . and [his] personalist and absolutist conception of authority." But in order to avoid misinterpretation of what he meant by "democracy," Alsogaray hastened to add that a "political solution" would depend on the "attainment of the goals of the Revolution."[6] The liberals, in other words, buoyed by the successes of the economic program, had no intention of calling elections at any time in the foreseeable future; there was still too much to be done, and the unfinished tasks demanded that they focus their attention on the power struggle within the state apparatus. Apparently unaware of the surrealistic overtones of the issue, the liberals, the leading periodicals, and most of the upper bourgeoisie were still asking whether the dictatorship was to be "democratic" or "corporatist." Having followed with undisguised hopes the confrontation between the "democratic" Alsogaray and the "corporatist" Onganía, the leading periodicals criticized the forced retirement of the former and, on the verge of discovering that the regime was "authoritarian," worried over the resulting "personalization of power."[†]

*Lanusse replaced Alsogaray on August 23, 1968. The information on these personal feelings comes from my interviews.
†The quoted words and phrases come from *La Nación*, August 25, 1968, p. 6, which warned that "the Revolution now risks the support of certain democratic sectors." Examples of approval of Alsogaray's statements may be found in *La Nación*, September 1, p. 6, and September 3, p. 6, 1968, and in *Primera Plana*, September 5 and 12, 1968. Meanwhile the paternalists did their best to widen the rift between themselves and their partners in the BA; see note *, p. 151. Also contributing to the deterioration of relations between paternalists and liberals were the "Community Councils," corporatist prototypes established in 1968 in the province of Córdoba by officers close to Onganía (*La Nación*, May 19, p. 6, and December 24, p. 1, 1968). But as *Economic Survey* expressed, the conflicts between the "corporatists" and "democrats" in the BA did not revolve around the issue of the return to political democracy: "The first task is to correct the fundamental distortions

Other liberal currents were also beginning to receive close attention. Alsogaray's dismissal and related events added resonance to the views of Admiral Isaac Rojas (vice president from 1955 to 1958), who from his pedestal of extreme anti-Peronism warned of the convergence of Onganía's corporatist tendencies and the Peronist affiliations of his interlocutors in the unions.[7] More important, however, were the activities of General Aramburu, who proposed a "civil-military front" that would pursue a "democratic solution" for the country.[8] Meanwhile, Daniel Paladino, Perón's "personal delegate" and newly appointed Secretary-General of Justicialism (the Peronist political party), initiated contacts aimed at the "reappearance of the politicians" that resulted in a series of meetings between Peronists and Radicals.[9]

Let us pause to consider the meaning of these episodes. The dismissal of the commanders in chief marked a point at which several tensions converged. One involved the considerable portion of the media that supported Alsogaray prior to his removal and endorsed the statements he made afterwards, all the while escalating their attacks on the corporatists in government. Another had to do with the complex processes within the CGT. Initially, the most important of these was the appearance of the *CGT de los Argentinos*. Despite its rapid loss of affiliates, this organization demonstrated the potential for protest beneath the oft-proclaimed "order." The focus later shifted to the struggle between the Vandorists and participationists for control of the *CGT-Azopardo*, which by the end of 1968 had secured the membership of the great majority of unions. Tensions also emerged from incipient phenomena that signaled a major break with the past: the radicalization of various sectors of the Catholic Church, local workers' activity under the leadership of left-wing activists, and the resumption of active contacts among the political parties. Finally, it was no coincidence that Onganía's above-mentioned announcement of the "imminent beginning" of the social phase came only a few days before Alsogaray's forced retirement and the storm of concerns it elicited.

---

that hinder the [economic] development of the nation. No constitutional government can do this as well as the government of the Argentine Revolution is doing it. This is a well-known fact abroad and has greatly contributed to the recovery of the prestige [Argentina] lost 25 years ago. . . . [Merely announcing the intention to return at some point to a constitutional government] would deal a fatal blow to the tasks of the present government, interrupt economic development and foster the resurrection of leftist demagoguery" (August 23, 1968, p. 8). Nor did Krieger Vasena wish to confuse matters; see his diatribes against "electoralism" in *Política económica*, vol. 2, p. 47.

Underlying this baroque polemic between corporatists who called themselves democratic and democrats who relegated elections and political parties to an indefinite future, two fundamental issues were at stake: first, whether the paternalists would move decisively toward realizing their corporatist and redistributive goals; and second, whether they would be able to obtain the support they needed to make such action effective. The first issue was the crucial one. The upper bourgeoisie, together with their allies in the government and the media, worried less that the paternalists would achieve their aims than that merely by trying to do so they would destroy what really mattered: the economic stability and growth that had been achieved under Krieger Vasena's leadership. According to these actors, conflict between the liberals and the paternalists had resulted in a "lack of institutional definition" that threatened to replace the "social peace" and high profits they were currently enjoying with the fluctuations and uncertainties of the previous period.* To underline their support for Krieger Vasena, on November 18, 1968, the organizations of the upper bourgeoisie paid collective tribute to the Economy Minister.† On the other side, the President had just announced that wage policy was "being studied"[10] in anticipation of the impending expiration of the wage freeze imposed at the beginning of Krieger Vasena's term in office. That the issue went beyond wage policy to the future of the whole economic program was apparent from the statements of union leaders, whose demands included a return to the system of collective bargaining. A return to sector-by-sector negotiations would give the unions far more leverage than they enjoyed under present conditions, where they confronted a government that since March 1967 had set wage levels and working conditions unilaterally.

Meanwhile, the leading periodicals turned their attention to the "rapprochement" between the paternalists and participationists, placing it in the context of the "corporatism" debate and noting that contacts between the two currents "confuse the political panorama [at a time when] a coherent and determined effort is being made to achieve eco-

---

*It was also argued that this lack of definition posed an obstacle to attracting long-term foreign loans and investments (*Economic Survey*, March 21, 1968, p. 1).

†*La Nación*, November 19, 1968, p. 1. Among the organizations represented at this meeting were the ACIEL, the CAC, the UIA, the Buenos Aires Stock Market, the Interamerican Council on Trade and Production (CICYP), and the FIEL. Even the SRA was present; in spite of its conflicts with the economic team, it knew well where it stood when it came to the alternative possibility.

nomic recovery."* At issue was the balance of forces that set the general direction of social and economic policy. Should the paternalists succeed in co-opting the CGT, they would acquire what they previously had lacked: a base of support in society upon which to pursue their goals for the social phase. The paternalists' impossible search for submissive but "authentically representative" labor bosses pointed out the incongruencies of their ideology, but it also marked the objective limits of the situation itself. Vandorism, though willing to negotiate, was unlikely to be a docile ally. Despite their overt and covert attempts to become the paternalists' recognized interlocutors,[11] the Vandorists obviously intended to exchange their support for something more substantial than an opportunity to provide the "technical and apolitical advice" that constituted the paternalists' definition of participation.† The participationists, on the other hand, could hardly be expected to become representative. The tide might turn toward Vandorism or toward the tempest that was forming around more radical currents, but it would not be restrained by collaborationists prepared to renounce politics and to accept with gratitude whatever benefits the paternalists might grant during the social phase. Consequently, the paternalists' efforts to deliver the CGT into the hands of the participationists‡ did little more than strengthen the Vandorists.

The upper bourgeoisie and the liberals needed no organized support from the unions. Their goal, as has already been noted, was rather to atomize the working class, to eliminate the Law of Professional Associations, and to establish "free" unions to which neither workers nor employers would be required to contribute. Without such reforms, there would be, in their view, no end to the threat that an excessively power-

---

*La Nación, April 14, 1968, p. 6. The following day, La Nación again demanded the repeal of the Law of Professional Associations and the restoration of "freedom of association" (p. 6). Similar demands are reported in La Nación, April 21, p. 6, and June 23, p. 6, 1968.

†Onganía pursued this theme doggedly: "The participation we advocate is technical, concerned with studying problems. . . that are neither political nor rhetorical" (at a meeting with participationist union leaders; La Nación, February 1, 1969, p. 1). "It is necessary to organize the community by means of programs that are very well orchestrated from the technical standpoint. This will enable us to establish liaisons with these organizations [of the community] and collect advice for government decisions" (La Nación, January 24, 1969, p. 1).

‡These efforts included Onganía's above-mentioned refusal to meet with the (Vandorist) CGT leadership, the government's inspection of union accounts (which turned up numerous "irregularities"; La Nación, November 6, 1968, p. 1), and the appointment by the government of a "normalizing delegate" to serve as a virtual superintendant of the CGT.

ful popular sector had posed for the past two decades. The upper bourgeoisie, momentarily defeated when Onganía prevailed over Alsogaray,
retained a basic line of defense in the Economy Ministry and another in
Lanusse, the new army commander in chief. For the moment, however,
the dismissal of Alsogaray gave the paternalists a reprieve from the
possibility of a liberal coup, which reinforced their illusions of "organizing the community."

In 1968, as we have seen, the economy resumed a high rate of
growth, and several indicators gave a promising outlook for the future.
Despite the turbulence in both CGTs and unrest among workers and
students in certain regions of the interior, strikes and other forms of
protest had also subsided. Why, then, if everything was going so well,
were such conflicts taking place within the BA and among the social
sectors allied with it? The reason is that both paternalists and liberals,
precisely because everything was going so well, prepared to king their
pieces and, in so doing, revealed that they were heading toward different sides of the board. The reduction of inflation, the improvement in
the balance of payments, and the government's improved fiscal situation suggested to the paternalists that the time was nearly ripe not only
for a more just distribution of resources but also for the implantation of
a comprehensive corporatist scheme. In order to achieve these goals,
Onganía said that "authentic representatives" would have to emerge
among the bourgeoisie as well as the workers and demonstrate a willingness to "amalgamate" their respective classes, imbued with a "spirit of
solidarity," into a staunchly paternalist state. On the other side, the goal
of the liberals and the upper bourgeoisie was to remove the remaining
political obstacles to the continuity of the economic and social domination they had reconstituted through the implantation of the BA. The
paternalists were viewed as the main such obstacle within the state
apparatus. In terms of class relations, the major impediment was perceived to be the organizational network of unionism, which in spite of
the blows it had suffered since early 1967 still seemed capable of reactivating the popular sector in directions antagonistic to the BA.

2. NEW PROBLEMS AND PROLEGOMENA
   TO THE EXPLOSION

With Alsogaray dismissed and Onganía temporarily free from the
danger of a liberal coup, the tensions outlined in the preceding para-
graphs crystallized around the issue of the wage and salary increases

that were due in December 1968. By announcing that collective bargaining would be restored by the end of 1969, Onganía managed to convince the upper bourgeoisie not only that the social phase was about to begin but also that he had no intention of doing away with one of the most effective and unifying resources available to the unions for negotiating wages and working conditions. Nonetheless, and in spite of rumors that Onganía was considering granting wage hikes larger than those proposed by the economic team, the increase finally decreed was so small that it failed to restore most real wages and salaries to their 1966 levels.[12] In the context of the paternalists' overtures to the unions and announcements that the social phase was about to begin, the upper bourgeoisie took this meager wage and salary hike not as a sign of Onganía's reasonableness, but as evidence that they had won an important victory, because Onganía could not do without Krieger Vasena and his team. For the Vandorists and participationists, on the other hand, the government's decision represented a clear defeat on the issue of most immediate concern to the rank and file of the unions they controlled. This defeat placed them in a difficult position that was further complicated by the reduced but persistent action of the *CGT de los Argentinos,* the radicalization of some sectors of the Catholic Church, the worker and student unrest in Córdoba, and a surge of wildcat strikes. It would not be long before the leaders of the CGT would have to pay as much attention to these trends as they did to their relations with the government. In controlling the national union apparatus at a time when a considerable part of the population did not appreciate the fine distinctions they made between Onganía and Krieger Vasena, the Vandorists and participationists stood in danger of opening a deep rift between themselves and their social bases. Accordingly, it was not just the *CGT de los Argentinos* but also the *CGT-Azopardo* that closed out the year with bitter criticisms of the wage and salary increases, though the latter was careful to hint that it might still be willing to reach an understanding with the paternalists.[13]

A few weeks later Onganía, always evenhanded, met first with members of the upper bourgeoisie, before whom he reiterated a number of time-worn themes,* and then with participationists, to whom he again expressed his support for a "strong" CGT (although not one with the

---

*See Onganía's speech in *La Nación,* January 24, 1969, p. 1, in which he again stressed the necessity of "reorganizing [the state and the entire] community in accordance with technical criteria," and repeated that the Revolution was "still [far from] the political phase."

"mark [of the] immediate past . . . in which there was an exaggerated preponderance of politics") that would also be "ready to participate." According to Onganía, participation had not yet occurred "because of the workers' lack of organization"[14]—which flatly contradicted what the liberals and the upper bourgeoisie thought of the matter. If the bourgeoisie needed additional evidence that Onganía's decisions on wages and salaries did not reflect a change in his overall goals, they received it when he announced that he would hold another meeting with the participationists to discuss the future economic plan. The participationist leaders made positive comments on the meeting, but their attendance was criticized by the Vandorists and harshly condemned by the CGT de los Argentinos and the classist unions. The participationists thus emerged from the meeting linked more closely than ever to the paternalists, but farther than ever from their own class and even from the Vandorist CGT-Azopardo. The Vandorist leaders, for their part, realizing that any collaborationist move with Onganía would be lethal so long as he remained unable to break with the economic team, were anxious to increase their support among a popular sector that was moving toward a full-fledged confrontation with the BA. Accordingly, they seized the occasion of May 1, 1969 (Labor Day), to issue tough statements calling for opposition to a government that sheltered within its economic apparatus persons who "starved" the pueblo, increased unemployment, and "sold out the national patrimony to [foreign] monopolies."[15]

As of April 1969 the paternalists had still not managed to co-opt more than the handful of unions associated with participationism. What limited them was that the BA was not viable without the confidence of an upper bourgeoisie that, drawing on the lessons of past decades, wanted the CGT disbanded and the unions atomized, not integrated into a comprehensive corporatist scheme that would also envelop their own organizations. Given their dependence on the upper bourgeoisie, the paternalists' corporatist illusions served only to underscore the archaic character of their ideology. The paternalists' political isolation, their fading influence in the armed forces, and the insufficiency of their entrenchment in the state apparatus were revealed as it became evident that the labor bosses and "apolitical politicians" they had tried to invent could at most gain control of organizations which, as a result of that control, were transformed into empty shells. Such unsuccessful efforts were costly in that they reinforced the hostility of the upper bourgeoisie and their allies toward the paternalists and their goals.

Several factors contributed to make 1968 a year of resurgent militance among university students: an unenlightened university administration, increasing discontent among the middle sectors, the radicalizing impact of the Theology of Liberation and the Movement of Third World Priests, and student hopes for a radical alliance with the new union currents. It was in this climate, also influenced by the events of the late 1960s in the United States and Western Europe, that guerrilla activity was born.* Tensions mounted on May 15, 1969, when a university student was killed by the police in a demonstration in the city of Corrientes. Protest spread quickly to other universities. In Rosario the death of another student sparked an uprising that spread through many parts of the city.[16]

May 1969 also saw a series of governmental errors that resulted in the withdrawal of various benefits enjoyed by industrial workers in Córdoba, Argentina's second-largest city and the principal site of classist unionism. On May 15, students and workers in Córdoba engaged in fierce confrontations with the police. The next day a general strike was called. The student movement in Córdoba, which had opposed the BA since the 1966 coup, rapidly gained momentum as news arrived of the demonstrations in other cities. These events culminated in the "Cordobazo" of May 28 and 29, when workers, allied with students and other middle sectors, launched a mass uprising. Assailed by rocks, Molotov cocktails, and an inflamed multitude, the police retreated, and the insurrection took over most of the city, focusing its attacks on targets whose symbolic implications escaped nobody: property of the government and of transnational corporations. The rebellion was not suppressed until the army forcibly occupied the city.†

---

*See Table 57 for monthly data on guerrilla activity. La Nación, April 12, p. 8; April 22, p. 4; and May 6, 1969, p. 20, gives reports and alarmed commentary on these episodes. Just a few days before the great urban explosions of May 1969, Borda stated that the emergence of guerrilla activity "[has] not in any way marred the image of order and tranquility emanating from the government of the Argentine Revolution" (La Nación, April 22, 1969, p. 8).

†The data in chapter 9 will permit us to examine how the popular challenges to the BA varied by region and social class. The focus of this book does not permit a full treatment of the local, national, and international factors that contributed to the Cordobazo. A number of studies afford an overview of this theme; see Francisco Delich, Crisis y protesta social, Córdoba 1969–1973 (Buenos Aires: Siglo XXI, 1974); Beva Balvé et al., Lucha de calles—lucha de clases. Elementos para su análisis (Córdoba 1969–1971) (Buenos Aires: Editorial La Rosa Blindada, 1972); Oscar Moreno, "La coyuntura política argentina de 1966 a 1970 y los movimientos populares reivindicativos de carácter regional," paper presented at a seminar on "The Regional Issue in Latin America," Mexico City, 1978; Ernesto Laclau, "Argentina: Anti-Imperialist Struggles and the May Crisis," New Left Review 62 (1970); Raúl Ávila, "El Cordobazo: la violencia y sus protagonistas," Papers no. 1, 1973. A good journalistic account is Siete Días Ilustrados, edición extra, May 1969. For reports on these episodes from organizations expressing solidarity with them, see Cristianismo y revolución, no. 18, July 10–15, 1969, and De Frente, 2nd phase, 1, no. 5, May 30, 1974.

The Cordobazo demolished the myth of order and authority. It also dealt a shattering blow to the upper bourgeoisie's confidence that the BA would be able to guarantee their long-term social domination. What did not happen in Brazil or Uruguay, what has not happened in Chile, and what happened to a more limited extent in Greece (leading in short order to the fall of the regime of the colonels) had mortally wounded the Argentine BA. From that moment on, the story of the successes and ambiguities associated with the emergence of this BA became the story of its demise.

As we have seen in preceding chapters, in all cases where the proponents of orthodoxy within the BA have tried to normalize the economy around the expansion of its most dynamic and transnationalized sectors, they have done so against the immediate interests not only of the popular sector but also of a good many middle sectors and of the weakest factions of the local bourgeoisie. The normalization of these capitalisms cannot fail to introduce reforms more efficientist and drastic than those a good part of the local bourgeoisie would like to see implemented. At the same time, policies aimed at rationalizing the public sector, reducing the fiscal deficit, and cutting back on state subsidies create severe hardships for many in the middle sectors. As typically attempted under the BAs, normalization creates profound disruptions for the entire society, including a substantial part of the local dominant classes, both urban and agrarian. In words more agreeable to the paternalists, the mission of this peculiar normalization is to restructure society (destroying or subordinating in the process its weakest capitalist segments) before reintegrating it into a new and stricter subordination to the state apparatus and the largest factions of capital.

Since normalization constitutes an attack on the interests of such broad segments of society, it is a formidable and uncertain task even for those who wield power as impressive as that concentrated in the BA. Nevertheless, the interests on which normalization tramples are not motivated automatically into political action. Social actors, for various reasons, may be unaware that their interests are in jeopardy. Even if aware, they may be incapable of converting this awareness into action. And even if they act in defense of their interests, they may do so outside of a framework of alliances that could make their opposition effective. To overcome the first obstacle, actors must be able to receive and interpret information and to attribute an attack on their interests to something other than fate or chance. Overcoming the second obstacle supposes the capacity to coordinate and allocate resources—information, leadership, money—for sustained collective action. The third obstacle poses the further requirement that diverse political actors, who may diagnose the situation in different ways and be oriented toward different medium-range goals, discern nonetheless a common adversary whose defeat is perceived by each to be necessary for its interests.[17]

A major impediment to overcoming the first and second obstacles is fear. Fear is a function of the level of threat that precedes each BA. To the extent that the prior crisis raises the specter of the abolition of capitalism, the bourgeoisie and various middle sectors will, at least in the short and medium run, consider the eradication of this threat to be sufficient compensation for the damage their immediate economic interests suffer after the BA is implanted. Moreover, a high level of threat implies that a significant part of the popular sector has adopted anticapitalist goals. For the bourgeoisie, opposition to the BA under these circumstances would mean allying with actors that have recently challenged their most fundamental interest as a class.

Threat and the fear that accompanies it have another consequence. The greater the threat prior to the implantation of the BA, the greater tends to be the subsequent repression and the government's willingness to apply it. By comparing the moderate level of repression in the case analyzed here with the higher level in Brazil and the even higher levels applied in post-1973 Chile and Uruguay and in post-1976 Argentina, it is possible to discern a crescendo of threat culminating, as discussed in chapter 1, in a crisis of social domination. High repression dismantles the organizations of the popular sector, increases the difficulty of creating new ones, and, more generally, raises the threshold for attempting collective action in opposition to the BA despite the hardships experienced by a broad range of sectors. The post-1966 Argentine case also suggests that a relatively mild previous threat can leave room in the BA for illusions of more or less immediate social integration. Such illusions can lead to delays and vacillation in applying coercion, in sharp contrast with the harshness that paternalists, nationalists, and liberals alike have shown in cases of significantly higher previous threat.

Finally, the achievement of the third condition for concerted action—the detection of common adversaries and mutual interests that prevail over longer-term differences—is also heavily influenced by the level of prior threat. The fundamental class interest of the bourgeoisie is not economic. It is to assure the existence of the political conditions that can guarantee its reproduction as a class. This basic interest is usually little in evidence, but it emerges with clarity when a crisis of social domination makes the subordinate classes a concrete threat to the very existence of the bourgeoisie as a class. In such situations, which are historically exceptional,* the bourgeoisie converge around their fundamental class interest, even when such an alignment runs against the economic interests of several or all of the fractions that constitute this class.† Furthermore, in terms of the direct relations between classes, the reestablishment of "order" by the BA rewards the bourgeoisie with the restoration of strict control over the workplace. The BA thus exposes itself in its basic condition as a state that guarantees the reproduction of social domination and, therefore, of the bourgeoisie as the dominant class. Consequently, when the crisis is at the very heart of social domination (as was the case prior to the implantation of the BAs of the 1970s), the bourgeoisie and the middle sectors are less willing, and take longer, to ally with the popular sector in opposition to the BA, even though the economic interests of many fractions of these classes and sectors may have been damaged severely.

A different pattern prevails in situations such as Argentina prior to 1966, where the crisis was mainly one of accumulation rather than social domination. In these circumstances the popular sector is not perceived as the immediate and purposeful bearer of a fundamental threat. The road is therefore open to an easier and more rapid alliance among all classes and sectors whose interests are affected negatively by the policies of the BA. But the breadth of this alliance imposes limits on its goals, which tend to revolve around a redistributionist revision of capitalism. Insofar as the goals of the alliance exceed these limits, its bourgeois and middle-sector components swing back toward the upper bourgeoisie, or the most radicalized sectors of the alliance are expelled in order to conserve its bourgeois component. The course of events in Argentina will allow us to examine this alternative.

I have argued that the implantation of the BA entails in all cases the crossing of a threshold marked by a significant level of crisis and consequent threat. A period (longer or shorter, according to the level of the preceding crisis) elapses before concerted oppositional actions are launched, during which the government finds itself in a political vacuum: indifference or discontent that is generalized but politically atom-

---

*But they are not alien to the European experience at the time of the emergence of fascism or to the South American situation prior to the coups of the 1970s.

†This choice, of course, involves both objective and subjective dimensions. There is little doubt that perceptions of the imminent collapse of society *qua* capitalist are usually exaggerated, in part by the fears generated by the crisis and in part by psychological action taken by those attempting to suppress it.

ized, and therefore impotent. On the one hand, given the conditions in which it has emerged, this vacuum provides the liberals and the upper bourgeoisie with the best possible conditions for carrying out economic normalization. On the other hand, as we have seen, this vacuum entails for the BA and its allies the risk of unexpected explosions which can reverse whatever successes may have been achieved during the period of order and tacit consensus. But this political vacuum, as long as it lasts, indicates the high degree of autonomy that the BA achieves with respect to most of society.

NOTES

1. For outlines of this "maximum program" see CAC, *La Nación*, March 28, p. 16, and December 21, pp. 1, 10, 1968; ACIEL, *La Nación*, October 10, 1968, pp. 1, 14; and UIA, *La Nación*, December 5, 1968, pp. 1, 20, and *Memoria Anual, 1968–1969* (Buenos Aires, 1969).

2. On these strikes and demonstrations see *La Nación*, May 2, p. 20; June 29, p. 1; October 18, p. 1; and November 11, p. 6, 1968. *La Nación*, December 11, 1968, p. 12, gives a clear picture of the decline of this organization.

3. *La Nación*, April 5, 1968, p. 10.

4. *La Nación*, August 13, 1968, p. 1.

5. *La Nación*, August 14, 1968, p. 11.

6. Statements in *La Nación*, August 31, 1968, pp. 1, 4.

7. Speech in *La Nación*, September 19, 1968, p. 10.

8. See *La Nación*, December 8, 1968, p. 6.

9. See *Primera Plana*, all issues of May and June, 1968. On Paladino's appointment as Secretary-General of Justicialism, see *La Nación*, May 21, 1968, p. 4.

10. *La Nación*, November 9, 1968, p. 1.

11. The existence of such efforts was reported in my interviews with Vandorists and paternalists.

12. See *La Nación*, December 24, 1968, p. 1, and the wage and salary data in chapter 4.

13. *La Nación*, December 30, 1968, p. 6.

14. *La Nación*, February 10, 1969, p. 6.

15. *Crónica*, May 2, 1969, pp. 5, 7.

16. *La Nación*, May 16, p. 1, and May 18, pp. 1, 24, 1969.

17. These considerations are inspired by Robert Dahl, *Modern Political Analysis* (Englewood Cliffs, N.J.: Prentice-Hall, 1969).

SIX

Crisis and Collapse

1. INITIAL REACTIONS TO THE CORDOBAZO

It would be hard to exaggerate the impact of the Cordobazo and the other protests of April and May 1969.* These massive uprisings in Argentina's major urban centers both expressed and intensified tensions that had been accumulating since the implantation of the BA. The

*To understand why the Cordobazo caused stunned surprise, it is useful to recall David Apter's observations in *Choice and the Politics of Allocation*. Apter notes that in a "bureaucratic regime"—which corresponds closely to the BA—the government and its allies suppress the channels of popular representation at the cost of losing information about the excluded sectors and the tendencies emerging within them. Accordingly, those who control the BA (behind its facade of power) remain vulnerable to dramatic surprises like the Cordobazo and have serious problems in implementing policies that require any cooperation from the excluded sectors. It is worth noting that events similar to those in Argentina in May 1969 preceded the fall of the Greek BA. Cf. Nikifouros Diamandouros, "The 1974 Transition from Authoritarian Rule in Greece: Background and Interpretation from a Southern European Perspective," in *Transitions from Authoritarian Rule*, ed. O'Donnell, Schmitter and Whitehead. Important (if less dramatic) surprises have accompanied even the partial reopening of the electoral arena to an opposition whose vote-getting capacity turns out to exceed all calculations. Argentina in 1973 (as we shall see in chapter 10) is a case in point, but an even clearer example is provided by the 1974 elections in Brazil. See Fernando H. Cardoso and Bolivar Lamounier, *Os Partidos e as Eleicões no Brasil* (Río de Janeiro: Paz e Terra, 1975), and Amaury de Souza and Bolivar Lamounier, "Governo e Sindicatos no Brasil: a Perspetiva dos anos 80," in *Dados* 24, no. 2, 1981. Sometimes the cost of these severe information losses is recognized by the BA's more perceptive leaders. This theme appears, for example, in the writings of General Alejandro Lanusse (*Mi Testimonio* [Buenos Aires: Editorial Laserre, 1977]) and in the lecture delivered by General Golbery de Couto e Silva to the Superior War College in Brazil ("Conjuntura Política Nacional: O Poder Executivo," Superior War College Publication T 202–80, Río de Janeiro, 1980).

Cordobazo showed in one spectacular blow that the order and the social peace the BA was supposed to guarantee had evaporated. The activity of the pre-1966 period was resumed with unprecedented force and aggressiveness, demolishing the argument that tacit consensus or a "longing for authority" could justify the BA.

Immediately after the Cordobazo, the BA's allies faced two options: they could abandon illusions of consensus, regroup, and try to impose social stability through systematic and much harsher repression, or they could offer selective benefits to the segments of society that they took to be indispensable supports for the new wave of opposition. A requisite for the first option was a high degree of cohesion among and within the upper bourgeoisie, the armed forces, and the government—at a time when the Cordobazo had shaken severely their tenuous cohesion. But the second option meant opening the BA to many of the sectors that had been excluded since 1966, a prospect that raised serious doubts about the continuity of normalization and risked antagonizing the upper bourgeoisie, the major social base of the BA. Both solutions were attempted. The result, as we shall see, was a dynamic very different from the one so far analyzed.

The BA's now-numerous adversaries saw the Cordobazo as a justified reaction to accumulated grievances. Since mass uprisings and collective violence had proved so effective in pummeling the BA, more than a few—the guerrilla groups prominent among them—favored continuing these forms of struggle. Guerrilla activity, for the most part, emerged after, not before, the Cordobazo.* Except in Córdoba itself, the events of May 1969 were less the culmination of an ongoing process than the starting point for new forms of protest and armed struggle that were much more active and violent than those practiced before 1966. This protest and violence would soon become part of the peculiar normality of Argentine politics.†

Sectors that had fought for access to the government—the CGE, the

---

*As noted in the preceding chapters, some guerrilla activity occurred during March and April 1969. Guerrilla organizations, however, do not seem to have played a role in the Cordobazo. On the other hand, the episodes in Rosario and Córdoba, by demonstrating popular willingness to engage in violent actions that many perceived as harbingers of revolution, stimulated the formation of several guerrilla organizations, including those that subsequently dominated this terrain. The role of the Cordobazo in catalyzing the formation of these guerrilla organizations was recognized in several of their publications, esp. *Militancia* 1, no. 3, June 28, 1973; *De Frente*, 2nd phase, no. 5, July 1973; and *Nuevo Hombre*, no. 24, January 11, 1972.

†Augusto Vandor's assassination shortly after the Cordobazo had enormous repercussions, as did other violent events to be examined later; see *La Nación*, July 1, 1969, pp. 1, 22.

participationists, and, despite their peculiarities, the Vandorists—attributed the Cordobazo to a "liberal" social and economic program that lacked "social content" and was conducive to "denationalization." These sectors favored a version of national development that would restrict, but not eliminate, the role of transnational capital,* a goal that implied replacing Krieger Vasena's team with another more congruent with the nationalist and populist—and often authoritarian—views of those sectors. The social base for this project would be an alliance among the armed forces, the workers, and the national entrepreneurs. It was clear, however, that neither the CGE nor the CGT wanted to pursue the radicalized path of those who, after the Cordobazo, engaged in violent struggles to overthrow the BA. The CGE and the CGT sought instead to use the repercussions of recent events to achieve a new and more advantageous accommodation with the BA, which entailed their participation in defeating the radical movements that followed the upheavals of May 1969.†

The leading periodicals and the upper bourgeoisie diagnosed the situation very differently. They too blamed the government for the Cordobazo and the subsequent wave of conflict and violence. But the problem, in their view, was that public policies had not gone far enough: rather than carrying out the maximum program of the upper bourgeoisie, the corporatists and nationalists within the BA had obstructed economic policy and had "vacillated" in their dealings with the unions. This had created a "political vacuum" conducive to subversion and insolent popular demands.[1] Accordingly, the leading periodicals and the upper bourgeoisie added to their maximum program a call for the full application of whatever repression proved necessary to extirpate the resurgent threat. Though they used the rhetoric of democracy (which they counterposed to the "totalitarianism" of the corporatists in the government and of those who had led the recent explosions of opposition), they were careful to stress that their aim was to "clarify the ultimate goals of the Revolution," not to call elections with "undue

---

*Such themes (as noted in chapter 5) had already been stressed by several national union organizations. The CGE, as we have also seen, had raised similar issues since 1967; see its *Memoria Anual, 1968–1969* and *1969–1970*, Buenos Aires. A synthesis of the CGE's position may be found in the interview with José Gelbard, "Three Years of Discouragement," *Confirmado*, April 8, 1970, p. 6.

†In June 1969, the CGE indicated its conciliatory stance by publicly inviting the government to engage in an "institutional dialogue with the participation of all representative organizations." "The CGE," it stated, "is ready as always to begin this great dialogue, which is aimed at achieving a 'Pact of National Construction and Pacification' " (*Cronista Comercial*, June 28, 1969, p. 6).

haste."[2] The urgency in their demands conveyed their perception that the problem was no longer one of consolidating gains, but of recovering lost ground and of setting things straight before the tendencies unleashed by the Cordobazo destroyed the achievements of 1967–69. Time was running out for everyone.

There had emerged with the Cordobazo an active and multiform opposition that thoroughly condemned the BA. But the classes and organizations unwilling to hurl themselves into the abyss of all-out opposition embarked on an effort to rescue the BA, each hoping to improve its position relative to the others. In so doing, however, they resurrected the conflicts inherent in the distinction between the government and its economic policies. Some sharply condemned those policies; others supported them and tried to fashion a government that would place fewer restrictions on their implementation. The agonies of the BA were prolonged by the impasses reached by the supporters of these alternative projects. To understand these conflicts we must analyze their relationship to the reactivation of the popular sector and the growth of political violence. Between June 1967 and April 1969, the popular sector had played a relatively minor role in conflicts among the BA's allies. But after the Cordobazo, the popular sector—and new forms of political action—began to exert a profound influence on the overall trajectory of the BA.

Onganía's first response to the Cordobazo was to condemn it vehemently and to announce severe sanctions against those who had taken part in it.* The paternalists reacted with stunned surprise to events so inconsistent with the tacit consensus and desire for authority they evidently had come to believe existed among the population.† Along with their paralysis, the Cordobazo implied disaster for those whose role in the BA was to preserve "social peace."

One immediate consequence of the Cordobazo was the resignation of several high officials, including Borda and Krieger Vasena. Borda was replaced by retired General Francisco Imaz, who was as much a corporatist as his predecessor and no less a paternalist than the president. To complicate matters further, Imaz had served on active duty during Perón's second presidency (1952–55) and was believed to have retained his Peronist sympathies. Onganía viewed Imaz's background as

---

*La Nación, June 5, 1969, pp. 1, 22. Law 18,234 was enacted the same day, broadening the applicability of the law for the "repression of communism" and increasing the penalties for violating it.

†Evidence for this reaction comes from my interviews, but it can easily be inferred from the public behavior of Onganía and other paternalists.

an asset, since he was now more than ever intent on controlling a unionism which for the most part claimed to be loyal to Perón. Imaz's sympathies, however, made him less than acceptable to the liberals, especially to the commander in chief of the army, General Alejandro Lanusse, who had spent four years in prison under Perón and was considered one of the most bitter opponents of Peronism. It was over the objections of the commanders in chief that Imaz was named Minister of the Interior. With his less than skillful conduct in office he remained a permanent source of friction with top military officers and an inviting target for attacks against the paternalists.

As successor to Krieger Vasena Onganía chose José María Dagnino Pastore. The new Economy Minister was not a member of the liberal establishment, but neither was he close to the CGE or the unions. Much more than his predecessor, Dagnino Pastore was an authentic *técnico*. His reputation as a capable economist had been made primarily in academic circles, and he had few contacts in the world of the upper bourgeoisie. Most of his appointees had backgrounds similar to his own, which meant that the new economic team boasted an array of doctorates from the world's most prestigious universities. Its problem was that while its policies differed little from those of its predecessor, it lacked two assets that Krieger Vasena and his team had enjoyed: easy and direct contacts with the upper bourgeoisie* and, more important, the confidence of that class in the future of Argentina.

A second and closely related consequence of the Cordobazo was that it demolished the confidence of the upper bourgeoisie. The preceding chapters have stressed the importance of the BA's role in guaranteeing the order that gives the upper bourgeoisie sufficient confidence to participate in—and benefit from—economic normalization. The Cordobazo demonstrated the BA's inability to maintain that order,† and the

---

*This point was stressed by many of the businessmen I interviewed. Dagnino Pastore and his collaborators gave them little cause for complaint, but as one of my interviewees put it, "things were just no longer the same." Krieger Vasena (as could also be said for most of his collaborators) had been one of them: someone they had known personally for a long time, with whom they socialized, and to whom they had easy access. Dagnino Pastore and his team, in the words of these businessmen, were "intellectuals" and "professors," undoubtedly "capable" and "well-intentioned," but lacking "sufficient contacts."

†Not long after the Cordobazo, another spectacular riot occurred in Rosario, where a mass uprising again overwhelmed the police and forced the army to intervene. On other such urban "explosions," see Lidia Aufgang, "Las puebladas; dos casos de protesta social. Las ciudades de Cipolletti y Casilda," CICSO, *Serie Estudios* no. 37 (Buenos Aires: 1979). On the enormous impact of these events, which seemed to confirm all the fears raised by the Cordobazo, see *Panorama*, September 23, 1969, pp. 6–10, and *Análisis*, September 30, 1969, pp. 7–9.

sudden eruption of an opposition of formidable strength and scope augured poorly for its capacity to maintain it in the future.

Various economic indicators reflected the erosion of confidence that followed the Cordobazo. There were serious doubts about the future stability of the peso. In 1969, exporting firms, despite an increase in their foreign exchange revenues, sold US$112 million less on the foreign exchange market than they had in 1968. Moreover, the demand for cash dollars on that market rose 34 percent over 1968. Negative expectations were also presumably responsible for an otherwise inexplicable increase in remittances abroad in payment for real services (which increased from US$116 million in 1968 to US$320 million in 1969) and for financial services and other undetermined capital movements (from US$587 million in 1968 to US$845 million in 1969). Significantly, all of these changes occurred after the Cordobazo; the patterns of these indicators in the first months of 1969 resembled those of 1968. The net result of these changes was to reduce the foreign exchange reserves of the Central Bank from US$665 million by the end of May to US$605 million in June and US$446 million at the end of 1969. Negative expectations were also reflected on the futures market for foreign currencies. In spite of the government's decision to raise the premium on the dollar significantly above the level of inflation, the demand for U.S. dollars on the foreign exchange futures market forced the Central Bank to commit US$115 million to future sales.[3]

Another indication of the erosion of confidence was the sharp reversal in the balance of short-term foreign capital flows. The positive balance of US$69 million for the first quarter of 1969 suggested a continuation of the positive balances achieved during the two previous years (US$268 million in 1968 and US$150 million in 1967). By contrast, the outflow of short-term funds after the Cordobazo resulted in a negative balance of US$44 million for the second quarter of the year.[4] Negative balances were also recorded in the third and fourth quarters of 1969 (US$66 million and US$37 million respectively), and the year ended with a negative balance of US$57 million.* Another sign that the Cordobazo had undermined confidence was the interruption of long-term foreign capital flows. The positive balance of US$52 million for 1969 was only slightly below the US$56 million balance of 1968, but

*The sources of these figures are given in chapter 8. Economy Minister Carlos Moyano Llerena later estimated that the Cordobazo was responsible for a net capital flight amounting to nearly US$1 billion, a figure that is probably more realistic than the official ones given above.

virtually all the long-term foreign capital invested in Argentina during 1969 resulted from transactions concluded prior to the Cordobazo.*

Other economic variables less closely connected to the sensitive foreign exchange market reacted in similar ways. Interest rates were driven up by the restrictive monetary policies adopted after the Cordobazo in an effort to curtail foreign currency speculation and to discourage further capital flight. The interest rate for thirty-day bank loans, which in the days preceding the Cordobazo had dropped to 17.7 percent per annum (its low for the period), had risen by the end of the year to 22.6 percent.[5] This increase both reflected and stimulated inflationary expectations, which reinforced the above-mentioned trends in the foreign currency market. Negative expectations also manifested themselves on the stock exchange: demand rose sharply for government bonds with guaranteed adjustments for inflation and declined for bonds and securities that lacked such provisions.†

From a more structural perspective, the Cordobazo and its sequels produced a significant break in what had been a growing rate of investment. Investment in machinery and equipment grew by 6.2 percent in the first quarter of 1969 and by 20.0 percent in the second quarter, but it fell in the third quarter by 5.8 percent and recovered in the fourth quarter by only 0.6 percent. Owing to these trends and to a decline in private construction investment, the overall figures for gross domestic investment for the four quarters of 1969 were 3.9 percent, 13.6 percent, 5.8 percent, and −6.5 percent respectively.‡

It would be difficult to argue that each of these changes was due entirely to the Cordobazo. Nevertheless, the timing and consistency of the general pattern strongly suggest that the Cordobazo was a turning

---

*This assertion is based on interviews with members of the economic team inaugurated in June 1969. (Figures for long-term capital flows to Argentina are published on an annual basis only.) In the course of these interviews I was also informed that several TNCs negotiating direct investments withdrew their offers after the Cordobazo, while others hardened their positions. The result was that for one reason or another most of the investments negotiated were not realized. Subsequent offers were few and insignificant.

†On this and related points, see Richard Mallon and Juan Sourrouille, *Economic Policy-Making in a Conflict Society*, p. 216. See also the complaints in various issues of *Economic Survey* about the "speculative hysteria" (June 17, 1969, p. 13) brought on by the Cordobazo.

‡These data are taken from the Ministry of Economy and Labor, *Informe económico 1970*, 4th trimester. As one official source put it, "This deceleration [of investment rates] is attributable to the delayed effect of the expectations of instability that appeared after May 1969. . . . [The fall in the investment rate] cannot but reflect the impact on investment decisions of the expectations that emerged last May in the wake of monetary fluctuations and the modification of the exchange rate" (Ministry of Economy and Labor, *Informe económico 1969*, 4th trimester, pp. 8–38).

point for the confidence of the bourgeoisie, and ultimately for the BA. Even though the new economic team proved able, as we shall see, to soften some of the Cordobazo's consequences, the problem of a deeply shaken confidence remained.

In addition to the changes in top government personnel and the erosion of the confidence of the upper bourgeoisie, another consequence of the Cordobazo was the emergence of broad popular opposition to the BA. Chapters 8 and 10 will examine this process in detail, but a brief sketch here will serve to underline those aspects most important for understanding the demise of the Onganía government. As we have seen, the events of May 1969 belied the impression that the BA rested on the tacit consensus of the population and exploded the belief that the government's social and economic policies were backed by immense power. A largely spontaneous* act of collective violence in Córdoba had overwhelmed the police, forced the army into an arduous intervention, brought on the resignation of Krieger Vasena's team, and conspicuously weakened the cohesion of the government and of its principal allies. For more than a few Argentines, the Cordobazo heralded the appearance of "the people in arms." Many expected—some with apprehension, others with buoyant anticipation—that the final revolutionary onslaught, the "Argentinazo," might be launched at any moment against a government that had been exposed as a paper tiger. This impression was reinforced by other urban riots and political assassinations.

Why wait, then? Why postpone the final assault on the Winter Palace? But, as we have seen, organized and sustained guerrilla activity did not precede the Cordobazo; it resulted from the hyper-radicalized interpretation that was given to this and similar events. The Cordobazo and its sequels were rhapsodized as preludes to an imminent revolution in search of an armed vanguard. A more diffuse but no less decisive lesson drawn from these episodes was that of the supreme efficacy of violence, an outlook which came to be shared not only by guerrillas (and antiguerrillas) but also by union leaders, members of the state apparatus, and a good many intellectuals. As violence began to mount in a dreadful

---

*The sources cited earlier corroborate the view that the Cordobazo was basically a spontaneous action. A number of paternalists later reproached the military authorities of the Córdoba region for having promoted, or at least failed to discourage, the demonstrations that precipitated that great upheaval (my interviews with paternalists). The presumption was that in seeking to alter to their own benefit the balance of forces within the government, the liberal military authorities had fomented disorders with a view toward discrediting the government appointees in the region, who were notoriously close to Onganía. See Roberto Roth, *Los años de Onganía*.

dialectic of reaction and counterreaction, it came to appear to those who used it—whether to promote or to prevent "revolution"—as a just violence in the service of a higher cause that could excuse any horror. Guerrillas attacked businessmen, members of the armed forces, and union leaders;* some unionists turned on guerrillas and even on militants from their own class;† right-wing death squads appeared; and the state's security apparatus began an assault on "subversion" defined so loosely that it threatened to encompass dissent in any form. Each felt its own opinion confirmed by the reactions that its own actions provoked. In this way what appeared initially as a bold expression of the people's grievances unleashed the monstrosity of widespread and ever-increasing violence that would become an element of Argentine daily life. From that point on, there is little that can be understood without taking into account the intense fear, almost always silent or expressed obliquely, that permeated all levels of Argentine society.

2. OTHER REPERCUSSIONS
   OF THE CORDOBAZO AND
   THEIR RELATIONSHIP TO
   PREEXISTING TENSIONS

It is necessary to examine more closely the reactions that the Cordobazo provoked within the armed forces. The nationalists pressed for special advantages and protection for national capital and sought to establish an alliance with union leaders. From a position obviously nostalgic for populism, they advocated a stronger economic role for the state apparatus, the appointment of "nationalist *técnicos*" to the main economic policy-making positions, an end to "economic denationalization," and the realization of the dream of a "union of the *pueblo* and the armed forces" that would marginalize both the "subversives" and the "anti-national" liberals. In the armed forces, some nationalist officers, antagonized by Onganía's appointments of liberals, had been plotting his ouster since early 1967. After the Cordobazo they redoubled their efforts, apparently finding strong support among

---

*Among the union leaders assassinated by guerrillas were Vandor and, shortly thereafter, Alonso. Their killers deemed both of them "enemies of the people" and "lackeys of imperialism."

†Some unions used gangster-like methods to suppress leaders and movements arising from their own bases.

junior officers.* The nationalists would not get their chance until 1970–71, but their initiatives in 1969 placed additional strain on an already fragile situation.

Probably out of fear of jeopardizing their positions in the command of the armed forces, liberal military officers on active duty were careful in expressing their views. But retired liberals such as generals Aramburu and Alsogaray were more impatient. With the support of the leading periodicals, the upper bourgeoisie, and numerous middle sectors that were increasingly sensitive to the negative consequences of government's authoritarianism, these retired generals were obviously intent on forcing the removal of Onganía and the paternalists. The reference to generals Aramburu and Alsogaray suggests a further, extremely important, consequence of the Cordobazo: the emergence of serious disagreements within the upper bourgeoisie and the liberal military current over what course to follow. Before the Cordobazo, when order seemed assured, these actors agreed that normalization had to be completed via the fulfillment of the maximum program of the upper bourgeoisie. They also agreed that implementing this program would soon require a version of the BA unencumbered by paternalists and presided over by a military liberal. The Cordobazo shattered this consensus. In the first place, the ensuing capital flight and decline in private investment made it clear that bourgeois confidence would have to be painstakingly restored before pursuing more ambitious economic goals. Second, the Cordobazo had sharpened dissent within the armed forces over which alliances to maintain and which new ones to forge. The result was that the armed forces lacked the cohesion necessary to apply the harsh and systematic repression that was perceived as necessary for restoring confidence. In this situation, Aramburu and his followers felt that the time was ripe to remove Onganía, call elections previously negotiated with the political parties, and back a presidential candidate for "national unity" (Aramburu himself). This candidate would offer the military and the upper bourgeoisie a credible guarantee that their interests would be safeguarded against "subversion" and "demagoguery." Alsogaray, on the other hand, represented those who advocated a highly repressive coup that would give the liberals full control of the BA without reopening the electoral arena.

*This information comes from my interviews. Nationalist conspiracies also received attention in the press, especially after a coup attempt that went no farther than a radio broadcast. See *La Nación*, July 31, pp. 1, 10; August 1, p. 1; and December 29, p. 10, 1969; *Primera Plana*, July 29, 1969, p. 10; and *Panorama*, December 30, 1969, p. 6.

Aramburu established contacts with the outlawed political parties, assigning them a role which, in Argentina, was hardly original: in exchange for a carefully circumscribed license to operate, the parties would furnish the votes necessary to elect a president who was acceptable to the dominant classes and the armed forces.[6] Although further setbacks would take place before this alternative prevailed within the armed forces, enthusiastic accounts of Aramburu's "democratic and constitutionalist convictions" began to appear in the leading periodicals.[7] Together with the evidence that accumulated after the Cordobazo of the extent and intensity of opposition to the BA, Aramburu's maneuvers breathed new life into the political parties. Party leaders, until recently marginalized by repression and by the indifference of most of the population, began to attract public attention. Foremost among these leaders was Perón, who from his exile in Spain called for massive and violent confrontations with the BA. Meanwhile, Peronist leaders in Argentina stepped up contact with the Radicals as well as with other minor parties.*

But the process begun by the discussion of an electoral way out was still embryonic. In the second half of 1969, most members of the armed forces apparently still regarded Aramburu's proposals as too bitter a pill to swallow. Such proposals, in their view, entailed acknowledging the failure of the BA and permitting the resurrection of the very political parties they had recently condemned as the root of all evil. But if, for these reasons, active-duty officers did not sufficiently support Aramburu's presidential aspirations, many were scarcely more attracted to the continuist alternative proposed by Alsogaray. This option, with its aggressive repudiation of the paternalists, would have etched deep cleavages into the armed forces at a time when many regarded high

---

*It is worth noting at this point that the experience of the Argentine BA following the Cordobazo stands in sharp contrast to that of the Brazilian BA in 1968–69. In the latter case, university student militance, several strikes, and the emergence of guerrilla organizations generated a repressive reaction that effectively liquidated these challenges. The Brazilian BA, unlike the Argentine, seemed willing and able to restore order through harsh repression, a perception that strengthened the confidence of the bourgeoisie. This confidence, together with the new economic team appointed in late 1967, initiated the period of large and sustained inflows of transnational capital associated with the Brazilian "economic miracle." Nevertheless, factors internal to each BA do not fully account for the differing responses to these challenges. The challenge posed by the Cordobazo and its sequels was much more massive and violent than the one posed by comparable episodes in Brazil. Accordingly, much harsher repression would have been required in Argentina—from an armed forces and government which, moreover, were more deeply divided at the time than their Brazilian counterparts—for similar results to have been achieved.

institutional cohesion as more necessary than ever for meeting the challenges that emerged after May 1969. Consequently, with both options for the moment unworkable, and with the previously excluded classes and sectors showing an increasing capacity to press for their goals, the upper bourgeoisie was forced to confront evidence that the offensive it had launched in 1967 faced an uncertain future, even in terms of military support. The actions of General Lanusse after May 1969 should be interpreted from this perspective. Shortly after the Cordobazo, Lanusse reaffirmed the army's support for the Argentine Revolution and for the government but at the same time stressed his own democratic convictions. His pronouncements were as vague as those of other officers and government officials, but the leading periodicals reported them as if the philosopher's stone had been discovered.[8]

In short, the armed forces suffered the vacillations and internal cleavages that the Cordobazo had caused within the dominant classes. At the same time, sectors previously peripheral to the BA—especially the CGE and some union currents—glimpsed an opportunity to carve out space inside it. These factors blocked each other so that the Onganía government had room to survive a bit longer. The new economic team attempted, with some success, to revive the economy from the shock it had received while trying to make it more compatible with greater social sensitivity. Meanwhile, the paternalists continued to use the carrot-and-stick approach in their dealings with the unions, though the carrot was now more evident than before. Even as the liberals were blaming the Cordobazo on the paternalists' indecisiveness and on their efforts to control the popular sector, the paternalists launched an all-out effort to create the "organized community." The corporatist ideology of General Onganía and his current was never so apparent as after the Cordobazo. They saw "participation"*—the corporatization of the entire society—

* On participation and related themes see (among many similar statements) Onganía's press conference reported in *La Nación* (September 12, 1969, pp. 1, 14). According to Onganía, "high levels of technical skill" would be needed to achieve the "organization of the community." This organization would involve "the incorporation of private political bodies into the state, which until now has been made up [exclusively] of public political bodies." At a time when the relation of forces had changed drastically, Onganía continued to insist that no timetable could be established for the beginning of the political phase until "solidarity" had been achieved. These themes may also be found in speeches by Onganía in *La Nación*, July 8, 1969, pp. 1, 16; September 21, 1969, pp. 1, 12; March 8, 1970, p. 1; and April 1, 1970, pp. 1, 14. As if to remove any doubts that considerable time would elapse before the inauguration of the political phase, Imaz added that it would be "necessary [beforehand] to establish a clear sense of organic unity within the community" (*La Nación*, April 3, 1970, p. 10), and that "as long as the goals of the Argentine Revolution remain unfulfilled, there will be no political opening" (*La Nación*, March 19, 1970, p. 1).

as the only way to stem the crisis and advance toward their stubborn utopia of integration and solidarity.* Given the weakened situation of the paternalists, the achievement of these goals implied the negotiated co-optation of the unions, together with the selective use of repression against unionists unwilling to restrict their activities to whatever form of participation they were offered. The reaction of the upper bourgeoisie to the paternalists' renewed pursuit of these goals was, not surprisingly, increased hostility toward them and toward the unions and heightened concern that the achievements of economic policy since 1967 were on the verge of evaporating.† This concern became even more acute when Onganía gave formal notice that he was aiming at the "unification" of the "authentic representatives" of the bourgeoisie in the full-fledged corporatist system he was stubbornly pursuing. If these goals showed little political acumen, they offered striking testimony to the power of ideology to shape almost automatically the responses of authoritarian minds to grave and unforeseen circumstances.

The retreat of the liberals and the upper bourgeoisie as the government cut most of its direct ties to them placed the paternalists much more fully in control of the state apparatus than they had been before the Cordobazo. But for this control they paid the heavy price of estranging the principal social base of this state. Meanwhile, their attempts to ally themselves with other sectors of society met with little success.

3. THE VICISSITUDES OF "PARTICIPATION"

As the vacillation and debates within the armed forces grew more pronounced, guerrilla activity and other forms of violence expanded

---

*The limitations of the paternalist ideology are pathetically clear from their calls for "technical" and "organic" participation: once the (corporatist) "community councils" had been established, they would have a "voice but not a vote, as voting would constitute interference in decision-making, which is the exclusive prerogative of the government" (Onganía, La Nación, September 14, 1969).

†After the Cordobazo, moreover, it was all the more unlikely that the upper bourgeoisie would find much comfort in Onganía's belief that "with respect to the economy, we have attained the basic goals set forth at the outset. We are now in a position to undertake changes in the social sphere that will assure peace and solidarity for the future." No less unsettling was his exhortation that "the workers . . . must unite rapidly in order to realize their aims, which are those of the government" (La Nación, July 8, 1969). Representative of the reactions these statements generated was an editorial in La Nación, November 20, 1969, p. 8, which came out against efforts to unify the CGT and again demanded the repeal of the "unfortunate Law of Professional Associations, whose existence has been a prime cause of the country's political instability."

markedly.* The popular irruption that followed the Cordobazo was changing the terms of all of the conflicts and alliances among sectors that supported or sought access to the BA.

After the Cordobazo, union leaders found the government more willing than before to engage in negotiations. At the same time, however, these leaders faced a popular activation, supported by many of their rank and file, which was growing more radical. Most national union leaders moved closer to an agreement with the paternalists, but this rapprochement followed a sinuous path; national union leaders could ill afford to appear too submissive to the paternalists or to lock their organizations openly in the lethal embrace of the paternalists' corporatist schemes.

In a new effort to unify the CGT under leaders sympathetic to the paternalists, law 18,281 was passed, providing for the appointment of a "normalizing delegate": a de facto intervenor charged with setting up a congress for the election of regular CGT officials. The national union movement, as we have seen, was divided at the time into the *CGT de los Argentinos,* which had been forced underground, and the *CGT-Azopardo,* which was directed by a Vandorist-dominated provisional commission (the "Twenty"). Both CGTs criticized the appointment, but it was not long before the Twenty announced that they were ready to hold negotiations with the president's delegate.

Reflecting the new emphasis on the carrot, in August 1969 the government issued Decree no. 4686, which provided for the future restoration of collective bargaining.[9] Shortly thereafter it announced guidelines for wage and salary increases including significantly higher allowances for family dependents. The costs of these increases were to be borne exclusively by employers. The government also announced the creation of an "Advisory Council on Prices and Wages," to be composed of representatives from the bourgeoisie, government, and labor.[10] Considering that the unions were pressing for wage and salary hikes ranging from 30 to 100 percent, it should come as no surprise that the bourgeoisie viewed these decisions as forerunners of even greater follies to come under the social phase.†

*Data on political violence will be found in chapter 9. In addition to assassinating Vandor and Alonso, guerrilla groups began to launch dramatic assaults on installations of the armed forces and other security forces. But massive uprisings in the cities of Cipolletti (*La Nación,* September 14, 1969, pp. 1, 22) and Rosario (*La Nación,* September 16 and 20, 1969) again showed that the guerrilla groups were not the only ones willing to use violence to oppose the BA.

†See, for example, the immediate reaction of the ACIEL in *La Nación,* August 26, 1969, p. 1. The general assembly of the UIA, for its part, opposed a return to collective bargaining, advocated holding wage and salary increases below five percent, and again

But it would be wrong to assume that these decisions made the popular sector more receptive to the paternalists' overtures. As already noted, the various forms of protest that emerged after the Cordobazo sent national union leaders scurrying for ways to ride the wave of popular activation that threatened to wash away both them and the BA's allies. The government's vagueness as to what ceilings, if any, would be placed upon the wage and salary increases to be negotiated through collective bargaining* gave the Twenty an opportunity to call a forty-eight-hour general strike "in view of the government's failure to respond to the [unions'] minimum demands, and in solidarity with all striking unions, for the defense of the national patrimony and for the sovereignty of the people."[11] The tone of this proclamation prompted a government response that was formally similar to its reaction to the CGT's 1967 Plan of Action: it convened CONASE, declared that it would "take drastic measures to curb any attempt at excesses," and announced its readiness to adopt "measures at the level and order of importance necessary to ensure that union organizations confine their actions to their proper ends."† As in 1967, the CGT leaders called off the strike.‡ But there were signs that the situation had changed profoundly. Onganía held two meetings with the Twenty before the strike was canceled;[12] prior to the Cordobazo, talks with those who had "placed themselves outside the law" would have been unthinkable. Furthermore, not only the CGT de los Argentinos and the most militant regional unions (such as those in Córdoba) but also the "62 Organizations"—the political expression of Peronism within the unions—decried the decision of the Twenty as "treason," and countered with preparations for a "week of struggle" and a general strike.[13] The 62 Organizations, like the Twenty, had been under the control of Vandor and his allies. But after Vandor's assassination, his followers split be-

---

asserted that what was needed was changes in the laws governing worker dismissals and the repeal of the Law of Professional Associations (La Nación, October 1, 1969, p. 1). In an effort to calm things down, Onganía assured the UIA Assembly that collective bargaining would remain "under state tutelage" (La Nación, October 30, 1969, pp. 1, 6). Economic Survey (September 23, 1969, p. 1) added to its criticism of the government's decrees complaints about the "loss of authority" brought on by the resurgence of labor conflict.

*The Labor Secretary stated on August 8 that the government would place no obstacles in the way of future wage negotiations. Recall, however, Onganía's promise to the UIA that such negotiations would remain under state "tutelage."

†La Nación, September 26, 1969, p. 1. Note the similarity between this statement and the communiqué of February, 1967, cited in chapter 3.

‡This decision was made by the Twenty (La Nación, September 28, 1969, p. 16).

tween those who were prepared to follow Perón's instructions (transmitted through the "62") to "strike hard," and those who preferred to act more cautiously so as not to jeopardize their positions within the unions and the CGT. For the paternalists, who were anxious to demonstrate their capacity to reassert authority, the apex of the CGT was an easier target than the guerrilla groups or wildcat strikes within individual factories. The result was that a substantial part of the Vandorists swung toward the participationists, who had been opposed all along to any such adventures.*

Once the Twenty had called off the general strike, Dagnino Pastore announced that the forthcoming collective agreements would not address the wage and salary issue. Instead, an across-the-board increase of 3,000 pesos (far less than the unions had expected) would take effect at the beginning of November 1969, to be followed in March 1970 by an additional 7 percent increment.[14] However, the clause holding employers responsible for absorbing the wage and salary hike ensured that Dagnino Pastore's recently proposed price accord among leading enterprises would be considerably less voluntary than its 1967 counterpart.[15] The organizations of the upper bourgeoisie raised new protests against state interventionism, which had been accepted gracefully when it served to freeze the wages of the popular sector but was rejected out of hand when it seemed to impinge (only symbolically, since the wage increases were soon translated into higher prices) on profits.[16]

Meanwhile, the new economic team was trying to revive the economy. But even apart from the obstacles posed by the direct consequences of the Cordobazo, this effort ran into two major complications. First, the stock-raising cycle, after almost two years of depressed prices and herd depletion, entered a phase in which cattle were kept off the market and beef prices began to rise rapidly. Second, utilization of installed productive capacity, having risen from the low levels registered when Krieger Vasena took office, was approaching its ceiling as a result of the recent economic growth. Partly because of this factor, unemployment had fallen to a new low.[†] The achievements of the policies launched in March 1967 had brought the economy to a point where

*Disregarding Perón's instructions (despite having distinguished themselves from the Vandorists by claiming staunch loyalty to Perón), the remnants of the 62 de Pie, formerly led by Alonso, also moved toward cooperation with the government.

†The unemployment rate in April 1969 was 4.5 percent of the labor force, the lowest level registered during the 1966–73 period (Ministerio de Trabajo, Boletín de Estadísticas Sociales, various issues [Buenos Aires]).

new productive investment was needed in order to sustain economic growth. Investment in intermediate and capital goods was viewed as particularly necessary, since imports in these sectors had risen significantly faster than overall exports and the GNP.*

But several requisites for these new investments had disappeared with the Cordobazo. In spite of an influx of short-term foreign loans toward the end of 1969 (partly compensating for the capital flight during the three months after the Cordobazo); in spite of assurances that new productive undertakings would be left to private activity; in spite of painstaking efforts to reassure transnational capital that, in accordance with the policies established in 1967, there would be no discrimination against foreign investment; and in spite of the announcement that adjustments to the economic conjuncture would not affect the continuity of the economic policies implemented between 1967 and 1969, the new economic team faced a number of obstacles. First, as was mentioned above, it lacked close contacts with the dominant fractions of capital. This meant that the upper bourgeoisie, though approving of the orthodoxy that informed most of the new team's policies,† lacked what they thought they needed now more than ever: smooth access to the state institutions. Second, the prevailing political conditions had made Argentina unattractive to potential long-term investors. With respect to private capital, the Cordobazo and its sequels created an image of disorder which effected a virtual stoppage of foreign direct investment and long-term loans. Moreover, any attempt by the state apparatus to compensate for the dearth of private investment would have exacerbated the fears of an upper bourgeoisie already apprehensive about statism. Third, the balance of payments deteriorated.[17] This factor led in the second half of 1969 to restrictive monetary and credit policies that contrasted with the rather loose ones that had prevailed in the preceding period. Tighter control of the money supply and of credit introduced new tensions, evident especially in the protests of the weakest fractions of the bourgeoisie, which as

---

*Dagnino Pastore proclaimed that "1969 marks the end of a stage based on the cyclical recovery of the level of economic activity. . . . Consequently, an increase in the level of production presupposes increasing installed capacity through an intense investment effort," aimed especially at "developing heavy industry" (*La Nación,* January 3, 1970, pp. 1, 22).

†See, for example, the statement of the UIA in *La Nación,* July 24, 1969, p. 1, which applauded the announcement that the March 1967 program would be continued but criticized the wage and salary increases, the possibility that collective bargaining would be restored, and "statism."

usual were those most adversely affected by the decline in liquidity and credit.* Fourth, these factors converged to drive up interest rates, compounding the financial distress of a significant part of the bourgeoisie and creating a new stimulus for inflation. Fifth, the announcement that collective bargaining would be resumed, together with the perception that the social phase of the Argentine Revolution was about to be launched in full, further eroded the confidence of the bourgeoisie and fueled inflationary expectations. Finally, the combined effect of the new inflationary expectations and the deterioration in the balance of payments produced a conspicuous overvaluation of the peso and, consequently, expectations of a new devaluation. In the wake of Krieger Vasena's solemn pledge that the March 1967 devaluation would be the last, the stability of the peso in relation to the dollar had become the epitome of everything that was proclaimed to have been achieved. This stability, about which the government had unwisely boasted, was shaken, like everything else, by the Cordobazo.

In view of these problems, the long-delayed appearance in February 1970 of the "National Plan for Development and Security" for the years 1970–74 came at a less than opportune time.[18] One basic thrust of this plan was to leave the state apparatus in charge of investment in infrastructure, while reserving large productive investments for private initiative. But with inconsistency that escaped nobody, the plan asserted that economic growth based largely on transnational capital was leading to rapid economic concentration and denationalization. In view of this, the plan stated a commitment to making this pattern of economic growth "compatible" with the promotion and strengthening of national capital. It also made provisions for important increases in wages and salaries. It did not, however, bother to detail how all these goals would be achieved. The upper bourgeoisie saw the plan as the ultimate distillation of the paternalists' estrangement from elementary economic rationality.

Despite the greater "social sensitivity" the paternalists had sought in their new *técnicos*, economic policy by and large continued to adhere to the framework and goals established under Krieger Vasena. But another goal now had to be added: to repair the damage that recent events had done to bourgeois confidence. The announced restoration of collective

---

*The protests were well founded: the total declared value of commercial bankruptcies soared from an index of 100.0 in 1966 to 237.3 in 1969 and 522.3 in 1970. The indices for 1967 and 1968 had been 154.6 and 182.7 respectively (data deflated by the wholesale domestic price index) (Ministerio de Hacienda, *Informe Económico* 1972, 4th trimester, pp. 82–83).

bargaining, together with the economic expectations this announcement had kindled within the popular sector, were the first casualties of this priority. But as if to compensate for its indefinite postponement of collective bargaining, the government announced that it was "studying" a law that would generate funds for social welfare by imposing a withholding tax of two percent on employers and one percent on workers, based on the gross wages or salaries of the latter. The enormous mass of resources generated by this tax would then be placed under union control.* The bourgeoisie, including the CGE, protested in unison against the strengthening of the union apparatus implicit in these arrangements.[19] Perón, probably worried about the autonomy this scheme would give to followers as unreliable as the union leaders, became more vehement in urging a total confrontation with the BA.[20]

It was no accident that such announcements coincided with a marked improvement in relations between the government and the leaders of the national unions. In December 1969, Onganía received a commission of twenty-five CGT leaders (mostly former Vandorists) and announced his decision to allow it to replace the "normalizing delegate" as the body in charge of finally bringing about the unification of the CGT.[21] The 62 Organizations, following Perón's instructions, remained in opposition, but their declining weight was evidenced by the support that the metalworkers, the most important union within the CGT and the central locus of Vandorism, gave to the Twenty-five.[†] After law 18,610 put the social welfare tax into effect,[22] the Twenty-five seemed ready to cooperate with the paternalists. True, the government had less authority and the unions more autonomy than the paternalists would have liked, but the moment seemed to them to be approaching at which they would consummate their impossible love with the organized workers.[‡] This seems to have influenced the timing of Onganía's ouster,[§] which occurred just before the official "normalization" of the CGT.

Meanwhile, as Dagnino Pastore adhered by and large to economic orthodoxy, the CGE witnessed the evaporation of the possibilities it had

---

*La Nación, November 2, 1969, p. 8. It was probably no coincidence that on the same page of this issue a call for elections appeared for the first time since the coup.

†La Nación, January 15, 1970, p. 22. The support that the metalworkers' union gave to the Twenty-five and to the efforts to unify the CGT weakened the "62 Organizations" significantly. Once again, Perón seemed on the verge of losing control over the unions.

‡Especially after Onganía met with the Twenty-five (La Nación, March 11, 1970, pp. 1, 24) and the latter used a very moderate tone to request new wage and salary increases and a "revision" of economic policy.

§According to several of the paternalists I interviewed.

envisioned immediately after the Cordobazo. With its constituents hemmed in by restrictive monetary and credit policies, the CGE criticized with renewed vigor the "strangulation of the national entrepreneurs" and the related processes of economic concentration and denationalization.[23] These protests, which were beyond suspicion of subversive intent, gave the opposition to the BA an element of bourgeois respectability, making it more difficult to repress than it would have been had it been limited to the popular and middle sectors. Furthermore, the protests revealed the potential for an accord between, on the one hand, the bourgeois factions represented by the CGE and, on the other, a national unionism which, even if profoundly tempted by the economic advantages that the paternalists offered them, was prepared to explore any alliance. The proponents of this accord converged with the liberals, albeit from opposite angles, in viewing Onganía's ouster as necessary for achieving their goals.

Meanwhile, the agrarian situation was getting out of hand. The Pampean organizations responded to the obvious weakness of the government by increasing their hostility toward it. Their complaints merged with those of other sectors in a chorus of protest that increasingly recalled the pre-1966 praetorian period.[24] The conflict escalated when the government decided to counter rising beef prices by imposing price ceilings on meat and other food products and by prohibiting periodically the sale of beef on the domestic market.[25] This interventionism got an unenthusiastic reception from the bourgeoisie as a whole and was greeted bitterly by all of the Pampean sectors (not just the Pampean bourgeoisie). These protests were heightened by the noisy resignations of the Secretary and Undersecretary of Agriculture and Livestock, both of whom had close ties to the Pampean bourgeoisie.[26] Furthermore, the undersecretary accompanied his resignation with an attack on the meat-packing industry and on policies enacted during the Krieger Vasena period which, he argued, had allowed it to grab the lion's share of the profits generated in the sector as a whole. Whether or not he was right, the economic and financial situation of the meat packers was far from good at the time of the undersecretary's resignation. A notable indication of this was the declaration of bankruptcy by the Swift company, which was owned by Deltec, a transnational group that counted Krieger Vasena as a member of its board of directors. Apparently precipitated by maneuvers that benefited the parent organization at the expense of local creditors, the Swift bankruptcy and the ensuing scandal raised to new heights the nationalist and moral undertones of the condemnations of the BA.

In contrast to the preceding period, the context of these conflicts within the BA and the dominant classes was, as already noted, marked by the resurgence of popular activation and by a new phenomenon: the urban guerrilla. There were numerous kidnappings, attacks on banks, takeovers of whole towns, and attempted assassinations (we shall review these in chapter 9).[27] These events were paralleled by increasingly aggressive student activism and by several violent strikes.* As we shall see, it was not only industrial workers, but also teachers, public employees, judicial employees, transportation workers, and even doctors and lawyers, who, after 1970, demonstrated through their strikes that the longing for order, which most of them had shown in 1966, had come to an end.

Even if the paternalists had come close to co-opting the union leadership they had fallen far short of controlling and taming the popular sector. The national unions absorbed some of the combativeness of the working class in Greater Buenos Aires, but they had much less influence over the middle sectors and the working class in other urban centers. The efforts of the leaders of the national unions did help focus popular demands on economic gains, thereby dampening some of the more radical possibilities of the situation. But even as this economism protected the bourgeoisie's basic class interest, it clashed with their economic interests. The bourgeoisie realized that the satisfaction of the demands of the national unions would come at the cost of a considerable part of their own accumulation and/or at the risk of new inflationary pressures. Either possibility, they were well aware, would mean the end of economic normalization.

4. THE FINAL CRISIS

A group of officials from the president's office, in conjunction with representatives from the three branches of the armed forces, were instructed to draw up the National Policies that would embody the major goals and strategies of the Argentine Revolution. The document went through several drafts[28] that failed to alter it in any fundamental way, though they did take the edge off its most explicitly corporatist pro-

---

*Chapter 9 provides data on protest and violence in the context of a broader overview of these processes. For accounts of strikes, occupations of hospitals and large factories, and other conflicts in Córdoba and Rosario, see *La Nación,* June 18, 1969, pp. 1, 10; June 29, 1969, pp. 1, 4; July 31, 1969, p. 7; September 16 and 17, 1969, p. 1; October 30, 1969, p. 1; May 16, 1970, p. 5; and June 3, 1970, p. 12.

visions.* The goals and strategies contained in the final version of this document were not much more specific than the ones set forth in the 1966 Directives of the Revolutionary Junta.† The document made no mention of the political future of the country save for the statement, which was very ambiguous in the context, that its goal would be to "construct a stable and efficient democratic political system,"‡ linked in some unspecified way to the "basic organizations of the community" (themselves the embodiment of "integration" and "spiritual solidarity"). The anguished allies of the BA found conspicuously absent from the document even the outline of a political strategy for putting out the flames.§

If this kind of proposal had met with widespread skepticism before the Cordobazo, in its aftermath it sounded nothing less than bizarre. Society was erupting from all sides. The paternalists responded with efforts to stabilize the economy and to co-opt the union apparatus, recording in both endeavors significant but insufficient successes. By 1970, public opinion had turned massively against the BA. The government had proved unable to control the various forms of protest that had emerged, and the guerrillas had become a most worrisome reality. Moreover, opposition from various sectors of the Catholic Church was lethal to a government which, reflecting the convictions of Onganía and his closest collaborators, had taken pains to present itself as embodying a "Christian conception of politics."‖ Meanwhile, the cost of living was rising rapidly,# and in the wake of the Swift-Deltec scandal the agrarian sector had further increased its hostility toward the government. The liberals, though still caught in the dilemma of whether to

*Nevertheless, the document reiterated the call for participation and stated explicitly the goal of promoting "the existence of solid [unified] labor, business, and professional structures that will assure authentic representation at all levels." These provisions were set forth with the aim of assuring "a just equilibrium among the aspirations of [these] sectors" (Policy 53, clause b).

†Policy 1: "Respect for human dignity"; Policy 2: "Achievement of the permanent preeminence of the national interest"; Policy 3: "Reform of cultural, social, and economic structures with a view toward achieving an Argentine community with its own creative and spiritually integrated personality, and with the aim of neutralizing the particularistic interests which stand in the way of these goals"; etc.

‡Policy 4.

§This anxiety is expressed vividly in Alejandro Lanusse, *Mi Testimonio*.

‖The decision to "dedicate Argentina publicly and solemnly, on November 30 [1969], as an act of grace to the Immaculate Heart of Mary" met with the approval of the upper echelons of the Catholic Church. However, it was not much help to the government: the ceremonies attracted a flood of sarcasm and criticism, even from several Catholic groups. The quotation is from a speech by Onganía in *La Nación*, November 17, 1969, p. 1.

#See Table 34.

adopt the minimalist solution represented by Aramburu* or a hard-line path that called for a highly repressive reconsolidation of the BA, agreed on the necessity of ousting Onganía. The nationalists, as we have seen, had their own reasons for wanting Onganía removed. The major political parties found new interlocutors and saw their statements and actions reported in the press with a breadth and sympathy unheard of during Krieger Vasena's term. The upper bourgeoisie and the leading periodicals focused their hopes for a coup on General Lanusse. Given the fluidity of the situation, there is no way to assess how much support Onganía still enjoyed within the armed forces.† It is clear, however, that before the Cordobazo such support had already been weakened by Onganía's insistence that "the armed forces neither govern nor co-govern, but only back the government," and by his application of this dictum as justification for not consulting the armed forces in such sensitive areas as the appointment of ministers and provincial governors. But following the Cordobazo, important aspects of the situation had changed. In particular, the armed forces now had to take direct charge of repression. Moreover, the Cordobazo and its sequels demonstrated that the civilian population put little stock in Onganía's distinctions between those who governed and those who merely backed the government. For the population, this was a military regime, and the armed forces were one of the favorite targets of an angry opposition. Many officers thus concluded that Onganía's arrangements imposed severe institutional costs on them while denying them the political weight that corresponded to such responsibilities.‡ Having made the bitter discovery that beneath the oft-proclaimed "tacit consensus" lay their own unpopularity, the armed forces placed the blame on a government that had to

*Probably anxious to precipitate the denouement, Aramburu issued harsh criticisms of the situation and offered a "democratic way out" (La Nación, December 17, 1969, p. 16).

†In one of their last acts of authority, the paternalists shut down publications (such as Primera Plana, on August 7, 1969) for covering disputes within the armed forces and for "alarmist" reporting of social conflicts. Lanusse, for his part, continued to express support for the government (in increasingly ambiguous terms), but missed no opportunity to affirm the "democratic mission" of the armed forces. He also insisted, in a rather obvious retort to the paternalists, that an essential aspect of the Argentine Revolution would be its culmination in a democracy "with parties and a parliament." The leading periodicals responded to these statements with outbursts of democratic fervor and elegies to Lanusse. See, for example, La Nación, October 7, 1969, p. 1; November 25, 1969, p. 1; February 28, 1970, p. 1; March 1, 1970, p. 6; and May 30, 1970, pp. 1, 22.

‡Lanusse stresses this point in Mi Testimonio (Buenos Aires: Editorial Lasserre, 1977). In taking this stand, these officers to some extent were trying to evade their own responsibilities. Nevertheless, my interviews suggested that at the time this feeling prevailed throughout the military.

rely on them to do the dirty work of extinguishing the fires of popular activation.

It was in these circumstances that the Argentine BA—installed in June 1966, refashioned in March 1967, and mortally wounded in May 1969—approached its demise during the first months of 1970. Liberal control of the BA's economic apparatus had resulted in some important successes, but it had also produced a multitude of oppositions. The liberals, who had failed in their efforts to fully dominate the higher governmental positions, were expelled after the Cordobazo from their economic policy-making positions, leaving them (and the upper bourgeoisie) few reasons to support Onganía's government. These changes took place in the climate of urgency produced by the strong resurgence of violence and popular activation. The solitude of the paternalists and their utopian goal of integrating society were blatantly inadequate to cope with the renewed threat. Thus, liberals and nationalists agreed that it was necessary to seal shut the abyss that the Cordobazo had opened, and that Onganía's ouster was the first step. But regardless of which alternative won out—the politically negotiated settlement represented by Aramburu, the capture of the BA by liberals ready to resume the course interrupted in May 1969, or the capture of the BA by the nationalists—everyone was faced with the same enigma: how to implement any of these alternatives, especially how to secure from the armed forces some reasonably cohesive support for it.

The first months of 1970 were replete with rumors of a coup, meetings of top military officials, "tours of inspection" by the commanders in chief, and hints in the media that the government was about to fall. For anyone able to recall the political climate of 1966, the meaning of all this was clear. As if anything more were needed, Aramburu was kidnapped on May 29, 1970, by a guerrilla group, the Montoneros.[29] His death was not confirmed until after Onganía's overthrow, but there were signals from the beginning that more than a ransom attempt was involved. Aramburu's kidnapping completed the destruction of the image of order and security.* Moreover, workers in

---

*To grasp the profound effect of the kidnapping and murder of Aramburu it is necessary only to consult any Argentine periodical issued after May 29, 1970. Shortly after the kidnapping, Onganía announced in a televised speech that the death penalty would be imposed for crimes against public order (La Nación, June 3, 1970, pp. 1, 12). This decree was insufficient, however, to alleviate the feeling that order and authority had collapsed for good. To make matters worse, the Minister of the Interior made the imprudent suggestion that Aramburu had arranged his own disappearance in order to compound the difficulties of the government (La Nación, June 30, 1970, p. 1).

Córdoba called a general strike and occupied several factories during the same week that the kidnapping took place,[30] heightening the clamor against a government that, as before the 1966 coup, seemed to many to be leading the country into chaos. It was in this climate that Onganía met with CONASE on June 5, 1970, to discuss the final revisions to the above-mentioned National Policies. The meeting focused on two issues: whether or not these policies were corporatist and, in response to a question by Lanusse, what political plan Onganía would implement. Onganía's response—that the "National Policies" and the political plan were one and the same—ended the meeting and set the coup in motion.*

On June 8, 1970, the three commanders in chief asked Onganía to resign. Onganía responded by relieving them of their commands. Several hours later, alone in the Government House except for a small group of collaborators, Onganía tendered his resignation[31] and exited down the path that the armed forces had forced Illia to walk four years earlier.

The central feature of the ensuing period, General Levingston's presidency, was an attempt to reorient the BA in a nationalist direction. This effort, which was abandoned even sooner and more decisively than its predecessor, marked the point at which the BA's death certificate was signed. Under General Lanusse, Levingston's successor, no serious attempt was made to resuscitate what remained of the BA. The Lanusse government sought instead to negotiate guarantees by which the dominant classes and the armed forces could entrench themselves against a violence and a popular activation that threatened to swallow much more than the ruins of the BA. But we shall examine this process in the chapters that follow.

5. THE BA DURING THE PERIOD OF NORMALIZATION

The Cordobazo and its sequels marked the turning point for the experiment initiated in June 1966. The preceding sections of this chapter have described how various actors interpreted those events. This

---

*This account is drawn from my interviews with participants in the meeting and coincides largely with that of Lanusse in *Mi Testimonio*. Although his government was in no way democratic, the accelerated timing and sequence of events that preceded Onganía's demise coincides in many respects with the analysis in Juan Linz's "Crisis, Breakdown, and Reequilibration," in Juan Linz and Alfred Stepan, eds., *The Breakdown of Democratic Regimes* (Baltimore: The Johns Hopkins University Press, 1978).

section is this author's interpretation, drawing on themes raised in earlier chapters.

Why did such profound convulsions overtake a society that previously had seemed content with, or powerless before, the BA and its allies? Fundamentally, because the BA is a last resort for classes which, once this state is implanted, pay the heavy price of sacrificing much of the stability and ideological fluidity of their domination. Bureaucratic authoritarianism always constitutes a severe defeat for the popular sector. Yet beneath its capacity for repression and its occasional successes, it also involves a serious risk for the dominant classes. This is because the BA is a reaction to political activation and threat which are channeled (at least in part) through classical political representation. By blocking these channels, by suspending rights of citizenship, and by prohibiting any appeals to *pueblo* or class, the BA dismantles crucial mediations between society and state, exposing itself and its social base to the risk of major social explosions.

Two fundamental consequences result from the fact that the BA is a system of exclusion. First, the BA lacks any mechanism to generate the illusion that it is representative of the popular sector and, thence, of the nation as a whole. Following a period in which many feel that the interests and demands of the popular sector have been taken too much into account, the implantation of the BA entails the denial of the state as representative of the whole of society. The second consequence is that the BA, by denying itself all semblance of representativeness, starkly reveals the ties that link its economic institutions and many of its top personnel, both civilian and military, to the dominant fractions of domestic and transnational capital. These fractions, which furnish the teams of *técnicos* that are placed in charge of economic policy, keep a jealous grip on the state's most important levers of policy making, shoving aside many middle sectors and fractions of the local bourgeoisie. In so doing, the BA exposes Gordian knots, which later serve as focal points for the attacks of the excluded classes and sectors.

Initially, the basic task of the BA—apart from the imposition of "order"—is economic normalization. Normalization, as was argued in chapter 1, demands obedience to a code that is the ideological distillation of the interests of the dynamic and transnationalized vanguard of the capitalism in which the BA emerges. Once the BA is implanted, this code entails not only the exclusion of the popular sector but also the restructuring of a substantial part of the local bourgeoisie. The memory of the threat that preceded the implantation of the BA allows the government a respite, longer or shorter depending basically on the level of previous threat, in which to attempt what I have called the normalization of the economy. But in pursuing this normalization, a profound cleavage is carved between the state apparatus and the upper bourgeoisie, on one side, and the rest of society on the other. This cleavage, combined with the suppression of other mediations between the state and society, leaves the BA and the upper bourgeoisie in an isolation that, though useful for attempting economic normalization, is conspicuous and therefore dangerous.

As was argued in chapter 1, the imposition of order under the BA entails more than the exclusion of certain actors from the political arena. It also reveals in a particularly transparent way that the BA is the organizer and guarantor of the relations of domination in society. Every state is the guarantor of a certain social order, but the degree to which this condition is apparent varies, as does the probability that a given state in the long run will be able to consolidate itself and the social order it guarantees. In this context, it is important to stress again that the BA is, historically, a specific type of capitalist state. The capitalist character of a state derives not from the will of social actors but from its objective condition as the support of a social order that presupposes the continuous reproduction of society *qua* capitalist. In its usual operation, the capitalist state rarely reveals the coercion behind its protection of this social order. This coercive backing, moreover, usually takes the form of the impersonal application of law.[32] The BA, by contrast, in addition to being based on an extremely narrow (and strongly transnationalized) alliance, operates through extensive and often arbitrary coercion, crudely revealing its condition as the guarantor of the existing social domination.

If its basic role is to restore "order," and if the crisis that precedes its implantation has extended to many of society's micro-contexts, then the BA faces an enormous task: penetrating as many of these contexts as possible and restoring "authority" there.* This is no mean feat, even with the aid of the numerous authoritarian tendencies that always exist

---

*The coercive "reestablishment of authority" applies in practice not just to the sphere of work, but to most societal contexts. Following the implantation of the BA, many micro-contexts—the family, the schools and universities, the communications media, and various professional associations, to name just a few—go through periods in which firm believers in the virtues of authoritarianism find ample room to impose their preferences. The extent to which such views permeate these micro-contexts seems also to vary with the depth of the preceding crisis and the corresponding level of previous threat. Studies at these "micro" levels are needed in order to better understand these processes.

within these micro-contexts. Consequently—in spite of the BA's shaky ideological foundations and its difficulties in dealing with the problem of presidential succession[33]—the BA's leaders have difficulty forseeing the end of their rule: there is no way to be sure that the subversive potential embodied in the preceding crisis has been truly eradicated (especially for those whose profound paranoia inspires them to take charge of this task).

We have already examined the reasons why, during the period of normalization, the apparatus of the BA isolates itself from most of society. This is the opposite of the previous democratic or praetorian state, which was open to all organized currents and sectors of society and whose policies danced to the tune of the changing forces among those currents and sectors. The state that preceded the BA had little autonomy from the country's social forces. By contrast, the BA, like all states born of a profound crisis (including the European fascisms), is in certain respects highly autonomous in relation to society as a whole, including the bourgeoisie. The more obviously it has saved the bourgeoisie as a class, the less this conspicuously capitalist state is a state *of* the bourgeoisie, although it is closely linked to some fractions of this class. Rather, as is underscored by the dramatic circumstances of its implantation, the BA is a state *for* the bourgeoisie: it supports and defends the most basic and long-term interests of this class, but it is not an apparatus colonized by the immediate interests of its various fractions. We have seen why the normalization programs implemented under the BA cannot but aim at restructuring a good part of *that* bourgeoisie, the one historically given in the dependent and uneven capitalisms that, when certain crises are triggered, the BA often comes to rescue. The exclusionary wall erected against the popular sector is obvious, and at this point in the analysis it should also be clear that a substantial portion of the middle sectors will inevitably become disillusioned with the BA. With respect to the popular sector and many middle sectors, the BA acts with almost sovereign autonomy.* But no less important is that the BA's economic policies are made independently of, and even against the expressed preferences of, a substantial part of the bourgeoisie.

The BA's relationship to one segment of society—the uppermost fractions of the bourgeoisie—is quite different. But in spite of the close ties

---

* "Almost" is inserted in recognition of the fact that some of the BA's policies are influenced by the fear of resuscitating popular activation. In this sense, the tacit presence of the excluded sectors remains important; see my "Tensions in the Bureaucratic-Authoritarian State."

between certain high public officials of the BA and the upper bourgeoisie, it would be simplistic to assume that normalization policies are designed conspiratorially to promote the interests of the dominant fractions of capital. Certainly, normalization policies lead to the expansion of the upper bourgeoisie, to an even larger expansion of its financial segment, to the pursuit of further transnationalization, and to the increased concentration and oligopolization of the productive structure. But as should be clear from the data and arguments presented here, such consequences are inevitable in the orthodox program, regardless of the intentions behind each policy. To restate this argument in different terms, the BA's economic institutions and policies during the normalization period have little autonomy with respect to the upper bourgeoisie and transnational capital. This low degree of autonomy, however, has little to do with the intentions or social origins of government personnel. It is not so much that those who conduct economic policy want to conform to the code or believe that it adequately represents reality (though most of them do). Neither is it that such officials are recruited from, and usually return to, top positions in the oligopolistic firms and major financial institutions, even though this lends credibility to their commitment to maintaining orthodox normalization policies. The crucial points are, first, that given the political and economic conditions under which the BAs are implanted, a viable—orthodox—normalization program permits little freedom for public policy and, second, that the consequences of such a program, and the decisions made in accordance with its code, objectively and fundamentally benefit the upper bourgeoisie and transnational capital.

It needs to be emphasized, in accordance with the argument in chapter 1, that it is meaningless to analyze the relative autonomy of the state at the level of the state *in* society. The issue of relative autonomy belongs instead at the level of the state apparatus as a center of public policy: i.e., as the locus of the decisions and non-decisions that determine the modes in which the various state institutions act upon society. Our discussion of the relative autonomy of the state apparatus has focused thus far on a single issue: economic policy—normalization—and its impact. To understand simultaneous variations in the autonomy of BA's apparatus in other spheres, it is necessary to consider the armed forces. It is their drastic intervention that rescues society *qua* capitalist, regardless of whether most members of the armed forces intend this consequence (usually they do not). This victory confers upon the leaders of the armed forces the right of access to the institutional apex of the state. The armed forces become the main institutional support of an order that is imposed through coercion and whose continuity is guaranteed in large measure by coercion. But the position of the armed forces within the BA is an imposition of a reality that is in many ways inconsistent with the orientations and perceived interests of the other actors who participate in its institutions and constitute its social base. Although both the armed forces and the liberal *técnicos,* with their respective tasks of maintaining order and pursuing normalization, are indispensable to the BA, this does not ensure their easy coexistence. Of all the actors entrenched in the BA's institutions, the *técnicos* uphold the most orthodox capitalistic views, while the armed forces have the least capitalistic outlook. If a typical ideological orientation exists within the armed forces, it is between nationalism and paternalism. Such an orientation is hardly consistent with the ideology and practices of the liberals and the upper bourgeoisie. The conflict between these outlooks becomes sharper with the consequences of normalization: the increasing centrality of financial capital, accelerated transnationalization, the dismantling or subordination of much of industry (especially its most unequivocally national segments), and increased consumption of luxury items in the face of an often pronounced drop in the living standards of large sectors of the population. Unlike the liberal *técnicos,* most members of the armed forces view these processes not as desired ends but as unfortunate, if inevitable, steps that must be taken in pursuit of a national interest that is broader—and less prosaic—than that envisioned by their civilian allies. Paradoxically, these orientations are reinforced by the implantation of the BA, which most members of the armed forces interpret as their successful response to a crisis which, in their view, has resulted not from a threat to society *qua* capitalist, but rather from the selfish, subversive, immoral and irresponsible behavior of most other social sectors—including the bourgeoisie. The armed forces' self-image as the incarnation of a rationality transcending the myopia and avarice of particularized interests injects a constant note of uncertainty into the support that they give to normalization. As a result, negotiation is constantly taking place over how much heterodoxy the liberal *técnicos* will have to concede in order to be allowed to maintain control of the main levers of economic policy.

There is certainly less inconsistency between the higher-ranking military officers and the liberal *técnicos.* The incumbents of these higher (and institutionally less introverted) roles are sometimes military liberals prepared to lend full support to normalization. To the extent that there exists an agreement between top military officers and the executors of the normalization program, the tensions and oppositions raised by normalization may take longer to erupt. Nevertheless, as the liberal *técnicos* and the upper bourgeoisie are well aware, the more or less imminent dangers that the armed forces pose to the consolidation of normalization can never fully be controlled. While the state apparatus has little autonomy from the upper bourgeoisie during the period of normalization, when the liberal *técnicos* are in charge of economic policy-making, the upper bourgeoisie remains in permanent danger of sudden shifts in government personnel and policies owing to the (at best) ambiguous acquiescence that many military officers give to these policies and their impacts. These shifts may bring about not only important gains in the autonomy of the state apparatus in relation to the upper bourgeoisie but also, as we shall see in the next chapter, policies which severely hinder the latter's interests. Consequently, the upper bourgeoisie finds itself under the BA in the paradoxical—and, in the long run, untenable—situation of having to rely on the institutional actor which coercively guarantees the "reimplantation of order," but is at the same time uncomfortable with the typical impacts of the social and economic domination that the upper bourgeoisie enjoys under the BA. Thus, even if the bourgeoisie as a whole (not just its upper fractions) views the implantation of the BA as the only way to preserve, and later on "normalize," the capitalist parameters of society, the BA remains for this class a suboptimal form of political domination.

The ideological orientations of many military personnel, in addition to producing the tensions just discussed, tend to transform the armed forces into an arena for the expression of grievances by the middle sectors and the fractions of the local bourgeoisie that bear part of the costs of normalization. Such grievances converge with the aspirations of the armed forces to enhance the decision-making powers of the country in the international arena, which are often perceived to be related to increased national (public and private) control of the economy. This convergence may form the basis for alternative projects of capitalist development, which supposedly would involve neither intense economic transnationalization nor the weakening of national sovereignty.

The pursuit of such a project requires, however, more than a convergence of the ideology prevailing in the armed forces and the perceived interests of many middle sectors and a good part of the local bourgeoisie. The case we are studying here grew out of a crisis of accumulation and, therefore, out of a relatively mild previous threat. Consequently, an alliance among these actors was reached rapidly on the basis of available political choices. This situation, as we have seen, created numerous uncertainties for the continuity of order and normalization. By contrast, when the previous crisis and threat are significantly deeper, the armed forces (in spite of what many officers may think) are much more dependent on the field of social forces in which they are embedded. In effect, as we saw, the deeper the crisis, the more difficult the economic situation faced by the normalization program and the more dangerous it is to stray from orthodoxy. Economic policy tends therefore to adhere more rigorously to orthodoxy, making the impacts of normalization more severe. In less critical situations, on the other hand—such as the one that prevailed in Argentina between 1966 and 1969—it is not long before many come to believe that departures from orthodoxy need not be very costly. An unorthodox turn in the BA's economic policies implies the restoration of at least a limited role for the popular sector, especially the unions. A reappearance of some institutional expressions of the popular sector may be acceptable to some of the BA's actors and allies insofar as they believe that it will not precipitate a new and deeper crisis. Under the Onganía government, as we have seen, the adherence of the unions and the popular sector to Peronism, which upheld a procapitalist ideology, made an alliance with them acceptable to some members of the bourgeoisie and of the armed forces. By contrast, in BAs where the memory of a crisis of domination is still fresh, the fear of reopening Pandora's box eliminates all thought of an alliance with the popular sector. When this memory recedes, or when it appears that the causes of the challenge to social domination have been eliminated, the local bourgeoisie and the armed forces, along with the middle sectors, may once again consider this alliance as possible. But in such cases, in contrast to the ones in which the previous threat was relatively mild, those who initially applauded the implantation of the BA and whose interests were later damaged severely by normalization take more time, and face more obstacles, in their approach toward the popular sector.

NOTES

1. See *La Nación* and *La Prensa,* both June 1, 1969, p. 6.
2. These and other calls for the consolidation of orthodox economic policies and for the application of more repression may be found in the *Memorias Anuales* of the UIA, of the ACIEL, and of the CAC, all 1969–1970.
3. Ministerio de Economia y Trabajo, *Informe económico 1969,* 4th trimester, Buenos Aires. This publication explicitly attributes these and other changes to the negative expectations generated by the Cordobazo.
4. BCRA, *Boletín Estadístico,* December 1969, p. 14.
5. Ministerio de Economia y Trabajo, *Informe económico 1969.*

6. On similar attempts during the 1955–66 period, see Guillermo O'Donnell, *Modernization and Bureaucratic-Authoritarianism*, chapters 2 and 4.

7. See, for example, *La Nación*, August 8, p. 1 and December 17, p. 16, 1969.

8. See, for example, *La Nación*, November 25, 1969, p. 1; March 1, 1970, p. 6; and May 30, 1970, pp. 1, 22.

9. *La Nación*, July 15, 1969, p. 1.

10. *La Nación*, September 5, 1969, pp. 1, 22.

11. *La Nación*, September 23, 1969, p. 1.

12. *La Nación*, September 25, p. 12 and September 27, p. 1, 1969. For a subsequent meeting see *La Nación*, October 4, 1969, p. 1.

13. *La Nación*, September 28, p. 1 and October 2, p. 1, 1969.

14. *La Nación*, October 10, 1969, p. 1.

15. *La Nación*, November 1, 1969, p. 1, gives the text of this "Accord."

16. See, among others, *La Nación*, August 26, 1969, p. 1 (ACIEL); October 1, 1969, p. 1 (UIA); October 5, 1969, p. 8 (UIA and CAC).

17. The data that support this assertion are given in chapter 9.

18. On the appearance of this development plan, see *La Nación*, February 20, 1970, pp. 1, 24; for the criticisms leveled at it by the UIA and the SRA, see *La Nación*, April 24, 1970, p. 9 and March 21, 1970, p. 9, respectively. Dagnino Pastore's public statements and speeches are reprinted in Ministerio de Economía y Trabajo, *Política Económica Argentina, 1969–1970*, Buenos Aires, 1970.

19. See the bitter reactions of the UIA (*La Nación*, December 18, 1969, p. 1 and January 30, 1970, p. 7) and of the ACIEL (*La Nación*, February 6, 1970, p. 9), as well as the CGE's criticisms (*La Nación*, January 31, 1970, p. 1).

20. This information comes from my interviews.

21. *La Nación*, December 5, 1969, pp. 1, 12.

22. *La Nación*, February 27, 1970, p. 1.

23. See esp. *La Nación*, January 12, 1970, p. 11.

24. For some of the protests of the Pampean bourgeoisie, see *La Nación*, July 27, p. 1; November 14, p. 1; November 22, pp. 1, 6; and December 19, p. 1, 1969.

25. *La Nación*, April 16, 1970, p. 1.

26. *La Nación*, April 15, p. 1 and April 16, p. 24, 1970. A good analysis of these issues is Nidia Margenat, "Las organizaciones corporativas del sector agrario." See also Gerardo Duejo, *El Capital monopolista y las contradicciones secondarias en la sociedad argentina* (Buenos Aires: Siglo XXI, 1973).

27. On these episodes, see *La Nación*, June 27, 1969, pp. 1, 18.

28. I have seen three slightly different drafts of this document.

29. *La Nación*, May 30, 1970, p. 1.

30. *La Nación*, June 3, p. 22 and June 6, pp. 1, 22, 1970.

31. *La Nación*, June 9, 1970, p. 1.

32. For a fuller development of these themes, see O'Donnell, "Apuntes para una teoría del estado."

33. These themes are discussed in O'Donnell, "Tensions in the Bureaucratic-Authoritarian State."

SEVEN

Levingston: The "Nationalization" of the Bureaucratic-Authoritarian State

1. A NEW PRESIDENT

There was as much support for the coup that ousted Onganía as for the one that had installed him in the presidency.[1] Dislodged from the apex of the state apparatus and neutralized within the armed forces, the paternalists had suffered a clear defeat. Naming the victors was not so easy: the composition and goals of the new government remained a matter of speculation. One point, however, was clear: the armed forces largely agreed that the purpose of the coup, despite its "anti-corporatist" aims,* had been to prolong the BA. No one was contemplating a headlong rush toward a political way out, which would have implied an admission of failure of the "modernization" of the country that had

---

*The junta's statement giving the reasons for Onganía's ouster stressed the "anti-corporatist" aims of the coup (*La Nación*, June 10, 1970, p. 1). After commending the Onganía government for various "modernizing" achievements, it said that "a renewal of social tensions and a clear sensation of public insecurity" had resulted from "the [government's] lack of clear ideas as to how the process of institutionalizing the country was to culminate within a reasonable length of time." It added that "the approach espoused by Lieutenant General Onganía ran the risk of producing a segmented representativeness incapable of guiding the currents of civilian opinion in accordance with Argentina's democratic traditions. At the same time, it fostered a concept of the state that might ultimately have deformed our republican essence." On the other hand, the junta's communiqué employed language that would not have been out of place in a statement by the paternalists (for example, it discussed "the necessity of achieving a just balance among the aspirations of the business, professional, and labor interests in determining the general interest"). The statement was also ambiguous in its attitude toward the existing political parties, proposing a "democratic and representative system based on the *formation* of truly responsible political parties" (emphasis added).

been claimed ostentatiously for the past four years. Besides, it was tempting to blame everything that had gone wrong on the blunders and ideology of Onganía and his current. The moment had arrived, thought many within the armed forces, to forge new alliances and to appoint officials better suited to achieving the grandiose goals set forth in 1966.

The murder of Aramburu had eliminated the only figure who seemed capable of guaranteeing that a political solution could be negotiated with the political parties without jeopardizing the basic interests of the upper bourgeoisie and the armed forces. The army, moreover, appeared to have united behind General Lanusse, an officer particularly congenial to the upper bourgeoisie and the liberals. Now that the liberals controlled the armed forces, the realization of the maximum program of the upper bourgeoisie seemed possible once again. The time was ripe to end the "weaknesses" and "incongruencies" that had allowed the "social peace" to be disturbed, and to build on the achievements of the Krieger Vasena period by implementing without hesitation the full range of economic and social policies favored by the upper bourgeoisie. Such a program would require, of course, the indefinite postponement of elections and political party activity. There was no need to confuse the issue: since the new stage of the Revolution would be controlled by the liberals, it would be democratic. Party activity and elections, however, would be relegated to the distant future—or so it was still believed.*

The nationalists were less noisy than the liberals in expressing their democratic convictions, perhaps because their views on the subject were suspiciously close to those of the paternalists. Besides, the mere mention of a specific date for elections, however distant, would have raised unnecessary complications in the formidable task that the nationalists planned to undertake: fashioning a government under their control, allied with the local bourgeoisie and, insofar as they would accept a subordinate role in the coalition, with the unions. The nationalists differed from the paternalists in envisioning a more dynamic economic role for the state apparatus, in seeking to confine transnational capital to specific areas of the economy, and in cultivating the support of the *pueblo* through the use of nationalist slogans and appeals to social justice. Whereas the liberals sought to maintain the proscription of the

---

*To ensure that the coup would not be misinterpreted, *La Nación,* after expressing its support for the junta's action, editorialized that "in the magnitude of our failures there is a special lesson for those impatient individuals who think it feasible to transform the endemic imbalances in our amply endowed country through the simple mechanism of an immature electoral process. . . . The roads to all dictatorships, including those of the majority, must be closed" (June 10, 1970, p. 8).

political parties, the nationalists contemplated a popular mobilization that would replace the parties with a government-controlled movement.

But by 1970, in contrast to 1966, a solid majority of public opinion favored holding elections without further delay.* Moreover, Onganía's efforts to distinguish the military from the government did not stop many Argentines from holding the armed forces responsible for the many things that had gone awry since the 1966 coup. Accordingly, many took a dim view of evidence that, regardless of whether the nationalists or the liberals prevailed, the continuation *sine die* of the "military regime" was being contemplated. But these changes in opinion still lacked solid support within the armed forces and class organizations. Even the unions, tempted as always to reach an accord with the government and not averse to a nationalist stage, carefully avoided the issue of parties and elections in stating their support for the coup.†

Another new aspect of the situation was that the armed forces announced their readiness to participate fully and in a variety of ways at all levels of government. One of the first acts of the junta of commanders in chief was to declare that it would decide jointly with the president all matters of "significant importance."[2] The president, however, had not yet been named. The commanders in chief and their respective branches of the armed forces had trouble agreeing on Onganía's successor, in part because of interservice rivalries and in part because of the importance that both nationalists and liberals attached to controlling the presidency. The announcement that this matter had been resolved came several days after the coup. To the surprise of almost everyone—including, apparently, the new president himself—the choice was Roberto M. Levingston, a junior general who was at the time heading the Argentine delegation to the Interamerican Defense Council in Washington, D.C. Levingston, who was largely unknown to the public, had played an important behind-the-scenes role as director of the army's intelligence service in the military struggles of 1962–63 which had culminated in the triumph of the legalists. Although he had never commanded a unit of military importance, his colleagues regarded him as an

*In a national survey of 3,000 people, taken between October and December of 1970, the Centro de Estudios Motivacionales and Sociales asked, "From the point of view of the country, do you think elections would be beneficial or inexpedient?" "Beneficial" was the response of 77.6 percent, and 8.9 percent responded "inexpedient"; 7.9 percent replied that it would "depend," while 5.6 percent did not answer. After four years of the Argentine Revolution, public opinion had almost completely reversed itself.

†See the statement of the Normalizing Commission of the CGT (the Twenty-five), which also expressed the hope that the 1970 coup would provide the opportunity for "the definitive reunion of the people and its armed forces" (*La Nación*, June 12, 1970, p. 6).

introverted but talented officer.[3] His reputation as an intellectual and his tendency to keep to himself made him something of a mystery to his fellow officers. It may be asked why the junta selected an officer who was not in command of troops, was unproven as a military leader, and was regarded as an enigma by his own colleagues. The answer is that he was chosen for precisely those characteristics. In the first place, the junta, now intent on fully militarizing the regime, saw the president basically as its delegate. Levingston would be in charge of the routine affairs of government but would be only one of four participants (and the only one without a military command) in making truly important decisions. In addition, selecting a president with little political weight of his own seemed to obviate a series of problems: no threat would be posed to Lanusse's control of the army, fears within the navy and air force that the army would gain excessive influence over the state apparatus would be diminished, and, since Levingston was identified as neither a liberal nor a nationalist, a reasonable balance would seem to have been struck between those two currents.

2. GOVERNMENTAL DECISIONS AND CONFLICTS

With Levingston's assumption of the presidency came the formation of a new cabinet, a process in which the junta had more say than Levingston. The Interior and Social Welfare ministries went respectively to Brigadier Eduardo McLoughlin and former naval officer Francisco Manrique, both liberals and both close to Lanusse. Appointments to the Public Works and Foreign Relations ministries were of a different sort. The new Minister of Public Works was Aldo Ferrer, a developmentalist *técnico* whose ideas were quite advanced for that current. José María de Pablo Pardo, the new foreign minister, came from the mainstream of traditional Catholic nationalism but was also closely connected to the liberals, particularly through his close ties with the navy. The Ministry of Economy and Labor was assigned to Carlos Moyano Llerena, who was reputed to have been the principal intellectual influence behind Krieger Vasena's program. These appointments were clearly biased toward the liberals, and the CGT and CGE were the first to express concern. When Levingston held his first public meeting with leaders of the CGT, the latter made no effort to disguise their lack of enthusiasm for the president's haughty demeanor and for what they termed his "reluctance to engage in dialogue."[4] The CGE, however, was mollified by a speech in which Levingston announced that the government would seek to reverse economic denationalization and to promote national capital, especially small and medium-sized enterprises.[5] Included in this speech and in the National Policies that the junta revised and issued after Onganía's ouster[6] were some familiar themes. Profound structural reforms and community participation through authentically representative basic organizations were again called for, and reference was made to the tremendous evils brought on by political parties and the electoral system. Such themes, punctuated as before with appeals to national grandeur and to the ultimately spiritual content of development, had previously provoked sarcasm and alarm. But since all the currents were for the moment preoccupied with establishing their positions with respect to the new government, and since each still expected to control it, these obvious continuities provoked few comments at the time.

Attention soon focused on the Ministry of Economy and Labor, where Moyano Llerena's decisions closely recalled the ones taken in March 1967. The peso was devalued from 350 to 400 to the U.S. dollar (although Moyano Llerena, unlike Krieger Vasena, would not claim that this would be the final devaluation); exports were again subjected to a withholding tax that allowed the state apparatus to absorb entirely the resulting foreign exchange windfall; import duties were lowered to compensate for the effects of the devaluation; and a new voluntary agreement on prices was proposed. Moyano Llerena argued that these policies would be a major step toward restoring confidence in the stability of the currency.[7] But conditions had changed since March 1967. Substantial sectors of the population were mobilizing against the BA, and union leaders were pressing aggressively for economic concessions. Moreover, the Cordobazo and its sequels* had undermined the government's capacity for coercion. Repression did not disappear, but its continuous and systematic use against the entire popular sector was no longer a credible possibility. Under these conditions, the government could not, as it had done in 1967, impose a wage freeze, and without a wage freeze Moyano Llerena's program was fundamentally compromised. Moreover, while in the summer of 1967 the government had viewed the union leaders as the principal agents of subversion, it now

---

*Violent incidents became more numerous and spectacular in the second half of 1970. Widespread strikes, together with guerrilla actions including takeovers of entire towns and assaults on military and security installations, suggested that the new government was far from finding a solution to the "disorder" that the junta had given as a reason for removing Onganía.

saw them as indispensable allies in containing the worrisome popular activation. Thus, not only did Moyano Llerena's policies include no mention of a wage freeze, they also earmarked the better part of the fiscal revenues from the devaluation to raising payments to pensioners. There is perhaps no better indication of the relation of forces prevailing after the Cordobazo than the contrast between Moyano Llerena's use of these funds and the way they were used by Krieger Vasena.

Moyano Llerena's reduction of import duties* and his association with the Krieger Vasena period soon moved the CGE and the nationalists to launch sharp attacks on the Economy Minister,† who got little support from the upper bourgeoisie and its organizations. Caught off balance by the devaluation, aware of the difference between the contexts of 1967 and 1970, and little moved by Moyano Llerena's concern for the pensioners, the organizations of the upper bourgeoisie criticized the devaluation, calling it an "unnecessary and suicidal" step that had destroyed what little confidence remained.[8] If policies similar to those of 1967 had been enacted with the hope of improving expectations, they had the opposite effect. Prices rose almost immediately and the recently devalued peso was placed under heavy pressure. Opposed by its natural adversaries, criticized by the upper bourgeoisie, and having produced effects the reverse of those intended, Moyano Llerena's administration soon ended with his resignation.

The Public Works Ministry performed more successfully, launching several important projects with widely publicized dynamism. But serious friction soon emerged in other areas of government. Levingston had appointed Francisco Luco, a former Peronist member of Congress, as Undersecretary of Labor. Luco's administration was subjected to wage demands it had no capacity to meet. Moreover, the new government divulged through Luco its unwillingness to repeal the Law of Professional Associations, proposing instead—once again—to build "structural bases" of support (this time for the nationalists) among the unions. The unexpected revival of this theme drew attacks with a distinct flavor of déjà vu.[9]

Another point of friction appeared in the Interior Ministry, where

---

*The reduction of import duties, like other orthodox policies resembling those adopted in 1967, got an unsympathetic reception (even from the upper bourgeoisie) in what was now a very different political and economic setting. See the protests of the UIA in *Periscopio*, October 1, 1970, p. 19.

†The CGE and the nationalists were soon joined in these attacks by the recently "normalized" CGT and its new secretary-general, José Rucci, a Vandorist member of the metalworkers' union (*La Nación*, July 14, 1970, p. 4).

McLoughlin, without mentioning a specific timetable, had clearly based the future political plan on an accord with the political parties along the lines of the one that Aramburu had attempted. McLoughlin hoped that the new government would achieve successes that would give it sufficient leverage to impose guarantees on the political parties that would prove satisfactory to the bourgeoisie and the armed forces. But the Undersecretary of the Interior, Ricardo Gilardi Novaro—who, like Luco, had been appointed by Levingston and not by the junta—acted independently of McLoughlin and in direct accord with the president. Levingston and Gilardi Novaro had in mind something very different from what McLoughlin envisioned. After four or five years of "deepening the revolution," a democracy, to be sure, would arise, with "constitution, parties, and elections." But this democracy, unlike its predecessor, would be neither "factionalized" nor "disordered": on the contrary, it would express the consensus achieved by the Revolution, thanks to which, in the words of Levingston, it would be "hierarchical" and "ordered."[10] Such a vision, with its less explicit but still noticeable corporatist components, was scarcely novel. However, it incorporated elements that attested to the distance separating the nationalists from the paternalists. The elimination of the old parties, for which even harsher words were reserved than in the Onganía period, was explicitly proposed. It was also made clear that those parties would be replaced by a very few new ones, no less "hierarchical" and "ordered" than the rest of the system being contemplated.[11] It was nowhere specified how many parties would exist, but the possibility that "few" meant only one was implicit in plans to create a "Movement of the Argentine Revolution" to embody and promote its "philosophy" during and after the military regime.* This movement would be the instrument for superseding the old parties, for mobilizing the *pueblo* behind the "National Revolution," and for channeling this mobilization in support of a state guaranteeing "national capitalism"

---

*To the dismay of many, Levingston announced that his government would last at least four or five years, after which the preexisting political parties would no longer have a role to play since "the party structures in effect prior to 1966 belong to the past. . . . I repeat: the dissolution of parties carried out by the Argentine Revolution is, for this government, an irrevocable decision." In place of the old parties there would be "a formula for neutralizing political atomization and for channeling opinion into great new party forces coexisting within the framework of a stable and efficient democracy." This would result from a successful effort to "deepen" the Argentine Revolution, which would require the "mobilization and participation of the entire population of the country" (speech by Levingston printed in *La Nación*, September 30, 1970, pp. 1, 14). Gilardi Novaro touched off a cabinet crisis by stating that a government-organized "movement," designed to "perpetuate the philosophy of the Revolution," would form the axis of the government's proposed political plan (*La Nación*, October 14, 1970, p. 1).

and an ordered, "hierarchical" society.* Evidently inspired by the Mexican PRI, this scheme, like the Moyano Llerena program, lacked a number of conditions for success. Most important, the movement would not originate in anything resembling a revolution. It would also have to contend with a popular sector that had already passed through a populist experience (the Perón governments) and that had moved toward an activation that far exceeded the limits contemplated by those who sought to mobilize it from what remained of the BA. If the political and organizational space for the project was virtually nonexistent,[12] Moyano Llerena's program (which, in spite of its inconsistencies, tried to conform to orthodoxy) ensured a scarcity of the economic payoffs that might have alleviated its difficulties. Moreover, when economic policy took a turn more consistent with the nationalists' aspirations, the ensuing crisis, as we shall see, created even more intractable problems.

The movement that the nationalists contemplated was fundamentally nonviable and went no further than attempts to recruit what came to be called the "intermediate generation," more or less youthful leaders of the traditional political parties whom the nationalists regarded as uncontaminated by the old politics.[13] These efforts demonstrated to the liberals that Levingston was no closer to them than Onganía had been and heightened the hostility of the increasingly active political parties (particularly the Peronists and the Radicals)† to the government. Moreover, Levingston's insistent references to hierarchy and authority, like his attacks against "politicians" (who in light of what had occurred since 1966 had risen considerably in public esteem), did not facilitate his efforts to demonstrate his "concern for the poor"[14] and to reach the people through clumsy "dialogues."[15] On top of this the nationalists re-

---

*Virtually every official statement expressed the inconsistencies between these illusions of mobilizing and the nationalists' "hierarchical" vision of society. The government's messages also manifested a reluctance (to say the least) to countenance new political parties, even in the future. For example: "We seek . . . a system of parties, or ideas, which is not yet fully defined, in which the currents of opinion in this country—which are not many—can find a channel of expression conducive to a more stable, responsible, and hierarchical political life" (Levingston's press conference in *La Nación*, October 13, 1970, p. 5).

†Statements by the Radical Party and by Daniel Paladino, Perón's delegate, noted acrimoniously that the new government, far from clearing the way for parties and elections, seemed intent on perpetuating itself through a scheme no less authoritarian than the one Onganía had developed. See *La Nación*, September 9, 1970, p. 11 and October 3, 1970, p. 5, and *Primera Plana*, October 6, 1970, p. 14. It should also be noted that the CGT was the first important class organization to demand democracy, elections, and the full restoration of the national constitution (*La Nación*, September 15, 1970, p. 11). This line was adopted subsequently by Peronism.

fused as firmly as their paternalist predecessors even to discuss a date for elections.*

The nationalists sought to manipulate the popular mobilization from the government, above and against the political parties. They were prepared to do the same against the unions if the latter proved unwilling to enter into subordinate collaboration with the government in return for selective benefits and policies more sensitive to the economic demands of their rank and file.

The nationalists' designs became the target of corrosive popular satire that focused on Levingston's arrogant style and increased the hostility of the liberals and the political parties toward the new president. Many concluded that if things had changed at all, it had not been for the better. This was certainly the viewpoint of most of the media, which hammered it home in the anti-Levingston offensive it soon launched. Popular activation very different from the sort that the government contemplated rose to higher levels, guerrilla activity gathered further momentum, and the unions pressed for wage increases which, if conceded, would only accelerate the collapse of Moyano Llerena's policies. The seven percent wage and salary increase granted in October 1970 was not enough for the CGT, which formulated a new Plan of Action and inaugurated it with widely observed general strikes on the ninth and twenty-second of that month. In November 1970, despite the announcement that collective bargaining would be resumed in March 1971 with no government-imposed limits on wage and salary hikes, and despite the fact that Moyano Llerena had already resigned, a thirty-six-hour general strike was called and widely heeded. These events demonstrated the government's difficulties in forging an alliance with the unions, at least so long as no major changes occurred in economic policy. Furthermore, it was clear that the government would not and could not use extensive repression against the unions: the strikes generated no sanctions, and the Interior Minister did no more than blame them on the "lack of representativeness" and "politicization" of a "small group of pseudo-leaders."† Nor could the generalized hostility toward the government be controlled.‡

---

*Levingston's refusal to discuss elections is evident in his previously cited speeches and statements. The monthly *Extra* published the question that many were asking: "Why, then, was Onganía ousted?" (insert to the front page of its October 1970 issue).

†For complaints about the "irresolute attitude of the government toward the strike," see *La Nación*, November 15, 1970, p. 8, and *Primera Plana*, November 17, 1970, p. 14.

‡The image of order and hierarchy was helped neither by riots in Tucumán, which ended only when troops were sent in from the neighboring province of Salta (*La Nación*,

Under these conditions, the organizations of the upper bourgeoisie bitterly criticized the wage and salary increases and the "lack of [political] guarantees." Moreover, the main economic indicators of an acute loss of confidence—a black market and a strong demand for foreign exchange—emerged once again. At the same time, beef and other agricultural prices continued to rise, stimulating a general price increase.[16] New and more severe restrictions on the domestic consumption of meat failed to solve the problem, but by adding the Pampean bourgeoisie to the government's opponents,[17] they worked the miracle of producing a unanimous chorus of opposition just three months after the new government had assumed office.

The situation took an important turn when the president seized an opportunity provided by the conflict between the Interior Minister and his undersecretary to secure the resignations of both, as well as that of the Economy Minister.[18] After a series of maneuvers and delays, Brigadier General Mario Cordón Aguirre, on active duty in the air force (the most nationalistic branch of the armed forces) was named Minister of the Interior. Ferrer moved in as Economy Minister. These changes, some reshufflings in the provincial governments, and Levingston's obvious efforts to acquire his own base of political and military support, showed the commanders in chief that the decision-making scheme they had sought to implement was not at all the one that Levingston had in mind. Far from content to accept the circumscribed role assigned to him, Levingston intended to assume leadership of the nationalist phase of the BA and to wrest control of the army from Lanusse. The commanders in chief (especially Lanusse, whose personality, civilian backing, and weight within the army made him primarily responsible for the situation) had to find a solution to this unexpected problem. This would involve some difficult choices. On the one hand, Levingston's ouster could no longer be reconciled with illusions of reviving the BA, a conclusion that many paternalists and nationalists within the armed forces still found difficult to accept. On the other hand, Levingston was launching what remained of the BA on a nationalist course, the implications of which would soon become evident. This thankless dilemma served to prolong the Levingston government from the October 1970 cabinet

---

November 14, 1970, p. 24), nor by a police strike in Catamarca that culminated in serious turmoil (*La Nación*, November 18, 1970, p. 1), nor by continued guerrilla activity, which included the assassination of José Alonso (*La Nación*, August 28, 1970, p. 1).

changes until March 1971, an extraordinarily long interval considering the circumstances.*

3. THE HOUR OF THE PEOPLE

On November 11, 1970, the Peronists, the Radicals, and several minor political parties issued a joint statement entitled *La Hora del Pueblo* (The Hour of the People).[19] The coalition announced by the signatories of the document came also to be known by that name. The statement called for a quick return to democracy and contained generic allusions to a future characterized by political stability, a more equal distribution of income, and protection of the nationally owned sectors of the economy. On the one hand, in demanding elections with "neither vetoes nor proscriptions," the document implied a commitment by the Radicals to supporting the reentry of Peronism into an electoral arena from which it had been excluded in various ways for the past fifteen years. On the other hand, by formalizing pledges to respect when in government the rights of minority parties, the document expressed a commitment by Peronism (which in the eyes of many was the only party likely to violate those rights) not to take undue advantage of its electoral clout.

La Hora del Pueblo had been a long time in the making. As it became clear to party leaders that the coup, in the eyes of paternalists, nationalists, and liberals alike, had been carried out to suppress all political parties for an extended period of time, many discovered a common interest in restoring the electoral system. This stance, to be sure, had not prevailed before 1966, when no party of even minimal importance had

---

*Rumors soon circulated that a new coup, headed by Lanusse, was in the making. Following a meeting of generals, however, Lanusse informed the media (*La Nación*, October 17, 1970, p. 1) that he remained in "total agreement" with the President and with the four- to five-year term the latter apparently envisioned for himself. Lanusse explained that "the length of this term is not arbitrary, but determined by the time it will take to achieve the social and economic objectives that are considered indispensable for assuring the stability and effectiveness of the democratic regime that they are intended to establish and preserve." Nevertheless, Lanusse and his closest collaborators were already involved discreetly in the initiatives that were soon to culminate in the public announcement of *La Hora del Pueblo*. Lanusse took the occasion to add, with involuntary irony that would soon become apparent, that "Mr. Juan Domingo Perón, whatever his achievements or errors in discharging the offices he has held in his public life, was appropriately disqualified for very serious offenses by a Special Tribunal made up of five of the Nation's Lieutenant Generals. This act remains in effect; its causes should not, and cannot, be forgotten by those who take pride in being soldiers."

failed to collaborate in promoting a military coup,* each presuming
that the intervention of the armed forces would install its personnel in
the government and/or constitute it as an eventual electoral heir.[20] By
1970, however, the major political parties† seemed to have learned from
experience: their demands for a return to elections were accompanied
by mutual promises to play by democratic rules both before and after
being seated (or not) in the government.

Arturo Mor Roig of the Radicals and Daniel Paladino of the Peronists were the most important figures in reaching this agreement. There
is little doubt that the timing of the public appearance of *La Hora del
Pueblo* (and its open appeal to the armed forces to reject Levingston's
project in favor of democratization) was the result of conversations
between the top leaders of its constituent parties and the current of the
armed forces led by Lanusse.[21] *La Hora del Pueblo* represented an
important convergence. On the one hand, growing social tensions and
the exhaustion of the "Argentine Revolution" had convinced the more
astute supporters of the BA that it was necessary to decompress the
situation by making government positions accessible to such parties as
the Radicals and the Peronists, which together could count on the
backing of a substantial majority of the population.[22] On the other
hand, the huge electoral majority constituted by the combined supporters of the Peronists and Radicals could serve as a safety valve for the
armed forces as well as for the sectors of the bourgeoisie which, so-
bered by the incongruities of the paternalists and the adventures of the
nationalists, were rediscovering their "democratic vocation." Not only
were the Peronists pledging not to alter the rules of the game if and
when they won an election,‡ they had also agreed with the Radicals on
a generic program of moderate redistributive nationalism that coin-

*For example, the Radicals actively supported the 1955 coup that ousted Perón, while
the Peronists helped promote the 1966 coup. Both supported the 1962 coup against
President Frondizi, who in turn was active in promoting the 1966 coup.

†Several parties with little electoral weight but some influence on public opinion (such
as the Developmentalists led by Arturo Frondizi, the Intransigents of Oscar Alende, and
the faction of Christian Democracy led by Horacio Sueldo) came out against reopening
the electoral process and in favor of "deepening the revolution." On the other side, the
Encuentro de los Argentinos (the Meeting of the Argentines) emerged to the left of *La
Hora del Pueblo*. It consisted of the Communist party, offshoots of the Socialist party,
some splinters of the major parties, and groups that had been linked to the *CGT de los
Argentinos*.

‡The Peronist representatives to *La Hora del Pueblo* who were party to this agreement
turned out to be less representative of Peronism (and of Perón) than had been hoped. But
this is a story we shall take up later.

cided with the policies favored by the local bourgeoisie and many military officers.*

Widespread disillusionment with military control of government, and the corresponding rise in the prestige of politicians, formed the context in which *La Hora del Pueblo* emerged and signaled the return of the parties as important actors in the processes that were unfolding.†\nThe reappearance of the parties and their de facto acceptance as actors in the political arena marked another turning point in the process we are analyzing. Together with the resurgence of popular activation and the significant gains in autonomy from the state apparatus that were being made by various organizations of civil society (particularly the unions), the reemergence of the parties marked the point at which the BA, according to the definition proposed in chapter 1, ceased to exist. The state, to be sure, was still authoritarian, but it was no longer the BA that has concerned us thus far. Its exclusionary character was dissolving rapidly, and the unstable and swiftly changing authoritarian hybrid typical of the transition took the place of its failed predecessor.

Once the BA is implanted, the politicians banned, and the excoriated politics suppressed, the politics that remains—aside from tugs of war among the currents in the state apparatus—consists of the raw expression of demands not easy to link to any general interest. With the political and economic exclusion of the popular sector, moreover, the articulation of these interests is monopolized by organizations that are notable for their skewed class composition. The exclusion of the popular sector and the suppression of political parties do more than reduce the number of actors in the political arena. Politics in the BA is an opaque politics of and within bureaucracies, in which highly disaggregated interests flow through the interstices of the state institutions, corroding the technical and neutral image that those who speak for the BA try so hard to create. Meanwhile, the hushed politics of an opposition still silenced beneath the mantle of repression and tacit consensus

---

*Another factor (mentioned in several of my interviews) apparently facilitated this convergence: many of the most prominent figures in *La Hora del Pueblo* were willing at the time to support a transitional president (Lanusse) in the period between the liquidation of the BA and the full operation of a democratic regime. The language used in the public announcement of *La Hora del Pueblo*, which left the door wide open to negotiations with the armed forces over the terms of the political solution, is worth noting.

†By that time, Levingston's fulminations against "the old politics" could only work to the parties' advantage.

can be heard only in places, and through signals which are not readily accessible to ears attuned only to conventional politics.

Two fundamental consequences result from the subsequent crumbling of the BA. The first involves the reappearance of political actors with characteristics, strategies, and goals very different from those that monopolized the scene under the BA. These actors include not just the political parties, but also a diverse set of neighborhood associations, church groups, professional organizations, regional movements and even, in the case studied here, guerrillas. Arising from this first consequence is a second one: a tremendous expansion of the political arena to encompass a broad range of actors in society. This expansion also involves the conversion of many social organizations, such as the ones just mentioned, into theaters where contending groups try to secure the positions that they deem important for affecting the direction of the political process. In the wake of the controls imposed by a BA, society recovers vigorously, inventing new institutions while repoliticizing and giving new meanings to old ones. Politics under the transitional authoritarian regime becomes immensely more complex than it was under the BA. From the perspective taken in this book, which considers the state first and foremost an aspect of the relations of domination within society and only secondarily a set of institutions, the transition from BA rule involves crucial changes in the relations of social domination. These changes have profound reverberations in the state apparatus and in the policies its incumbents do or do not decide to implement.

The collapse of the BA and the reappearance of the political parties thus resulted from (and in turn greatly encouraged) the repoliticization of most of society in the direction of strong opposition. The agony of the Levingston government and the failure of its efforts to resuscitate the BA were the obverse face of a process that radically changed the relations between state and society that had existed under the BA. This tumultuous, uncertain and ultimately fateful process is the theme of the rest of this book.

4. THE "NATIONALIZATION"—AND
    COLLAPSE—OF THE BA

The appointment of Ferrer to head the Ministry of Economy and Labor gave the nationalists, at long last, access to this part of the state apparatus. Ferrer and most of his collaborators did not come from the nationalist right; they were developmentalist *técnicos* with a reformist orientation. Like the liberals, they had international links, but these were more with development organizations like the UN Economic Commission for Latin America, the Andean Group, and the Interamerican Development Bank than with transnational corporations and international financial agencies. The nationalism of this group was different from that of Levingston and his current, who had few connections with and a marked antipathy toward all sorts of international organizations and considerable hostility toward big business per se. Nevertheless, Ferrer and Levingston shared a commitment to the tutelage of national capital, moderate income redistribution, close control of transnational firms operating in the domestic market, and the expansion of the state apparatus, including as a producer. Such programs, they hoped, would generate broad popular support for the ideology of national invigoration which they held in common.

The goals of the new economic team are summarized in the National Development and Security Plan for 1971–75, which replaced the earlier one prepared by the Onganía government. This document, while hardly innovative in many respects, evidenced considerable concern for protecting national enterprise and for promoting the state apparatus as a direct producer, particularly of industrial inputs.* The plan also provided for the creation of a public agency to support small and medium-sized firms and to promote domestic capital formation, with a view toward equipping local entrepreneurs to compete and negotiate more successfully with transnational capital.

Both the development plan and Ferrer in his inaugural address were careful to stress the importance of private initiative and to insist that transnational capital was welcome—in economic activities to be delimited by the government.† These ideas were soon converted into policies:

---

*The plan advocated "the consolidation and expansion of nationally owned enterprises, particularly in the dynamic sectors." The state would be involved in "promoting the concentration" of these enterprises and in "helping to organize their finances," for which preferential funding would be provided (*Plan Nacional de Seguridad y Desarrollo*, Presidencia de la Nación, Buenos Aires, 1971, pp. 34 and 108). In addition, public investment would be increased significantly and channeled primarily toward the industrial sector rather than (as in the Krieger Vasena period) toward the physical infrastructure. The state was to "assume the functions of a producer and participate to varying degrees in the capital stock of [private] enterprises" (*Plan Nacional*, p. 109). Not surprisingly, the upper bourgeoisie and the leading periodicals made strong objections to such "collectivist" and "socializing" proposals (see, for example, *La Prensa*, February 8, 1971, p. 4).

†For the text of Ferrer's address, see *La Nación*, October 28, 1970, pp. 1, 10. Ferrer also announced that capital goods industries were to be modernized and that an increase in the minimum wage was being considered (which did not prevent the CGT from proceeding with the thirty-six-hour general strike mentioned earlier). In addition, he made two

import duties were raised,[23] signaling a strong emphasis on the protection of local industry; the National Industrial Bank was transformed into a National Development Bank with expanded resources for medium- and long-term financing of industrial projects;[24] several investment projects were approved for the production of industrial inputs; and a law was passed obliging state enterprises to buy preferentially from local suppliers.[25] None of these policies was in fact detrimental to the upper bourgeoisie or to transnational capital already operating in the domestic market. The same could not be said for potential new foreign investors, but there were few who still found Argentina an attractive market.*

Despite the fact that industrial capital benefited (at least in the short run) from these policies, toward the end of 1970 the UIA and other organizations of the upper bourgeoisie launched a bitter campaign against them. They denounced in a typically overdramatized tone the statism of the new policies, arguing that it foreshadowed the suppression of "freedom and private initiative" and, ultimately, the arrival of "totalitarian collectivism."[26] At the same time, they criticized the government for its inability to control the popular activation—above all (once again) in Córdoba.†

Partly because of policies that for the first time seemed seriously concerned with raising the incomes of the best organized segments of the popular sector, Ferrer's administration managed to reduce the number of strikes declared by the national unions.‡ At the same time, Levingston and Luco entered negotiations with a "non aligned" group of union leaders.[27] These leaders, in large measure successors to the

---

promises that he was soon obliged to rescind: that the peso would not be devalued, and that unrestricted collective bargaining would be restored shortly (on the latter see also *La Nación*, November 14, 1970, p. 5).

*The figures in chapter 9 show that foreign direct investment practically dried up in 1970 (as well as in 1971 and 1972).

†Especially noteworthy were the strikes at the Fiat and IKA–Renault automobile factories, during which some thirty executives were held hostage; see *La Nación*, January 16, pp. 1, 5, and February 21, p. 4, 1971. A "week of struggle" was also declared in Córdoba (*La Nación*, January 17, 1971, p. 5) during which a series of "active stoppages" took place, frequently involving the holding of managerial personnel as hostages (*La Nación*, January 24, p. 10; February 25, p. 6; February 28, p. 11; March 4, p. 5; and March 19, p. 1, 1971). For the UIA's demands that the government intensify repression, see *La Nación*, January 21, pp. 1, 7, and March 12, p. 1, 1971.

‡Also contributing to lower levels of strike activity at the national level were promises by the economic team to restore unrestricted collective bargaining (i.e. without government-fixed ceilings on wage and salary increases), and to provide frequent cost-of-living adjustments to wages and salaries (*La Nación*, December 30, 1970, pp. 1, 6).

participationists, were as incapable as ever of delivering the CGT and its affiliated unions into the hands of the government. The Vandorists, in another déjà vu, retained a firm grip on the CGT, and it was with them that the nationalists would have to deal if they wished to acquire an organized base of support. But the Vandorists—worried by the activation of their rank and file and now under pressure from Peronism, whose expressions of opposition to the government ranged from *La Hora del Pueblo* to the guerrillas—agreed only to a kind of cease-fire, which took the form of a temporary decline in strike activity and some moderation of the CGT's economic demands. This response was a far cry from the active support that the nationalists sought from the unions.

The CGE, which had decried the concentration and transnationalization of capital that had taken place under Krieger Vasena, could not but applaud the nationalist-statist aims of the new government. Tutelage of national industry, stimulation of internal consumption, increased state investment in industry, and various direct and indirect subsidies to the local bourgeoisie were, after all, policies that the CGE had long advocated. Furthermore, as we saw before, the CGE had denounced since 1967 not only the domestic expansion of the "international monopolies" and the government's indifference to "denationalization," but also the "financial suffocation" of local capital that reinforced those processes.[28] It was no secret that transnational capital operating in the Argentine market received a substantial part of its financing from the domestic financial system, and that its intimate links to that system, together with its solvency, allowed it access to a disproportionate share of the cheapest available credit. It was against this background that the government made a decision that deeply antagonized transnational capital and the various bourgeois factions linked to it: it decreed that any future increases in bank assets available for lending would be channeled exclusively to nationally owned firms.* Bank credit for foreign firms was virtually frozen by this decree and, in view of the significant inflation that now prevailed, it began to diminish rapidly in real terms. Foreign enterprises would now have to obtain new credit abroad, which the Central Bank facilitated by adopting a liberal policy of swaps. This mechanism produced an influx of short-term foreign capital that greatly

---

*For Ferrer's announcement of the "Argentinization of credit," see *La Nación*, December 30, 1970, pp. 1, 6. Ferrer stated that "foreign firms should finance themselves with their own resources and with credit obtained abroad. The savings of Argentines are for supporting what is Argentine. . . . [It is necessary to stop] the growing denationalization of the productive apparatus, which is often financed with Argentine credit and backed by guarantees from the national state."

increased the public sector's foreign debt. Since the Argentine government guaranteed such transactions, transnational corporations could supply their subsidiaries with working capital whose repatriation was protected against exchange fluctuations. In short, the government's new credit policies succeeded in giving local capital a greater share of domestic financing, but only at the expense of encouraging transnational capital to acquire a rather large debt to itself that was guaranteed by the Argentine state. Under the circumstances, these arrangements were an excellent, no-risk transaction for transnational capital and a source of severe indebtedness for Argentina.

Nevertheless, the discrimination against foreign capital embodied in these policies violated one of the sacred precepts of orthodoxy and gave rise to a chorus of protests.[29] It soon became clear, however, that the government's credit policies were only the beginning. Levingston loudly denounced "distortions" which, even in the state banks, had benefited the "international monopolies" at the expense of "national enterprises," and he announced that the government was contemplating an investigation of all banks and financial institutions operating in Argentina.[30] These episodes, the angry criticisms directed at them, and certain expressions of vehement support for the "anti-monopolist" and "anti-denationalizing" implications of existing and subsequent policies[31] moved the center of gravity from the economic team to the president and his immediate collaborators.

It was clear that Levingston intended to create a political movement—not a party—to support and prolong his presidency. In December 1970 he unveiled the "Bases of the Political Plan," which proposed "a profound effort to create and consolidate a national and revolutionary spirit," again made derogatory references to the "old politics," and stressed the importance of "achieving popular consensus to facilitate revolutionary action." These objectives, the document continued, would necessitate the indefinite extension of prohibitions against political party activity and a search for "alternatives that will assure the continuity of the philosophy of the Argentine Revolution."[32] The press received these and similar pronouncements[33] with a mixture of alarm and sarcasm: Levingston really sounded ridiculous.[34] A more aggressive response came from the parties grouped in *La Hora del Pueblo*, which, in a public statement addressed to the armed forces, termed the political plan a "deplorable document" of "continuist design" that made a mockery of the reasons that had been given for deposing Onganía.[35] The cabinet changes, the economic policies, the virulent attacks on the political parties, and the calls for the creation of a "revolutionary spirit" to nourish the forthcoming movement elicited from most of the media a condemnation of the "continuist adventure." The armed forces, the media insinuated, had created this Frankenstein, and it was up to them to destroy it.[36]

Given the resurgence of the political parties, the hostility of nearly all organizations of society,* and the massive public opposition to the government, efforts to excite the above-mentioned spirit and to produce the longed-for movement were obviously futile. How, then, should they be understood, apart from the personal predilections of Levingston and his closest collaborators? Many of the nationalists' policies had emerged in response to those of the Onganía government. Above all, the transnationalizing and efficientist orientations of Krieger Vasena and Dagnino Pastore had produced a strong nationalist reaction in the armed forces and in many social sectors. This reaction gave rise to the view that the national entrepreneurs who controlled the smaller and less dynamic firms were ready to lead, in alliance with a nationalist-controlled state, an alternative pattern of capitalist development. The *pueblo* was expected to lend active but disciplined support to this alliance, which would finally bring about the "national grandeur" that the internationalism of the liberals had so far prevented the country from achieving. These populist illusions found fertile soil not just in the government, but also in the CGE, a substantial proportion of union leaders, and more than a few political parties—notably Peronism, whose dynamic resurgence seemed to demonstrate the viability of the nationalist and populist policies it had enacted while in government some twenty years before. Increased receptivity to such views did not, however, translate into support for the Levingston government. Instead, it helped to stimulate the extraordinary growth of Peronism that will occupy us in the next three chapters.

Meanwhile, Levingston and his close collaborators focused their attacks on financial capital. Employing a moralistic tone containing strong anti-usury connotations, they attributed the numerous economic scandals that surfaced during the period to the "foreignness" of the largest fractions of capital. No fascist solution was in store for Argentina, but some middle sectors and some segments of the armed forces, as

---

*Including the CGE, which despite its support for many of the policies adopted kept its distance from both Levingston and Ferrer. See, for example, Gelbard's cautious statements in *La Nación*, January 30, 1971, p. 5. See also the conclusions of the Annual Congress of the CGE, which focused on the shakiness of the overall economic situation and minimized the importance of the new policies, which, it argued, "do not signal a real and coherent change" (*La Nación*, March 12, 1971, p. 4).

the preceding discussion suggests, were moving closer to a syndrome characterized by nationalism, rejection of big business, appeals to small entrepreneurs exploited by the large firms, moralistic diatribes against usury, strident condemnations of liberalism, and appeals to a *pueblo* first denied existence as a class.* Furthermore—as if to complete a proto-fascist syndrome that would later reappear, as we shall see, under rather surprising circumstances—the same sectors brandished a fervent anticommunism and claimed that only they could put down the "subversive potential" of the popular activation.

But not all hopes for a nationalist alternative for Argentine capitalism were an expression of this syndrome. The developmentalist reformism of Ferrer and his team pointed toward something closer to European social democracy. But the structural and political conditions prevailing in Argentina were even less auspicious for this alternative than for the implantation of a fascist state. Accordingly, the economic team, initially the driving force behind the government, found itself compelled to coexist with the particular version of nationalism upheld by Levingston and his immediate collaborators. In this uncomfortable position, and under heavy fire from the upper bourgeoisie and most of the media, the economic team greeted the coup that deposed Levingston with obvious relief.

In its final months, the Levingston government reached a level of confrontation with the upper bourgeoisie that went substantially beyond the one contemplated by many of those who advocated a nationalist solution, including Ferrer and his team and the CGE. As noted in chapter 1, most of the firms affiliated with the CGE were small or medium-sized, technologically backward, nationally owned, and without links to transnational capital. Few of the CGE's leaders controlled the large, oligopolistic enterprises which, according to the definitions proposed in chapter 1, would have qualified them as members of the upper bourgeoisie. Rather, the CGE leadership came largely from firms of a still different order, which reflected the position of some segments of the local bourgeoisie in Argentina's capitalism: they constituted an ascendant fraction within the bourgeoisie, in control of dynamic, medium-sized, and often recently created enterprises using modern technology, with numerous backward and forward linkages to the TNCs. The economic interests of these fractions are harmed, as are those of the rest of the local bourgeoi-

---

*In its final days, the Levingston government gave a further indication of its pro-fascist ideological leanings by creating a State Secretariat for Youth (*Análisis*, March 23, 1971, p. 10).

sie, when state tutelage is withdrawn and when discrimination against transnational capital is eliminated. These changes allow transnational capital to expand its operations in the domestic market, and contract it for parts of the local bourgeoisie. They also strengthen the TNC's bargaining position with respect to the ascendant fractions of the local bourgeoisie in the continuous renegotiation of the latter's subordinate linkages to the former. In such circumstances, those fractions, not in spite of but precisely because of their close links with (and ultimately their dependence on) transnational capital, may become an influential nationalist voice. This voice expresses the specific grievances not so much of the ascendant segments as of the weaker, and more properly national, layers of the local bourgeoisie. The willingness of the ascendant segments to take nationalist positions results in part from a perception that the entire local bourgeoisie shares a common interest in restoring state tutelage and in checking the unfettered expansion of transnational capital. It is also reinforced by the prior existence in Argentina of an organization—the CGE—that had already formed around convergences within the local bourgeoisie as a whole. Nevertheless, the dynamic segments of the local bourgeoisie are so deeply intertwined with transnational capital that there is a point beyond which this nationalism will not be taken. The pursuit of a stronger bargaining position with respect to transnational capital in no way entails excluding it from the domestic market. Any such exclusion would provoke what these ascendant fractions, together with the whole bourgeoisie of which they are a part, desire least: the collapse of the economy and/or a leap toward some kind of socialism. There exists for these fractions a delicate balance between improving their bargaining position and precipitating this disaster. Furthermore, they feel that in order to preserve this balance it helps to have strong influence over a state apparatus that provides them with tutelage but at the same time prevents "nationalist excesses."

Levingston's attacks against transnational capital transgressed the limits of this bourgeois nationalism. Consequently, his appeals to the local bourgeoisie to rally behind his government were met with an eloquent silence. There are indications (such as the expressions of support he received from some provincial industrialists' organizations) that Levingston's appeals reached the weaker and most authentically national fractions of the bourgeoisie, but this support mattered little in the political process. In fact, Levingston's assault on transnational capital encouraged the CGE to explore the other prominent alternative: the class alliances that revolved around the electoral road embodied in *La*

Hora del Pueblo. The union leadership, which also wanted to keep a prudent distance between itself and the government, reached a similar conclusion. The resulting rapprochement between the CGE and the CGT was closely related to the growing activity of the parties of *La Hora del Pueblo,* which in February 1971 published a new manifesto urging elections and reiterating their promises of fair play. It also implied that these parties were prepared to grant guarantees to the currents in the BA and in the upper bourgeoisie that would support the political solution they were advocating.[37] These activities were in turn connected to the coup against Levingston that was in progress. *La Hora del Pueblo* offered the arguments—and the votes—to make palatable what was now inevitable: that the armed forces and the bourgeoisie would shelve the aspirations that had survived Onganía's overthrow, issue the BA's death certificate, and retrench to salvage their fundamental interests.

Like Onganía, but more rapidly and in more critical circumstances (including a rapidly deteriorating economy), Levingston was isolated by forces that united tactically in spite of their disagreements over less immediate goals. And again, as with Onganía, it was events in Córdoba that gave the Levingston government its final push. Social conflict, as noted above, had grown more widespread and intense toward the end of 1970 and the beginning of 1971. In February 1971, Levingston secured the resignation of Francisco Manrique, the Social Welfare Minister, who was the last remaining cabinet member close to Lanusse.* Levingston also forced the governor of Córdoba to resign, replacing him with one of the most reactionary members of the very reactionary right wing in that province. The new governor began imprudently with a virulent diatribe against the political activation in the region[38] just as a new explosion of strikes and factory occupations was taking place. These events culminated in a new uprising in the city of Córdoba that was no less widespread and violent than the one of the previous year but which involved significantly more radical leadership and slogans.[39] If Onganía's apoliticism and his (more or less willing) support for the efficientist economic policies had produced a massive and violent reaction, Levingston's nationalism had fared no better.

With the rapprochement among the armed forces, the CGE, the CGT, and *La Hora del Pueblo,* and with the upper bourgeoisie now

---

La Nación, February 10, 1971, p. 1. After this departure, very few doubted that a coup led by Lanusse was in the making.

seeking only to consolidate defensive positions, the second Cordobazo was the last straw for the military liberals. The issue was no longer to "achieve the goals of the Revolution," but to find bases for negotiations that could guarantee reasonable terms for the liquidation of the BA and for the withdrawal of the armed forces to their "specific functions." After a week, Levingston was deposed. At that point the armed forces, incapable of reviving the BA and deserted by a bourgeoisie that had lost the last vestiges of confidence, began its retreat under a liberal leadership that extended—at last—to the apex of the government.

5.   THE NATIONALIST BA EXCEEDS ITS LIMITS

There can be little doubt that a lack of political acumen contributed greatly to the demise of Levingston's government, as it had with Onganía's. But other, less circumstantial, factors were also operating in that direction.

Following the 1966 coup, several factors enabled the paternalists to gain important positions in the institutional system of the state. Among the most important was the recent institutional history of the armed forces, which made Onganía the almost obligatory choice for president in 1966. This did not prevent the liberals from controlling the economic apparatus (albeit after a six-month delay), but the weight of the presidency—and, above all, evidence that Onganía and his current intended to assume full control of the government—left the upper bourgeoisie and transnational capital with serious doubts. On another level, the relative mildness of the economic crisis that preceded the implantation of the BA in 1966, together with the special characteristics and comparative advantages of Argentina's major export sector, allowed economic growth to be resumed much more rapidly than has been the case in other BAs. In one important sense the economic program was too successful, since it encouraged the paternalists to press almost immediately for redistributive policies that clashed with the interests and demands of the upper bourgeoisie. This attempt, together with the paternalists' clumsy but worrisome efforts to co-opt the unions, created serious apprehension among the upper bourgeoisie and its allies—not so much because these efforts were likely to succeed, but because they had the potential to destroy the achievements of the normalization program. Accordingly, the leading periodicals, liberal military officers, liberal *técnicos,* and the organizations of the upper bourgeoisie launched a relentless attack against the paternalists. But with the departure of Krieger Vasena, the paternalists gained a high degree of control over the institutional system of the BA. Their demise, however, occurred soon afterward, with the opening of the Pandora's box of a massive popular opposition that greatly sharpened preexisting conflicts within the BA.

The nationalists, with Levingston at the helm, rose to government with this opposition already in full swing and fell as it reached new and violent heights. In the first part of its short term in office (up to the departure of McLoughlin), Levingston's government was a chorus of dissonances: Moyano Llerena's poor imitation of Krieger Vasena's program, the efficient performance of Ferrer and his team in the Ministry of Public Works, the fruitless efforts of the military junta to maintain Levingston as its delegate, and the inconsistencies of Levingston's efforts to demonstrate social sensitivity while mobilizing society in pursuit of a hierarchical vision that was at least as hostile to politics as Onganía's. Like the paternalists, the nationalists expelled the liberals in the closing moments of their government, assumed a high degree of control over the state apparatus, and moved according to their ideology. The local bourgeoisie and the unions declined to follow them to the precipice, and the little confidence that remained among the upper bourgeoisie and transnational capital evaporated. Moreover, once the nationalism of Levingston and his current was transformed from an ethereal discourse into discriminatory and statizing policies, numerous fractions of the local bourgeoisie also added their voices to the opposition.

First under the paternalists, and later under the nationalists' government, confidence was shaken so severely that normalization was aborted. Moreover, the nationalism of the Levingston government, despite being massively rejected by the population, fueled a popular activation whose main ideological axis was an exasperated nationalist reaction to the transnationalization and "loss of national spirit" that were alleged to have taken place during the preceding years. Mindful of this reaction, segments of the upper bourgeoisie, until recently the strongest support of the BA, now desired its euthanasia. The loosening of the social relations of domination (or, according to the definitions set forth in chapter 1, the beginnings of a crisis of social domination) that began in the last year of Onganía's government added a note of urgency to this discovery. As workers became more "undisciplined" in factories and in the streets, national union leaders—threatened by the same processes and in an attempt to absorb them—lodged high wage and salary demands to which the government could respond only with vacuous statements and promises. The BA that the liberals and the upper bourgeoisie, with the grudging collaboration of the paternalists, had launched on a triumphant voyage in March 1967 had sailed into stormy seas. By the end of 1970, its supporters were trying to guide it safely to shore before the winds blew in even more dangerous directions.

6. ECONOMIC MISADVENTURES OF THE NATIONALIST TURN

By the time of the Cordobazo, industrial production was approaching the limits of installed capacity. Private investment in machinery and equipment had risen substantially in the first half of 1969, and direct foreign investment also increased. These trends seemed to indicate that the state apparatus could relinquish its role as the motor of economic activity and embark on the long-term consolidation of the achievements of the normalization program. We have seen, however, that such possibilities vanished abruptly with the events of May 1969. The Dagnino Pastore administration, and to a lesser extent that of Moyano Llerena, managed to cushion some of the impacts of the Cordobazo, but the data presented in chapter 9 demonstrate that this episode was as much an economic as a political turning point. Other variables support this assertion. Imports rose as a consequence of the economic growth experienced during 1968 and 1969, exhibiting (as is typical in these productive structures) a high elasticity in relation to domestic economic growth. After the Cordobazo, however, imports took a speculative leap as forecasts of political, monetary, and exchange instability appeared. As a result, 1969 closed with a large deficit in the balance of payments and a negligible balance-of-trade surplus.[40]

Confronted with an overheated economy, Dagnino Pastore's team, as we have seen, clamped down on credit and the money supply. At the same time, it attempted to relieve social tensions by allowing real wages and salaries to rise above the depressed levels prevailing in the second half of 1968 and the first half of 1969. As we saw in chapter 5, however, these increases did little to pacify the popular sector. They also produced an important rise in consumer demand that was hardly congruent with the attempt to cool the economy. Moreover, the second half of 1969 saw the rise of a new complication: a significant rise in domestic beef prices, the result of a strong increase in international meat prices and a reduction in domestic cattle sales. In Argentina, beef is not only the mainstay of the popular diet, it also exerts an important lead effect on the prices of its substitutes.[41] In the uncertainty produced by the Cordobazo, the rise in meat prices and its impact on the prices of other basic foodstuffs worked together with pressures on the balance of payments (and consequent expectations of a new devaluation), and with wage and salary demands (and the government's apparent inability to contain them), to give inflation, which in the triumphal moments of the Krieger Vasena period some had thought was gone for good, a strong upward push. The Dagnino Pastore and Moyano Llerena ministries placed restrictions on meat sales and prices, temporarily slowing the price hikes. These controls, however, failed to strike at the root of the problem, and they launched the Pampean bourgeoisie and its organizations on a new round of protests.

These darkening expectations were improved little by Moyano Llerena's inexpedient replication of Krieger Vasena's program at a time when the relation of social forces had changed profoundly. Dagnino Pastore finally began to stress the need for a new push toward deepening the productive structure. He advocated launching an ambitious program of import substitution directed mainly at the intermediate and capital goods that had accounted for a disproportionate share of the rise in total imports.[42] Such a program would require large investments, not, as in the previous period, in the physical infrastructure, but in productive activities capable of advancing substantially the vertical integration of Argentine industry. But with the negative expectations that prevailed after the Cordobazo, there was little prospect of increasing private domestic investment, which went instead toward defensive, short-term placements. Still less could be expected from private transnational capital; as we have seen, medium- and long-term inflows from abroad fell abruptly after May 1969. Public investment remained the available option. By 1970, however, the fiscal situation began to deteriorate. Moreover, any move to channel state investments toward directly productive activities would have antagonized the upper bourgeoisie. The latter had not objected to the infrastructural investments of the Krieger Vasena period, but it would be another matter—the excoriated "statism"—should the state turn to direct investment in productive sectors. In short, Dagnino Pastore and Moyano Llerena, for all their nuances, tried hard to follow the path that Krieger Vasena had taken. In the new political and economic context, however, their efforts were doomed to exacerbate the crisis they were trying to mute.

This was the situation of the Argentine economy when Levingston moved to imprint a nationalist stamp on the Argentine Revolution.

Disregarding the orthodox restraints accepted by his predecessors, Ferrer decided that the above-mentioned investments would flow not only from private initiative but also from the state apparatus, and he announced that the state would also provide active tutelage for private national capital. He accompanied these decisions with a visible (and unsuccessful) effort to dispel misgivings* arising from the "leftist" views he had expressed in his academic publications, and from his past performance (1958–60) as Economy Minister for the Province of Buenos Aires, when he had tried, and failed, to impose a tax on potential land rent. Accordingly, one of his first decisions was to lift the restrictions on domestic sale and prices of meat. This measure received from the Pampean bourgeoisie some applause, but nothing compared to their rage when, in response to rising inflation and meat prices, Ferrer imposed controls even stricter than the ones he had just removed. Other policies enacted more with an eye toward relieving social tensions than ensuring a consistent economic program included substantial wage and salary increases, the (unfulfilled) promise to reinstitute unrestricted collective bargaining, and a loose monetary policy. Finally, the decision to encourage swap transactions soon led to serious strain on the foreign exchange reserves of the Central Bank.† All of these factors made it easy to foresee new devaluations and inflationary spirals.

The effort to move the Argentine Revolution in a nationalist direction and the misgivings of the Pampean and upper bourgeoisies about Ferrer's appointment as Economy Minister reinforced the negative tendencies that already existed, and made October 1970, the month in which Ferrer assumed his post, an economic conjuncture almost as

*These misgivings were well expressed by La Nación (October 19, 1970, p. 6), in an article entitled "The Most Pressing Problem: Confidence." "The most urgent task facing Dr. Aldo Ferrer and his collaborators on the economic team is undoubtedly that of demonstrating that his ideas and actions are compatible with policies capable of inspiring confidence. Several weeks ago, a serious run on the foreign exchange market was precipitated by the mere announcement of a vague plan suggestive of large wage increases, a major expansion of credit, the nationalization of bank deposits, and control of exchange operations. . . . Once it became known that Dr. Moyano Llerena might resign, concern emerged once again in financial circles at the prospect of that ominous plan. . . . It will not be easy [for Ferrer's team] to restore confidence. The announcement of that plan and the general feeling that it will inspire the new policies have created expectations that will be difficult to dispel, even though Dr. Ferrer's views do not involve the closed-minded statism advocated in some quarters."

†Just prior to Ferrer's appointment as Economy Minister, the BCRA debt on futures operations in the foreign exchange market was US$101 million. By December 31, 1970, it was US$225 million. By the end of 1971—after Ferrer had left office, but due to transactions concluded during his term—it had risen to US$485 million (Ministerio de Economía, Informe Económico, 1970, 4th trimester [Buenos Aires, 1971]; and Ministerio de Hacienda, Informe Económico, 1971, 4th trimester [Buenos Aires, 1972]).

important as the Cordobazo. Data presented in chapter 9 show that this month was a major turning point for such crucial variables as the rate of inflation and the prices of meat and other foodstuffs. Moreover, it was in October 1970 that black-market rates for foreign exchange began to rise sharply in relation to official quotations. The same month saw an analogous leap in the rate of the U.S. dollar on the futures market.

When early in 1971 Levingston removed all doubts about the direction in which he intended to move the "Revolution," these unpromising initial reactions gave way to accelerated economic deterioration. Suffice it to say that while the budget prepared for 1971 assumed a 15 percent annual rate of inflation, prices rose by 12 percent in the first three months of that year alone. Accordingly, the "fiscal discipline" of the 1967–69 period gave way to the budgetary chaos of 1971–72, which we shall examine in chapter 9. These problems were compounded by the unions' renewed capacity for pressure, reinforced by what the bourgeoisie understood as the "dangerous demagoguery" of a government seeking support for its nationalist project. Expectations fell still further with the prospect that unrestricted collective bargaining (promised for the summer of 1971) would result in substantial wage and salary hikes and in new rounds of inflation. It was to preclude this possibility that Ferrer, contrary to his previous announcements, issued a decree imposing a 12 percent limit on the wage and salary increases that could be "freely" negotiated. This decree was greeted angrily by the unions and the popular sector but did little to calm the bourgeoisie, which had more than enough to worry about with the nationalist policies being enacted at the time.

The attempt to set the BA on a nationalist course came at a time of deep political crisis and particularly unpropitious economic conditions. Moreover, a number of crucial variables—in a pattern similar to that observed just prior to the 1966 coup and immediately following the Cordobazo—responded with remarkable speed and sensitivity to Ferrer's appointment as Economy Minister and to the signals that the government was taking a nationalist turn. So rapid was this response that it coincided with Ferrer's first and largely ceremonial acts, making it even less likely that the nationalists' policies would succeed.

NOTES

1. See especially the special edition of *Panorama*, June 10, 1970.
2. Amendment to the "Acts of the Argentine Revolution" in *La Nación*, June 21, 1970, p. 1.

3. This assessment of how Levingston was viewed by his comrades is based on my interviews.

4. *La Nación*, June 18, p. 6, and July 24, pp. 1, 6, 1970.

5. *La Nación*, June 25, 1970, p. 5.

6. *La Nación*, June 21, 1970, pp. 1, 20.

7. *La Nación*, June 30, 1970, pp. 1, 6.

8. Statements of the CAC, UIA, and the Buenos Aires Stock Exchange in *La Nación*, June 29, 1970, pp. 1, 4.

9. See, among others, *Economic Survey*, July 21, 1970, p. 1.

10. See Levingston's speeches in *La Nación*, July 13, pp. 1, 5 and September 28, pp. 1, 3, 1970; see also the interview with Levingston in *Confirmado*, September 23, 1970, pp. 14, 18.

11. See Levingston's press conference in *La Nación*, October 11, 1970, p. 14, and his speech in *La Nación*, September 30, 1970, pp. 1, 12.

12. For an excellent analysis of the theme of political space, see Alfred Stepan, *The State and Society: Peru in Comparative Perspective* (Princeton: Princeton University Press, 1978).

13. See *La Nación*, November 27, p. 1 and November 29, p. 9, 1970.

14. See, among others, *Primera Plana*, December 15, 1970, p. 15.

15. For example, *La Razón*, September 29, 1970, p. 16.

16. On these and related themes see the data in chapter 9. For the alarm these trends caused, see *Economic Survey*, October 6, p. 1; November 3, p. 6; November 10, p. 1 (which also expressed concern about the "tremendous prospects for inflation"); and December 9, p. 7, 1970.

17. See the angry complaints of CARBAP in *La Nación*, July 27, 1970, p. 4, and of the "Assembly of Agricultural and Livestock Producers" (which included the SRA and CARBAP) in *La Nación*, November 18, 1970, pp. 1, 6.

18. *La Nación*, October 14, 1970, p. 1. For a review of the events leading to these resignations, see *Panorama*, October 16, 1970, pp. 1, 6.

19. *La Nación*, November 12, 1970, p. 6.

20. On this theme see O'Donnell, *Modernization and Bureaucratic-Authoritarianism*, chapter 3, and "Modernization and Military Coups."

21. Dealings between the parties in *La Hora del Pueblo* and the military liberals were widely rumored and were confirmed in my interviews.

22. Lanusse, *Mi Testimonio*.

23. *La Nación*, November 10, 1970, pp. 1, 22.

24. *La Nación*, January 2, 1971, pp. 1, 18.

25. For Levingston's announcement of the upcoming enactment of the "buy national" law as part of an effort to "Argentinize the economy," see *La Nación*, December 24, 1970, p. 22.

26. See the UIA in *La Nación*, December 29, 1970, p. 14, the ACIEL in *La Nación*, January 6, 1971, p. 3, and the CAC in *La Nación*, January 16, 1971, p. 7.

27. *La Nación*, January 31, 1971, p. 10.

28. See the CGE's *Memoria anual, 1968–1969* and *1969–1970*.

29. Perhaps the most persistent criticism of these policies came from *Economic Survey* between November 1970 and March 1971.

30. See Levingston's speech in *La Nación*, February 5, 1971, pp. 1, 7, and his press conference in *La Nación*, March 20, 1971, p. 4.

31. *La Nación*, January 23, 1971, pp. 1, 16.

32. Text in *La Nación*, December 5, 1970, pp. 1, 22.

33. See *La Nación*, December 17, 1970, pp. 1, 6.

34. See for example *La Nación*, December 6, 1970, p. 6, and *Primera Plana*, December 15, 1970, pp. 14, 15.

35. *La Nación*, December 12, 1970, p. 6.

36. See among others *La Nación*, January 17, p. 8 and February 28, p. 8, 1971; *Análisis*, February 16, 1970, pp. 7, 10; and *Panorama*, February 16, pp. 8, 10; March 2, pp. 16, 20; and March 9, pp. 8, 13, 1971.

37. *La Nación*, February 17, 1971, p. 4.

38. *La Nación*, March 3, 1971, p. 3.

39. *La Nación*, March 16, 1971, pp. 1, 22. On this episode, see Balvé et al., *Lucha de calles—lucha de clases*.

40. The data referred to here and in the rest of this section are included in the complete series for the whole period, presented in chapter 9.

41. See Reca and Gaba, "Poder adquisitivo," and Juan Carlos de Pablo, *Política Antiinflacionaria en la Argentina, 1967–1970* (Buenos Aires: Amorrortu Editores, 1972).

42. See Dagnino Patore's *Discursos* (Ministry of Economy and Labor, Buenos Aires, 1970).

EIGHT

The Garden of the Diverging Paths

1. INITIAL EUPHORIA

The coup that deposed Levingston and brought Lanusse to the presidency was at long last, according to its authors, democratic. Its goal was the full restoration of democratic institutions, which the armed forces now claimed, rather unconvincingly, had been the main objective of the 1966 coup. To this end, political parties and political activity were rehabilitated, the parties' real estate was returned to them, and a solemn promise was made that proscriptions and electoral fraud had ended for good. The new government, according to the junta of commanders in chief, was prepared to negotiate "a broad and generous accord [that would] overcome the antinomies of the past" and usher in an era of "fair play," beginning with the election of a constitutional government and culminating in a "stable and efficient democracy."[1] To facilitate these goals, the policies of the newly established government "would center on political matters, with special social sensitivity."[2]

As a token of these intentions, Arturo Mor Roig—Radical party leader, past president of the Chamber of Deputies (1963–66),* and one

---

*Mor Roig's term as president of the Chamber of Deputies was cut short by the 1966 coup. At that point he began graduate studies in political science at the Catholic University of Buenos Aires, where he wrote a memorable paper on Machiavelli for one of my classes. During this period his ideas acquired a Social Christian tint that distanced him somewhat from his Radical party colleagues but at the same time brought him close to quite a few military officers. On Mor Roig's intellectual evolution, see *Confirmado*, August 19, 1970, p. 19.

of the main architects of *La Hora del Pueblo*—was appointed to head the Interior Ministry. Aldo Ferrer, who stayed on as Economy Minister, was commissioned to implement what the junta termed a "policy of profound social sensitivity," beginning with wage and salary increases and yet another pledge to restore collective bargaining unrestricted by government-imposed ceilings.[3] So that no one had cause for complaint, the Central Bank allocated special funds to help compensate employers for their higher wage and salary costs,[4] and price controls on meat were eliminated.[5]

The CGT and the CGE appeared favorably inclined toward the new government. At a joint meeting with Lanusse, they expressed their support for the new stage and proposed a "truce" in the form of a tripartite "social pact" among "workers, entrepreneurs, and the state" to expedite the transition to democracy.[6] The organizations of the upper bourgeoisie, complaining that they were being left out, demanded "participation" in government policy making,* but their request, like the outcries of bitterly anti-Peronist sectors that saw on the horizon the return of the "fugitive tyrant," mattered little in the face of the enthusiasm that the new situation unleashed. This enthusiasm was shared by the major political parties, the CGE, numerous middle sector associations, and even the considerable number of military officers who by then seemed anxious to rid themselves of the thankless task of defending the BA against near-unanimous opposition. Indeed, by opting for an electoral solution, the military liberals could take advantage of the anti-militarist sentiments that the BA had generated. On the other hand, the upper bourgeoisie, faced with the end of all efforts to normalize the economy, had few reasons to rejoice. Nonetheless, they saw the road that the military liberals had chosen as less worrisome than the precipice toward which the nationalists had seemed determined to bring society.

Lanusse, now president not of the "Argentine Revolution" but of the "Government of the Armed Forces," had much to do with the prevailing enthusiasm. As a member of a family that controlled important enterprises in both the urban and rural sectors and as an old adversary

---

*A few weeks after the coup, the UIA issued a statement condemning the "pernicious statism" of the government's economic policy and warning against the "dangerous uncertainty and lack of confidence" prevailing at the time. The statement concluded that "all of [this] is indissolubly linked to a political process which is fickle, vacillating, and difficult to resolve." Since "this fragile scheme [would] only accentuate social distress and give solid support to disorder and extremism," the UIA demanded that the government allow it "participation in major economic, social, and political decisions" (*La Nación*, April 16, 1971, p. 10). Times had clearly changed.

of Peronism, Lanusse was seen by anti-Peronists as someone who could be trusted in future negotiations with Perón. Moreover, Lanusse had won great military prestige as a cavalry commander in the military confrontations of 1962 and 1963, in which generals Alcides López Aufranc and Tomás Sánchez de Bustamante, his closest military collaborators in the government Lanusse formed, had also figured prominently. Lanusse's personal characteristics also contributed to his positive image among the military and civilians. A handsome man who spoke in a straightforward and eloquent manner, Lanusse had obvious zest, and not insignificant talent, for political maneuver—attributes that Onganía and Levingston had conspicuously lacked. Lanusse was the only military leader of the period who could reasonably hope to gain significant popular support. His liberalism, though a far cry from the paternalism and nationalism of his predecessors, was flexible enough to allow him to adopt socially sensitive policies, with which he hoped to pave the way for his political operation. In addition, his gestures of "inter-American solidarity" while commander in chief of the army and his "anti-communist" background held him in good standing with the government of the United States. Lanusse had a sharp temper and could not be accused of underestimating the personal qualifications that made him—aside from Perón, of course—the most complex and interesting political personality of the period.

Beyond the announcement that Argentina would soon reach a "democracy without exclusions" through a "Great National Accord" (GAN), what did Lanusse's government involve? Its basic goal was to negotiate with the political parties, the bourgeoisie, and the unions a political solution to the collapse of the BA. Otherwise, in the assessment of Lanusse and his current, "subversion" would abolish the capitalist parameters of Argentine society and the country's affiliation with the "Western world."[7] The solution to the collapse of the BA would be attempted by the military current that was most clear-sighted, most politicized, and most closely connected to society's dominant classes and political forces: the liberals, who looked to Lanusse as their undisputed leader. In so doing they would have to take account of the following aspects of the situation: (1) opposition to the BA, mostly under the banner of Peronism, had erupted from all sides; (2) Peronism had expanded beyond the CGT, the CGE, and its traditional political leaders to encompass two new and very important components: broad segments of the middle sectors, and some of the most active (and violent) guerrilla organizations; (3) Peronism's electoral weight was difficult to estimate, but clearly constituted at least the first plurality of the electorate; (4) Perón himself, for reasons we shall examine, exercised more control over his heterogeneous following than in the recent past; (5) the emergence of radicalized goals and strategies that challenged not only the BA but also capitalism and whatever regime—democratic or not—implied its survival; and (6) the belief that Perón, by repudiating the sectors that advocated such goals and strategies, could contribute decisively to their defeat.

A major task for the new government was thus to eliminate guerrilla activity, wildcat strikes, factory occupations, the taking of hostages, and massive urban uprisings. More generally, it sought to reverse the population's widespread hostility to the armed forces.[8] By 1971, the military and the dominant classes faced a much greater threat than the one they had tried to eradicate five years earlier, and the armed forces were exhausted and fraught with internal conflicts. Furthermore, it was far from clear what strategy could minimize the risks of the task at hand.

This situation generated evident concern, as much among those who supported the strategy we are about to study as among those who demanded, "before it is too late," the application of the massive repression that would have been necessary to reimpose a ghastly order. During a praetorian period, the perception of threat generates reactions that lead to the implantation of the BA. As we are now seeing, however, the collapse of the BA can appear even more threatening, in part because the coercive institutions indispensable for reimposing order are enervated or fragmented, and in part because the popular activation may rise to new heights. In such cases, the collapse of the BA's walls of exclusion seems to leave the innermost bastions of society exposed to a final assault by a radicalized and multitudinous opposition. In these circumstances the more astute actors within the BA tend to seek negotiations with the more moderate leaders of the previously excluded sectors, in the hope of isolating and eventually defeating the radicalized currents of opposition. This, in a nutshell, was the goal of the operation that Lanusse tried to conduct.

2. COMPLEXITY AND CHANGES WITHIN PERONISM

At this point it will be useful to explore the relationship between Peronism, a movement that encompassed the largest part of the popular sector, and Perón, who jealously guarded his role and repeatedly purged his movement of persons who might have shared his leadership.* By sketching out these interactions, we can place in proper perspective the role played by Perón's personal characteristics: his extraordinary tactical skill and flexibility; his talent for rapidly perceiving changes in Argentine society and in the aspirations of the popular and middle sectors; his personal appeal; and his populist, nationalist and corporatist ideology, which, however, was vague and flexible enough to incorporate elements of more radicalized views.

Let us begin by posing a question that the actors of the period often raised: What did Perón really want, and what could he actually do in relation to the most dynamic and autonomous components of his movement—in particular, the unions and guerrilla organizations? To put the question somewhat differently, to what extent was Perón's brilliant maneuvering not much more than skillful adaptation to actors and conditions that were heading in directions he realized he could not alter?

Peronism grew enormously and became much more complex as it incorporated many who had been antagonized by the BA, but it never acquired any real institutional structure. To understand why Peronism evolved in this way, it is important to examine each of its diverse currents. First, the unions. After the 1955 coup that ended Perón's second government, the unions, with their organizational base and the Peronist allegiance of their rank and file, became—as their leaders and Perón often stressed—the backbone of the movement. As we have seen, however, the unions and their leadership were far from homogeneous. One current, encompassing several variants of participationism, anxiously sought agreements with each successive government. A second current, Vandorism, almost always prevailed over the participationists in controlling the CGT and the more influential unions and made several attempts, most visibly during the Radical government of 1963–66, to form a union-based political party independent of the old leader. The Vandorists sought to force from the dominant classes more permanent accommodations as well as additional economic and institutional advantages for their unions by combining the organizational strength of the unions and the CGT, the widespread Peronist allegiance of the popular sector and, on repeated occasions, the tough pressure tactics that distinguished them from the participationists. A third current within the

---

*A serious problem for our analysis is that despite the decisive role that Peronism has played in modern Argentina, there exists as yet no study that does justice to its complexities and changes over time.

unions, the Peronist left, was more sporadic. Despite its important influence in some provinces, this current managed only occasionally to gain control of national-level unions (as happened during the period we are studying, with the CGT *de los Argentinos*). It was composed of groups that rejected the ultimately accommodationist strategies of Vandorism in favor of a (thoroughly confused) "revolutionary" stance with which they hoped to gain the support of the "national entrepreneurs" and the armed forces in their struggles against the "monopolies." Finally, there arose after 1969, especially in the interior, a quite heterogeneous current that criticized, from various Marxist standpoints, all Peronist currents as prisoners of a bourgeois ideology that could not fail to betray the real interests of the working class. This current was never coordinated effectively at the national level, and did not attract more than a small portion of the working class. But the militancy of both this current and the Peronist left placed them at the forefront of the factory occupations, hostage-takings, and urban riots that created so much apprehension among the armed forces and the dominant classes.[9]

Peronism also included what I shall term its *political personnel,* professional politicians mainly of middle-sector or (often provincial) upper-class extraction. Since Peronism, in part because of repression and in part because of Perón's stern opposition, had never been institutionalized as a political party, these political personnel, unlike the unionists, lacked organizational bases. No less than the unionists, they were subject to the jealous vigilance of Perón, who sought to identify "traitors" who might try to usurp the leadership of his movement. With Perón in exile, these personnel were subject after 1955 to repeated temptations (to which nearly all succumbed at one time or another) to channel Peronist votes to the various political solutions attempted by successive governments.[10] Had such attempts to form neo-Peronisms succeeded, they would have divided the movement and probably ended its electoral supremacy. But they always failed. The history of Perón's relations with these political personnel was, as with the unionists, one of mutual dependency, distrust, and frequent "betrayals" of the leader's instructions. The few, like Héctor Cámpora, who obediently played the games that Perón wanted, would be rewarded for their loyalty when Perón needed representatives capable of resisting the temptations offered by Lanusse and the enormous interests supporting the "Great National Accord."

The volatile relations between Perón and his main followers took place in the context of repeated attempts by governments and the dominant classes to pulverize Peronism. These factors, together with Perón's tactical skills, led the latter to adopt a pendular strategy within his movement. By supporting some Peronist political or union currents against others that he felt were becoming too independent, by weakening those which had emerged victorious with his support, and occasionally by backing the political personnel against the union leaders (or vice versa), Perón performed the remarkable feat of leading a movement that by 1971 was shot through with internal divisions but in which all currents claimed unconditional loyalty to him. By 1971, moreover, a new phenomenon was under way: the "Peronization" of many middle sectors which, not long before, had been stern anti-Peronists and had applauded Onganía's promises of order and authority. This process occurred as many middle sectors, especially university students and members of various groups affiliated with or closely tied to the Catholic Church (including the guerrilla organizations, whose membership came largely from these cohorts), were becoming radicalized. These new currents saw* in Perón a revolutionary leader who, in conjunction with the armed strength of the guerrilla organizations and the "people in arms," would spearhead the "Argentinazo"—the great and violent revolution that would usher in the era of "national socialism" *(socialismo nacional)*. These groups challenged not only the BA and its allies but also many other currents within Peronism. With intransigent purity, these young segments of the middle sectors excoriated the "union bureaucracy" and, with few exceptions, the "political bureaucracy" of Peronism, as "traitors" always ready to sell out their movement through cynical negotiations with the government currently in office. Perón encouraged these groups (including the Montoneros, the main Peronist guerrilla organization), telling them what they wanted to hear and accepting them as interlocutors on an equal footing with the unionists and the political personnel.†

---

*Or claimed to see. There is little doubt that the vast majority of those who belonged to these radicalized currents really did perceive Perón as a revolutionary leader. At the leadership level, however, the situation was more complex. Some leaders of these currents, recognizing that Perón retained enormous influence within the popular sector and that his ambiguities and oscillations would serve at least to keep the "bureaucrats" continually off balance, declared allegiance to Perón as an expedient way to increase their own influence within the popular sector. To the best of my knowledge, however, only a minority of the leaders took this instrumentalist view of Perón's role.

†Perón's relations with the radicalized sectors of his movement deserve careful analysis. In the absence of such a study (though it is worth consulting Daniel James, "The Peronist Left, 1955–1975," *Journal of Latin American Studies* 8, no. 2, 1978), it should be noted that Perón, whose communications with union leaders were consistent with his usual discourse (see esp. the 1971 and 1972 issues of the monthly *Las Bases,* the official organ of Peronism), used quite different language and discussed quite different themes in

The appearance of these new radicalized currents, who came primarily from the middle sectors, coincided with the reactivation of the popular sector. Much of this radicalization was expressed in the assertion of the nation and *pueblo* as a locus of identification in the struggle against imperialism, the "monopolies," the "oligarchy," and the domestic agents of "denationalization" *(entreguismo)*, as well as against the union and political "bureaucracies" of Peronism. The more aggressive themes in this discourse* (many of which were said to derive from the never more vivid memory of Eva Perón and her somewhat mythical radicalism) concluded with calls for a national socialism that would reject both the reactionary road of a new military coup and the "farce" of elections. Grounded in Perón's "third position" (which declared itself to be as alien to liberalism as to Marxism, both rather peculiarly defined), and in the vision of an organized community in which Perón distilled his corporatist ideology, national socialism was defined so vaguely that some of its advocates cited Guevara, Mao, and Fanon as well as Perón, while others, such as Perón's influential personal secretary José López Rega, associated it with "other national liberation movements": the European fascisms.

Despite the disagreements within Peronism, the reactivation of the

---

his messages to the radicalized sectors of his movement. In the latter, Perón characterized the situation as one of revolutionary war. He endorsed the "special formations"—the guerrilla organizations—as the vanguard of this struggle and welcomed them as full-fledged Peronists. See, among many other documents, Perón's statements in *Panorama*, May 18, 1971, p. 9, and the very influential—both for its direct impact and because it foreshadowed the tone of later communications—*"Carta a la juventud"* ("Letter to youth"), which was published in a number of periodicals, including *Nuevo Hombre*, no. 2, July 28, 1971, and *Cristianismo y Revolución*, no. 29, July 1971. But perhaps the most influential of these communications, and the most enduring in its lethal consequences, was the letter that Perón sent to the Montoneros congratulating them for the "execution" of Aramburu: "I entirely agree with, and praise, what you have done. Nothing could be farther from the truth [than to say that by murdering Aramburu] you ruined my tactical plans, because there is no way that *an action desired by all Peronists* could interfere with the Peronist leadership" (Perón's emphasis) (Jorge L. Bernetti, *El peronismo de la victoria* [Buenos Aires: Editorial Legasa, 1982], p. 40). The guerrilla and other radicalized groups saw the situation as one requiring violent and unyielding struggle. Among the many documents and statements premised on this point of view, see the interview with Rodolfo Galimberti in *Primera Plana*, August 1, 1972, p. 9. For a study written from this perspective, see Donald Hodges, *Argentina, 1943–1976: The National Revolution and Resistance* (Albuquerque: University of New Mexico Press, 1976).

*These themes were taken up and radicalized by such well-known intellectuals as John William Cooke, Héctor Hernández Arregui, and Rodolfo Puiggrós, all of whom were especially influential during the period we are examining; see Juan E. Corradi, "Between Corporatism and Insurgency: Some Sources of Ideological Tension in Peronism," in *Terms of Conflict: Ideology in Latin American Politics*, ed. Morris Blachman and Ronald Hellman (Philadelphia: Institute for the Study of Human Issues, 1977).

popular sector and the radicalization of various middle sectors converged in a massive—and angry—national popular current within
which Perón would have to move if he wanted to preserve his leadership. This was what worried Lanusse and the liberals. When Perón
told an interlocutor, "I have two hands and I use them both,"[11] he
was probably alluding not only to a tactic at which he excelled but
also to the fact that after the Cordobazo his movement was permeated
at both the leadership and base levels not only by union and political
bureaucrats but also by tendencies and possibilities that were profoundly (if, as we shall see, ambiguously) radicalized. Peronism's traditional currents—the union leaders and the political personnel, ready to
negotiate with the armed forces and the dominant classes—had by no
means disappeared. But the radicalization of Peronism's new currents
opened the way for what Perón, a military man to the end, termed
"pursuing the enemy": an all-out effort to harass, and finally defeat,
his opponents.

3.   PARAMETERS OF THE SITUATION

Let us return to a crucial point. As many (including Lanusse) saw the
situation at the beginning of Lanusse's presidency, the central problem
was to forge an agreement between the government and Peronism's
political personnel and union leaders. If Perón endorsed such an agreement, the radicalized currents that claimed allegiance to his movement
would no longer be able to wave the Peronist banner before a popular
sector whose further radicalization was immensely worrisome. Considering that the "Government of the Armed Forces" had much to offer
these unionists and political personnel in the way of institutional advantages and future governmental positions, and given the very anti-
Peronist assumption that Perón was, above all, corrupt, there seemed to
be a good chance that such an agreement could be reached. At any rate,
elections would have to be called within a rather brief span of time if the
political solution was to work, and no electoral calculus could fail to
take Peronism into account. This equation seemed to have few un-
knowns. First, the political personnel of Peronism (and of the other
political parties) were prepared to support a process that would restore
institutional recognition to their roles and allow them access to governmental positions. Second, national union leaders were willing, as always, to opt for the electoral route if by so doing they could expect to
strengthen their positions, and this political solution seemed to provide

them with an opportunity to regain the influence they had lost and never fully recovered after the 1966 coup. On the other hand, there was little doubt that Peronism's radicalized currents would staunchly oppose any attempt to save the system. Indeed, the only unknown was Perón himself.

The search for a political solution occurred not because the liberals had suddenly rediscovered the virtues of democracy, but because fundamental institutional and class interests were at stake. In order to defend those interests, it seemed that the future constitutional government would have to satisfy some crucial conditions. It would have to (1) firmly combat all "extremist" or "subversive" currents; (2) leave ample room for domestic and transnational private initiative; (3) respect the inroads that the armed forces had made since 1966 into many parts of the state apparatus; (4) conduct no investigations into and take no reprisals for the handling of public affairs since 1966; and (5) refrain from interfering in what the armed forces chose to define, under the broad guidelines set forth in the Doctrine of National Security, as their specific responsibilities. These conditions tacitly implied a further guarantee: that the future constitutional government would not use a parliamentary majority to abrogate them.* These provisions were aimed quite obviously at Peronism, the only significant electoral force whose willingness to respect them was in doubt.

As described in the preceding chapter, the BA expired with the Levingston presidency. Its remnants were swept away by the government's negotiations with the main political parties, which ended the political exclusion of the popular sector. Due to the supreme importance that the political arena acquires in any such rescue operation and to the intimate relationship between that arena and the alarming irruption of social forces, the fit between politics and economics became much looser during the Lanusse presidency than in the period we have studied up to this point. The price that the dominant classes and the armed forces had to pay for their retreat was the transition from a situation in which the state apparatus was closely linked with the upper bourgeoisie and highly autonomous from the rest of society, to one in which various social actors, including those previously excluded, re-

---

*These conditions, which taken together may be termed the optimal outcome of the retreat in which the armed forces and the upper bourgeoisie were engaged, were recounted to me, with slight variations, in several of my interviews. They are also readily recognizable in the speeches and statements of Lanusse and Mor Roig during their first months in office, as well as in Lanusse's *Mi Testimonio* (Buenos Aires: Editorial Lasserre, 1977).

gained access to a state apparatus that once again, together with society as a whole, was acquiring praetorian characteristics. Furthermore, the search for a political solution following the collapse of the BA meant that the armed forces now took the political initiative with a high degree of independence from the preferences of the upper bourgeoisie. The interests of the upper bourgeoisie, like the institutional interests of the armed forces, would now be safeguarded (under very threatening conditions) in the ways that the liberal leadership of the latter saw fit.

This situation was marked by several far-reaching changes. On the economic front, the government's aim was to prevent the economic crisis from getting out of hand. But even this modest objective was subordinated to the goal of preventing further explosions of opposition. If the risk of such explosions could be reduced by mismanaging the economy, it seemed to the new rulers to be well worth the cost. But the change in the relation of forces that led to the search for a political solution could not but affect important immediate interests of the bourgeoisie. Expectations that a policy of greater social sensitivity would involve significant concessions to the popular sector accentuated the problems of an economy already under severe strain. This resulted in the resurgence of severe economic uncertainties. Moreover, the state apparatus was no longer protected by a solid wall of exclusion. On the contrary, the state institutions would be parceled out and colonized as part of the booty with which various social forces were to be appeased for facilitating the transition. But the resulting disintegration of these institutions diminished the government's capacity to impose its political solution and gave new impetus to the economic crisis. These problems, which, as we shall see, became more acute almost every month, placed severe obstacles in the way of the political solution (or, as I shall also call it, the *exit* or *rescue operation*) sought by the Lanusse government.

The upper bourgeoisie was trapped between two abysses: the popular activation on one side, and the risk of new military coups on the other. Since the liberals had opted for the exit, those most likely to instigate the coup were a mixture of paternalists and nationalists, with whom the upper bourgeoisie, after their experience with Onganía and Levingston, felt they had had enough. Lacking a political program of their own, the upper bourgeoisie had to moor themselves to the shaky boat in which the military liberals attempted to navigate the storms of the political exit. The bourgeoisie demonstrated once again that they require the political guidance of the state apparatus to survive as the economically dominant class, even if such guidance demands the sacrifice of many of their immediate interests. Prior to the Cordobazo, when the upper bourgeoisie were in full offensive, they had established close ties with important segments of the state apparatus and participated actively in the conflicts between paternalists and liberals. They had demonstrated during that period a capacity to take the initiative not only in promoting their own economic interests but also on the political front, where they advocated prolonging the BA under liberal rule. After Levingston's ouster, by contrast, the upper bourgeoisie were compelled to sacrifice their maximum program and more than a few of their immediate interests in order to permit a rescue operation whose final outcome was far from clear.

The path proposed by the military liberals would surely have been rejected had anyone foreseen the turns it was going to take. The pace and tactics of the rescue were conditioned by the fact that those who conducted it reflected the interests, views, and biases of the armed forces, an institution riddled with tensions which by then were not easily reconcilable with views and preferences of the upper bourgeoisie. This synthesized the temporary political defeat of a class that remained socially and economically dominant at a time when the conjuncture's center of gravity—as if to compensate for the exclusionary and bureaucratic character of politics in and under the BA—was shifting to an expanding and highly conflictual political arena.[12]

4. INITIAL CONDITIONS FOR THE "POLITICAL EXIT"

Having outlined the situation at the beginning of Lanusse's presidency, let us examine some of the problems that his government confronted. One was how to ensure that the process would lead neither to totalitarianism, which more than a few expected to arise from a Peronist government, nor to collectivism and demagoguery, which so distressed the upper bourgeoisie, nor to subversion, which was the primary concern of the armed forces. As Lanusse and his collaborators stressed time and again, the coming elections would not be a mere exit: they would constitute a solution upon which a stable and efficient democracy would be based. Consequently, there was no question of permitting any candidate, supporting any program, to run. As Lanusse put it repeatedly, no one was contemplating a leap into the void. On the contrary, it was necessary to reach an agreement—the Great National Accord—in which "voice and vote" would be given to the political parties, to the "organizations of the community" and, of course, to the armed forces.[13] Without this accord there could be no solution, and without this solution the armed forces would be forced to conclude that, since the conditions for the restoration of democracy had not been satisfied, the military regime would have to persist indefinitely.*

According to the proposed agreement, the first elected government was to be one of "consolidation": i.e., of transition toward the firmly seated democracy that would arise only with its successor. And, since there had to be reliable guarantees that all parties to the agreement would comply with its terms, the president of the first constitutional government would have to be . . . Lanusse.† The political parties could return to the scene with no constraints on their activities, except those they had previously accepted as signers of the Great National Accord—which included not presenting their own presidential candidates in the coming elections. Anti-Peronists and the upper bourgeoisie would also have to make concessions if the Great National Accord was to work. The former would have to accept the return of Peronism (and Perón) to a central role in Argentine politics, while the latter would have to defer to a period of social sensitivity in the interest of relieving social tensions.

Votes did not seem to constitute a problem. In exchange for their electoral support, the Peronists and Radicals would have their parties legalized, gain access to thousands of elective offices, and have the opportunity to compete for the presidency after the first constitutional government.‡ Lanusse, moreover, seemed capable of adding an apprecia-

---

*Implicit in these statements was the threat of an *autogolpe* (a coup mounted by Lanusse and his current with the goal of interrupting the emerging political process and perpetuating themselves in government for an indefinite period). As early as April 7, 1971, Lanusse told a gathering of union leaders: "I have yet to take myself for a fool. . . . If the conditions of the accord are not met before elections are called, make no mistake: there will be no elections" (*Primera Plana,* March 21, 1972, p. 14).

†See Lanusse's speech in *La Nación,* May 2, 1971, p. 1. Actually, neither Lanusse nor his government ever admitted publicly that the preferred solution involved making Lanusse himself the next constitutional president. Even in his *Mi Testimonio* Lanusse, informative and explicit on other issues, carefully avoids denying or confirming this point. There were important reasons for maintaining this ambiguity, one being that numerous military officers suspected Lanusse of excessive personal ambition. Nevertheless, the signals issued by Lanusse and his immediate collaborators convinced many actors and observers of the period (and all of the persons I interviewed) that Lanusse's sights were fixed on a constitutional presidency, even after this objective had become completely unrealistic. The media was also convinced that Lanusse aspired to a constitutional presidency; see, for example, *Primera Plana,* November 2, 1971, p. 8, March 21, 1972, p. 14, and June 22, 1972, p. 12; and *La Nación,* February 2, 1972, p. 10 (which noted that "the only presidential candidacy that is widely discussed is that of Lanusse") and June 16, 1972, p. 6.

‡From the government's point of view, there was an additional advantage to preventing the Peronists from entering a presidential race until after the first elected government: the likelihood that Perón, an old man, would die in the interim.

ble block of votes of his own. If the image of Franco had hovered over Onganía's presidency and that of the PRI over the Levingston period, Lanusse—the aristocratic military leader rescuing the nation by means of a quasi-plebiscitary election—tried hard, and initially with some success, to evoke the memory of de Gaulle. His grand coalition would even include the unions, partly by way of the agreements to be reached with the Peronists and partly due to economic policies concerned with alleviating social tensions. The upper bourgeoisie would have to content itself with the guarantee implicit in Lanusse's background, while the armed forces could ask for no better guarantee than the prospect of seeing Lanusse become the constitutional president. In any case, the armed forces, as noted above, appeared to hold the trump card: if for some reason the parties failed to abide by the Accord, they would on no account allow the country to make a leap into the void. Rather, they would launch a new coup that would postpone indefinitely any democratic solution.

Another aspect of the Great National Accord involved the elimination of proscriptions against Peronism, which would be allowed to field candidates below the presidential level.* Moreover, Perón would receive economic and honorific compensations, in exchange for which he would have to explicitly renounce his ties with the guerrillas, with radicalized unionism, and more generally with all the "non-moderate" sectors of Peronism. Assuming that the Peronists, as the *La Hora del Pueblo* documents suggested, were genuinely committed to the restoration of democracy, this scheme did not seem unreasonable. That the government's paramount concern was to restrain the popular activation and—above all—to isolate the guerrillas and the leftist (both Peronist and non-Peronist) currents within unionism is highlighted by the fact that a proposal along these lines was among the first contacts the government made with Perón.[14]

But several other conditions would have to be met if the political exit was to succeed. First and foremost, Peronism (or more precisely, Perón) would have to negotiate according to the terms proposed by Lanusse. Second, the Peronists and the government would have to succeed in a joint effort to redirect the popular activation into more tranquil chan-

---

*Before the elections, the Peronists and Radicals were expected to endorse the Lanusse government publicly and to participate in a coalition or "national conciliation" cabinet. This arrangement, with Lanusse as president and Radicals and Peronists in high government positions, would be the makeup of the first, transitional constitutional government. See *La Nación*, June 27, 1971, p. 6, and *Panorama*, July 17, 1971, p. 9.

nels. Third, it was crucial that Lanusse's government should not become too unpopular; widespread popular hostility would mean electoral suicide for any party suspected of collaborating with the government. Fourth, and closely connected with the preceding condition, the economic situation could not be allowed to deteriorate to the point where the popular sector would again be set against the government, as had happened under Ongania and Levingston. Finally, the entire process, with its inevitable ups and downs, would have to be supported by the armed forces.

Only the last of these conditions was met, and that with serious problems. As a result, everything evolved and ended very differently from the way things were initially anticipated.

5. THE GAME BECOMES MORE COMPLICATED

First, and most important, Perón did not play by the rules that the government proposed. Rather than repudiating the guerrillas, his messages, some more explicitly than others, referred approvingly to their activities.* Furthermore, he neither agreed nor declined to renounce his eventual presidential candidacy, nor did he assent in the designation of a national union candidate. Indeed, it was not clear, except perhaps to those who thought that personal rewards would suffice to secure his compliance, why the proposed terms should have attracted him. On the other hand, the possibilities implicit in the reopening of the electoral system gave the Peronist political personnel strong reasons to accept the government's conditions, especially in view of the fact that most were as worried as the armed forces by the new forms of militancy. Most union leaders, for their part, were unprepared to confront the government head-on. Perón, however, was hardly enthusiastic about the rewards— and temptations—that a political solution held for his followers. Should he renounce his eventual presidential candidacy, Perón would in effect be conceding to the next (non-Peronist) president a wide range of co-optation opportunities, implying the risk of losing control of his move-

---

*Having endorsed Aramburu's assassination, Perón now refrained from condemning such guerrilla acts as the kidnapping and murder of Oberdán Sallustro, head of the Argentine Fiat subsidiary, and the almost simultaneous assassination of four-star general Juan Carlos Sánchez. Even though Peronist union leaders and political personnel were among the many who deplored these acts (*La Nación*, April 15, 1972, p. 1), the government was unsuccessful in its demand that Perón add his voice to the outcry; see *Panorama*, April 6, p. 12, April 13, pp. 8, 16, and April 20, pp. 16, 21, 1972; and *La Opinión*, March 30, 1972, p. 7.

ment. Nor could he afford to ignore the growing strength of the radicalized Peronist currents (which openly rejected Lanusse's solution* and would not take kindly to Perón's support for it,†) if only with a view toward later converging with them in an electoral process tilted in his favor. Perón's reluctance to play this game probably also had to do with Lanusse, who with his family background and his anti-Peronist past epitomized the persons, ideas, and classes that Perón had every reason to detest. In addition, given Lanusse's potential popularity and the centrifugal forces that were always at work within Peronism, it was not inconceivable that many Peronists, if Perón or a Peronist candidate were forbidden to run, could be attracted to the parties coalescing around Lanusse.‡

In view of these possibilities, why should the old leader invest his political capital to save elements of Argentine society—the armed forces, the liberals, and the upper bourgeoisie—that had long been so hostile to him? Perón might have been induced to cooperate had he been offered the central role in a grand project of national reconciliation that would vindicate his past governments, link them symbolically to the future, and allow him to assume the role of an elder statesman above the cares and obligations of the presidency. But the strong anti-Peronist sentiments within and outside the armed forces made this intolerable. Lanusse and his collaborators chose to offer Perón personal rewards in exchange for votes and the excommunication of the guerrillas.§

---

*The slogan "no coup, no election: revolution" expressed the position of these currents. An interesting compilation of their slogans and songs is Jorge Pinedo, *Consignas y lucha popular en el proceso revolucionario Argentino, 1955–1973* (Buenos Aires: Editorial Freeland, 1974).

†It is quite clear from the correspondence between Perón and the Montoneros, as well as from the August 1972 *Primera Plana* interview with Rodolfo Galimberti, the leader of the Peronist Youth, that these radicalized sectors were not prepared to give unconditional support to Perón's decisions.

‡Considering that Perón, without having relinquished his nationalist and corporatist ideology of the organized community, was attempting to navigate among the new radicalized currents, his behavior is easier to understand. While Perón declined to sever his ties to the "special formations," his preferred objective was most probably a victory on the political-electoral plane, as evidenced by such statements as: "The path of armed struggle is indispensable. Every time the *muchachos* deal a blow, they strike for our side at the negotiating table and strengthen the position of those who seek a clear and clean electoral process. Without the Viet Cong guerrillas' relentless attacks in the jungles, the Vietnamese delegation in Paris would have had to pack their bags and go home" (*Panorama*, June 29, 1971, p. 9).

§When I interviewed him later, one of the key members of Lanusse's political team complained that the negotiations with Perón were "like deals among gangsters" in which it was erroneously assumed that Perón would ultimately base his decisions on prospects for personal economic gain. As we shall see, this was not the only serious miscalculation rooted in the establishment's contempt for Perón and Peronism.

If Lanusse's aims were transparent, Perón's were not. At the time, even his closest collaborators (according to interviews and informal conversations I held with some of them) did not know where he stood. For one reason or another, he seemed unwilling to accept the proposals he was offered. It is important to stress, however, that he did not reject them outright. Perón's criticisms of the government during 1971 and 1972 sounded at times as if he was heading towards a drastic break with it, and at others that he was merely angling for a better bargaining position. These oscillations gave each current within Peronism reason to believe that Perón would ultimately endorse its own positions. This state of affairs continued from March 1971 until the March 1973 elections. In the meantime, a series of factors changed the initial panorama: most notably, the intensification of social conflicts, of the economic crisis, and of guerrilla activity. The last, evidenced not only in the number of actions but also in the growing operational capacity that they demonstrated,[15] drew an increase in repression, while numerous cruelties on both sides inflamed the confrontations.*

Another problem was the rapid deterioration of the economy. In May 1971, Ferrer and his team left the Economy Ministry. Indeed, it may be said that they took the ministry with them, for upon their departure the junta of commanders in chief dismantled it, arguing that it had amassed too much power.[16] The broad decision-making powers which had resided in the ministry were farmed out to various secretariats that were supposed to be overseen and coordinated by the president and the junta. Nothing better exemplifies the reversal of the centralizing tendencies that had predominated since 1966† or reveals more clearly

---

*As already noted, the expansion of guerrilla activity was marked not only by kidnappings and assassinations, but by other spectacular acts, such as takeovers of medium-sized towns and military installations. The government responded by establishing special courts to try cases of "subversion" (*La Nación*, May 29, 1971, p. 1), as well as by recourse to nasty procedures that circumvented existing legislation (for a list of persons allegedly wronged by such procedures, see *Primera Plana*, December 14, 1972, p. 16). The massacre of sixteen guerrillas recaptured shortly after their escape from prison did as much to increase the hatred and violence of the situation as did the assassinations of Aramburu, Vandor, Sánchez and Sallustro (*Panorama*, August 23, 1972, p. 4, and *La Nación*, August 23, 1972, pp. 1, 16).

†CARBAP, an organization of the Pampean bourgeoisie, submitted the initial proposal to break up the Economy Ministry, arguing that statism would increase if the Ministry were left intact (*Economic Survey*, April 27, 1971, p. 5). The organizations of the upper bourgeoisie apparently saw the ensuing period as one in which (in contrast to the period of Krieger Vasena's ministry) the centralization of decision making in the state's economic apparatus was unlikely to work to their advantage. "Liberal circles . . . introduced the idea that the fragmentation of the [Economy] Ministry would ensure that a deliberative stage would precede the making of major decisions, thus diminishing the government's executive capacity. The result would be reduced state intervention and increased 'free-

the change in priorities from economic normalization to the quest for a political exit. This decision, of course, accelerated the state's institutional disintegration and increased its permeability to all organized groups in society; praetorianism again reared its head.

Another major problem was the armed forces themselves. Implicit in the search for a political solution was their admission of political defeat. This led to tensions that moved Lanusse to act quickly to head off a potential coup.* Moreover, the economic situation, as we shall see in chapter 9, deteriorated greatly during 1971 and 1972; social conflicts continued unabated, and the agreement with Peronism did not materialize. To make matters worse, all indications were that Lanusse's popularity, which was probably quite high at the beginning of his presidency, was evaporating rapidly. All of these aspects of the situation led paternalists and nationalists in the armed forces to agitate against the liberals' "betrayal" of their institutional mission and of the "goals of the Argentine Revolution." In their view, the BA had failed not because it had been too authoritarian, but because it had conceded too much to everything that represented the old Argentina: liberals (both civilian and military), politicians, unions, bourgeois organizations, and the leading periodicals. However, the National Revolution was still possible: all that was needed was the courage to break with the past.

These feelings were distilled in the ultra-nationalist coup of October 1971. Targeted at Lanusse and those who supported the political exit, the purpose of the coup was not only to revive the BA but also to dismantle virtually all existing social organizations, which, in the view

---

dom' for the 'play of economic forces' " (*Primera Plana,* June 1, 1971, p. 10). This position converged with Lanusse's hopes of appeasing everyone by parceling out the state apparatus, in a sort of reverse corporatism, among the "representative sectors" of society. As *Primera Plana* (June 29, 1971, p. 10) put it, "Lanusse intends to replace [the Economy Ministry] with a perpetual dialogue whose interlocutors would be the real powers . . . ; to award the Central Bank to the financial 'establishment'; [the Secretariat of] Industry to a protectionist team favorable to the growth of manufactures; [the Secretariat of] Labor to persons receptive to the demands of the CGT; [the Secretariat of] Agriculture, to someone who genuinely speaks for rural producers."

*Lanusse forced the retirement of seven colonels who were among those most highly qualified for promotion (*Panorama,* May 18, 1971, cover story entitled "The Military Plot," which also reported unrest in the air force, p. 8). This action, however, did not eliminate the concern raised by General Labanca's well-known efforts to mount a nationalist coup, whose goals made the Levingston period seem like a timid prelude (cf. *Confirmado,* May 25, p. 8 and June 29, p. 8, 1971). For indications of a potential air force rebellion, see *Confirmado,* August 17, 1971, p. 8; and for premonitions of what became the unsuccessful coup of October 1971, see *Confirmado,* September 7, 1971, p. 8 (see also the cover story entitled "Argentina: The Military Temperature"); see also *Primera Plana,* September 14, 1971, p. 8 and *La Nación,* September 16, 1971, p. 6.

of those who mounted the coup, had been contaminated by the twin evils of "subversive Marxism" and "anti-national liberalism." In a situation that seemed on the verge of repeating the armed clashes of 1962 and 1963, the uprising was suppressed after the government deployed superior troops against the rebels. It is significant that once the ideology and goals of the insurrection were known, nearly all organizations and sectors of society—the CGT, the CGE, the organizations of the upper bourgeoisie, *La Hora del Pueblo*, the *Encuentro de Los Argentinos*, the media, the Radicals, and the Peronists, among others—repudiated the attempt and rushed to express their support for democracy and the continuation of the Lanusse government.* In the face of evidence that the rebels intended to eliminate democracy for good, it is also important that Lanusse and the liberals, speaking for the armed forces, reaffirmed their promise that the era of authoritarianism in Argentina had ended and that an irrevocable commitment had been made to the expression of the "popular will," "freely and without exclusions," in the forthcoming elections for a constitutional government.[17]

Although the uprising was limited to two army regiments, it clearly had broader support within the armed forces. This meant that no one from then on could ignore the possibility that another coup might be attempted. Another important aspect of the October 1971 attempt was that it revealed the ultra-nationalist orientation of the military that might overthrow Lanusse's government. This ratified the feelings of the upper bourgeoisie that the road taken by the military liberals, however risky and unpleasant, was the only one with a chance of averting catastrophe.† For their part, politicians of all stripes could not ignore that an ultra-nationalist coup would close the electoral arena for a long time to come. The CGE wanted no more of the excesses that the Levingston government had perpetrated during its last months in office. Even the national union leaders, who had never been inoculated against the populist temptation of a "union of the *pueblo* and the armed forces," would not accept a coup that had as one of its goals the elimination of practically all existing social organizations.

The failed coup attempt thus served Lanusse as an eloquent reminder to his interlocutors that the road he proposed was flanked to one side by

---

*For a good synopsis of this unanimous rejection, see *Análisis,* October 15, 1971, p. 16. As the UIA put it (*La Nación,* October 10, 1971, p. 10), "We want no more revolutions, regardless of their slogans or protagonists."

†My interviews. Also, the leading periodicals expressed this view quite explicitly in the weeks immediately after the October coup attempt.

the overflowing of popular activation and to the other by the reaction-ary and irrational tendencies in the armed forces. By acting swiftly to defeat the rebellion, moreover, Lanusse showed that he was capable of standing up to the type of challenge that had toppled his two predeces-sors. But these advantages came at a cost. In the first place—and this is a price that the victors in such attempts always seem to pay—the military officers who had helped Lanusse now felt entitled to a greater say in matters outside the strict domain of the armed forces.[18] Another, even more costly, consequence was that in crushing the October rebellion, Lanusse and his current had committed themselves irrevocably against any other coup.* From that point on, what probably had been a bluff all along was revealed as one: there existed no longer a credible possibility that Lanusse and his current would themselves stage a coup, postponing the elections indefinitely, if the Great National Accord was rejected. There remained, to be sure, a significant chance that a coup would occur, but in the event that it did, its targets would include Lanusse and his current, not just the process leading toward elections. In other words, the threat of an *autogolpe* no longer existed. Lanusse had lost the ace in the hole with which he expected to force Peronism to agree to his terms for the political exit. Meanwhile, Perón's card—his decision as to whether or not to condemn the radicalized Peronist currents—remained as mysterious as ever. The victory won in October 1971 thus came at the cost of leaving the upper bourgeoisie tied to a partner who had already played his trump card. From that point on, bayonets alone could not force the political parties to comply with Lanusse's demands to sit around a bargaining table.

After the abortive insurrection a number of Peronist leaders moved nearer to Lanusse. The big problem was that Perón might not want elections—at least on Lanusse's terms—and that he might even prefer a military coup from the extreme right.† This hypothesis was not prepos-

---

*Lanusse himself, writing later in *Mi Testimonio*, noted that "the politicians—particularly the Peronists—were convinced that since a coup was impossible and the institutional process was guaranteed, they could all rest on their laurels and gather votes amidst the outcry of opposition, leaving the government to defend both itself and them as best it could. Many things happened within a short span of time [after the October 1971 coup], including Perón's replacement of his delegate Jorge Daniel Paladino, a man inclined toward dialogue, by Héctor J. Cámpora, the spearhead of *Montonerismo* and of the most virulent opposition. The experience of October 8 demonstrated the degree to which the war could be won without advancing the goal of peace" (*Mi Testimonio*, p. 250).

†There are indications that Perón, playing all his cards, sent encouraging signals to the leaders of the October attempt via his personal secretary, López Rega (*Primera Plana*, November 14, 1971, p. 8).

terous if it was assumed that Perón's highest priority was to maintain control over his movement, or given the premise (dear to the radicalized sectors of Peronism) that Perón might favor a right-wing coup in order to further "sharpen the contradictions." Whether or not Perón really favored elections at the time (I believe that up until the last moment he was open to all possibilities) the important point is that the other participants in this game did not know what he thought.*

There were signals toward the end of 1971 that Perón was hardening his position. One was his replacement of Daniel Paladino, his personal delegate,† by Héctor J. Cámpora, one of the few Peronist politicians with a reputation of solid loyalty to Perón. From that point on, Perón and Cámpora, when asked whether they would enter negotiations with the government, insisted with unassailable logic that if the government really had, as it asserted, a democratic vocation, and if it was genuinely committed, as the people demanded, to calling free elections ("with neither tricks nor exclusions," as Lanusse had said), then they did not see what there was to negotiate: the government had only to call elections and the majority would choose the president they preferred. Nor did they see the need, if proscriptions and vetoes were truly to be abolished, of agreeing as to who would be the presidential candidate.[19] According to Cámpora, moreover, it was not that Perón wanted to be

---

*As one source put it, "The unknown factor has a name. No one knows for sure what Perón wants" (*Primera Plana*, August 31, 1971, p. 9). In a game where the other players had put all their cards on the table, the master tactician was not about to reveal his.

†According to contemporary observers, Perón removed Paladino (who appeared at times to be less his representative than an intermediary between him and Lanusse) not only because of his growing distrust of him but also as a signal that he would be taking a harder line in the future. Thereafter, Perón (both directly and via Cámpora) gave ever more explicit encouragement to the radicalized Peronists, who viewed Paladino's demise as an important victory. By then, as *Primera Plana* commented (January 11, 1972, p. 6), "[Perón's] public statements were all tinged with guerrillism." See also *Primera Plana*, January 25, 1972, p. 8 (article entitled "The Hour of the Hard-Liners"), which reprinted a pamphlet in which the Montonero guerrillas announced that they would accept elections only if they were held "with Perón in the country and as a candidate [supporting] a program in which a nationalist revolutionary government would nationalize all key economic sectors, expropriate the landholding oligarchy, the industrial bourgeoisie, and the international monopolies; in which a revolutionary state would initiate comprehensive economic planning; and in which there would be workers' control of production." This position went well beyond what Perón himself ever wanted or claimed to want. The complexity of the field of forces in which Perón operated, his pendular strategy, and his personal preferences are apparent in the proposal he circulated at the same time for the formation of a "Civic Front for National Liberation," which would embrace the parties of *La Hora del Pueblo* and the *Encuentro de los Argentinos* as well as the CGT and the CGE. The proposal came out in favor of a very moderate socioeconomic program and advocated "clean and pure elections . . . within the shortest time possible" (*Primera Plana*, February 22, 1972, p. 7).

president of Argentina again, but that many wished him to do so, and he had always done "what the people wanted."*

Perón's reticence placed him squarely at the center of attention and greatly helped him to increase his influence over his followers. Although many Peronists had an obvious interest in proceeding with the elections according to the terms proposed by Lanusse, any public disagreement with Perón's instructions was tantamount to political suicide. Rather, the best way to gain influence within Peronism seemed to be to outdo everyone else in proclaiming one's unshakable loyalty to Perón, which meant relinquishing any possibility of influencing Perón's decisions. The result was that all currents within Peronism, even as many winked at Lanusse, went out of their way to demand that Perón be allowed to return to Argentina and to stand as their presidential candidate. It was ambiguous what effect this tactic would have. On the one hand, to demand Perón's return ran the risk of igniting the anti-Peronism always simmering within the armed forces and provoking another coup. On the other hand, many moderate Peronists, in part because they needed to believe it, continued privately to assure the government and the armed forces that Perón, in raising the specter of his candidacy, was merely trying to strengthen his hand before entering the long-awaited negotiations.†

But more serious complications stemmed from Perón's refusal to condemn, and his occasional statements of support for, the guerrillas and other radicalized groups. This resulted in a situation where Peronist politicians and union leaders found themselves crowded together with those groups under an umbrella that their leader refused to close. Insofar as it was believed that Perón could effectively marginalize his radicalized followers by condemning them, he seemed capable of striking where it hurt the most. What would be the use of an agreement between

---

*To reduce the likelihood of a coup, some Peronists pressured Perón, at the cost of their political careers, to proscribe his own candidacy. The tone in which Cámpora implicitly responded to such suggestions did little to diffuse anti-Peronist sentiments: "Only one thing need be said about Perón's candidacy: the Justicialists, the people, demand that Perón be a candidate, and the General has always done what the people want" (*La Nación*, April 22, 1972, p. 12). José Rucci, the secretary-general of the CGT (who, like Cámpora, lacked a solid base of his own, but whose loyalty to Perón went well beyond that of most other union leaders), announced that "the choice is between elections with Perón as a candidate and civil war" (*La Nación*, May 27, 1972, p. 5).

†In my interviews with government officials, as well as with Peronist politicians and unionists, reference was made repeatedly to such private assurances on the part of those who publicly declared non-negotiable their demand that Perón be allowed to run for president. Moreover, between mid-1971 and mid-1972 such weeklies as *Primera Plana*, *Confirmado*, and *Panorama* hinted repeatedly that such assurances were being made.

Lanusse and some Peronist leaders if Perón refused to endorse it and instead placed his full support behind the guerrillas?* Time was running out for the government. Elections could not be postponed much longer, but the conditions had not been met whereby the institutional interests of the armed forces, and the class interests behind them, could be considered to be reasonably guaranteed. This evoked loud laments from the bourgeoisie and encouraged the speculative behavior that contributed to further deterioration of the economy. As will be seen in chapter 9, the familiar economic problems of the 1955–66 period reappeared with a vengeance in 1971. They grew even more acute in 1972, aggravated by numerous cabinet crises, price truces and accords that did not even begin to come to fruition,† price freezes and anti-speculation campaigns that fueled the complaints of the upper bourgeoisie,‡ an outright ban on

---

*A similar problem surrounded proposals to bring Radicals and Peronists into a coalition cabinet, which Lanusse and Mor Roig advocated as a means of breathing political life into their government and preparing the way for its constitutional successor. See Lanusse, *Mi Testimonio,* p. 223 passim, and *Primera Plana,* August 31, 1971, p. 9. Such proposals failed because "the Radicals would never agree to join [the cabinet] unless the *Justicialistas* [Peronists] accompanied them, and the latter would not [participate in such a cabinet] without Perón's authorization" (*Primera Plana,* September 28, 1971, p. 9). Perón was pulling the strings once again: any Peronist who joined the proposed cabinet without his consent would be guilty of "treason," undermining the effect that the coalition cabinet was meant to achieve. Should the Radicals enter the cabinet on their own, their image as an official party, which was already crystallizing due to Mor Roig's ministry, would be enhanced to the detriment of their electoral chances. For evidence that the Radicals were aware of this problem, see *La Nación,* September 23, 1971, p. 9.

†*Economic Survey,* September 7, 1971, p. 9. The upper bourgeoisie did not take kindly to "price truces" aimed at slowing the rise in the cost of living. The UIA and CAC complained that "price freezes in conjunction with wage and salary hikes make not for a truce but for a plain and simple redistribution of income" (*Análisis,* September 24, 1971, p. 17). The tone of such criticisms, however, differed from that of previous years. The president of the UIA, aware of the changes that had taken place in the relation of forces, added comments that would have been unthinkable a short time before: "The UIA is convinced that an accord between the government, labor, and business will serve at least to decelerate the disconcerting pace of price increases. . . . It will be necessary to formulate an incomes policy on the basis of good will from all quarters" (*Análisis,* August 31, 1971, p. 16). The industrial upper bourgeoisie, now on the defensive, employed language that seemed to have been lifted straight from the documents of the CGE. The UIA, demonstrating a degree of flexibility that was not to be found among the non-industrial segments of the upper bourgeoisie, removed itself from the ACIEL, a stronghold of virulent anti-Peronism and economic orthodoxy (*La Nación,* September 30, 1972, p. 10). In addition, the UIA, to the surprise of many, commented favorably on the state's role in the economy and on supporting small and medium-sized enterprises (*La Nación,* October 24, 1972, p. 6, and UIA, *Memoria anual, 1972–1973,* Buenos Aires, 1973).

‡In addition to the previously cited complaints of the upper bourgeoisie and the leading periodicals about the deterioration of the economy and the growing misfortunes of the political solution, see *Economic Survey,* August 17, 1971, pp. 1, 5, April 11, 1972, pp. 1, 4, and June 27, 1972, p. 7: "More than anything else, the Argentine economy suffers from a severe investment crisis that is due less to the economic situation than to the brutal uncertainty of the Great National Accord." See also *La Prensa,* July 29, 1972, p. 8.

imports to alleviate temporarily the shortage of international reserves,* and hurried trips abroad by government officials seeking credits with which to head off default on the country's international debt.

Furthermore, the recurrent wage and salary demands fueled by the rising inflation resulted in numerous strikes. National work stoppages called by the CGT achieved widespread participation.† Much to the concern of the bourgeoisie, the government was not backing them against the increasingly demanding positions of the unions. This was due both to the government's fading capacity for repression (which was focused primarily on the guerrillas) and to the fact that Lanusse's political hopes depended in no insignificant measure on the good will of the (Peronist) national union leaders. These problems were exacerbated by the economic crisis, and in particular by a strong decline in overall liquidity and credit (traceable to capital flight), black-market transactions, speculation in inventories, and the government's absorption of a substantial part of the increase in the money supply to finance its own

---

*La Nación, September 16, 1971, p. 1. Import restrictions remained in effect until October 31, 1971.

†These national work stoppages are covered in La Nación, September 29, 1971, pp. 1, 16, February 29, 1972, p. 1, and March 1, 1972, p. 1; Panorama, October 5, 1971, p. 8; and Primera Plana, March 7, 1972, pp. 10, 12. For reports on the unions' criticisms of the government's economic policies and "political tricks," see Las Bases, January 4, 1972, p. 3. But see also Las Bases, May 4, 1972, p. 4, for statements by Rucci, who also sought to distance himself from the other side by condeming the "dirty Bolshies." See also the CGT's statement of July 6, 1972 (Primera Plana, July 11, 1972, p. 54), which, after criticizing the armed forces, added that "if any attempt is made to deceive the people by tampering with the upcoming popular consultations, the people, finding the road to a peaceful solution blocked, will opt for the bloody road of violent revolution as the only way to realize their destiny. The responsibility [for this choice] will fall on those who have refused to respect the sovereign will of the people. . . . Let us hope that the armed forces know how to assume their historical responsibilities" (emphasis in the original). In the same statement, however, the CGT made a characteristic turnabout by affirming that "the workers' organizations and the workers themselves today constitute the providential backbone of ideological security. . . . Were the Forces of Labor or the Armed Forces to falter in the dangerous circumstances of the present day, we do not wish even to contemplate the prospects for the country and the citizenry." The government responded to this statement by freezing union funds, suspending the legal recognition of the CGT, and imposing other sanctions (La Nación, July 8, 1972, p. 1). But as might have been predicted under the circumstances, these penalties were soon revoked (La Nación, July 15, p. 1 and July 26, p. 1, 1972). In addition, new riots took place in cities of the interior: Neuquén (La Nación, December 2, 1971, p. 1); Mendoza (La Nación, April 5, 1972, p. 1); Malargüe (La Nación, July 7, 1972, p. 1); and General Roca (La Nación, July 8, 1972, p. 1). These episodes required the intervention of the army. On the riot in Mendoza, see "El Mendozinazo: Crónica, análisis y relatos," Cuadernos de antropología Tercer Mundo (Buenos Aires, 1972). In addition, numerous strikes were called by university and secondary school students, some of which resulted in campus occupations and police repression. Various protests organized by the Movement of Third World Priests should also be noted; see Andrew Graham-Yooll, Tiempo de tragedia, especially pp. 66 and 108–19, and Michael Dodson, "Priests and Peronists: Radical Clergy in Argentine Politics," Latin American Perspectives, no. 3 (Autumn, 1974).

deficit. Once again, it was the weakest factions of the bourgeoisie that paid the heaviest price for these problems. Accordingly, the CGE added its voice to the chorus of protest.* Moving ever closer to the CGT, it joined that organization in demanding wage and salary hikes and easier access to credit for national enterprises.† The upper bourgeoisie reacted predictably by pointing out that such policies would result in higher inflation, larger fiscal deficits, and further balance-of-payments problems. The tone of their counterproposals for renewed orthodoxy, however, made clear that the upper bourgeoisie had little hope of being heard.[20] The government, for its part, made room for all sorts of demands—from the most redistributionist to the most orthodox—which canceled each other out and hardly ever were implemented. With the suppression of the Ministry of Economy and Labor, only through an abuse of language can it be said that an economic policy existed during this period. The government's actions in the economic field focused almost exclusively on doing what was deemed on a day-to-day basis to facilitate the political exit—the prospects for which became even more remote with the ensuing economic crisis.‡

The government's hopes were dealt an additional blow by the activation of the popular sector, which terrified the dominant classes both in

*In addition to criticizing economic policy, the CGE attempted to organize nationwide "business protests" (*La Nación*, January 11, 1972, p. 1). Although not widely adhered to, these protests reinforced the impression that the government was incapable of controlling any sector of society.

†As an important manifestation of this convergence, a meeting called by the CGE, which was attended by representatives of the CGT and of nearly all political parties, produced a unanimous call for the acceleration of the process toward elections "without restrictions or conditions." Implicit in this proposal was a rejection of the terms that the government and the armed forces were seeking to impose (*Panorama*, March 14, 1972, p. 12). The CGE also joined with the CGT in a pact that called for the "reactivation of industry," higher wages, the "recovery of purchasing power in the domestic market," "bank credit to alleviate the suffocation of business," tax reductions, protection of national industry, and a "lessening of international pressure on the domestic market." These proposals, which were consistent with Perón's position, concluded with a demand for the "immediate legitimation of power through the free expression of the popular will" (*Panorama*, September 14, 1972, p. 13). The text of this pact (entitled "Bases for Social Peace and National Reconstruction") is reprinted in *La Nación*, September 9, 1972, pp. 1, 5.

‡The government underscored its impotence by voicing its concern over the deteriorating economy and by asserting (ineffectively) its intention to maintain real wages and salaries and existing levels of economic activity. See *La Nación*, July 2, pp. 1, 12, November 18, p. 1, December 2, pp. 1, 20, 1971 (in which Lanusse was quoted as saying that "the corollary of maintaining real wages will be social peace"), and February 5, 1972, p. 1 (where it was announced in an odd martial tone that "the government will fight against the cost of living"). To make matters worse, the president of the Central Bank, while attempting to secure balance-of-payments assistance from the IMF and a consortium of international banks, had the less-than-astute idea of announcing that the country was on the "verge of bankruptcy" (*Panorama*, August 17, 1971, p. 8, story entitled "The Flight of Dollars"). For the reactions these remarks provoked, see *Análisis*, December 2, 1971, p. 9, and *Economic Survey*, November 23, 1971, p. 2.

itself and because it seemed to provide fertile ground for the guerrillas. Nonetheless, and testifying to their lack of political alternatives, the dominant classes did not promote Lanusse's ouster but accompanied him, albeit grudgingly, to the bitter end of the attempted exit. With the military liberals committed to this operation, with the potential coup-makers ready to take the country in an extreme nationalistic direction, with the majority of voters leaning toward the Radicals and the Peronists, and with the emergence of radicalized currents, which challenged their very existence as a class, the bourgeoisie (increasingly the whole of this class, not just its upper segment) had little choice but to follow their military tutors along an uncertain path.

A further problem was Lanusse's loss of popularity. At the least opportune time for the success of their rescue operation, both Lanusse and the armed forces were receiving unmistakable signals of widespread popular hostility.* By mid-1972, having grappled for more than a year with Perón's ambiguous responses to his proposals, Lanusse, irrevocably committed to elections, changed his original position. If (or as long as) Peronism stood in the way of the Great National Accord and his own semiplebiscitarian constitutional presidency, Lanusse would again become an ardent foe of Peronism and Perón.[21] Lanusse hoped that in this way he could win the electoral support of anti-Peronist voters and of the still uncommitted who would supposedly opt out of the rash adventure entailed by a Peronist government. Lanusse thus returned to his old anti-Peronist stance, in the expression of which he accused Perón of "cowardice" for remaining in exile and refusing to face Argentina's problems in Argentina.† Lanusse's new position did little to improve

---

*Evidence for the declining popularity of Lanusse and his government may be found in *Primera Plana,* March 14, 1972, p. 6, and *Panorama,* May 11, 1972, p. 5. As is clear from *Mi Testimonio,* p. 232, Lanusse was aware of his growing unpopularity and the risks it posed: "The army (together with its sister forces) had its back to the wall. . . . The lack of oxygen was total. As was demonstrated time after time, the country was either indifferent or hostile en masse to the government. How was the army supposed to recuperate [institutionally] in the long run? . . . Could it be supposed that the pressures closing in on us would diminish *little by little?*" (emphasis in the original). It became apparent that Lanusse's unpopularity ruled out his candidacy, as well as increasing his difficulties in bargaining with any strength with the major political parties (*La Nación,* March 19, 1972, p. 6).

†The subsequent exchange of insults between Lanusse and Perón can be followed in *Panorama,* July 1, p. 12, and August 3, p. 8, 1972, and *La Nación,* May 21, p. 5; July 15, p. 1; July 26, pp. 1, 12; August 25, p. 1; October 25, p. 1; October 28, pp. 1, 14; October 29, p. 1, 1972. One of Lanusse's speeches (*La Nación,* July 26, 1972) is noteworthy for a passage that soon boomeranged: "Don't come running to me, or to any other Argentine, saying that Perón does not come back [to Argentina] because he cannot. You may say that it is because he does not want to, but deep in my heart I know that it is because he does not have the guts."

whatever chances might have remained for an accord that would include Peronism. It also ran the risk of provoking Perón's return to Argentina, although Lanusse, whose scorn for Perón as cowardly and corrupt was typical of many anti-Peronists, seems not to have seriously contemplated this possibility.

Now that Lanusse was aiming to become the anti-Peronist candidate, Peronism would have to be either proscribed or defeated at the polls. Given the solemn promises and widespread expectations that Peronism would be allowed to participate in the elections* and the belief that full electoral proscription might drive Perón toward total support for the radicalized currents, the first option was almost unthinkable. It was clear, moreover, that any such decision would deprive Lanusse's government of any meaning and provoke its fall at the hands of the military officers who from the beginning had opposed a "political adventure." The second option, however, appeared possible. Opinion polls, some taken a few days prior to the elections, seemed encouraging: at most 40 percent of the respondents expressed the intention of voting for Peronism.[22] Such figures should have merited methodological skepticism (since they were arrived at via dubious sampling procedures and since approximately 30 percent of the respondents in various polls declared themselves undecided), but they helped convince Lanusse and his advisers that an electoral victory was possible. However, survey data focused less directly on the respondent's intended party vote (see Table 30) could have suggested quite different conclusions.

We see first that most respondents rejected any formula implying the continuity of the existing regime. Second, there existed a strong positive relation between a respondent's likelihood of expressing positive feelings toward Perón (i.e., of responding affirmatively when asked whether Perón's return to Argentina would benefit the country) and his/her membership in the popular sector. Third, given this distribution of opinions, the high percentage of "lower strata" and "lower-middle strata" respondents expressing a desire for "elections as soon as possible" (72.3 percent and 60.7 percent respectively) could have suggested—as proved to be the case—a much higher percentage of Peronist votes than was forecast by surveys directly addressing questions of party preference.†

---

*By that stage, the initial promises that the upcoming elections would be based on "fair play" and would involve "neither exclusions nor proscriptions" had been ratified explicitly by both Lanusse and Mor Roig. See La Nación, July 8, 1971, pp. 1, 16, and December 31, 1971, pp. 1, 12.

†Other significant sources of data include an IPSA survey taken around October 1972, which asked respondents to express their opinions about the government. Seventy-five

TABLE 30   POLITICAL OPINIONS IN ARGENTINA, 1971

	Upper Strata (%)	Upper Middle Strata (%)	Lower Middle Strata (%)	Lower Strata (%)	Total (%)
If Perón were to return, would it be advantageous or disadvantageous for the country?					
Advantageous	14.1	25.6	35.8	57.4	40.9
Disadvantageous	57.7	55.6	38.5	19.4	35.3
Don't know, no answer	28.2	18.8	25.7	23.2	23.8
In the confusion we are in everyone proposes a different path for the country. Of all of these proposed paths, which do you prefer?					
Elections as soon as possible	43.5	46.9	60.7	72.3	59.2
Elections within three years	33.6	26.3	19.1	11.1	19.7
Continuance of present government for more than three years	10.7	10.6	6.9	6.5	8.7
Other responses	12.2	16.2	13.2	10.1	12.4

SOURCE: Computer printouts from a nationwide survey (N=4,000) taken in cities with more than 20,000 inhabitants during July and August of 1971, by the Centro de Estudios Motivacionales y Sociales. I am indebted to its director, Dr. José E. Miguens, for facilitating my access to these printouts.

It still seemed possible that Perón's rejection of the proposed accord was a tactic aimed at improving his bargaining position. If this had been the case, Lanusse's new strategy of appealing to anti-Peronist sentiments might have bettered his hand in the anticipated negotiations. The main problem with this strategy was that the unfolding social and economic crisis was evaporating Lanusse's chances of obtaining a significant portion of the vote on his own. A possible solution would have involved Lanusse becoming the presidential candidate of the Radical Party, the historical rival of Peronism. The Radicals, however, had been the vic-

percent responded with negative evaluations, as expressed in their agreement with the propositions that the armed forces should, in the words of the survey, "return to the barracks" and/or "hand over the government to the politicians." Only four percent were favorably disposed toward the military government and/or advocated its continuation (figures compiled from data kindly supplied to me by Frederick Turner). For these and other pertinent data, and for a discussion of the methodology employed in their collection, see Frederick Turner, "The Study of Argentine Politics through Survey Research."

tims of the 1966 coup, in which Lanusse and other military liberals had played an active role. Moreover, it was not obvious to the Radicals why, if the presidency was to be won by a coalition of non-Peronists, their own party should not furnish the candidate. Still another problem was that the presence in the Interior Ministry of a prominent Radical leader such as Mor Roig was already making the Radicals look suspiciously like the "official party," an image that augured poorly for their electoral chances. In short, the Radical party was not disposed to offer its electoral machinery and votes to Lanusse's candidacy.

There remained another possibility. An optimistic interpretation of the above-mentioned polls suggested that in the upcoming elections Peronism would win the first plurality, but not the majority, of the votes cast. If this happened, the rest of the parties might have reason to prefer an "impartial" or "nonpartisan"—i.e., non-Peronist—president. To set the stage for this scenario, it was necessary to make some changes in the existing legislation. In particular, electoral procedures were redrawn to introduce a system of *ballotage,* or second round. The key provision of this system was that if no candidate obtained the majority of the votes cast, a second election would take place between the two parties (or coalitions of parties) which had received the most votes. The new electoral legislation,[23] while not precisely congruent with the proclaimed goal of national unity, did seem to have the merit of keeping alive Lanusse's hopes for a constitutional presidency. Decried as evidence of fraudulent and continuist intentions, the legislation was implemented, and the March 1973 elections took place under it.

But there were other obstacles along Lanusse's road to a constitutional presidency. If Lanusse could be portrayed as a nonpartisan candidate,* so could many others. In particular, if the prime concern was to have a constitutional president who could ensure continuity between the armed forces and a government based on the political parties, then why not choose some other high-ranking officer? After all, Lanusse's popularity had plummeted so much by mid-1972 that even being a relatively unknown military officer would perhaps be an asset for such a candidacy.† Moreover, Lanusse, with considerable energy but at high

---

*Lanusse was required by law to run as the candidate of some political party. This requirement provided the incentive for the creation of the *Federación de Partidos Provinciales* (Federation of Provincial Parties), which would later make a dismal showing with another government-sponsored candidate.

†When I interviewed him later, a key member of Lanusse's political team would lament that the proliferation of presidential aspirants within the armed forces had made it impossible for the government to present a united front in its negotiations with Peronism (as

cost (including to his health), was both the president and the commander in chief of the army; it would have been difficult to add to these
responsibilities those of an electoral candidate.

As of mid-1972, Perón showed no signs of renouncing the presidential candidacy on which his partisans were insisting.* The Radicals were
in the difficult position of trying to distinguish their positions from
those of the government while supporting the process that was to culminate in elections. Meanwhile, virtually all the organizations of society
found a motive for protest in the deepening economic crisis.

In June and July of 1972 all of the symptoms of an imminent coup
were once again present, and it was clear that the intense anti-Peronist
sentiments of a good part of the armed forces would now reinforce the
currents involved in the October 1971 attempt. The burning issues
were, first, the undeclared but ever-present candidacy of Lanusse, at this
point as nonviable from a military as from an electoral standpoint; and
second, the insistently advocated candidacy of Perón, which he had still
neither accepted nor rejected. With a coup seemingly imminent, Lanusse
made a speech at San Nicolás (the site of the nineteenth-century inter-
provincial pact that prepared the way for the ratification of the National Constitution) in which he announced more explicitly than ever
that the Great National Accord was a necessary step toward the "institutionalization" of the country.[24] First, the political solution entailed by
the holding of elections had to be negotiated with, and approved by, the
armed forces. Second, the same requirement applied to the basic orientations of the subsequent government's social and economic policies.†
Third, the tutelary role of the armed forces would extend throughout
the next constitutional government, which was defined as transitional.
Fourth, if the participants in the accord (basically the major political

---

well as with other political parties), thus eliminating all possibility of reaching a negotiated solution prior to the elections. The same person was convinced that more than a few
politicians and union leaders had raised the presidential hopes of several high-ranking
military officers in order to hinder Lanusse's aims.

*See the previously cited statements of Perón, Cámpora, and Rucci. The proclamation
of Perón's candidacy at the Justicialist party convention in Buenos Aires was not legally
valid, but it created quite a stir (*La Nación*, June 26, 1972, p. 4).

†These first two conditions only served to publicize positions already well known to
the major political actors. Lanusse himself, in his *Mi Testimonio* (p. 228), notes that he
had specified in an April 7, 1972, memorandum to the commanders in chief of the navy
and air force that the Great National Accord was designed with the following objectives in
mind: "(a) the [political-electoral] solution must at no time signify a leap into the void; (b)
the solution must *necessarily* be approved [by the armed forces]; and (c) the presidential
candidate must be acceptable to the armed forces" (emphasis in the original). Note
Lanusse's reference to the "candidate" in the singular.

parties, especially Peronism) did not abide by these stipulations, the only alternative left to the armed forces would be to postpone the process indefinitely.*

Lanusse's speech succeeded in annoying most political parties, but it did little to dispel the dangerous climate prevailing in the armed forces. Moreover, discontent within the military was heightened by new violent episodes, including urban riots. On July 7, 1972, when in his own words "the coup was almost at hand"[25] and just after all of the four-star generals had "advised" him to forget his electoral aspirations, Lanusse made a decisive speech.[26] After confirming that elections would be held on March 25, 1973, he repeated some well-worn themes: "The purpose of the *mesa del acuerdo* [the accord to which the political parties were again summoned] is to achieve the minimum of agreements [between those parties and the armed forces] that is necessary to assure the stability that the future government will need in order to complete its constitutional term. These agreements will involve basic and fundamental aspects of the national interest upon which it is indispensable to agree. . . . It is indispensable that political leaders clarify their attitudes and positions and that the government lay its cards on the table in such a way as to ensure that no doubts remain." More important, Lanusse announced that the junta of commanders in chief had resolved that any government official who had not resigned his position by August 25, 1972, or any person who by that date had not established residency in the country, would be ineligible to run for office in the upcoming elections.† Implicit in this arrangement was the proscription of the exiled Perón, as well as the so-called self-proscription of Lanusse after August 24. The indignation of the Peronists, the apprehension of other political actors,[27] and the end to all reasonable hopes of imposing his own constitutional presidency was the price Lanusse paid for forestalling the imminent coup.

Seven months before the elections, the only serious presidential contenders had disappeared with a stroke of the pen. For good reasons of internal politics, the Radical party selected as its candidate Ricardo

---

*Or, as Lanusse said in this speech, "If we Argentines are incapable of finding a solution that can reasonably be crystalized by means of an accord, I ask myself: what other course remains that will not have been attempted? Or can it be that the solution consists in the armed forces' imposing what we Argentines cannot agree upon?" (*La Nación,* June 1, 1972, pp. 1, 20).

†In another attempt to allay concern within the armed forces, Lanusse also announced in this speech that the CGT's legal recognition had been withdrawn and that union funds had been frozen in retaliation for this organization's meddling in "politics." These sanctions, as already noted, were promptly rescinded.

Balbín, who epitomized the "old politics" and was unlikely to help his party surpass the approximately 25 percent of the vote it had averaged prior to 1966. A proliferation of nonpartisan presidential aspirants moved in to fill the resulting vacuum, some hoping to be the candidate that the armed forces would somehow impose upon Peronism, others seeing themselves as the candidates of various coalitions of miniscule parties which would be blessed with the votes of a proscribed Peronism. Although on a more modest scale than Lanusse, these aspirants also tried to present themselves as attractive enough to voters to win the elections and as capable of supplying solid guarantees to the armed forces and an increasingly skeptical bourgeoisie. More important than the emergence of this group of presidential hopefuls was the rise to prominence of Francisco Manrique, whom Lanusse had reinstated as the Minister of Social Welfare. Manrique's mission had been to utilize the ministry's patronage resources to alleviate social tensions and, incidentally, to grease the wheels of Lanusse's presidential candidacy. Manrique's success in these endeavors is demonstrated by the fact that by mid-1972 he was the only government official with popular support. Given these circumstances, and since Lanusse's candidacy was no longer viable, Manrique felt that it would be a pity to possess such assets without investing them in a presidential campaign. Accordingly, he resigned his post before the August 25 deadline.[28] In his new role as a politician with votes in hand, Manrique was not long in finding parties without votes that were willing to make him their candidate. To the right of Manrique, Álvaro Alsogaray and his *Nueva Fuerza* party began a noisy and expensive "North American–style" campaign—complete with cheerleaders and TV jingles—that centered on the themes dear to orthodox liberalism. To crown it all, Lanusse, disgusted by Manrique's "desertion," imposed (at the last minute and virtually without any party machinery) on air force general Ezequiel Martínez, another liberal, the thankless task of becoming the candidate ostensibly supported by the government and therefore condemned to compete with *Nueva Fuerza* for a paltry percentage of the vote.* To the left of these parties and candidates, and with the support of the Communist party, Oscar Alende and Horacio Sueldo, leaders of offshoots of the Radicals and Christian Democrats respectively, forged an alliance fraught with byzantine debates over the content and degree of its leftism—a position for which

---

Nueva Fuerza was to obtain two percent and Martínez three percent of the votes cast.

various parties of socialist origin held better credentials, if far fewer votes. Finally, diverse small parties such as the Popular Conservatives, the Developmentalists of ex-President Frondizi, the other half of the Christian Democrats, some Radical and Socialist splinter groups, and a number of provincial parties joined Peronism in the Frente Justicialista de Liberación, FREJULI (the Justicialist Liberation Front).

But the main question remained what the Peronists—especially Perón—would do. Perón responded to the implicit proscription of his candidacy and to Lanusse's ad hominem attacks by hardening his position.* He insisted that an accord was superfluous since the government needed only to abide by its promise to call elections without vetoes or proscriptions.† Nonetheless, Perón, in keeping with his pendular strategy, dispatched Cámpora[29] to the junta of commanders in chief‡ with a document, notable for its moderation, entitled *"Bases Mínimas para el Acuerdo de Reconstrucción Nacional"* (Minimum Bases for an Agreement on National Reconstruction).§ Although it gave rise to endless speculation as to whether Perón had finally accepted Lanusse's injunc-

---

*Perón's reactions are covered in *Panorama*, July 13, 1972, p. 16 (in which Perón instructed Galimberti to "confront the dictatorship head-on") and August 23, 1972, pp. 10, 12.

†See esp. the joint statement by Perón and Cámpora entitled "To the Argentine People and the Armed Forces," in *Las Bases*, August 22, 1972, p. 3, and Perón's *"Cartas"* in *Las Bases*, September 15, pp. 4, 7, and October 5, pp. 5, 8, 1972, where he stated that "the famous Great National Accord has failed because of the meanness of its objective: to solve the problems of the Armed Forces," and added that "nobody can normalize with permanence and stability the institutional life of the country without taking *Justicialismo* into account."

‡Not to Lanusse, arguing that it was the armed forces, not Lanusse and his "palace clique," who could help resolve the problems of the nation.

§*Las Bases*, October 5, 1972, p. 6. As was noted by almost every commentator, only two of the clauses in this document would be difficult for the armed forces to swallow: Point 9, which demanded the "lifting of the state of siege and the release of all political and union prisoners," and, to a lesser degree, Point 7, which called for Interior Minister Mor Roig to be replaced by a military officer "in order to remove all suspicion" of improprieties in the upcoming elections. The remaining clauses were either purely rhetorical (Point 1) or obviously negotiable, such as the demand for a "reexamination" of amendments to the constitution and of the "restrictive clauses" pertaining to the upcoming elections (Point 5); for the formation of an interparty commission to guarantee "equality of opportunity" for all the parties participating in the elections (Point 8); for consultation with "all political forces" over the legislation under which the elections would be held (Point 10); and for the entitlement of the subsequent government to decide according to the constitution whether political prisoners should be given amnesty and whether revisions should be made to the "anti-subversive" legislation enacted after 1966 (Point 6). The social and economic goals set forth in the document were similarly moderate: implementation of the "pact" between the CGT and the CGE (Point 2), and the immediate creation along corporatist lines of a "social and economic council" in which representatives were supposed "to discuss and elaborate a project for national reconstruction, which will be the principal and unavoidable task of the future constitutional government" (Point 3).

tions to enter the Great National Accord, the document lacked a commitment by Perón to negotiate with the existing government either the role of the armed forces in its constitutional successor or the candidacies to be permitted in the upcoming elections. Meanwhile, in an aggressive tone that reflected their desperation at the approach of the solemnly affirmed election date, Lanusse and Mor Roig insisted on the "indispensable necessity" of settling these issues *before* the elections *in order* for them to take place.* Some of these exhortations became formal if ineffective decisions.† Finally, Mor Roig summoned all the political parties to begin negotiations for the Great National Accord. On the basis of a document drawn up by the government ("Bases for a Program of National Unity"), party leaders were to determine the program of the next government in conjunction with representatives of the government and the armed forces. A less explicit but crucial item on the agenda was the expected agreement between the parties and the "government of the armed forces" on a presidential candidate. Other points raised in this document ranged from broad statements about the national destiny to such matters as the commitment of the future government to continued action against the guerrillas, the inviolability of the judiciary (especially of the special courts established in 1971 to deal with "subversive activities"), the future status of the commanders in chief as members of the national cabinet, the stipulation that the constitutional government would not be allowed to change promotion rules and decisions made by the armed forces, and the preservation of the control that the armed forces had gained since 1966 over most major public enterprises.

*Mor Roig exhorted the political parties "to define a program of national union" in conjunction with the armed forces, which would have to "participate in elaborating the agreement if it is to be sound and enduring" (*La Nación*, July 26, 1972, pp. 1, 12). Shortly thereafter Lanusse reaffirmed that the "political solution" would have to be "agreed upon" with the armed forces prior to the elections (*La Nación*, July 29, 1972, p. 4). In subsequent speeches Lanusse stressed that the armed forces "are not, nor will they be, left out of" the Great National Accord or of the government it was designed to produce (*La Nación*, September 30, 1972, pp. 1, 6). Similar statements by Lanusse followed in rapid succession: *La Nación*, October 7, 1972, pp. 1, 10 (on the necessity of achieving "a minimum program of agreement and a commitment by the next constitutional government to abide by its terms," and announcing "the decision of the armed forces to participate during the gestation of this program and also to participate [once the subsequent government had been inaugurated] during the stage of its completion and execution"); and *La Nación*, October 26, 1972, p. 16 (for Lanusse's speech to the UIA: "It is worthwhile repeating—so that nobody can claim to have been ill informed—that the process of institutionalization, the goal of which is national union, will necessarily be achieved by way of concordances [with the armed forces] prior to elections").

†Some of which sounded curiously unreal, such as the resolution by the commanders in chief that they would have the rank of cabinet ministers during the subsequent government (*La Nación*, October 18, 1972, p. 1).

It soon became clear that it would not be easy to persuade the major parties to sign any accord. First, some parties, including the Peronists and Radicals, had just concluded in the context of *La Hora del Pueblo* their own "Pact of Guarantees," in which they again promised each other to respect democratic liberties.* Moreover, the Peronists continued to insist that there was nothing to agree upon with the government, and that the elections should be held without the eligibility requirements adopted in July. This position made the Radicals—anxious to avoid being seen as too acquiescent or as too closely linked to an unpopular government—even less inclined to enter the proposed accord. Without the two major parties, the government's initiative plainly made no sense, even if several minor parties were more than willing to abide by its terms.† In fact, the only chance of imposing such an accord resided in the threat of a coup, which Lanusse did not fail to make. But as already argued, this was a card Lanusse could no longer play convincingly following the October 1971 rebellion, and even less so after the decisions he had been obliged to make in July 1972. There remained to the end, however, the possibility that a coup would be mounted against Lanusse and the process leading toward elections. Lanusse expended considerable effort and displayed remarkable dexterity in fending off such a coup, at the expense of making his own bluff even more evident.

NOTES

1. Statement of the military junta upon taking charge of the government (*La Nación*, March 24, 1971, p. 1).
2. See the "Guidelines for Governmental Action" that Lanusse imparted to the cabinet (*La Nación*, April 1, 1971, p. 1).
3. *La Nación*, March 25, 1971, p. 1. Once again, this promise went unfulfilled; collective bargaining was not reintroduced until 1973.
4. *La Nación*, March 30, 1971, p. 1.

*This pact was made in the context of *La Hora del Pueblo* (*La Nación*, July 20, 1972, pp. 1, 6).
†Lanusse could not be accused of lacking forthrightness when he expressed his concern over the refusal of the Peronists (and consequently the Radicals) to enter into the proposed accord. See *La Nación*, October 28, 1972, pp. 1, 18: "I feel compelled to express my bafflement and dismay that the leaders of certain political groupings have not seen fit . . . to respond in an appropriate manner to the desires of the government and the armed forces—and, I add with calm and studied conviction, to the deep hopes of the Argentine people. . . . We have stressed repeatedly the necessity of an accord. . . . However—and a warning is naturally and logically in order here—time is running out." Time was indeed running out, but Lanusse's opponents correctly viewed this factor as working to their advantage.

5. *La Nación*, April 24, 1971, p. 1.

6. *La Nación*, April 14, 1971, p. 1.

7. My interviews. Lanusse, in his *Mi Testimonio*, elaborates on these and related themes.

8. Lanusse, *Mi Testimonio*.

9. A good approximation to the positions of these radicalized sectors may be found in *Cristianismo y Revolución*, no. 29 (July 1971), pp. 11–14. See also the 1971 issues of *Jerónimo*, especially numbers 4 and 5; *América Latina*, no. 12 (July 1971), no. 13 (September 1971), and no. 14 (November 1971); !*Ya!* no. 8 (August 16, 1973); and *Nuevo Hombre*, August 28, September 8, and November 3, 1971. On Córdoba unions that would become the most important expressions of classist, non-Peronist, working-class rank-and-file movements, see Natalia Duval, "Argentina: sindicatos y movimientos de masas," *Historia del movimiento obrero*, no. 95 (1974); Juan Carlos Torre, "Una nueva opción social," *Los libros*, August 1971; the text of "El programa de SITRAC-SITRAM" in *Los libros*, August 1971; Zorrilla, *Estructura dinámica del sindicalismo argentino;* and Delich, *Crisis y protesta social,* and "Córdoba, la movilización permanente," *Los libros*, August 1971.

10. On these attempted "political solutions" during the 1955–66 period see Guillermo O'Donnell, *Modernization and Bureaucratic-Authoritarianism*, chaps. 3 and 4, and "State and Alliances in Argentina."

11. *Primera Plana*, September 7, 1971, p. 9.

12. Increasingly hopeless complaints by the organizations of the upper and Pampean bourgeoisies over political and economic prospects may be found in *La Nación:* June 25, 1971, p. 6 (ACIEL); September 3, 1971, p. 6 (UIA); September 16, 1971, p. 3 (UIA and SRA); September 17, 1971, p. 10 (CAC, asserting nostalgically that "the fundamental cause of the present situation is the abandonment of the economic policies initiated on March 13, 1967"); October 27, 1971, p. 5 (UIA); November 6, 1971, p. 6 (editorial summary of many of these complaints); November 27, 1971, p. 1 (CARBAP); December 11, 1971, p. 14 (Buenos Aires Stock Exchange); December 17, 1971, p. 1 (SRA); December 23, 1971, pp. 1, 9 (SRA); January 5, 1972, p. 1 (SRA); January 12, 1972, pp. 1, 12 (CAC and UIA); February 12, 1972, p. 1 (SRA); March 3, 1972, p. 12 (CAC); July 19, 1972, pp. 1, 12 (UIA); July 20, 1972, pp. 1, 10 (CAC); August 16, 1972, p. 10 (UIA); September 5, 1972, p. 10 (UIA); September 11, 1972, p. 1 (joint statement of the UIA, SRA, CAC, and Buenos Aires Stock Exchange); and September 21, 1972, p. 6 (CAC).

13. For statements to this effect by Lanusse in the first stage of his government, see *La Nación*, April 14, p. 2 and May 2, p. 1, 1971.

14. Information on the content of these first proposals to Perón comes from the meeting that took place in Madrid between one of Lanusse's military aides and Perón and Lopez Rega. The meeting was recorded, and parts of it were made public about a year later.

15. We shall examine in chapter 9 the data on guerrilla activity. For an incomplete but eloquent inventory of the most spectacular guerrilla actions, see Donald Hodges, *Argentina, 1943–1976;* Charles Russell, James Miller and James Schenkel, "Urban Guerrillas in Argentina: A Select Bibliography," *Latin*

American Research Review 9, no. 3 (Autumn, 1974); and James Kohl and John Litt, *Urban Guerrilla Warfare in Latin America* (Cambridge: MIT Press, 1974). See also the chronology compiled by Andrew Graham-Yooll in *Tiempo de tragedia. Cronología de la revolución Argentina* (Buenos Aires: Ediciones de la Flor, 1972).

16. *La Nación,* May 27, 1971, p. 1.

17. *La Nación,* October 9, p. 1 and October 10, p. 1, 1971.

18. These feelings of entitlement were expressed in my interviews and, more obliquely, in Lanusse's *Mi Testimonio.*

19. Among many similar statements, see *Las Bases,* September 10, 1972, p. 5 and *La Nación,* July 5, 1972, p. 10.

20. See the joint statement by the UIA, the CAC, the SRA, and the Buenos Aires Stock Exchange in *La Nación,* September 11, 1972, p. 1 (see also note 12).

21. On this theme, see Botana et al., *El régimen militar, 1966–1973.*

22. Some of these surveys may be found in *Panorama,* February 8, 1973, p. 19 (which gives the results of a survey predicting that Peronism would obtain only 29 percent of the vote) and March 8, 1973, pp. 14, 18; *La Nación,* January 25, p. 8, and March 4, p. 6, 1973; and *Análisis–Confirmado,* December 19, 1972, p. 10 and February 13, 1973, pp. 10, 13.

23. The text of this legislation may be found in *La Nación,* September 26, 1971, pp. 1, 14.

24. *La Nación,* June 1, 1972, pp. 1, 16.

25. Lanusse, *Mi Testimonio,* p. 288. The possibility of a coup was being openly discussed (*La Nación,* July 6, 1972, pp. 1, 20).

26. *La Nación,* July 8, 1972, p. 1, 20.

27. For these protests see *La Nación,* July 14, 1972, p. 6.

28. *La Nación,* September 20, 1972, p. 1.

29. *La Nación,* November 1, 1972, pp. 1, 16.

Economic Crisis and Political Violence

1. ECONOMIC MISADVENTURES OF THE POLITICAL RESCUE

We leave our narrative at the end of 1972, close to the culmination of the process that began in June 1966. This chapter provides an overview of various aspects of the 1966–72 period, beginning with socioeconomic data that chart with remarkable sensitivity the successes and subsequent misfortunes of the BA. Next, we turn to a phenomenon that was central to the crisis of 1971 and 1972: the unfolding of the political violence that virtually destroyed the fabric of Argentine society.

The uneasy marriage between paternalists and liberals during the Onganía government was an attempt to subordinate politics to the pursuit of economic normalization and, behind that, to the offensive of the upper bourgeoisie. The Levingston government tried to push the economy toward a nationalism and statism that went far beyond what the existing relation of social and political forces would bear. Lanusse's term, during which the economy was subordinated to the rescue operation launched with the 1971 coup, was marked by numerous changes and inconsistencies as the government tried to ward off social explosions by granting concessions to previously excluded sectors. Such concessions were expected to generate enough political support to enable Lanusse to win a constitutional presidency, or at least to force Peronism into carefully restricted negotiations regarding the composition and policies of the next civilian government.

TABLE 31   INDUSTRIAL WAGES
(in 1966 pesos) (index 1966 = 100.0)

	(1) Average Annual Industrial Wage According to ex-Instituto Nacional de Estadística y Censos (INDEC)	(2) Average Hourly Industrial Wage (INDEC sample)	(3) Average Industrial Wage (BCRA data)	(4) Legal Minimum Wage for Day-Laborer (weighted average for unmarried and married workers)
1966	100.0	100.0	100.0	100.0
1967	99.7	99.1	98.1	98.6
1968	94.4	93.2	90.3	94.9
1969	99.4	96.8	98.3	98.5
1970	99.1	97.5	97.2	99.6
1971	102.1	98.9	103.2	98.4
1972	91.7	90.1	94.5	91.3
Average 1967–1972	97.7	95.9	96.9	96.9

SOURCES: Columns 1 and 2 calculated from Instituto Nacional de Estadística y Censos, *Boletín Estadístico Trimestral,* various issues. Column 3 calculated from unpublished worksheets of the Banco Central de la República Argentina. Column 4 calculated from de Pablo, "Políticas de estabilización," pp. 401–7.

NOTE: Data deflated by the cost-of-living index for Buenos Aires.

In keeping with these priorities, one of the first decisions of the Lanusse government was to repeal the law that limited the wage and salary increases attainable through collective bargaining. Shortly thereafter, however, inflationary pressures forced a return to the practice of setting wage and salary increases by decree. The raises thus granted by the new government were designed to demonstrate its social sensitivity and were reflected in an improvement in real wages (tables 31 and 32) and salaries (Table 33) during 1971.

By examining the monthly figures presented graphically in Figure 3* additional insight can be gained into the evolution of wages and salaries. The data for 1971 and 1972 present a jagged profile, contrasting

*Figure 3 depicts the changes in the legal minimum wage, adjusted for inflation, for unmarried industrial workers. The other wage and salary series used in the preceding tables show a similar profile.

TABLE 32   NONINDUSTRIAL WAGES
(in 1966 pesos) (index 1966=100.0)

	Minimum Wage for Construction Workers	Minimum Wage for Mine and Quarry Workers	Minimum Wage for Workers in Agriculture and Stockraising
1966	100.0	100.0	100.0
1967	100.9	104.7	101.6
1968	92.8	92.0	92.2
1969	94.7	92.7	96.6
1970	97.3	97.3	107.0
1971	98.3	102.0	121.4
1972	87.0	91.2	105.4
Average 1967–1972	95.2	96.6	104.0

SOURCE: Unpublished worksheets of the Consejo Nacional de Desarrollo.
NOTE: Data deflated by the cost-of-living index for Buenos Aires.

with the smoother contours found during the 1967–69 period but resembling the pattern prior to the 1966 coup. While the annual data in tables 31, 32 and 33 indicate that average annual wages and salaries rose slightly in 1971 before plunging steeply in 1972, Figure 3 shows that these annual figures are the aggregate expression of a monthly pattern consisting of ever more frequent raises followed by increasingly severe declines. In other words, the sharp and frequent fluctuations in real wages and salaries characteristic of the pre-1966 period recurred as workers and employees fought to protect their incomes against rising inflation.

Another similarity between the Lanusse period and the era that many believed Krieger Vasena's administration had eliminated for good was that a trend toward lower real wages and salaries accompanied the ever-wider fluctuations in inflation and in wages and salaries. As can be seen from tables 31, 32 and 33, 1972 was the year of the largest decline in real wages and salaries for the entire period we are examining. Moreover, despite the greater frequency of pay raises in 1972 as compared with the previous year, the decline in real wages and salaries became more pronounced as 1972 progressed. This phenomenon was closely connected to the rising inflation portrayed in Table 34 and in Figure 4.

These monthly series indicate that a sharp if irregular decline in

TABLE 33   SALARIES OF LOWER-MIDDLE SECTORS
(in 1966 pesos) (index 1966=100.0)

	(1) Basic Salary[a] of Lower-level Employee in the Central Government	(2) Basic Salary of Primary School Teacher	(3) Basic Salary of Commercial Employee	(4) Basic Salary of Lower-level Bank Employee	(5) Basic Salary of Driver of Public Transport Vehicles	(6) Basic Salary of Lower-level Employee of the National Institute of Agricultural and Livestock Technology
1966	100.0	100.0	100.0	100.0	100.0	100.0
1967	92.5	89.0	97.1	99.4	102.9	78.1
1968	84.4	76.6	86.7	89.6	88.6	73.2
1969	85.5	85.0	88.7	91.7	90.3	79.6
1970	91.6	87.7	93.5	95.6	92.1	74.7
1971	83.3	93.0	99.8	97.6	92.3	83.7
1972	78.6	97.0	89.8	87.0	81.1	83.9 (Oct.)
Average 1967–1972	86.0	88.0	92.6	93.5	91.2	95.4

SOURCES: Column 1 calculated from unpublished worksheets of the Secretaría de Hacienda. Columns 2–5 calculated from unpublished worksheets of the Consejo Nacional de Desarrollo, and Ministerio (or in some periods Secretaría) de Trabajo, *Boletín de estadísticas sociales*, various issues. Column 6: Centro de Investigaciones en Administración Pública, Instituto Torcuato di Tella, "Determinación de objetivos," p. 246.

NOTE: Figures deflated by the cost-of-living index for Buenos Aires.

[a]"Basic salary" refers to the salary received by an employee with no dependents.

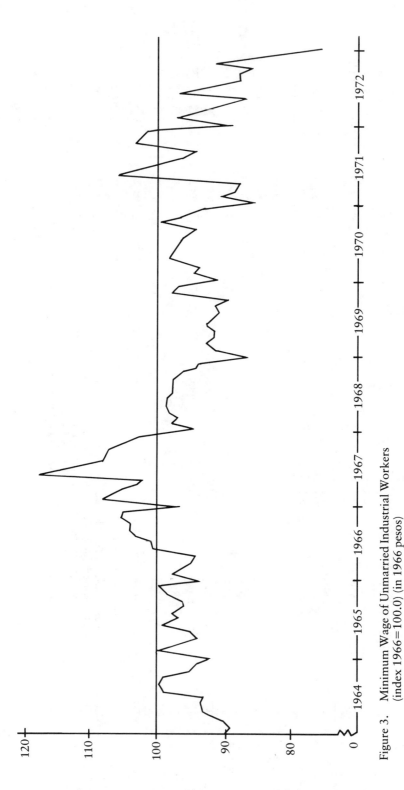

Figure 3. Minimum Wage of Unmarried Industrial Workers
(index 1966=100.0) (in 1966 pesos)

SOURCE: Ministerio de Economía y Trabajo (*or* Ministerio de Hacienda, according to the period), *Boletín Estadístico Trimestral*, various issues.

NOTE: Data deflated by the cost-of-living index for Buenos Aires.

TABLE 34 INFLATION IN THE COST OF LIVING FOR BUENOS AIRES
(% change each month from the same month of the preceding year)

	1963	1964	1965	1966	1967	1968	1969	1970	1971	1972
January	30.8	28.5	14.3	40.2	26.7	29.0	8.2	6.5	27.4	46.8
February	24.5	26.4	20.7	36.7	26.6	27.6	5.7	9.5	29.9	47.2
March	35.3	20.3	24.0	36.4	26.7 (Krieger)	24.0	7.7	9.6	29.6 (Lan.)	51.8
April	32.6	23.0	20.7	37.8	25.6	22.0	8.2	10.5	29.8	57.8
May	24.5	23.2	23.1	36.3	25.5	21.0	6.6 (Cordb.)	12.7	31.9	56.5
June	23.1	23.5	26.3	32.1 (Ong.)	29.9	16.4	7.3	12.5 (Lev.)	35.1	60.1
July	18.9	22.1	31.3	28.6	34.2	10.8	8.8	12.3	39.2	61.2
August	16.2	21.0	34.9	27.3	33.1	10.6	10.3	14.5	41.2	56.8
September	15.6	20.4	35.4	27.3	31.7	11.6	9.1	14.7	39.6	59.2
October	17.6 (Illia)	21.4	33.7	28.1	31.3	10.6	9.1	17.4 (Ferrer)	35.7	65.2
November	21.9	19.7	36.9	26.5	31.2	8.5	9.0	19.6	35.8	68.7
December	27.6	18.1	38.2	29.9	27.3	9.6	9.0	22.8	39.1	64.1

SOURCE: Calculated from Dirección Nacional de Estadística y Censos, *Boletín Estadístico Trimestral* and *Índice de precios el consumidor-capital federal*, various issues.

NOTE: "Illia" appears in the month in which Dr. Illia assumed the presidency; "Ong." the month in which Lt. General Onganía assumed the presidency; "Krieger" the beginning of the 1967 economic program; "Cordb." the month of the first Cordobazo; "Lev." the month in which General Levingston assumed the presidency; "Ferrer" the month in which Aldo Ferrer became Economy Minister; "Lan." the month in which Lt. General Lanusse assumed the presidency.

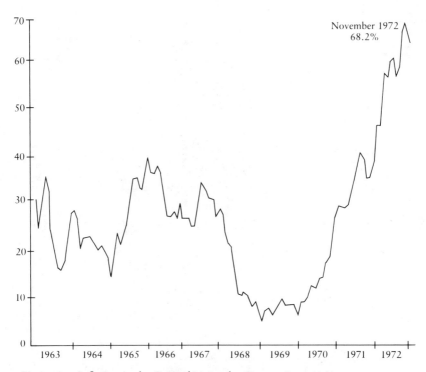

Figure 4.   Inflation in the Cost of Living for Greater Buenos Aires
(% change each month from the same month of the preceding year)

SOURCE: Ministerio de Economía y Trabajo (or Ministerio de Hacienda, depending
on the period), Boletín Estadístico Trimestral, various issues.

wages and salaries occurred precisely when problems on this front were
the last thing Lanusse's rescue operation needed. The tables also show
that the incomes of the lower middle sectors, already pinched severely
under Krieger Vasena, again declined faster than those of industrial
workers. This absolute and relative drop in the income of the middle
sectors was probably related to the radicalization that we began to
analyze in the preceding chapter.

Wage and salary increases were by no means the only source of
inflation. Surely more important was the shift in relative prices that was
already visible in 1970 but became much more pronounced in 1971 and
1972. Table 35 indicates that in 1971 and 1972 the Pampean bourgeoisie took ample revenge (especially through higher beef prices) for the
depressed prices it had suffered in the preceding period.

Closer analysis of the relationship between wage levels and food

TABLE 35   RELATIVE PRICES OF BEEF, GRAIN, AND FLAX
(index 1966=100.0)

	Wholesale Beef Prices relative to Non-agrarian Wholesale Prices (index)	Wholesale Grain and Flax Prices relative to Non-agrarian Wholesale Prices (index)	Retail Beef Prices* in the Federal Capital (index)	Heads of Cattle Sold on the Major Markets (index)
1966	100.0	100.0	100.0	100.0
1967	100.7	101.0	89.0	102.2
1968	98.6	101.2	94.2	97.9
1969	95.2	104.3	93.4	104.6
1970	120.0	106.4	120.6	93.8
1971	152.5	115.7	160.7	62.3
1972	150.4	134.7	153.1	61.5

SOURCE: Calculated from data in the *Boletines* of the Junta Nacional de Carnes (data deflated by the non-agrarian wholesale price index); Ministerio de Hacienda, *Informe Económico, 1972* (fourth quarter), Statistical Appendix; and Instituto Nacional de Estadísticas y Censos, *Boletín Estadístico Trimestral* and *Precios al por Mayor,* various issues.
*Deflated by the cost-of-living index for Buenos Aires.

prices reveals that the impact of the decline in the former was actually more severe than is suggested by the data presented above. Column 1 of Table 36 reproduces column 4 of Table 31, which presents the index of the yearly weighted average of the legal minimum wage for married and unmarried industrial workers taken together. As is customary, the inflation rate (estimated by the cost-of-living index for Greater Buenos Aires) was used in Table 31 to deflate nominal wages to their approximate real values. But this index assumes unrealistically that consumption patterns do not vary significantly across social classes. When nominal wages are deflated instead by various indices of food prices (as is done in the remaining three columns of Table 36), the decline in real wages is even more pronounced. Since members of the popular sector spend a relatively high proportion of their incomes on food, the reduction in their living standards was certainly more severe than is suggested by the figures that show minimum wages deflated by the overall rate of inflation.*

*Conversely, the slight decline in retail food prices during 1967 and 1968 means that real wages in those years were slightly higher than is suggested by the data in chapter 4.

TABLE 36   RATIO OF MINIMUM WAGE OF INDUSTRIAL
WORKERS TO PRICES OF FOOD AND AGRICULTURAL PRODUCTS
(index 1966 = 100.0)

	(1) Legal Mini- mum Wage (weighted aver- age for unmar- ried and mar- ried workers)	(2) Ratio of (1) to Retail Price of Beef	(3) Ratio of (1) to Wholesale Prices for Agri- cultural and Livestock Goods	(4) Ratio of (1) to Wholesale Prices of Indus- trial Food Products
1966	100.0	100.0	100.0	100.0
1967	98.6	101.8	99.8	98.8
1968	94.9	106.5	105.4	99.1
1969	98.5	117.4	106.0	106.5
1970	99.6	94.9	101.8	96.1
1971	98.4	72.4	85.8	86.0
1972	91.3	65.5	73.2	78.9

SOURCE: Calculated from INDEC, *Boletín Estadístico Trimestral* and *Índice de precios al consumidor;* and Ministerio de Economía y Trabajo (or in some periods Ministerio de Hacienda), *Informe Económico,* various issues.
NOTE: Data in columns 1 and 2, as well as the wage data component of 3 and 4, deflated by the cost-of-living index for Buenos Aires. Wholesale data are deflated by their respective price indices.

Another consequence of these shifts in relative prices deserves to be considered. Table 37 shows that in 1971 retail food prices rose considerably more than other prices, including those of retail industrial goods. In 1972, by contrast, the latter rose more than the former. This suggests that in 1972, despite the major relative price shift toward agricultural goods at the wholesale level, the industrial and commercial bourgeoisies managed, at the expense of consumers, to keep their retail prices ahead of those for foodstuffs.

The preceding data suggest that in 1971 the urban bourgeoisie were forced to relinquish part of their accumulation to the Pampean bourgeoisie. In 1972, however, the urban bourgeoisie pushed their prices to levels that were once again at rough parity with those of the Pampean bourgeoisie. The wage and salary data leave little doubt as to who paid the bill for these adjustments. Furthermore, prices in the "general services" category of the cost-of-living index rose considerably less than those for food and industrial goods. This indicates that another big loser of the period was, as is typical in such circumstances, the state apparatus.

This inference is supported by the data in Table 38, which show that

TABLE 37   DISAGGREGATION OF THE COST-OF-LIVING INDEX FOR BUENOS AIRES
(index 1966 = 100.0)

	Cost-of-Living Index	Annual Change (%)	Cost-of-Living Index for Food	Annual Change (%)	Cost-of-Living Index for Industrial Goods (Exclusive of Food and Services)	Annual Change (%)
1966	100.0		100.0		100.0	
1967	129.2	29.2	129.0	29.0	131.5	31.5
1968	150.2	16.2	149.4	15.8	152.0	15.6
1969	161.6	7.6	158.6	6.2	164.2	8.0
1970	183.5	13.6	184.7	16.5	185.7	13.1
1971	247.2	34.7	261.7	41.7	236.4	27.3
1972	391.7	58.5	426.9	63.1	398.5	68.6

SOURCE: Calculated from Instituto Nacional de Estadísticas y Censos, *Boletín Estadístico Trimestral* and *Índice de precios al consumidor*, various issues.

TABLE 38   THE BUDGET OF THE NATIONAL GOVERNMENT
(in 1966 pesos) (index 1966=100.0)

	(1) Total Revenue	(2) Total Expenditures	(3) Current Expenditures	(4) Capital Expenditures	(5) Deficit	(6) Deficit as % of Total Expenditures	(7) Deficit as % of Gross Domestic Product	(8) National Government Savings* (in millions of pesos)	(9) Transfers to Provincial Governments (in millions of pesos)
1966	100.0	100.0	100.0	100.0	100.0	29.9	3.0	−501.9	n.d.
1967	124.8	104.9	95.1	153.0	57.9	16.5	1.7	836.0	1
1968	134.7	102.4	90.9	166.4	26.5	7.7	0.7	653.8	116
1969	144.5	108.5	97.9	170.1	23.9	6.6	0.6	486.1	152
1970	149.8	113.0	99.6	170.4	26.6	3.2	0.6	477.7	215
1971	139.1	123.0	111.6	175.4	85.2	20.7	2.0	−198.3	468
1972	134.2	122.0	105.1	200.3	93.2	22.8	2.2	−400.4	665

SOURCES: Calculated from Ministerio de Económica and Ministerio de Hacienda, *Informe Económico*, various issues; Ministerio de Hacienda, *Boletín Mensual*, various issues; and Ministerio de Hacienda, Superintendencia del Tesoro, worksheets for the preparation of the budget of the National Government. For Column 8: BCRA, *Sistema de cuentas de producto e ingreso*, vol. 3.

NOTE: Data deflated by the non-agrarian wholesale price index.

*"Savings" refers to the difference between current expenditures and revenues.

TABLE 39   TAX REVENUES OF THE NATIONAL GOVERNMENT
(in 1966 pesos) (index 1966 = 100.0)

	(1) Central Government Revenues from Indirect Taxes	(2) Central Government Revenues from Direct Taxes	(3) Direct Taxes as % of Gross Domestic Product	(4) Tax Pressure[a] as % of Gross Domestic Product
1964			1.5	14.8
1965	84.9	80.8	2.4	16.3
1966	100.0	100.0	2.6	18.0
1967	80.3	113.7	2.7	20.9
1968	134.3	87.8	2.2	20.4
1969	141.9	86.1	2.1	19.1
1970	142.0	85.9	2.0	18.7
1971	132.7	75.1	1.7	17.5
1972	121.5	64.4	1.5	15.6

SOURCE: Calculated from BCRA, *Sistema de cuentas de producto e ingreso*, vol. 2.
NOTE: Data deflated by the national non-agrarian wholesale price index.
[a]"Tax pressure" equals columns 1 + 2 + contributions to the social security system.

the financial position of the state apparatus began to worsen in 1970 and deteriorated at an accelerated pace in 1971. By 1972, the fiscal situation was even worse than in the years preceding the BA. Only the most important aspects of these data need be summarized here: (1) a decline in total public-sector income (column 1 of Table 38), (2) a spectacular increase in the fiscal deficit, both in real terms and as a percentage of the GDP (columns 5, 6, and 7), and (3) strong increases in transfers from the central to the provincial governments, which in 1971 and 1972 consisted mainly of funds for current expenditures (basically salaries) rather than investment funds, which had constituted the bulk of such transfers before 1970. In terms of these and related aspects, the contrast with the Krieger Vasena years and the similarities to the pre-1966 period could not be more evident.[*]

Turning to the central government's major sources of revenue, columns 1 and 2 of Table 39 show that revenues from indirect taxes fell in

[*]The deterioration of the fiscal situation of the state apparatus is corroborated by the downward trend in the weighted average of prices charged by state enterprises. As will be recalled from chapter 4, this mean rose from an index of 1966 = 100.0 to a peak of 118.7 in 1967, declining to 116.1 in 1968, 110.0 in 1969, and 104.4 in 1970. It then plunged to 95.7 in 1971 and 90.3 in 1972 (data from Núñez Miñana and Porto, "Análisis de la evolución de precios de empresas publicas").

1972 from the levels attained in the previous years but rose in relation to direct tax revenues, which plummeted. The increase in the relative weight of indirect taxes probably accentuated the trend toward a more regressive distribution of income, but it did not prevent a major drop in the overall tax income of the central government (column 4 of Table 39). Nevertheless, the government maintained high levels of public investment and capital expenditures (column 4 of Table 38), contributing to the increase in the fiscal deficit.

   The effort to maintain a high level of public expenditure reflected the government's goal of postponing the recession that had appeared on the horizon toward the end of 1970 and which threatened to place additional obstacles in the way of Lanusse's project. The balance-of-payments crunch that emerged in 1971 showed that this was no easy task. Balance-of-payments problems had been mounting since 1970, but they worsened considerably in 1971 until in November of that year (the month of the failed coup attempt against Lanusse) the BCRA found itself with negative available foreign reserves. From that point on, as Table 40 shows, the foreign exchange position of the BCRA was consistently negative, expressing strains that led to such primitive policies as the temporary suspension of all imports.

TABLE 40   NET FOREIGN EXCHANGE RESERVES OF THE
ARGENTINE CENTRAL BANK
(in millions of current U.S. dollars)

	1966	1967	1968	1969	1970	1971	1972
January	145.8	155.6	486.7	613.8	507.0	474.7	− 137.4
February	146.9	151.7	476.8	657.0	535.4	359.0	− 203.2
March	182.4	203.5	490.9	672.2	614.8	282.7	− 137.5
April	188.8	292.5	517.5	694.3	569.1	243.2	− 197.0
May	208.9	395.5	525.3	665.0	706.0	154.7	− 230.8
June	224.2	465.9	539.8	605.4	735.0	76.6	− 135.9
July	199.8	494.0	537.0	652.9	804.0	116.6	− 149.6
August	219.8	497.6	535.7	636.5	803.4	95.4	− 164.4
September	197.0	494.7	562.2	569.1	748.0	44.3	− 218.6
October	177.3	481.6	553.4	497.3	751.9	2.6	− 232.6
November	161.3	482.2	590.0	482.0	708.0	− 44.0	− 131.6
December	176.9	500.9	593.3	446.1	567.8	− 124.9	11.1

SOURCE: BCRA, *Boletín Estadístico*, various issues.

These difficulties were due to various factors. First, as the second column of Table 41 indicates, the flight of short-term foreign capital in 1971 was even more pronounced than it was immediately after the Cordobazo. Second, foreign investment in Argentina came to a virtual standstill after 1970 (Table 42). Third, the balance of payments suffered from a speculative demand for imports as those who enjoyed access to dollars at official exchange rates (well below those on the black market) used them to expand their inventories as a hedge against inflation. The resulting deterioration in the balance of trade is evident from the figures in Table 43.

These and similar trends could not be controlled despite the important loans that were obtained, with the help of the United States government, from public financial institutions in 1971 and 1972 (Table 44). These inflows helped prevent the paralysis of the economy but increased significantly the country's foreign debt.

The fiscal and monetary "discipline" demanded by the international lending agencies in exchange for the balance-of-payments credits was implemented only partially, basically with cuts in the money supply and in the salaries of public employees. Such policies, as we saw, did little to reduce the fiscal deficit. One factor that temporarily sustained the level of economic activity was the defensive speculative behavior that emerged with rapid inflation. As buyers anticipated higher prices, the demand for consumer durables rose.* For similar reasons, and also because of the subsidy implicit in the official dollar exchange rate, domestic private investment in (mostly imported) equipment increased.† Inventories increased even more rapidly (Table 45). The government for its part maintained high levels of public works expenditures at a time when private investment in construction had fallen sharply, and increased its investment in transport equipment.

These responses to inflation could do little more than delay the recession, but this was not what worried a government that looked only to the very short term. As we have seen, large and frequent pay hikes did not prevent a decline in real wages and salaries that grew more

*For a candid discussion of the causes of the transitory euphoria in the consumer durables market, see Ministerio de Hacienda, *Informe Económico 1972,* 4th quarter (Buenos Aires, 1971).

†The strong speculative component in the short-lived surge in private investment in equipment and in the pronounced expansion of inventories is emphasized in FIEL-UIA, *Evolución de la actividad industrial. Encuesta de coyuntura,* nos. 15 (3rd quarter) and 16 (4th quarter), 1971 (Buenos Aires, 1971).

TABLE 41 BALANCE OF PAYMENTS: NET CAPITAL MOVEMENTS
(in millions of U.S. dollars)

		Net Balance of Long-term Capital	Net Balance of Short-term Capital	Change in the International Reserves of the Central Bank
1966		−105	−76	−5
1967	1st quarter			5
	2nd quarter			425
	3rd quarter			11
	4th quarter			13
	Yearly balance	4	268	480
1968	1st quarter	1	−15	−2
	2nd quarter	−10	0	78
	3rd quarter	0	67	40
	4th quarter	7	76	44
	Yearly balance	27	150	57
1969	1st quarter	−1	69	77
	2nd quarter	13	−44	−82
	3rd quarter	29	−66	−83
	4th quarter	30	−37	−171
	Yearly balance	57	−57	−260
1970	1st quarter	14	68	115
	2nd quarter	12	83	133
	3rd quarter	41	8	8
	4th quarter	25	55	−70
	Yearly balance	144	185	185
1971	1st quarter	8	−48	−60
	2nd quarter	39	−75	−41
	3rd quarter	41	−94	−88
	4th quarter	−22	−180	−196
	Yearly balance	66	−393	−385
1972	1st quarter	5	−85	−16
	2nd quarter	53	−63	−2
	3rd quarter	49	−10	−30
	4th quarter	30	49	214
	Yearly balance	137	−109	167

SOURCE: BCRA, *Boletín Estadístico*, various issues.

TABLE 42   DIRECT FOREIGN INVESTMENT AUTHORIZED UNDER
THE REGIME OF INDUSTRIAL PROMOTION
(including oil and construction, and excluding reinvestment)
(in millions of current U.S. dollars)

1960	111.7
1961	133.4
1962	85.8
1963	34.6
1964	33.8
1965	6.3
1966	2.6
1967	31.6
1968	56.4
1969	52.1
1970	9.8
1971	9.8
1972	8.9

SOURCE: Ministerio de Economía y Trabajo y Ministerio de Hacienda, *Informe Económico*, various issues.

TABLE 43   ARGENTINE FOREIGN TRADE
(in millions of current U.S. dollars)

	Exports	Imports	Balance of Trade
1966	1,593	1,124	469
1967	1,464	1,095	369
1968	1,368	1,169	199
1969	1,612	1,576	36
1970	1,773	1,694	79
1971	1,740	1,868	− 127.8
1972	1,868	1,840	28

SOURCE: BCRA, *Boletín Estadístico*, various issues.

pronounced in 1972. At the same time, the emergence of black markets (not only in foreign exchange), and the repeated frustration of attempts to impose wage and price "truces," showed the extent to which the government had lost control of crucial economic variables. In addition, food and textile consumption declined throughout 1972, unlike the

TABLE 44   FOREIGN LOANS TO THE ARGENTINE GOVERNMENT
AND FOREIGN DEBT
(in millions of current U.S. dollars)

	Foreign Loans to the BCRA and the National Government	Accumulated Foreign Debt (Public and Private)
1966	129	3,300
1967	253	3,200
1968	108	3,394
1969	107	3,969
1970	149	4,765
1971	434	5,297
1972	630	6,082

SOURCES: Foreign loans: BCRA, *Boletín Estadístico,* various issues. Foreign debt: BCRA, *Anexo al Boletín Estadístico,* July 1973, and for 1972, *Economic Survey,* October 7, 1976, p. 3.

previous year, when purchases of these typical mass-consumption items had risen in response to the increase in wages and salaries.*

It should come as no surprise, then, that data on the growth of the economy and its principal sectors display a profile quite different from that of the 1967–69 period. Table 46 shows that GDP growth and per-capita consumption slowed considerably in 1972.

The data presented in this section show the return in 1971 and 1972 of the uncertainty, fluctuations, and negative expectations of the years prior to the 1966 coup. Once again, moreover, and even more acutely than in the pre-1966 period, these phenomena coincided with the appearance of an active black market in foreign exchange and with the sharp rise of the dollar on that market (Table 47).

The same processes were reflected in the large increases during 1971 and 1972 in the rate of the dollar on the futures market (Table 48).

The foregoing attests to the collapse of a project that between 1967 and 1969, despite the conflicts and impasses between the paternalists and liberals, seemed to have come close to eliminating the fluctuations

---

*As Ministerio de Hacienda, *Informe económico 1972,* remarks, these data strongly suggest that although some consumers had enough resources to shield themselves from inflation after participating in the run on durable consumer goods, many members of the popular sector whose incomes had diminished had to reduce their purchases of food and textiles.

TABLE 45 INVESTMENT
(index 1966=100.0)

	Gross Fixed Domestic Investment	Investment in Construction		Investment in Equipment		Change in Inventories
		Private	Public	Transport Equipment	Machinery and Other	
1965	100.7	91.8	100.6	108.9	91.9	1425.9
1966	100.0	100.0	100.0	100.0	100.0	100.0
1967	101.2	102.8	120.9	102.8	102.5	46.5
1968	104.2	115.8	149.3	107.9	115.2	−176.2
1969	111.5	132.9	196.1	122.9	140.9	− 5.4
1970	116.0	138.0	216.5	123.0	149.9	364.3
1971	119.9	133.5	222.9	139.2	179.3	541.1
1972	122.0	126.0	253.4	147.5	192.2	563.8

SOURCE: BCRA, *Sistema de cuentas de producto e ingreso*, vol. 2, pp. 126–27.

TABLE 46   GROSS DOMESTIC PRODUCT AND PRIVATE
CONSUMPTION
(in 1966 pesos) (index 1966 = 100.0)

	Gross Domestic Product per Capita (index)	Annual Change (%)	Private Consumption per Capita (index)	Annual Change (%)
1964	93.6	8.8	94.2	10.0
1965	100.7	7.6	101.1	7.4
1966	100.0	−0.7	100.0	−1.1
1967	101.2	1.2	101.2	1.2
1968	104.2	2.9	103.8	2.5
1969	111.5	7.1	108.9	4.9
1970	116.0	4.0	111.8	2.7
1971	119.9	3.4	117.6	5.2
1972	122.0	1.8	118.8	1.1

SOURCE: Calculated from BCRA, *Sistema de cuentas de producto e ingreso*, estimating a 1.3% rate of population growth.
NOTE: Data deflated by the overall wholesale price index.

of the economy. But it should be stressed that the full return to earlier trends, which by 1971–72 had become indisputable, was prefigured by earlier discontinuities in the series we have examined: in 1969, immediately after the Cordobazo, and in late 1970, when the BA took a nationalist turn. On the basis of these data, and from the standpoint of the economy and of political factors connected to it, the processes studied in this book can be periodized as follows: (1) the period prior to the 1966 coup, in which we observed an economy marked by sharp fluctuations and widespread speculative behavior, and by its correlate, the praetorian state; (2) the inaugural period of the Argentine Revolution, when Salimei was Economy Minister and when most of the variables we examined behaved as in the pre-1966 period; (3) the spectacular move toward stabilization of these variables and the resumption of economic growth that occurred under Krieger Vasena; (4) the turning point of the Cordobazo, at which various indicators registered with remarkable speed and sensitivity the shift from incipient confidence to the uncertainties brought on by that event and its sequels; (5) the period between the last half of 1969 and September 1970, during which Dagnino Pastore and (to a lesser extent) Moyano Llerena, in spite of an uncertain politi-

TABLE 47   RATIO OF BLACK MARKET RATE TO OFFICIAL
MARKET RATE FOR THE U.S. DOLLAR

	1966	1967	1968	1969	1970	1971	1972
January	129.7	114.7	100.0	100.0	99.9	106.9	105.7
February	126.0	115.5	100.0	99.9	100.0	104.4	107.6
March	121.1	98.6 (Krieger)	99.9	99.8	99.6	108.4 (Lan.)	102.6
April	117.9	99.5	99.8	100.1	99.8	114.7	102.8
May	116.0	99.6	100.0	100.5 (Cordb.)	100.3	116.6	120.7
June	117.1 (Ong.)	99.8	99.8	100.5	105.5 (Lev.)	119.4	118.1
July	111.6	100.0	99.8	100.3	100.3	114.4	112.1
August	105.6	99.9	100.0	100.5	100.2	116.1	130.3
September	113.7	99.9	100.0	100.5	100.4	104.4	137.3
October	117.3	99.8	100.0	100.4	104.1 (Ferrer)	114.9	129.4
November	108.7	99.8	100.0	100.4	107.2	120.7	119.0
December	108.7	100.0	100.0	100.6	108.4	113.9	112.9

SOURCE: Calculated from FIEL, *Informe de coyuntura,* various issues.
NOTE: "Ong." refers to the month in which Lt. General Onganía assumed the presidency; "Krieger" the month in which the 1967 economic program was implemented; "Cordb." the month of the first Cordobazo; "Lev." the month in which General Levingston assumed the presidency; "Ferrer" the month in which Aldo Ferrer became Economy Minister; "Lan." the month in which Lt. General Lanusse assumed the presidency.

cal climate, were able to dampen somewhat the reverberations of the Cordobazo; (6) the second turning point, October 1970, when the nationalist turn was taken; and (7) the full-fledged crisis of 1971–72.

Another similarity between the pre-1966 years and the 1971–72 period was that parts of the urban bourgeoisie achieved important profits—in spite of the relative price gains made by the Pampean sector—in the midst of the effervescence, speculation, and relative price shifts typical of situations of high uncertainty and inflation. But it can be inferred from the data that the bulk of these profits, as is typically the case in such situations, was channeled not into investments reproductive of capital but into speculative activities, including capital flight abroad that was surely more extensive than what was registered in the official statistics. These movements of capital were the aggregate expression of very nega-

TABLE 48   INTEREST RATES FOR THE U.S. DOLLAR ON THE
30-DAY FUTURES MARKET
(% above the cash quotation)

	1966	1967	1968	1969	1970	1971	1972
January	5.9	9.5	6.4	1.6	1.2	6.4	21.6
February	4.7	19.2	5.8	1.2	0.4	8.6	21.1
March	15.4	3.6	4.0	1.2	0.5	9.8	20.6
April	30.2	0.0	4.4	1.6	1.2	10.9	20.2
May	47.9	0.6	4.0	2.9	1.1	12.0	21.3
June	13.3	2.0	3.0	3.9	3.4	13.5	20.4
July	28.2	3.2	5.7	3.3	2.6	14.1	21.6
August	16.6	4.8	5.4	3.2	1.8	13.9	20.9
September	21.1	7.2	3.9	3.4	1.9	14.7	20.1
October	30.5	4.9	2.4	6.1	4.1	16.0	20.7
November	14.9	1.2	0.6	2.1	5.3	18.1	19.3
December	7.9	6.2	0.8	3.7	6.0	21.6	14.7

SOURCE: Calculated from BCRA, *Boletín estadística,* and FIEL, *Indicadores de coyuntura,* various issues.

tive expectations about the future. A substantial part of the bourgeoisie probably managed to protect their short-term economic interests by means of speculative decisions. But they were in a sense too successful at this, for such speculation gave decisive momentum to the economic crisis and undermined still further Lanusse's political solution.

The state at this time was still capitalist and authoritarian, but its governing personnel were so centrally preoccupied with carrying out the political rescue of the fundamental interests of the bourgeoisie and the armed forces that they practically disregarded the functioning of the economy. But economic problems returned with a vengeance, leading to the reemergence of an economy of plunder and a crisis which, especially in 1972, placed enormous obstacles in the path of a government that was facing most serious problems on the political plane.

Before examining these problems in more detail, let us review from a more structural perspective the changes in capital accumulation that corresponded to the demise of the BA between 1970 and 1972. Table 49 displays gross profit rates in each of the major economic sectors. As a first approximation of the degree to which the BA's collapse affected the overall accumulation of capital, observe that while the gross rate of

TABLE 49   GROSS PROFITS OF MAJOR ECONOMIC SECTORS
(in 1966 pesos) (index 1966=100.0)

	All Economic Activities	Industry	Finance Insurance, and Real Estate	Construction	Commerce	Agriculture, Livestock, Hunting and Fishing
1966	100.0	100.0	100.0	100.0	100.0	100.0
1969	117.5	109.3	159.9	156.7	113.5	98.0
1970	118.8	111.0	200.4	151.1	104.9	114.2
1971	118.7	115.6	175.3	82.8	101.7	142.1
1972	120.0	132.4	147.2	111.7	99.6	156.4

SOURCE: Calculated from BCRA, *Sistema de cuentas de producto e ingreso*, vol. 2.

NOTES: Data deflated by the respective wholesale price indices.

Gross profits calculated by deducting intermediate consumption, indirect taxes (minus subsidies), and expenditures for wages and salaries from the gross value of production.

Data for 1964–69 will be found in Table 24.

profit in the economy as a whole grew 17.5 percent between 1966 and 1969, it grew only 1.2 percent in 1970–72. It should be noted, however, that this figure is the aggregate expression of important changes both within and across the various sectors of the economy. In the first place, the gross rate of profit in industry increased greatly in 1972, a year of sharply declining wages and salaries. As argued in chapter 1, an economy of plunder does not rule out the making of large profits, even though economic growth may be reduced or reversed, inflation may rise, and capital may either exit abroad or find its way into the speculative placements with which a frightened bourgeoisie seeks to maximize its short-term gains.

Another beneficiary of the wage decline of 1972 was the labor-intensive construction sector, in which profit rates registered a net gain after a big drop in 1971. Financial capital, which after reaping huge profits in 1970 was subjected to various statist controls, fared considerably worse. The less than brilliant performance of commerce parallels the fall in mass consumption that took place in 1972. The agricultural sector, on the other hand, took revenge for the fall in its profits during the Krieger Vasena years.

Let us turn to the 1970–72 data on productivity and the rate of exploitation,* presented in Table 50. Here we find something significant. Productivity tumbled from 1969 levels in finance, commerce, and construction.† So did the rate of exploitation, which by 1972 had fallen below 1969 levels in each of these sectors, despite the decline of wages and salaries during that year. Industry presents a different picture. In that sector the growth of productivity between 1970 and 1972 was virtually equal to that of the 1966–69 period. Moreover, the rate of exploitation in industry, in contrast to the other sectors, continued to rise after 1969. But despite the marked increase in this rate in 1972, the exploitation rate in industry grew 14.5 percent in the 1970–72 period as compared with 25.2 percent between 1966 and 1969.

It is important to disaggregate the data pertaining to various subsectors of the industrial bourgeoisie, as was done in chapter 4. Table 51 shows that the performance of these subsectors was as heterogeneous during the collapse of the BA as it was in the 1966–69 period. In particular, we find once again a clear difference between the nondurable

---

*These variables were defined in chapter 4, section 4.

†As explained in chapter 4, methodological problems necessitate the exclusion of the agricultural sector from the exploitation and productivity data.

TABLE 50   PRODUCTIVITY AND EXPLOITATION RATES FOR
            ECONOMIC SECTORS
            (index 1966=100.0)

	Industry	Finance	Commerce	Construction
Productivity				
1966	100.0	100.0	100.0	100.0
1969	117.3	141.0	112.1	105.1
1970	124.0	146.4	105.6	105.1
1971	132.9	133.6	101.6	100.2
1972	134.1	108.5	93.9	92.4
Exploitation				
1966	100.0	100.0	100.0	100.0
1969	125.2	151.5	126.4	111.0
1970	128.0	155.5	112.9	108.0
1971	131.9	141.2	101.8	102.0
1972	142.5	129.0	104.5	106.2

SOURCE: Calculated from data in BCRA, *Sistema de cuentas de producto e ingreso*, vol. 2; and unpublished worksheets of the same institution.

NOTES: Value added data deflated by the wholesale price index for the corresponding sector.

Wage and salary figures deflated by the cost-of-living index for Buenos Aires.

The agricultural and livestock sector has been excluded due to the scarcity and unreliability of wage data.

consumer goods subsector and the other, more dynamic and concentrated subsectors of industry. While value added in the former grew a significant 28.2 percent between 1966 and 1972, the mean increase in the dynamic subsectors was 2.3 times as great. Also, while productivity and exploitation rates in the consumer nondurables subsector rose in that period at a rate that barely surpassed 1 percent per annum, the mean annual increase for the dynamic sectors was 6.8 times as great in productivity and 9 times as great in exploitation. By 1972, when the three dynamic subsectors are taken together, productivity had risen 48.6 percent and exploitation 62.2 percent over 1966 levels, while in consumer nondurables these indices had risen 7.1 and 6.9 percent respectively. The consumer nondurables sector registered its greatest gains in productivity and exploitation in 1970, but in 1971 and 1972 these rates fell, despite the fall in wages in 1972. In the dynamic sectors, on the other hand, these rates continued to climb throughout the period.

TABLE 51   VALUE ADDED, PRODUCTIVITY, AND EXPLOITATION
RATES FOR SUBSECTORS OF ARGENTINE INDUSTRY
(index 1966 = 100.0)

	Nondurable Consumer Goods	Durable Consumer Goods	Intermediate Goods	Capital Goods
Value added				
1966	100.0	100.0	100.0	100.0
1969	112.9	125.5	123.2	120.0
1970	118.7	134.7	131.7	130.2
1971	124.0	156.3	146.5	153.2
1972	128.2	169.7	155.5	166.2
Productivity				
1966	100.0	100.0	100.0	100.0
1969	104.0	126.9	124.1	124.1
1970	108.8	141.0	131.2	130.1
1971	107.6	158.2	146.2	146.9
1972	107.1	148.0	152.2	145.7
Exploitation				
1966	100.0	100.0	100.0	100.0
1969	109.2	131.6	132.2	134.0
1970	111.0	137.0	135.6	136.7
1971	105.8	154.4	149.1	138.4
1972	106.9	160.9	166.7	159.0

SOURCE: Calculated from unpublished worksheets of the Banco Central de la República Argentina.
NOTES: Value added data deflated by the wholesale price index for industrial products.
Wage data deflated by the cost-of-living index for Buenos Aires.

Once again, it is evident that the cleavages within the urban bourgeoisie
had quite concrete economic correlates. Moreover, the data in this chapter allow us to dispel the apparent paradox that arises when we consider
that it was the weakest fractions of the urban bourgeoisie—those who felt
wage and salary increases most acutely—that forged an alliance with the
unions and, in no small part, inserted themselves into Peronism. They
saw in such alliances a chance to improve their own share of capital
accumulation by means of policies that would restrict the growth of what

they called the monopolies and promote the expansion of the domestic market, even if a concomitant of the latter had to be increases in wages and salaries. In short, both the normalization program of 1967–69 and the plunder economy of 1970–72 revealed, albeit in different ways, the weakness of these factions in relation to the upper bourgeoisie.

2. PROTEST: STRIKES AND DEMONSTRATIONS

I have made numerous references to social protest and political violence. We are now in a position to analyze the data that pertain to these themes, first by looking at episodes of social protest, and then by examining the side of political violence for which I was able to gather reasonably reliable data: the actions of organizations that initiated a bitter process of urban guerrilla warfare and repression. The data used in this section are limited in that they have been compiled exclusively from periodical sources.* Bearing this in mind, let us turn first to the monthly totals of acts of social protest and political violence,† which are recorded in Table 52.

A pronounced rise in the number of such events occurred under the Radical government, indicating the not insignificant level of threat that preceded the 1966 coup. This increase was followed by a considerable decline under Onganía, which, it should be noted, began only in early 1967, after the defeat of the unions and the launching of Krieger Vasena's program. The overall level of conflict fell even more in 1968, the year that recorded by far the lowest total in the series. But the average number of acts of protest and violence during the first four months of 1969 was even lower than the monthly average in 1968. Then, in May 1969, the Cordobazo took place. The significance of the Cordobazo as a turning point is underscored not only by the jump that the series register in that month, but also by the continued rise from then on, until levels were reached in 1971 and 1972 that surpassed those of the Radical period by a substantial margin.

The data in Table 52 provide a general overview of the degree of conflict that prevailed during those thirteen troubled years. More detailed analysis is required, however. Let us look first at the most traditional form of social protest: strikes.

*For details see the Methodological Appendix.
†For the reasons given in the Methodological Appendix, workplace occupations of factories are not included in the figures in Table 52.

TABLE 52   ACTS OF PROTEST AND VIOLENCE
(excluding workplace occupations)

	1960	1961	1962	1963	1964	1965	1966	1967	1968	1969	1970	1971	1972
January	30	14	25	21	25	44	43	37	11	11	27	57	50
February	31	23	24	6	18	56	33	45	11	12	33	62	51
March	32	19	32	22	34	77	58	40	17	18	40	86 (Lan.)	57
April	29	35	9	31	42	43	66	22	8	24	53	79	46
May	28	64	48	33	52	69	64	20	18	92 (Cordb.)	83	120	68
June	25	40	40	44	76	51	56 (Ong.)	42	31	83	45 (Lev.)	120	105
July	31	40	46	27	38	36	14	30	8	50	53	118	177
August	34	36	117	10	42	32	37	20	20	40	37	70	133
September	39	36	31	20	39	30	71	15	25	91	70	95	86
October	60	37	84	28 (Illia)	77	59	65	34	58	85	143	111	200
November	39	60	46	26	53	63	38	19	16	70	76	45	59
December	26	40	43	9	136	29	51	12	16	23	64	73	77
Annual Total	404	444	545	177	632	589	596	336	239	599	724	1,036	1,109

SOURCE: See the Methodological Appendix.

NOTE: "Illia" refers to the month in which Dr. Illia assumed the presidency; "Ong." the month in which Lt. General Onganía assumed the presidency; "Cordb." the month of the first Cordobazo; "Lev." the month in which General Levingston assumed the presidency; "Lan." the month in which Lt. General Lanusse assumed the presidency.

TABLE 53   STRIKES AND WORK STOPPAGES

	Overall total	Strikes and Stoppages in the Interior as % of the National Total	Strikes and Stoppages by White-Collar Employees as % of the National Total of Strikes and Stoppages	Strikes and Stoppages by State Employees as % of the National Total of Strikes and Stoppages
Average 1956–59	133	57.9	52.4	36.5
Average 1960–63	186	54.5	61.5	46.7
Average 1964–66	273	56.7	63.5	43.4
1967	68	63.8	26.5	14.3
1968	50	63.3	37.5	25.0
1969	93	71.8	55.9	41.2
1970	116	76.4	58.2	32.6
1971	237	67.5	73.6	53.6
1972	187	55.1	78.8	60.9

SOURCE: See Appendix.
NOTE: "Interior" refers to all regions of the country outside of Greater Buenos Aires.

Table 53 shows that the annual total of strikes diminished after 1967, paralleling the decline in overall conflict. This trend, like many others we have observed, was reversed in May 1969, but yearly strike totals between 1970 and 1972 remained below those observed under the Radical government of 1963–66, even though acts of protest and violence occurred more frequently in 1970–72 than in the pre-1963 period. Evidently, patterns of conflict underwent profound changes between 1960 and 1972.

We can explore these changes by asking who went on strike. The second column of Table 53 shows there was a fair share of strike activity in the Greater Buenos Aires area before 1966. Between 1967 and 1971, however, the interior of the country took the lead in the context of an overall decline in strike activity. It should be recalled that local unions and the union rank and file are more tightly controlled by the

CGT and the national-level unions in the Greater Buenos Aires area than they are in the interior. Moreover, unions tend to be organized more bureaucratically in Greater Buenos Aires than in the interior and are usually able to supply their affiliates with a fairly comprehensive range of social services. It is no coincidence, then, that both the Vandorists and the participationists found their firmest bases of support in the national-level unions, especially in their organizational extensions in the Greater Buenos Aires region.* After the defeat of the unions in March 1967, each of these currents sought in its own way to come to terms with the nationalist and paternalist currents within the BA, which helps to explain why strike activity shifted more toward the interior between 1967 and 1971. Many of the strikes called in that period represented a challenge not only to the government but also to the national union leaders.† Only in 1972 did the regional distribution of strikes return to a pattern more consistent with the pre-1967 years, and only then—with state repression focused on the guerrillas, with the diminished credibility of the government's threats to repress the strikes, and with inflation producing wide fluctuations in wage and salary levels—did national union leaders again take the lead in promoting strike activity.

The question of who went on strike can also be answered from another angle. By looking at the data for blue-collar workers separately from that for white-collar employees, it is possible to rectify interpretations of recent Argentine history that portray the working class as the major if not the only dissenting actor since the fall of Peronism in 1955. Although in 1971 and 1972 blue-collar workers went on strike more frequently than during the 1966–70 period, they did so less frequently than under the previous, Radical government, indicating that the opposition and threat prior to the 1966 coup had a strong working-class

---

*Juan C. Torre develops an interpretation of these changing patterns of strikes and other protest activities that is congruent with the one set forth here in his "Sindicatos y trabajadores bajo el último gobierno peronista," Instituto Torcuato di Tella (Buenos Aires, 1979), mimeo.

†The question of who went on strike can also be answered by considering the decision-making level at which the strikes were called. Between 1955 and 1966, strikes declared outside the national unions and the CGT (that is, at the plant or local union levels) constituted 55.2 percent of the total. Under the Onganía government, however, the percentage of plant or local strikes shot up to 67.2 percent and remained at comparable levels during the governments of Levingston (69.4 percent) and Lanusse (71.4 percent). Once again, we see that workers and employees as a whole were far from passive adherents of the more conciliatory tendencies exhibited by their national-level leadership. For a comparative analysis of these and related issues, see Elizabeth Jelin, La protesta obrera, Nueva Visión, Buenos Aires, 1974.

component. In 1967 and 1968, which together with the first four months of 1969 comprised the period when the state seemed willing and able to employ rather harsh repression, blue-collar workers, especially in the interior of the country, accounted for a high proportion of the relatively few strikes called (see the third column of Table 53). Apparently, those workers were willing to take risks that neither the employees nor the national-level unions seemed ready for. In 1969 and 1970, the proportion of strikes called by blue-collar workers relative to white-collar employees returned to values normal for the 1956–66 period. This situation was reversed, however, in 1971 and especially in 1972, when white-collar employees accounted for more strikes than blue-collar workers. To grasp why this happened, it should be noted that *employees* refers basically to unionized lower-middle-class sectors— which, as we have seen, experienced pronounced income losses under the normalization program and even greater losses in 1972. More specifically, this category refers in large measure to state employees, who alone were responsible for more than half of the strikes called in 1971 and 1972 (see the fourth column of Table 53). During 1971 and 1972, strikes by state employees rose even faster as a percentage of total strikes than strikes by all white-collar employees. This coincided with a turn toward support for Peronism on the part of large segments of the middle sectors and with echoes among many of those segments of the ambiguous radicalization we shall soon examine.

The high incidence of employees' strikes is important also for what it suggests about Argentina's class structure. Argentina is extensively industrialized. This industrialization has generated, as we have seen, a working class of important economic and political weight. But it has also created, through numerous disequilibria in the country's productive structure and the consequent vicissitudes of its economic growth, a broad range of middle sectors, many of which depend on state salaries which are usually as erratic as they are low.* The recurrent and always unsuccessful normalization programs attempted in Argentina since 1952—the most systematic and most nearly successful of which has been examined in this book—have been, on the whole, more costly to these employees than to the working class. The result has been their recurrent protest and often ambiguous radicalization. But in part be-

---

*State employees, including those working in provincial and municipal governments and in public enterprises, constitute close to 30 percent of Argentina's economically active population (José C. Calvar et al., "Resultados preliminares de una investigación del sector público argentino").

cause many members of the armed forces come from these middle sectors, their strikes have proved more difficult to repress than those of the workers. In addition, the strikes of state employees tend more than workers' strikes to have strong public repercussions: by paralyzing the courts, the schools, the administrative tasks of the government at both the national and local levels, and other public services without which urban life is seriously disrupted, state employees' strikes usually present a more dramatic impediment to the functioning of society than do strikes by blue-collar workers.

The foregoing allows us to understand better the pressures that in 1971–72 led national union leaders, taking advantage of the state's reduced capacity for repression, to press their economic and corporate demands, seek bases of accommodation with the government, and use violence to combat radical tendencies within their rank and file. The national union leaders' apprehension over the growing radicalization and autonomy of their bases was shared, of course, by the armed forces and the dominant classes. This shared perception heightened the capacity of these union leaders to negotiate with the government and the dominant classes, both as unionists and as members of the "reasonable" sectors of Peronism. It was precisely this capacity that paternalists, liberals, and nationalists, each in their own way, had so recently tried to eliminate. The organizational and economic weight of the national union apparatus made it, as its leaders often said, a "wall of containment against subversion." But in order to play this role, the national unions pressed hard for what their bureaucratic weight best suited them for: benefits for their own organizations and higher wages and salaries.

As we have seen, in 1972 there was a return to the pattern of strikes that prevailed prior to 1966. Behind this shift lay an increase in the national union leaders' capacity for pressure, which they used to obtain wage and salary hikes which, as the data we have examined indicate, were both frequent and ineffective in maintaining the real income of the popular sector. These wage and salary increases fed the inflation that contributed to the economy of plunder, discouraged the bourgeoisie, and helped evaporate the conditions necessary for Lanusse's rescue operation. But if by pressing their demands these union leaders seemed hostile to the bourgeoisie and the government, in riding the wave of popular activation they were also what they proclaimed themselves to be: a crucial barrier against the radical tendencies of the industrial workers and various middle sectors.

Let us return to the data. Most of the events we have considered so far occurred in the workplace. Another type of behavior and, presumably, of motivation is involved in taking to the streets to protest. Here we are concerned primarily with street demonstrations oriented explicitly around political actors or issues. Table 54 gives figures for the annual totals of such demonstrations in the 1960–72 period. The general profile of these data is smoother than that of the strike figures, although once again we see a strong rise in 1969 (after the Cordobazo) and a peak in 1971–72.

The regional breakdown in Table 54 shows a significant convergence between the data for strikes and for street demonstrations: in both cases, the center of activity shifted toward the interior between 1968 and 1970, and moved back toward Greater Buenos Aires in 1972. Once again, the figures suggest that the initial challenges to the BA came from outside Greater Buenos Aires. Moreover, the data on the proportion of such demonstrations involving property damage—usually to buildings and vehicles—show the interior of the country to have been the site of a higher proportion of violent demonstrations. The data also show that beginning in 1969 the proportion of demonstrations all over the country that were violent was significantly higher than in the past.

TABLE 54   STREET DEMONSTRATIONS

	Total	Demonstrations in the Interior as % of the Total	Percentage of Demonstrations in Greater Buenos Aires Involving Property Damage	Percentage of Demonstrations in the Interior Involving Property Damage
Average 1960–66	71	48.9	45.9	57.3
1967	117	46.1	36.5	50.0
1968	105	60.9	56.0	84.4
1969	151	86.0	72.2	76.9
1970	140	72.1	65.8	84.1
1971	165	73.3	88.6	84.3
1972	164	59.7	56.0	81.6

SOURCE: See Appendix.
NOTE: "Interior" refers to all regions of the country outside of Greater Buenos Aires.

TABLE 55   ACTS OF POLITICAL VIOLENCE
(annual totals)

	(1) Total Number of Acts of Political Violence	(2) Bombings	(3) Number of Acts of Armed Political Violence (exclusive of bombings)
1960	223	212	11
1961	169	154	15
1962	309	291	18
1963	87	66	21
1964	215	194	21
1965	173	166	7
1966	158	142	16
1967	146	139	5
1968	84	77	7
1969	349	300	49
1970	443	287	156
1971	619	344	275
1972	745	539	206

SOURCE: See Appendix.

3. POLITICAL VIOLENCE

Turning to political violence, let us begin by examining the data at a relatively aggregated level. Column 1 of Table 55 gives the annual total of acts of political violence between 1960 and 1972. This category includes bombings, assassination attempts for allegedly political reasons, kidnappings, robberies declared by their executors to have been for the purpose of financing guerrilla operations, and various acts of armed propaganda.* The high level of this series throughout the entire 1960–72 period is quite remarkable. Moreover, it is not surprising, in view of the trends observed in the previous tables, that political violence declined in 1967–68, rose at the time of the Cordobazo, exceeded

*By armed propaganda I mean actions whose central purpose was to produce a major propagandistic effect. Such actions ranged from the capture of entire towns and the seizing of radio or television stations to relatively minor acts such as the hijacking of food trucks and the distribution of their contents in poor neighborhoods. See the Methodological Appendix for more details on these data.

significantly in 1970 the levels recorded in all of the preceding years, and reached exceptionally high levels in 1971 and 1972.

The data in column 1 of Table 55 include bombings, which caused considerable damage and commotion* but usually did not require a complex, militarized organization. The data in column 3, which exclude bombings, allow us to focus on actions requiring a higher level of organizational capacity and logistical support: those carried out by what may properly be called guerrilla organizations. These actions form a pattern quite different from that displayed by the more aggregated data presented in column 1. Prior to April 1969, most of the violent actions recorded were bombings; other acts of violence remained at relatively low levels. After the Cordobazo, however, violent actions exclusive of bombings rose impressively, peaking in 1971 but remaining at a high level throughout 1972. It is worthwhile examining the monthly data for these series, which are presented in Table 56 (the monthly count of all acts of political violence) and in Table 57 (the monthly count of acts of armed political violence, i.e., exclusive of bombings).

These monthly figures indicate that, from the Cordobazo onward, the population was confronted almost daily with news of disturbing and violent events. To these incidents of guerrilla activity must be added the actions of the state's security apparatus and its increasing recourse to extralegal and often spectacular procedures. There is, unfortunately, no reliable source of data on such actions and procedures, but taking them into account is indispensable for understanding the crucial place that violence, and the fear of violence, came to occupy in the lives of Argentines.

Another way to measure the intensity of this violence is to record the number of persons killed for allegedly political reasons. The yearly total of such killings, which averaged 5 in the 1960–68 period, rose to 39 in 1969, 41 in 1970, 64 in 1971, and 68 in 1972. Moreover, very few acts of armed propaganda occurred before 1969, when the total reached 15 (only one of which took place before the Cordobazo), whereas 36 such acts occurred in 1970, 47 in 1971, and 39 in 1972. It should be added that in those years such acts included, in an impressive display of organizational and quasi-military capacity, several seizures of medium-sized cities. Equally important, attempts on the lives of military officers and

---

*Qualitative examination of these data reveals that most of the bombs exploded prior to 1969 were relatively weak and constructed with rather primitive technologies. Thereafter, as was the case with other aspects of violence, significant "progress" was made in the technological sophistication and the destructive capacity of bombs.

TABLE 56   ACTS OF POLITICAL VIOLENCE
(monthly count)

	1960	1961	1962	1963	1964	1965	1966	1967	1968	1969	1970	1971	1972
January	7	0	10	7	4	15	16	8	2	6	12	42	34
February	20	3	7	0	1	21	13	14	3	6	11	38	33
March	17	5	20	9	17	26	10	27	7	4	20	52 (Lan.)	38
April	14	5	4	13	6	12	15	4	3	16 (Cordb.)	36	44	20
May	20	34	38	3	17	15	8	6	7	27	33	55	43
June	14	12	9	27	23	13	17 (Ong.)	26	6	52	25 (Lev.)	75	54
July	13	8	21	6	13	6	2	14	1	32	37	84	127
August	20	10	93	1	21	14	5	10	4	30	19	45	91
September	28	13	18	4	8	8	19	7	6	52	49	57	56
October	35	16	52	4 (Illia)	8	17	22	17	26	68	109	60	163
November	24	43	28	13	20	19	7	10	10	45	45	26	36
December	11	20	9	0	77	7	24	3	9	11	47	41	50
Annual Total	223	169	309	87	215	173	158	146	84	349	443	619	745

SOURCE: See Appendix.
NOTE: "Illia" refers to the month in which Dr. Illia assumed the presidency; "Ong." the month in which Lt. General Onganía assumed the presidency; "Cordb." the month of the first Cordobazo; "Lev." the month in which General Levingston assumed the presidency; "Lan." the month in which Lt. General Lanusse assumed the presidency.

TABLE 57 GUERRILLA ACTIONS: ACTS OF ARMED POLITICAL VIOLENCE EXCLUSIVE OF BOMBINGS
(monthly count)

	1965	1966	1967	1968	1969	1970	1971	1972
January	0	1	0	0	2	3	28	25
February	1	2	1	0	1	7	26	14
March	0	2	0	1	0	10	23 (Lan.)	14
April	2	3	0	1	16 (Cordb.)	9	22	12
May	0	1 (Ong.)	0	1	2	7	15	20
June	1	2	2	1	4	4 (Lev.)	42	11
July	1	1	1	0	3	12	36	23
August	1	0	0	1	4	7	23	24
September	0	1	0	0	5	16	17	17
October	0	1	0	0	6	22	23	19
November	1	0	0	1	4	28	10	10
December	0	2	1	1	6	31	10	17
Annual Total	7	16	5	7	49	156	275	206

SOURCE: See the Appendix.
NOTE: "Ong." refers to the month in which Lt. General Onganía assumed the presidency; "Cordb." the month of the first Cordobazo; "Lev." the month in which General Levingston assumed the presidency; and "Lan." the month in which Lt. General Lanusse assumed the presidency.

members of other security forces were rare before 1969, when 5 such attempts occurred. From that year forward, the number of such assassination attempts increased to 33 in 1970, 54 in 1971, and 44 in 1972, and a large proportion of them resulted in the deaths of high-ranking officers of the armed forces. These assassinations conveyed dramatically the degree to which the collapse of the BA represented an extreme threat not only to the armed forces' institutional interests but also to the lives of military officers. This risk wrought marked changes in the lifestyles of these persons and their families and reinforced their feeling that a cruel war had to be fought against a ubiquitous enemy.

In this chapter we have succinctly reviewed data on economic processes as well as on protest and violence. While not easy reading, it seems the best way to situate the quantitative side of this investigation in the context of the analysis of the implantation, impacts, and collapse of the 1966 Argentine BA. We have seen that after two years (those of the Onganía–Krieger Vasena period) in which all indicators deviated from the patterns of the previous years, patterns similar to those of the pre-1966 period reappeared during 1969 and 1970 and strongly reasserted themselves in 1971 and 1972. What in the pre-1966 years had been (in terms of the definitions proposed in chapter 1) a crisis of government, regime, and accumulation, became in 1971–72 (as we shall see in the next chapter) nothing less than a crisis of social domination. This crisis was reinforced by the challenge that the guerrillas posed to the coercive supremacy of the state apparatus, and its reverberations deepened the crises of regime and accumulation. What is more, we have seen only one side of political violence, the one opposed to the state, and have examined only its most quantitative aspects. The next chapter will situate this information in the context of the radicalization these events expressed and of the reactions they generated. This will bring us, in turn, to the final misfortunes of the Lanusse government.

TEN

A Curious End to a Sad Story

Having analyzed data on violence and on the economic crisis of 1971–72, we must now examine the ways in which these phenomena were related to the political scene. Our task is complicated by several factors. First, unlike the relatively simple politics of the initial phase of the BA—which, owing basically to the exclusion of the popular sector, is a politics of and within bureaucracies—we are now dealing with a multiplicity of events interacting in complex ways on various planes of society and the state apparatus. The situation examined in this chapter is typical of such transitions: little remains of the BA, but much remains to be done to consolidate a democratic alternative—if indeed such a consolidation is to occur.[1]

A second complication is specific to the case we are studying: the immense complexity that Peronism assumed as it engulfed a vast range of social sectors. By 1972, major actors within Peronism included guerrilla organizations, union leaders of a wide variety of outlooks, leaders of the CGE, and quite traditional and conservative politicians—as well as Perón himself, who had his own games to play. This convergence was at once the hope and the terror of the armed forces and the bourgeoisie. While all of the currents within Peronism claimed loyalty to Perón, it would be erroneous to consider Peronism a unified actor interacting with others: these currents were so diverse, and their goals and potential alliances so heterogeneous, that Peronism introjected a significant part of the conflicts and violence of the period.

A third problem, also specific to the present case, is posed by the analysis of the political correlates of the violence of the 1969–73 period. These years were marked by death, by fear, and by the brutal arrogance of those who, from the most diverse persuasions and at times with generous motives, engaged in violence limited only by the force that the "enemy" could muster.* Argentina is not yet rid of the hatreds born of the violence of these and subsequent years. I cannot analyze dispassionately this part of my country's history. But the tragedy that these events meant for Argentina makes it imperative to put forth a critical analysis of them, even if it is sure to infuriate those who, having questioned nothing and having learned nothing, still cling to the hatreds they have so effectively generated.

1. TOWARD A CRISIS OF SOCIAL
   DOMINATION

Bearing in mind the data in chapter 9, let us examine more closely the resurgence of popular activation and the consequent emergence of threat at a significantly higher level than that which preceded the 1966 coup. One of the central features of this activation is impossible to estimate with the types of sources and data used elsewhere in this volume. Behind the conflicts of the major political actors, in offices and factories, sometimes in conjunction with threats from guerrilla organizations or through the fear of violence which the state apparatus seemed powerless to stop (and thus at a point when even the last vestiges of order had evaporated), the bourgeoisie made a bitter discovery: little was left of the social domination they had thought consolidated during the recent, yet so remote, Krieger Vasena years. The problem for the bourgeoisie was not only, nor so much, to adjust to the economic crisis, but to maintain control of the work process and to preserve a minimum of discipline among workers and employees. As the BA disintegrated, the goal on which paternalists, liberals and nationalists had agreed—the implantation of "order and authority" in various social contexts, particularly the workplace—tottered with a crisis that extended well beyond the deterioration of the economy and the political misfortunes of the government.

Here we face a serious methodological problem. During Lanusse's

---

*I refer, above all, to the sad destiny of a generation then about eighteen to twenty-five years old, many members of which lost their lives. The responsibility for what happened to those young people, and for what some of them did, rests with older generations that should have known better, or at least should have refrained from encouraging the hatred for which the passionate young people of that generation were sacrificed.

government, a heavy silence settled over the spiral of armed action and violent retribution. Silence, as is clear from the interviews and informal conversations I conducted and from my own observations, became the usual response to a violence that began to permeate all levels of Argentine society. So it was, of course, for those who committed this violence. And so it became for those who for one reason or another (and there always seemed to be a reason) feared being picked as targets of violence, especially once it became clear that to show fear, or to speak of danger, was to make what was dreaded all the more likely to occur. The bourgeoisie were among the many who shared this fear. The state apparatus offered little protection against the danger of being gunned down or abducted, or having a member of one's family kidnapped, in retaliation for conflicts within the enterprise, or because someone was considered too harsh with workers, or simply because of the ransom expected. These risks were higher for owners and managers of large enterprises, both because such firms were more prone to engage in conflicts with their workers and employees and because they were expected to hand over more in ransom. As a consequence, all of the persons I interviewed who were owners or managers of large firms drastically changed their own lives and those of their families. They had to learn to live at home and to send their children to school with bodyguards, to change day to day the route they took to work, and to live in constant fear, under threats and blackmail attempts whose seriousness they could not determine. Some even moved their homes to Montevideo, across the River Plate, and commuted by plane every weekday to their offices in Buenos Aires. Moreover, the families of those who were kidnapped tried desperately to conceal the abduction from the police and even from their friends, convinced that their best hope was to pay the ransom in silence.* Since everyone knew this tactic of concealment, nobody could really be sure how many had gone through such ordeals; this uncertainty probably led everyone to exaggerate their own chances of being abducted and perhaps murdered.

Another consequence of the mounting fear and violence was that numerous enterprises made payments to guerrilla groups in the hope of shielding themselves from their attacks. But too many such groups ex-

---

*It was not until much later that this mantle of silence was lifted. Referring to this practice, José Martínez de Hoz, a prominent member of the upper bourgeoisie and Minister of Economy (1976–81) during the second Argentine BA, declared in 1985 that "in those years the kidnappings and ransoms were a most delicate matter, which everyone handled with the utmost secrecy. Not even the closest friends were informed of what was happening" (El Periodista, February 15, 1985, p. 4).

isted, and there also flourished apolitical blackmailers who camouflaged themselves as revolutionary in order to make their own windfall. Everyone knew about this, but it was never discussed in public or by the media.* In this way, the simultaneous emergence of guerrilla actions and innumerable plant-level conflicts—the connections between which were sometimes real, sometimes threatened by workers or outsiders attempting to strengthen their bargaining positions, and sometimes only imagined by the owners and managers of enterprises—became for the owners and managers not only a crucial political and economic problem, but the source of profound change in their daily lives.

Leaving behind the grey and bureaucratic order of the recent past, society exploded on all sides. As challenges emerged not only in the more public arenas, but also in universities, high schools, workplaces and neighborhoods, the armed forces were faced with the prospect of applying repression on a gigantic scale. In 1971 and 1972, however, the armed forces, too demoralized and preoccupied by the political conflicts of the period to act with the high degree of cohesion that would have been necessary for such repression, continued to vacillate between this route and the one down which Lanusse was traveling.† It was not until March 1976, after the violence had escalated still further, that the armed forces again united around the repressive option and inaugurated a new BA, much more violent and destructive than the one studied here.

What was the meaning of these events? Behind the violence of guerrillas and anti-guerrillas, and the fear experienced by almost everyone, lay a major intensification of class struggles. Several aspects of these struggles deserve examination. First, the challenges to social domination at the cellular level of society did not take shape as a national movement. Rather, they were distributed unevenly according to region, neighbor-

---

*One exception is an article in the September 26, 1972, issue of *Economic Survey* (p. 1): "A medal for heroism should go to any businessman who, in seeking to place any limits whatsoever on the demands of the workers, risks turning his establishment into a battlefield or being kidnapped by terrorists." The article goes on to say that "the military administration claims that it is trying to institutionalize the country. What it is on the verge of institutionalizing, however, is its own moral and material bankruptcy." What Juan C. Torre ("Sindicatos y trabajadores," pp. 52–53) has written in reference to the 1973–76 period is indicative of a situation that was already visible in 1971 and 1972: "We are not stretching the truth if we say that in those years the factories were in a state of rebellion. . . . It was often the case that, in disputes over working conditions, the workers would decide unilaterally what criteria should be used to resolve the contested issues, presenting the management with a *fait accompli.*"

†Not that Lanusse's government did not employ a good deal of repression. But since it maintained that elections and a constitutional government were necessary steps toward eliminating those challenges, the application of unrestricted repression, as well as a full militarization of the regime, were ruled out.

hood, firm type and size, and other social contexts about which it is difficult to generalize owing to the scarcity of reliable information. Second, many of the employees and the vast majority of the workers who occupied workplaces, went on strike, determined their own pace of work, continually escalated wage and salary demands, and tried to run some factories were identified as Peronists. Third, most important actors within Peronism—Perón, the political personnel, the national-level unions, and the leaders of the CGT and CGE—were not at all interested in supporting such challenges. In fact, a not insignificant part of the violence that occurred in the years we are studying was directed by the national union leaders against radicalized militants from among the rank and file. Fourth, and largely as a consequence of the previous points, these challenges seldom found expression in national-level politics and remained uncoordinated on a national or even regional basis. Fifth, the guerrilla organizations tried persistently to insert themselves into the struggles of workers, employees, and popular-sector neighborhoods. For obvious reasons, there is scarce information concerning the results of these efforts, but it seems clear that the guerrillas' success in penetrating such movements varied greatly from case to case. However, it is equally clear that the guerrilla organizations succeeded in convincing the class adversaries of these movements that the cellular challenges and guerrilla activity were tied closely together. This popular activation certainly posed a significant threat in itself, and in various instances its links to the guerrillas were not imaginary. But, sixth, this activation was characterized in most cases by methods and goals quite different from, and certainly more peaceful and democratic than, those of the guerrilla organizations.[2] Finally, and because of the combination of the preceding factors, these popular sector movements were doomed to suffer the cruel repression provoked by the "revolutionary violence" that the guerrillas perpetrated on their behalf. These popular challenges, lacking expression in the national political arena and devoid of a strategy for dealing with the dominant classes and their allies, were doomed in part to be absorbed by more moderate components of Peronism—the CGT and the national unions—and in part to share the suicidal fate of the guerrillas.

2. AN AMBIGUOUS RADICALIZATION

The collapse of the BA not only generated a severe political and economic crisis, it also jeopardized the entire system of social domination.

But the paradox of the situation was that more than a few of those who contributed to this deepest of threats—the Peronist guerrilla organizations, and particularly the Montoneros, the most important of them*— seemed unaware that class struggles were endangering the most basic social relations. Who belonged to these organizations and to the unarmed groups allied with them? Although no available data answer this question precisely, it is clear that the vast majority of their adherents were youthful (and thus recently politicized) members of the same middle sectors that, during the period we are studying, repudiated a long history of anti-Peronism and joined their former adversaries with the fervor of the newly converted. Furthermore, the majority of the leaders of these organizations shared another important characteristic: prior membership in groups of the Catholic and nationalist extreme right.

It is difficult to reconstruct an ideological climate that seems so far removed from the present day. We have seen how Perón, in his messages to these currents, urged them to "use all the means available to us" and to "wage struggle on all fronts," claiming that their victory would entail not only the defeat of the "dictatorship," but also the supersession of the "liberal-capitalist system." We have also seen that Perón, by cultivating the revolutionary image that some of his followers bestowed on him, channeled toward himself most of the popular activation and violent radicalization of the period.[†] In so doing, he greatly increased the chances that Peronism would come to encompass most of the oppositions to the BA and that he himself would become the axis of whatever political arrangement was finally reached. By the same token, he made it more likely that most of this activation and radicalization would remain within his movement's—and particularly his own—ideological limitations. These pointed not toward some sort of socialism, but to an organicistic and corporatist vision of society that rejected both "Marxism" and "Liberalism" and favored the building of an "organized community" around harmonious relations between "national entrepreneurs" and the "organized working class."[3]

Let us return to some themes outlined in chapter 8. Among the

---

*After their first spectacular deed, the abduction and assassination of Aramburu, the Montoneros grew until they dominated forces partially distinguishable from them: other guerrilla organizations, some of which (particularly the ERP) placed themselves outside the Peronist camp, and various organizations of working-class, and especially middle-class, Peronist youth.

†To repeated pleas by the government and by members of his own movement that he condemn the guerrillas, Perón responded with a silence that was interpreted by the guerrillas and their allies as expressing his solidarity with them.

youthful sectors of Peronism, the echoes of Perón's ideology were combined with readings of Mao, Fanon, and Guevara, as well as of national authors who attempted to transform Peronism into the historical agent of *socialismo nacional* (national socialism).[4] The result was a Tower of Babel: "neither Marxists nor Liberals," "third [international] position," "national socialism," "principal contradiction," "organized community," etc., whose synthesis was to be achieved through "direct [violent] action," the magic road to "national revolution." These orientations— hostility to foreigners per se; an extraordinarily chauvinistic affirmation of the nation; exaltation of the leader in the person of Perón; the worship of violence not only as an effective strategy but also as a purificatory catharsis; and militant hostility to both Marxism and liberalism (both characterized in peculiar ways)—together with the class origins of those who held them, gave the Peronist guerrilla groups a striking resemblance to a seldom recognized precursor: the radical wings of the European fascist movements,[5] those which never succeeded in governing or which, as in Italy, continued to dream of a "second wave" in which "their" revolution would be consummated.

The main difference between these European fascist currents and the groups that concern us here was that the former supplied shock troops that liquidated workers' activation and parties, while the guerrillas in Argentina attempted, with some success, to insert and strengthen themselves in working-class and popular movements. But this difference does not detract from the significance of their ideological convergences, to which we should add the profoundly militarist, authoritarian and elitist conception that all of these movements had of politics and of their own organizations.*

The return of Perón and Peronism to power (i.e. to government) would mark the beginning of the "National Revolution."† To help bring this about, every effort had to be made to sharpen the contradictions and to eliminate the numerous enemies, both inside of and external to Peronism, who obstructed the path toward the National Revolution.

---

*The writings of exiled Montonero leaders who later withdrew from that organization provide further insight into these views. See esp. Rodolfo Galimberti, "El peronismo y la crisis de la dictadura" N.p., June 9, 1981. This text, which came to my attention too late to be used in preparing this book, strongly supports what I am saying about the ideological orientations of the Montoneros and the consequences for that organization's internal characteristics and conception of politics.

†This "apparatist" and fetishized (as I used the term in chapter 1) view of political power as ultimately residing in the state apparatus is characteristic of (though not confined to) the ideology I am trying to delineate; see O'Donnell, "Apuntes para una teoría del estado."

This was Peronism as a movement, not as a party, a "liberal" invention that could serve at best as the movement's appendage and that remained perpetually vulnerable to conquest by the host of "traitors" that could be found in the "union bureaucracy"[6] and among the political personnel. What doubt could there be of an imminent revolutionary victory if Perón had made this goal his own, and if the *pueblo* was on the verge of launching the "Argentinazo," the great social explosion that would consummate the revolution in the jubilant reunion of leader, *pueblo*, and guerrilla organizations? And, if victory was imminent, why bother forging alliances, least of all with those who, in remaining outside Peronism, demonstrated their colossal ignorance of the direction of history, not to mention their anti-national leanings? Why, then, worry about the armed forces and the bourgeoisie, whom these organizations terrified with no thought toward the terrible reactions that were forming within those bastions of coercion and social domination?

"Liberal," "bolshie," "bureaucrat," "imperialist lackey," and other epithets marked, for the guerrillas and their allied currents, the broad ensemble of "traitors to the nation." Only the veneration of both Perón and violence could certify one as belonging to the correct camp. With leader and *pueblo* on the move, the great victory seemed closer with every snag encountered by the Lanusse government. Meanwhile, this euphoria fed terrible hatreds through the ugly episodes in which the guerrillas lost their image as daring Robin Hoods, and their opponents, acting in the name of the state or not, began to lose even the appearance of abiding by legal rules and procedures.

Survey data from 1971 and 1972 show that the guerrillas during this period enjoyed the support, or at least the sympathy, of a remarkable proportion of the population. Responses to questions on political violence have been aggregated into an "index of attitudes toward terrorism," depicted in Table 58. I have been unable to assess the reliability of these data, but even reserving a large margin for error, the percentage of the population expressing sympathy or support for the armed organizations is remarkably high.* This proportion was highest in the cities of Córdoba and Rosario, epicenters of the most tumultuous and radicalized opposition. Data from the same source allows us to see how these sympathies were distributed in March 1971 among various categories of respondents.[7] As Table 59 shows, support for armed organizations

---

*It should be noted, however, that on the basis of data from later surveys by the same agency, Frederick Turner remarks (without specifying percentages) that this sympathy declined in 1972 ("The Study of Argentine Politics through Survey Research," p. 92).

TABLE 58   ATTITUDES TOWARD TERRORISM

	Greater Buenos Aires	Overall Interior	Rosario	Córdoba
Justified	41.5%	49.5%	51.0%	53.0%
Unjustified	51.5%	48.5%	48.0%	46.0%
Unclassifiable	4.0%	2.5%	1.0%	1.0%

SOURCE: Photocopies of reports produced by IPSA (the agency that conducted the survey): "Opiniómetro-Medición sistemática de tendencias de la opinión pública (Ola I, Ola II)," IPSA S.A., Buenos Aires, n.d. I thank Frederick Turner (see also his "The Study of Argentine Politics through Survey Research") for allowing me to examine these documents, which are not easily available to Argentines.
NOTES: N = 1878
The above figures cover indices on the basis of two surveys, taken in March and October of 1971.

was least pronounced among the working class, which, though it would suffer disproportionately from the reactions that the acts of these organizations provoked, was occupied with other forms of struggle. By contrast, those whom the survey classifies as middle class and upper class were more likely to express a favorable attitude toward the guerrillas.

Even with a dose of skepticism about the startlingly high figures for the upper class in Rosario and about the criteria according to which respondents were assigned to the various categories,* it seems clear that at the beginning of 1971 support or sympathy for the guerrillas was high throughout the country, but highest among the middle and/or upper classes, among the younger respondents, and in the interior of the country.

If much less had sufficed to precipitate the 1966 coup, why is it that no new coup interrupted the process that culminated in the 1973 elections? The answer must be sought in the confusion of the armed forces and the upper bourgeoisie following the demise of the Onganía and Levingston governments, and above all in their disagreements over how to prevent what was most worrisome of all: a full linkage between the popular activation and the guerrillas. Lanusse's proposed political solution appeared initially as a promising way to isolate the guerrillas and the more radical leaders of the popular activation, and to guide the rest of this activation into channels conducive to the survival of the basic parameters of society. By contrast, the alternative of a coup raised the

*It would have been interesting to cross-tabulate age with social position, but I have not had access to the original data.

TABLE 59   RESPONDENTS WHO FEEL THAT TERRORISM IS JUSTIFIED
(by region, social position, and age)

| | Social Position | | | Age | | | |
	High	Middle	Low	18–24	25–34	35–49	50+
Greater Buenos Aires	43%	43%	37%	53%	48%	42%	28%
Interior as a whole	62%	54%	46%	66%	55%	49%	45%
Rosario	80%	55%	51%	76%	64%	47%	56%
Córdoba	51%	59%	51%	68%	61%	55%	39%

SOURCE: "Opiniómetro," IPSA S.A.

specter of a massive popular reaction, the legendary "Argentinazo." Lanusse's option, which was clearly the most lucid, failed. But its failure did not bring about the dreaded collapse. Perón stepped in, not to play the role that Lanusse had assigned him but to perform a sleight of hand that encouraged the guerrillas but at the same time made himself and his movement, not Lanusse, the real hope of absorbing the popular activation and liquidating the guerrillas.

3. THE HUNDRED FACES OF JANUS

Let us recapitulate. Around 1971 Peronism and Perón became the focal points of an extraordinary convergence of the most diverse currents, all pledging loyalty to the "indisputable leader." These currents included most of the working class; many recently "Peronized" middle sectors; most of the guerrillas; all currents within the CGT and the national unions; assorted groups led by intellectuals convinced of their ability to channel the *pueblo* toward all sorts of goals on both the left and right; politicians of the center and right, many engaged in traditional clientelist practices; and groups (including armed groups waging war against the guerrillas) that rallied behind the openly fascist brand of "national socialism" espoused by José López Rega. Peronism was multifaceted as never before.*

We saw that many guerrilla groups, a substantial portion of the newly radicalized segments of the middle sectors, and some combative currents in the working class had pinned their hopes on Peronism. However, another face of Janus still needs to be examined. The remarkable ideological ambiguity of Peronism, which allowed it to embrace a broad range of social and political forces, was one of its major assets. Perón, as already mentioned, refrained from condemning or rejecting any of these currents. Nonetheless, it was clear to anyone who bothered to look that Perón retained his long-standing corporatist, populist, and nationalist ideology,† although some of its most conservative

---

*It says much about the confusions of the time that no small part of the 1966–73 violence (and an even larger part of later violence) took place between the "conservative fascist" currents led by López Rega and the radicalized version of the same ideology embodied by the Montoneros.

†Despite Perón's use of revolutionary language in his messages to guerrilla and youth organizations, these orientations stand out in his writings of the epoch as well as in the numerous editions of his earlier works that appeared during this period. These texts are filled with wrath against those who had overthrown his government in 1955 and whose subsequent policies constituted short-sighted revenge against Peronism and Perón himself: above all, the "oligarchy" currents in the armed forces, which, like Lanusse, had a long

elements had been filtered out by the vigorous activation of his main social base, as well as by his interpretation while in Spain of his most admired personage—again, de Gaulle—and of social democracy. Within this ideological domain, the last hopes of the upper bourgeoisie by 1972 rested upon the more moderate sectors of Peronism: a good part of its political personnel, the leadership of the national unions and the CGT, and the bourgeoisie associated with the CGE, only recently mocked by the upper bourgeoisie as "artificial," "opportunist" . . . and Peronist. The upper bourgeoisie and the leading periodicals thus raised no cries of outrage when in manifestly corporatist language the CGT and the CGE proclaimed themselves the "pillars of the future social pact."* Would it not be acceptable, after all, for the bourgeoisie as a whole to fall back on the Peronism of *La Hora del Pueblo,* which repeatedly emphasized its respect for the democratic game and for minorities, and even on the Peronism of union leaders who fought vigorously for economic gains but were threatened by the same enemies as the bourgeoisie?

If Peronism was to succeed where Lanusse was failing as the rescuer of social domination, Perón's role was seen as crucial. Many believed that only his immense personal magnetism could guarantee the acceptance by a majority of the popular and middle sectors of a nonviolent and nonrevolutionary option. That Perón might choose this path once he had politically defeated Lanusse could have been inferred from his statements and writings, as well as from the frequent signals that the Peronist political personnel and union leaders were sending to the armed forces and the bourgeoisie to the effect that once installed in the government, they would settle accounts with "the subversives."

---

history of intense anti-Peronism. Nowhere in these writings is there evidence that Perón ever was the revolutionary leader that his radicalized followers wanted to see in him—unless his encouragement of violence defined him as such. A separate issue is why these groups considered Perón a revolutionary leader. I am not in a position to answer this, but I suspect the reason involves Perón's skill at adjusting his language to suit his audiences as well as the extreme ambiguity of the revolution these groups advocated, which consisted in not much more than the myth of violence as a revolutionary method. We are dealing with an extraordinary case of selective perception that may be understood as a compulsion to eliminate cognitive dissonance by those who had made an immense emotional investment in armed struggle.

*In a conversation with the author, one paternalist who had occupied high positions in the Onganía government remarked bitterly that the leading periodicals and the organizations of the bourgeoisie, which only recently had bristled at terms like "organized community" and its corporatist connotations, now had no apparent objections to them.

Peronism thus became simultaneously the source of the deepest fears of the bourgeoisie and their only apparent hope of allaying those fears.*

Many of those who placed the highest value on the construction of a democratic order also converged toward this fantastic alchemy, though in the end they had little influence over the course of events. The obvious—and correct—lesson that they drew from Argentine history was that nothing could be achieved until Peronism, whether or not it comprised a majority, was fully incorporated into the democratic game from which it had been coercively and fraudulently excluded for so many years. It was also clear to those who shared this view that for such a reincorporation to occur, Perón would have to reject both the guerrilla organizations and those who proclaimed themselves the heirs of European fascism.

The result of these convergences was that Peronism, to its great electoral advantage but with effects that would subsequently prove catastrophic, internalized practically all the conflicts of Argentine society. In these years it was Peronism, not the state apparatus, that was the site of convergence for virtually all of the country's lines of conflict, including its classes, its political alignments, and much of its violence. This extraordinary situation resulted from the constellation of factors we have discussed: the popular sector's tradition of expressing itself politically through Peronism; the disoriented retreat of the upper bourgeoisie and the armed forces following the collapse of the BA; the worship of violence that began with the reactions to the Cordobazo; the codes of fear and hatred that profoundly clouded and distorted the political scene; the ambiguous ideological radicalization associated with the "Peronization" of many middle sectors; and the rapid decline of the prospects for success of the operation launched by Lanusse.

---

*For various reasons ranging from personal fear to the unpopularity left over from their arrogant offensive of 1967–69, members and organizations of the upper bourgeoisie were unwilling to affirm publicly that they had pinned their hopes on Peronism. That quite a few of them had done so was clear from my interviews, which also indicated that many members of that bourgeoisie, frightened by the prospect of an immense social explosion, collaborated with Lanusse in warding off a coup. Corroborating this information, Frederick Turner notes that among the 120 entrepreneurs he interviewed in 1973, Peronism had "gained significant support among the industrialists and even among the landowners." This support was based on the perception of these respondents that Perón had an "ability to control the masses" ("The Study of Argentine Politics through Survey Research," pp. 95–96).

4. PERÓN'S RETURN AND THE DEMISE OF
THE GREAT NATIONAL ACCORD

In October 1972, shortly after Cámpora presented the "Minimum Bases for an Agreement on National Reconstruction," it was announced (for the umpteenth time) that Perón would return to Argentina.[8] Many believed up to the last moment that this announcement was another ploy by Perón.[9] But Perón returned to Argentina in November 1972, after seventeen years in exile. The enormous impact of his arrival was evident in the exultation of the Peronists, whose leader had at long last come home ("in search of peace," as he was careful to stress),* putting the lie to Lanusse's taunts that he would never dare risk his life by returning to Argentina. A huge crowd tried to greet Perón at the airport but was thwarted by military forces. Perón was obliged to stay at the airport hotel. It was not clear whether he was being held there as a prisoner or, as the government argued, to prevent an attempt on his life, but television newscasts, which showed the hotel surrounded by soldiers with their guns aimed at the building, gave the impression that the former was closer to the truth.[10] Shortly thereafter he moved to a private residence, and on December 14, without previous announcement, Perón departed for Paraguay without having held the massive gatherings that many had anticipated, and in circumstances indicative of sharp conflicts within Peronism.† His followers' expectations seemed to have been disappointed, and many of his adversaries, anxious to believe that this was true, congratulated themselves on the failure of his return and the damage it had supposedly done to Peronism's electoral prospects.[11]

Though much of what had been expected did not occur, a different interpretation would have emerged had some additional factors been

---

*See the statements by Cámpora in *La Nación*, October 3, p. 6 and October 22, p. 18, 1972. Just before he returned to Argentina, Perón reaffirmed his peaceful intentions: "I feel neither hatred nor rancor. This is no time to be thinking of revenge. I return as a peacemaker. . . . They call me, I come. Whoever believes that I have a taste for discord is mistaken. I have no taste for discord and no thirst for power. It matters little whether I become President; I only seek to serve my country in whatever way I can, in whatever capacity I am needed. The discord must end" (*La Nación*, November 1, 1972, p. 12). Despite these assurances, the guerrilla and various youthful sectors viewed Perón's homecoming in combative terms, greatly increasing the tension of the situation. For example, on November 9 Galimberti gave the following advice to those welcoming Perón at the airport: "Whoever has stones, bring stones; whoever has something else, bring something else" (*La Opinión*, November 11, 1973, p. 2). Because the radicalized sectors took charge of organizing the large crowds that went to greet Perón at the airport, the union leaders remained conspicuously inactive during these events.

†Most notably, those pitting the youthful sectors against union leaders, which became explicit the day that Perón moved to a private residence (*La Nación*, November 19, 1972, pp. 1, 20) and continued thereafter, often with considerable violence. On these confrontations, see *Primera Plana*, February 8, 1973, p. 10.

taken into consideration. In the first place, Perón, in a de facto negation of Lanusse's efforts to force him into a government-sponsored accord, held a meeting with representatives of most of the political parties. All who attended the meeting went out of their way to express support for democratization "without exclusions," and to announce their commitment to "national" and "popular" policies—a position that was symbolized by the participation of representatives of the CGT and CGE.[12] Perón was not exaggerating when he claimed that with that meeting, a few days after his arrival in Argentina, *he* had produced the Great National Accord. A second sign that Perón's opponents had been too quick to rejoice was the formal constitution of FREJULI, and soon afterward the announcement that Cámpora would be the Peronist candidate for president (and hence the candidate of the FREJULI coalition), and Vicente Solano Lima, of the Popular Conservative party, the candidate for vice-president.

This candidacy was imposed by Perón, who left Cámpora's name in a sealed envelope moments before leaving Argentina. The announcement of the candidacy gave rise to a tumultuous meeting of the Justicialist Party, at which most union leaders expressed opposition to Cámpora and proposed instead that Perón himself run for president. This motion was rejected by a majority composed of political personnel and the Peronist Youth, who argued, not without reason, that deciding on Perón's candidacy at that stage of the process was tantamount to provoking a coup. Cámpora's image, of a mediocre politician whose main distinction was his iron loyalty to Perón, also dismayed the other parties in the coalition. Moreover, Vicente Solano Lima, with his conservative background, displeased many radicalized sectors.*

*See *Análisis-Confirmado*, December 19, 1972, p. 12. The government (and most political observers) seriously miscalculated the number of votes the Cámpora–Solano Lima ticket would draw. This estimation was based on surveys, which were analyzed in a very unsophisticated way. According to those surveys, the Cámpora–Solano Lima ticket had no chance of receiving more than 40 percent of the vote and would most likely get about 35 percent (*La Nación*, December 23, 1972, p. 6). Under the new electoral law, those figures made a second round certain, thus opening the way for a variety of possibilities that centered on either replacing Cámpora with someone more palatable or defeating him with a second-round coalition among the Radicals, Manrique, and several minor anti-Peronist parties. For examples of such speculation, see *Análisis-Confirmado*, January 16, pp. 4, 6, February 20, pp. 5, 11, and February 27, pp. 7, 11, 1973; *Panorama*, February 8, 1973, p. 12; and *La Nación*, which as late as March 4, 1973 (p. 8) asserted that "a second round appears inevitable." Mor Roig, just prior to the elections, also took it for granted that a second round would be held (*Panorama*, March 8, 1973, p. 14). Lanusse admits this error in *Mi Testimonio* (p. 274). Interestingly, these incorrect assessments of the electoral strength of the Cámpora–Solano Lima ticket reduced the probability of a coup during the crucial months that preceded the election.

A third factor was that, according to all indications, the sheer fact that Perón had returned gave an enormous boost to his followers. Many probably reasoned that if their old leader had not held the massive rallies they had anticipated, it was because he had already won the game and could afford to sit out the brief time remaining before the government changed hands. Finally, Perón's presence in Argentina, sending conciliatory messages by television, embracing the leaders of other political parties, voicing the widespread discontent with the liberals and the military, and projecting the image of a good-natured old man who had risen above personal ambition, probably drew into the FREJULI camp an important bloc of still undecided voters.

To the obvious dismay of the armed forces, and in spite of Lanusse's persistent calls for a government-controlled transition,* the last vestiges of hope for an accord between the political parties and the armed forces disappeared with Perón's return.† By the end of 1972 all the political parties had nominated their candidates, and the electoral campaign began in earnest. Even though the proscription of Perón had removed the major obstacle to the elections, the possibility of a coup was discussed right up to the last minute.‡ The Peronists' refusal to participate in the defunct accord partly accounts for this uncertainty, but other factors were also responsible. One was the alarming campaign of

---

*Lanusse, reiterating some well-known themes, said, "Neither now nor in the future will the armed forces be shoved aside; they will participate in the process both at present and after the electoral act. . . . The armed forces seek and must reach a compromise with the next constitutional government, a common program of tasks to be accomplished. In so doing we shall be performing a service for our people by guaranteeing the security of what must be the political and institutional stability of the political future of the country" (*La Nación*, December 5, 1972, pp. 1, 24). When these calls went unheeded, Lanusse made other statements that sounded less like threats than expressions of the government's impotence: "Without denying the errors that the government has committed . . . I feel an obligation to affirm today my hope for ultimate success, despite events that have tarnished that hope and have caused me deep concern. . . . Our country has enough common sense to demand that the political parties adopt a responsible attitude, even at a certain political price. . . . Is it really possible to dispense with the military institutions which, at the risk of their own breakdown, engineered a truce in a struggle that could only have led to tyranny or anarchy?" (*La Nación*, December 30, 1972, pp. 1, 20). For subsequent statements, see *La Opinión*, January 26, 1973, p. 13.

†As mentioned earlier, Peronism (and later FREJULI) repeatedly declined to participate in such an accord. After the "Pact of Guarantees" had been signed in the context of *La Hora del Pueblo* and a meeting in Buenos Aires between Balbín and Perón had produced a joint proposal for "national pacification" (*La Nación*, November 22, 1972, p. 1), Radicalism also made it known that it would not enter any agreement with the government (*La Nación*, January 19, 1973, pp. 1, 6).

‡This uncertainty can be traced in *Panorama*, January 4, p. 12, February 8, p. 12, February 15, p. 12, February 22, p. 12, and March 8, p. 10, 1973. A few days before the election, *La Nación* (March 1, 1973, p. 6), in an article entitled "The Doubt Is Not Dispelled," again raised the question of whether a coup would occur.

Cámpora and (surprisingly, given his conservative background) of Solano Lima,* which was organized and promoted by the youthful and radicalized sectors of Peronism—including guerrilla organizations—whose participation became all the more visible with the consequent retreat of the national union leaders into the background. Another factor was the verbal offensive that Perón launched after leaving the country, which contrasted with the conciliatory tone he had maintained in Argentina and which led some observers to speculate that his goal was to provoke a coup in order to conceal the electoral weakness of Peronism.†

There were also rumors that the armed forces, instead of mounting a coup, might decide to hold elections after proscribing FREJULI or vetoing its candidates.‡ But arguments against risking a social explosion weighed as convincingly against a veto as they did against a coup. What happened instead was that Lanusse and his group, inspired by their Brazilian colleagues, explored the possibility of promulgating unilaterally an "Institutional Act" that would impose "legal obligations" on the next government—basically the same ones they had tried to obtain through the "Great National Accord."[13] They soon realized, however, that such obligations would be impossible to enforce. With these options apparently unworkable, the commanders in chief finally issued a statement in which they pledged themselves and their branches of the armed forces to abide in the future by a set of provisions, which did little more than indicate how far the armed forces had retreated in so short a

---

*The FREJULI candidates made enthusiastic references to the guerrilla organizations, whose songs, slogans, and banners were very visible in the electoral campaign. This conspicuous presence of the guerrillas gave rise to much alarmed commentary (*Panorama*, February 1, 1973, p. 14, *Análisis–Confirmado*, January 30, 1973, p. 5, and *La Nación*, January 21, 1973, pp. 1 and 7). When Perón named Cámpora as the presidential candidate, and union leaders and some of Peronism's political personnel attempted to sabotage the candidacy, the radicalized sectors gave up their earlier anti-election stance and threw themselves fully into the electoral contest.

†Perón went so far as to say that "the military are all idiots" (*Panorama*, February 8, 1973, p. 13) and that "they are good for nothing but riding horses" (*Panorama*, March 1, 1973, p. 14, in a statement that included elegies to Mao). The radicalized sectors, for their part, saw in statements such as these the true Perón, and interpreted the electoral road as a clever strategy by which Perón would increase his power in order to set in motion the "National Revolution." For speculation that Perón's goal was to trigger a coup and about the motivations that might lie behind this alleged objective, see, for example, *Análisis–Confirmado*, February 20, 1973, p. 5.

‡This alternative is discussed in the sources cited in the preceding notes. The now-famous possibility that Lanusse would launch an *autogolpe* was still discussed, but Perón made explicit what many now realized: "Lanusse has no interest in a new coup; it would come at his own expense" (*Panorama*, February 15, 1973, p. 12).

time.* When the admirals, brigadiers, and generals on active duty were asked to endorse this document (in the expectation that the next government would select commanders in chief from among those who signed), only the generals assented,[14] underlining how much support Lanusse had lost within the armed forces. The navy, a bastion of anti-Peronism, took the opportunity to express its disgust at the way in which the army had handled the situation, while the air force, in which the nationalists predominated, seized the occasion to break publicly with the military liberals. Thus, Lanusse and his group saw the process they had initiated through to its end, but under conditions very different from those they had anticipated.†

In February 1973 Lanusse, in a last-ditch effort to resurrect the accord, made an agonizing visit to Spain to meet personally with Perón,[15] who had returned there after a short stay in Paraguay. The meeting never took place. No agreement was reached, and the Spanish government arranged some embarrassing diplomatic ceremonies to impart some semblance of meaning to this curious visit. By March 1973, the accord and the guarantees had come to nought. Worse yet, with the union leaders and the more moderate Peronist personages having withdrawn from the FREJULI campaign, it was the radicalized sectors of Peronism that set the campaign's dominant tone and provided its major impetus.‡

*La Nación, January 25, 1973, pp. 1, 20. In this statement the commanders in chief agreed "(1) to respect and maintain into the future the full operation of representative institutions, in order to assure an authentic democracy that allows for the exercise of the rights of the inhabitants and the full enjoyment of liberty; (2) to assure the independence and permanence of the Judiciary as a guarantee of the provisions, rights and principles embodied in the constitution; (3) to rule out the granting of an indiscriminate amnesty for those duly convicted of crimes relating to subversion or terrorism; (4) to share, as members of the national cabinet, the responsibilities of the government produced by the expression of the popular will, in such capacities as are fixed by the law and by other provisions, especially those relating to internal and external security."

†In an effort to do something and, probably, to reduce the likelihood of a coup, the commanders in chief issued a decree (La Nación, February 7, 1972, pp. 1, 16) prohibiting Perón from returning to Argentina until the new government was in office. They also initiated judicial proceedings against FREJULI for the slogan "Cámpora to government, Perón to power," and for allegedly violating legislation that prohibited expressions of sympathy for acts of violence and terrorist organizations (La Nación, February 6, 1972, pp. 1, 12). These proceedings languished and no decision was made about them until the elections, when they were dismissed.

‡As already noted, the fears of the armed forces and the upper bourgeoisie were to some extent alleviated by the Peronist political personnel and union leaders, who gave confidential assurances that both they and Perón, once installed in the government, would put in their place the groups that for the moment neither they nor Perón could control (my interviews). Statements by the CGT and the 62 Organizations (La Nación, February 16, 1973, p. 10) calling for "national pacification" and making friendly references to the armed forces had a similar effect.

On March 11, 1973, in an atmosphere thick with rumors of a coup, the Cámpora–Solano Lima ticket came within a hair's breadth of winning fifty percent of the total vote cast. This margin obviated the need for a runoff election, and the Radical party, which had run a distant second, conceded defeat. So did the government, which looked with trepidation on the prospect of another, even more explosive and hopeless, electoral contest.

The military personnel attending Cámpora's May 25, 1973, inauguration received a crude reminder of the hostility that had accumulated against them with the insults and chants of the assembled multitude, which sang, "They're gone, they're gone, and never shall return," and hailed guerrilla groups parading in military formation. The radicalized Peronist sectors gained decisive influence in the presidency, the Interior Ministry, several important provincial governments, and other areas. An amnesty was extended immediately to all political prisoners. The "antisubversive" courts established during Lanusse's government were dismantled. A new army commander in chief was appointed, forcing most generals into early retirement. Civilians were appointed to many of the state institutions and public enterprises that the armed forces had dominated since the overthrow of Perón in 1955. These decisions meant that none of the conditions that Lanusse and the armed forces had tried to impose had survived the great wave that brought Cámpora to the presidency. José Otero, a leader of the metalworkers' union—the bastion of Vandorism—was named Labor Minister, and José Gelbard, the leader of the CGE, was appointed Economy Minister. Despite the woeful tone in which the upper bourgeoisie lamented this series of misfortunes, they stood by their hapless military tutors until the end. The long-awaited unification of business organizations occurred, but under the command of the CGE, which, through Gelbard's ministry, wielded as much control over the state's economic apparatus as Krieger Vasena had exercised during his now incredibly remote term in office. If any doubts remained about the extent to which things had changed, they were dispelled when the presidents of Chile and Cuba, Allende and Dorticós, were given prominent roles in the presidential inauguration ceremonies.

5. WHAT DID NOT HAPPEN AND WHAT WAS NOT SAID

The collapse of the authoritarian experiment of 1966 and the multiform popular irruption that followed it might have been an extraordinary opportunity not only to implant a political democracy but also to advance the construction of a more egalitarian society. But as we have seen in examining the main political and ideological tendencies at work, a catastrophic denouement was more likely. Barrington Moore writes of "suppressed historical alternatives,"[16] difficult but not impossible options cast aside in favor of others that ultimately lead to tragic consequences. The historical context to which Moore refers—Germany after the First World War—is not that dissimilar to the one that concerns us here. In both cases too many actors ignored, or discovered too late, that by playing the game proposed by abundant and powerful authoritarian currents, and by failing at crucial junctures to affirm unequivocally their commitment to democratic and socially progressive values, they could not but abandon to a terrible fate the social sectors they claimed to represent.

Why did this happen? Why did so many, from such diverse perspectives, generate the worst possible conditions for democracy? In seeking to answer these questions, we undertake the formidable challenge of trying to explain why something did *not* occur. One reason that democracy had such slim chances was that the collapse of the BA did not alter the inflexibility of the armed forces and the upper bourgeoisie. This was demonstrated by their failure to recognize that the best political solution once Onganía had been deposed, even in terms of their own interests, would have been to support democratization. Worse still, the Levingston experience, coming in the wake of Onganía and the Cordobazo, led not only to the rapid disillusionment of the military and the dominant classes but also to the ratification of the widespread perception that only violence would be effective in combatting those who had entrenched themselves in the state apparatus—an impression seemingly corroborated by the second Cordobazo and Levingston's subsequent downfall. Only then, with a broad and wrathful opposition and a deteriorating economic situation—was Lanusse's proposal made,* only to acquire in short order a not undeserved image as a manipulation centered on the complex personalities and ambitions of Lanusse and Perón. Limited, late, and ambiguous as it was, this call for democracy might have been effectively appropriated by political parties. But two factors were absent that might have facilitated this outcome: a reasonably

---

*In Brazil in 1973–74, President Geisel, whose government faced neither an armed challenge nor intense popular activation, proposed a "slow, gradual and secure opening." If even Geisel soon ran into unexpected hitches (such as the victory of the opposition party in the 1974 elections), Lanusse and his advisers were in for a far rougher future.

strong party system and an unequivocal commitment to democracy on the part of the parties that had the support of a decisive proportion of the electorate. (The latter comprised only the Peronists and the Radicals; none of the others had carried more than ten percent of the vote in previous elections.)

Perón held an unabashedly nationalist and corporatist vision of state and society. His 1946–55 governments had opened the way for the activation of the popular sector and for fundamental advances in its social and economic position, but they had never been renowned for adherence to democratic practices. It was not from Perón that one could expect an unequivocal commitment to a democratic regime. During the 1969–72 period, Perón uttered not a single word that raised the issue of democracy, except for his sharp criticism of the quasi-plebiscitarian and military-controlled version that Lanusse proposed. By deriding the very idea of political democracy as "liberal"—a term that in Argentina harks back to anti-popular and socially regressive positions—many of Perón's statements reinforced the authoritarian convictions of many currents within his movement. Moreover, the guerrilla groups and other organizations that set the dominant ideological tone for many youthful and middle-sector Peronists were viscerally anti-democratic in their ideas, practices, and goals. The Peronist political personnel, most of whom were attuned to Perón's ideology and biases, did not convey the image that their support for electoral processes went beyond their desire for government positions. The union leaders, for their part, had made it clear all too often that their main concern was whether whatever state or regime happened to exist at the moment would permit them to advance their own goals and the immediate economic interests of their constituents.

The Radicals had failed for several decades to obtain more than twenty-five percent of the vote. Moreover, they were unable to decide whether to become the party that would give some continuity to the "Argentine Revolution" or to oppose vigorously what remained of it. The first option smacked of the official position that had cost the Radicals dearly in the 1958 elections, which Frondizi had won with Peronist support. Furthermore, it was a Radical government, after all, that had been overthrown in 1966. Full-fledged opposition, on the other hand, was hampered by the presence of Mor Roig and other Radicals in the Lanusse government, as well as by the reluctance of the party's leadership to do anything that might precipitate another coup. This caution led to some tactical successes but prevented the Radicals from facing the crucial question of what sort of democracy, if any, it would be possible to construct. In consequence the main channel was closed through which opposition to the BA might have converged with aspirations which, behind so much violence and fear, probably existed in Argentine society for, to put it simply, a more civilized coexistence.

For these reasons, the cautious discourse of the Radical party had little chance of finding a receptive audience. Most of the smaller parties likewise did little to enhance the prospects for democracy. Some had staked their chances on a very undemocratic proscription of Peronism, hoping to become the beneficiaries of a last-minute transfer of Peronist votes. Others, anxious to ride the coattails of a Peronist electoral victory, refrained from doing anything that might irritate Perón or the main currents in his movement—such as expressing an unequivocally pro-democratic position. No bigger contribution to democracy was made by the candidacies of Manrique, Alsogaray, and Martínez, whose backgrounds could be traced either to the BA implanted in 1966 or to prior authoritarian experiences in recent Argentine history. Even the democratic credentials of the center-left coalition made up of Alende's party, the faction of the Christian Democrats led by Sueldo, and the Communist party—which, apart from Manrique, the Peronists and the Radicals, could alone aspire to more than five percent of the vote—were open to question. Sueldo and Alende had been among the few political leaders who had publicly expressed support for Levingston's nationalist adventure, and were therefore the quickest to condemn Lanusse's proposed transition as a farce. In short, even the parties constituted an uncongenial milieu for the democratic discourse that might possibly have turned the country away from the abyss toward which it was sliding.

I have argued[17] that the history of Argentina is viewed from the most diverse standpoints as one of repeated failure. Everyone seeks to identify, according to his or her own biases, the moment at which the great country that might have been was led astray by the treachery of their chosen culprits, ranging from "oligarchs" to "populist demagogues." The shared feeling of frustration that a great national potential has been squandered has fed a particularly paranoid imagination, out of which have come the bitter stories of the right and the left, of nationalists and liberals, of oligarchs and populists, each blaming the other for the country's real or imagined failures.[18] These views have exerted enormous influence on the formation of Argentine culture and, behind it, on the myths that have shaped the harsh conflicts of this country. Such recriminations intensified greatly toward the end of the 1960s, until they dominated the ideological climate in which the political currents of the epoch defined their positions. Following the events of 1969, recriminations pervaded the discourse of reactionaries and liberals seeking to account for the irruption of a threatening "rabble," and that of the currents that converged toward Peronism, captured by a mood of aggressive and chauvinistic nationalism. The latter contributed yet another trait to their syndrome of fascist radicalization: the profound anti-intellectualism of their intellectuals. The imperative was to act according to the dictates of Perón and the most radical and violent organizations. To think was viewed as damnable desertion. There were many anti-intellectual intellectuals, eager to plunge into revolutionary praxis, who fomented the idolization of violence to which many young persons proved suicidally receptive. Few—too few—intellectuals condemned unequivocally this verbal violence and the actual horrors it bred. This silence, born of fear and confusion, contributed to the unfolding of a situation where force of arms became the only way to defend one's position, and in which any argument against violence was viewed as a betrayal of some grandiose cause.

Undoubtedly, it was violent events like the Cordobazo that mortally wounded the BA. But it was not inevitable that such episodes would lead to the widespread belief that violence was the key to every door. When this conclusion was reached, and when it had been validated by the words and the silence of most of the intelligentsia, an entire society prostrated itself before the deeds and discourses of violence. With violence imposing itself on society, and in the absence of political actors and intellectuals who stood publicly and explicitly for other values, the rancor inherited from Argentine history eliminated the last chances of avoiding the precipice.

To be sure, there were elections in March 1973, won cleanly by the majority, which put to rest what little remained of the BA. But if these elections signaled the transitory defeat of the classes, factions, military officers and *técnicos* that had implanted and tried to consolidate the BA, they did not imply a victory for those who had done the most to defeat them. This discovery was made when the Cámpora government was terminated by a palace coup just a few weeks after its inauguration. This event, supported by the armed forces, the union leaders, and a bourgeoisie terrified by a radicalization which during that brief government surpassed what we have examined here, opened the way—culminating the irony of this story—for Perón's third presidency. Only then did Perón detach himself from the guerrillas, condemn the violence, and announce his commitment to democracy. It was too late. A few months later he died, leaving the presidency to his widow and the most governmental power to López Rega, as the war of all against all reached its climax. In this vortex, fed by a peculiar palace irrationality and by violence, fear, and brutalization more widespread and cruel than what we have studied here, Argentina entered its darkest night.

NOTES

1. Adam Przeworski, "Some Problems in the Study of the Transition to Democracy," in *Transitions from Authoritarian Rule: Prospects for Democracy,* ed. O'Donnell, Schmitter, and Whitehead (Baltimore: Johns Hopkins University Press, 1986); and Guillermo O'Donnell, "Notas para el estudio de procesos de democratización a partir del Estado burocratico-autoritario," *Estudios CEDES,* Buenos Aires, 1979.

2. A contemporary analysis of the characteristics and potential of what the source terms the "new social opposition" is given in *Pasado y Presente* 4, no. 1 (esp. pp. 3–29) and no. 2 (esp. pp. 179–203) (Buenos Aires: 1973).

3. Among the numerous collections of Perón's speeches and statements that were published or reprinted during this period, the ones that bear most directly on the themes discussed here are *La comunidad organizada* (Buenos Aires: Editorial CEPE, 1973), *Doctrina peronista* (Buenos Aires: Ediciones Macacha Güemes, 1973), *La tercera posición* (Buenos Aires: Ediciones Argentinas, 1974), and *Perón y los empresarios* (Buenos Aires: Confederación General Económica, 1973).

4. For an analysis from this perspective, see *Antropología Tercer Mundo,* no. 11 (December 1972) and no. 12 (February/March 1973). This source is noteworthy because it combines a quite lucid discussion of some of the contradictions and ambiguities of those radicalized tendencies with an exaltation of Perón and typical expressions of hostility toward the "union bureaucracy" and the Peronist political personnel.

5. Among the abundant literature on this theme see esp. Walter Laqueur, ed., *Fascism: A Reader's Guide. Analyses, Interpretations, Bibliography* (Berkeley and Los Angeles: University of California Press, 1976).

6. An illustrative diatribe against these "bureaucrats" is Jorge Correa's *Los Jerarcas sindicales* (Buenos Aires: Editorial Obrador, 1974).

7. Among the data to which I had access, only the survey of March 1971 contains this disaggregation.

8. *La Nación,* October 3, 1972, p. 6, among many others.

9. See, for example, *La Nación,* October 7, p. 6 and October 22, p. 6, 1972, the latter reporting what was confirmed in my interviews: neither the government nor the political parties thought Perón would return.

10. *La Nación,* November 17 and 18, 1972. A good account of these events may be found in the "Cultural Supplement" of *La Opinión,* November 11, 1973, pp. 1–7.

11. See, among many others, *La Nación*, December 31, 1972, p. 6, and January 21, 1973, p. 6, and *Análisis-Confirmado*, January 16, 1973, p. 8.

12. *La Nación*, November 21, 1972, p. 1.

13. *La Nación*, January 14, 1973, p. 8.

14. *La Nación*, February 8, 1973, pp. 1, 18. Only one army general declined to sign.

15. According to my interviews. On this trip, see *La Nación*, February 24, 1972, p. 1.

16. Barrington Moore, *On Injustice: The Social Bases of Obedience and Revolt* (New York: M. E. Sharp, 1978), p. 376.

17. Guillermo O'Donnell, *Modernization and Bureaucratic-Authoritarianism*.

18. For a good discussion of this theme and related ones, see Tulio Halperín Donghi, *Argentina en el callejón* (Montevideo: Editorial Arcos, 1964).

Methodological Appendix

This book is based on a large quantity and a wide variety of data. Their sources, treatment, and limitations are discussed in this appendix.

I. QUANTITATIVE DATA

The quantitative data consist primarily of time series for the 1966–72 period. Where the interpretation of longer-range trends was important to the analysis, the series were extended back to 1955 or 1956.* I have used monthly data wherever possible, since annual data are of limited use (and are sometimes misleading) in tracing the rapidly shifting conflicts and alliances described in this book.

Five data sets may be distinguished.

(1) The largest, covering various types of protest, was compiled from the January 1955 to December 1972 issues of the daily newspaper *La Razón*.† Each event was registered separately, but I subsequently aggregated the data on a monthly basis in order to facilitate the analysis. Time series were compiled for several forms of protest: (a) strikes and work stoppages;‡ (b) workplace occupa-

---

*These time series are stored on magnetic tape with approximately 10,000 records. For help in putting this data into machine-readable form, I thank the University of Michigan and Ricardo Milutin in Buenos Aires.

†A comparison of several daily newspapers revealed that *La Razón* had the best coverage of such events over the period as a whole.

‡A *work stoppage* refers to a period not longer than one day in which labor is voluntarily withheld. It should be noted that newspaper coverage of work stoppages and other forms of protest most probably underrepresents events in the interior of the country, with the likely exception of guerrilla activity. Unfortunately, there is no better source for such data. The alternative, the *Boletín de estadísticas sociales* (published by the Ministry of Labor), provides figures for strikes and work stoppages in the federal capital but not for the country as a whole or even for the Greater Buenos Aires area. Furthermore, these data

tions by workers and employees;* (c) demonstrations organized for ostensibly political purposes and/or by unions or political organizations; (d) acts of protest by university students; and (e) acts of armed violence.† I thank Carlos Alberto Giori, Jean-Noel Grau and Lila Milutin for their help in the arduous task of compiling these data.

(2) Time series for economic and financial data, presented wherever possible on a monthly basis. The sources for these data (and for those in categories 3, 4, and 5) are identified below the tables in which they are presented.

(3) Monthly and annual time series for public finances, in the compilation of which I had the assistance of Luis Ros.

(4) Monthly and annual time series for wages and salaries.

(5) National accounts data and annual time series for various industrial sectors and subsectors. I compiled these series from internal documents of the Banco Central de la República Argentina (BCRA); Andrés Fontana collaborated with me in analyzing them.

II. DOCUMENTARY SOURCES

(1) Business organizations: annual reports, various other publications, and statements in daily newspapers and other periodicals. The organizations covered include the Unión Industrial Argentina (UIA), Cámara Argentina de Comercio (CAC), Asociación Coordinadora de Instituciones Empresarias Libres (ACIEL), Sociedad Rural Argentina (SRA), Confederación de Asociaciones Rurales de La Pampa y Buenos Aires (CARBAP), and the Confederación General Economica (CGE).

(2) Workers' organizations: statements and documents published by the Confederación General de Trabajo (CGT) and statements by the CGT and the unions in the dailies *La Nación, La Razón,* and *Crónica.* I thank Ana María Barone, Emilia Basso, and Inés Holler for their help in assembling these data.

(3) Political parties and movements: various statements and documents.

---

are reported by the Labor Ministry just as they are received from the firms involved and only when the firms see fit to submit them. Using newspapers as a source for these data presents an additional problem: in many instances a newspaper will report the beginning of a strike but not the date on which it ended or the number of participants. Owing to the high incidence of missing values on these latter aspects, I analyzed strikes and work stoppages only in terms of their number and geographical location.

*Data for 1964 (the year the CGT launched its "Plan of Action") were excluded from the analysis because the daily newspapers were simply unable to register the thousands of workplace occupations that took place during that year.

†Acts of armed violence refer to: (1) the explosion of bombs with the obvious intention of intimidating or injuring persons and/or causing damage to property; (2) assassinations and assassination attempts allegedly motivated by political aims; (3) kidnappings for allegedly political reasons; (4) robberies expressly for the purpose of financing guerrilla operations; and (5) various acts of "armed propaganda": principally, the capture of radio or television stations, the hijacking of trucks carrying food or clothing and the distribution of their contents among poor populations, and—most important—temporary takeovers of cities and towns.

(4) Officials of the national government: speeches, statements and press conferences published in *La Nación* or by official sources; editorials and articles in the dailies *La Nación, La Prensa, Clarín,* and *La Opinión;* in the weeklies *Primera Plana, Confirmado, Análisis,* and *Panorama;* and in other publications cited in the text (though only in the case of those listed here did I examine all the issues throughout the period studied in this book).

III. INTERVIEWS

I conducted interviews with persons who played important parts in the processes analyzed in this book and/or who had access to privileged information concerning those processes. Several aspects of these interviews should be mentioned.

(1) Interviewees were selected on the basis of the positions they occupied and what I believed they knew about issues I found important or intriguing.

(2) Since the interviews were conducted as conversations in which I tried to make the key questions as inconspicuous as possible, all questions were open-ended and were asked with no questionnaire in view.

(3) Since the interviewees tended to become reluctant when I used a tape recorder, I confined myself to taking notes as well as I could, completing them immediately after each interview. In two cases even my note-taking caused the interviewee considerable nervousness.

(4) I was previously acquainted with approximately half of the interviewees.

(5) All interviewees were assured complete anonymity, which was demanded not just by elementary professional ethics but also by the ever-present danger of violence and by the fact that many had held or were holding top posts in government, class organizations or political parties. Consequently, the information that forms the basis for some of the findings and conjectures of this analysis must remain in the half-light. This limitation is less serious than it seems at first: the main function of the interviews was to alert me to processes that were unfolding or had unfolded, and to suggest how crucial actors of the period perceived and evaluated those processes. Many of these processes may be detected in readily accessible sources, which I quote whenever pertinent.

(6) I conducted the interviews with several types of actors: (a) seventy-two civilian and military personnel who served between June 1966 and March 1973 as top officials in the national government, including presidents of the Republic, cabinet ministers, secretaries and undersecretaries, cabinet advisers, and national directors of various ministries. These seventy-two interviewees represented about 20 percent of the top government officials. Twenty-seven of the seventy-two interviews involved two meetings. Thirty of those officials were current office-holders. In only four cases did persons decline to be interviewed. In six other cases the interviewee was so reluctant or evidently uncandid that I decided not to use the information I gathered in the interview. (b) Forty-six union leaders, leaders of business organizations, and top officials of political parties (specifically, those parties which in the pre-1966 period had enjoyed the most electoral support). I was previously acquainted with all of these persons.

(c) Directors of large enterprises: presidents of boards of directors and general managers or financial managers of thirty-four large industrial firms, twenty-two of which were TNC subsidiaries and twelve of which were among the hundred largest firms controlled by private Argentine capital. (d) Top leaders in the armed forces, most of them in the army. In addition to fourteen formal interviews conducted during 1971 and 1972, I held extensive conversations with approximately thirty other such officials throughout the 1966–72 period.

Index

ACIEL, 34–35, 146n, 154n, 196n19, 249n, 328
Agriculture, 103–5; profits in, 124–25, 285–86; wages in, 266. *See also* Pampean bourgeoisie
Air force, 52, 53n, 152, 200, 206; nationalists in, 318
Alemann, Roberto, 67n, 72–73
Alende, Oscar, 208n, 258, 322
Alonso, José, 68, 172n, 177n, 179n, 206n
Alsogaray, Álvaro, 57, 63–72, 258
Alsogaray, Julio, 39, 56–58, 63, 67, 146–56, 173, 322
Anídjar, Leonardo, 118
Anti-Peronism, 34, 153, 306, 312, 315n, 318
Anticommunism, 216, 229
Apter, David, xv, 21, 37n14, 164n
Aramburu, Pedro, 72, 203; assassination of, 187, 198, 234n, 241n, 243n, 306n; and presidency, 146, 153, 173–74, 186–87
Argentina: as capitalist economy, 22; social transformation in, 8–10
"Argentinazo", 233, 308, 311
Argentine Revolution, 58–59, 62–64, 147n, 198, 214; and armed forces, 145, 175; economic phase of, 59, 63, 75–76, 139, 140n; end of, 208; goals of, 184, 186n, 244; and nationalism, 222–24; and political parties, 74–75, 203, 321; political phase of, 59, 74–75, 146, 175n, 203, 321; social phase

of, 59, 75, 146–47, 153, 155, 157, 181; unions and, 68, 84
Armed forces: and Argentine Revolution, 145, 166, 175, 184; and BAs, 28, 33n, 304, 313; and Cámpora government, 319, 323; coercion by, 138–39, 192–93, 294; after Cordobazo, 171–75; and coup of (1966), 39, 227; and elections, 249, 256–57, 317–18; factions in, 44, 51–58; and government, 32, 48–49, 165, 173–74, 192–94, 199, 219, 236–39, 255, 284; and guerrillas, 172, 308; and Lanusse government, 236–40, 318; and Onganía government, 67, 69, 188, 195; and paternalists, 140, 158, 197; and Peronism, 47, 51, 232, 242, 248, 256, 301, 311n; and political parties, 60, 203, 209n, 214–15; and *pueblo*, 172, 245; support of, 187, 230, 241, 254n, 258. *See also* Military liberals
Army, 52, 58, 67, 152, 159, 200, 250n, 319; and Lanusse, 198
Arregui, Héctor Hernández, 234n
Assassinations, 171, 172n, 241n, 243n, 296, 300, 328n
Aufgang, Lidia, 168n
Ávila, Raúl, 159n
Ayza, Juan, 37n10

BA (bureaucratic authoritarianism), 31–33; and capitalism, 2–6, 194; end of, 209, 219, 236, 286, 300–313, 320, 323; opposition to, 164–67, 171–74,

182–85, 215, 229, 322; threat preceding, 29–31, 45, 58, 97, 103, 141–43, 161, 189–90, 194–95, 289
Bacha, Edmar, 100n5
Balbín, Ricardo, 257–58
Beef prices, 120–21, 179, 183, 206, 221–24, 270–71
Bisio, Raúl H., 47n
Blachman, Morris, 234n
Black market, 49, 206, 250, 277, 279–80; dollar on, 283
Bombings, 296–97, 328n
Borda, Guillermo, 67, 73, 75n, 83n, 146n, 159n; resignation of, 167
Borón, Atilio, 33n
Bourgeoisie, 2–3, 12, 13, 30–33, 42, 50, 67, 72, 272; and Cámpora government, 323; class interest of, 161–62, 184; industrial, 132, 286; and inflation, 92–93, 283; local, 33–35, 56, 90, 123, 125, 127, 160, 189, 194, 195, 209, 213, 216–17, 220; and nationalism, 224; and normalization, 135–42; and political parties, 203, 208, 301; and unions, 224, 250, 288; and violence, 303, 308. See also CGE; Pampean bourgeoisie; Upper bourgeoisie
Brazil, 6, 10, 22, 27–29, 40, 58, 77, 89, 320n; agrarian class in, 141; BA in, xiii, 117, 139, 144, 160, 161, 174n; economy in, 14n, 92, 97, 103, 134n
Brodersohn, Mario, 102n33
Buenos Aires, 63–64, 184; protest in, 291–92, 327n
Buenos Aires Stock Exchange, 33–34, 154n
Bureaucratic authoritarianism. See BA

CAC (Camara Argentina de Comercio), 33–35, 63n, 154n, 249n, 328
Calvar, José C., 293n
Cámpora, Héctor J., 232, 246n, 247, 259, 314–17; candidacy of, 316–19; government of, 319, 323
Canitrot, Adolfo, 100n6
Capital: commercial, 133, 138; concentration of, 213; domestic, 76, 126, 172, 201, 211; financial, 91, 93–94, 109, 132, 142–43, 193, 215, 286 (see also Speculation); foreign, 66, 117–18, 169–70, 213–14 (see also Transnational capital); industrial, 34–35, 91, 138, 212; long-term, 110, 278; private, 32–33, 63–64, 223, 330; restrictions on, 50, 166; short-term, 110, 278

Capital flight, 20, 169n, 170, 250, 277, 283; after Cordobazo, 173
Capitalism, 2–6, 8, 11–17; and BA, 78, 194; national, 11–12, 203; and nationalism, 150–51; and paternalism, 55; and Peronism, 195; state, 139, 190; threat to, 161
CARBAP, 34, 86n, 243n, 328
Cardoso, Fernando Henrique, xiv, 10n, 36n, 37n7, 164n
Castelo Branco, 58, 70n10, 77
Catholic Church, 55, 60, 148n, 153, 157, 185, 233, 306
Cavalcanti, Leonardo, 37n9
Cavarozzi, Marcelo, xiv, 7n, 8n, 69n2
Ceresole, Norberto, 44n
CGE (Confederación General Económica), 34–35, 80, 132n, 165–66, 175, 182–83, 213–17; and CGT, 218, 251, 259n; and Lanusse, 228–29, 245; leaders of, 216, 305, 319; and Levingston government, 200–202; and normalization, 86n, 125–28, 139, 150; and Peronism, 247n, 301, 312. See also Bourgeoisie, local
CGI, 34–36, 86n
CGT (Confederación General de Trabajo), 34, 47–48, 79–85, 153, 155–58, 176–79, 200, 204n, 250–51, 292, 315; and BA, 166, 213, 228; and CGE, 218, 259n; dissolution of, 83, 147–49; and Lanusse government, 244n, 245; leadership of, 64–68, 177, 305; legal recognition of, 257n; and Onganía government, 62n; and Peronism, 80, 229, 231, 247n, 311, 318n; and Plan of Action, 79–82, 178, 205, 328n. See also Unions
CGT de los Argentinos, 149–53, 157–58, 177, 178, 208n, 232
CGT-Calle Azopardo, 149–58, 177
Chile, 9–10, 27–29, 40, 134n, 319; BA in, xiii, 6, 160, 161; economy in, 22, 28, 77, 89, 97, 103, 134n, 141
Christian Democrats, 66, 208n, 258–59, 322
Citizenship, 1, 5–10, 32; rights of, 189
Clarín, 34
Classes, social, 12, 89, 141–42, 293; domination of, 2–6, 14; relations among, 2, 30, 162. See also Bourgeoisie; Popular sector
Collective bargaining, 154, 157, 177–82, 205, 212, 223–24, 228, 265
Collier, David, xiv, 7n, 36n, 101n19
Collier, Ruth Berins, 7n, 101n19

Communism, 45, 55, 70n15; fear of, 125, 141, 167n
Communist party, 208n, 258, 322
CONASE (National Security Council), 53n, 62, 79, 178, 188
Conceição Tavares, Maria de, 100n5
Confirmado, 34
Congress, 50; disbanding of, 62
Consejo Empresario Argentino, 133n
Construction, 103, 287; investment in, 107, 118n, 281; profits in, 123–29, 132, 285–86; wages in, 266
Construction workers' union, 84n, 150n
Cooke, John William, 234n
Córdoba, 159, 165, 212, 218; unions in, 149, 178, 188; violence in, 54, 67, 157, 308–10. See also Cordobazo
Cordobazo, 159–60, 171, 289, 295–97, 320; and BA, 188–89, 323; effect of, 164–76, 201–2, 221–22, 235, 277, 282–83, 313; second, 218–19
Cordone, Héctor, 47n
Corradi, Juan E., 234n
Correa, Jorge, 324n6
Credit cooperatives, 123, 125, 132
Crisis of accumulation, 25–29, 42, 138–39, 162, 194, 300
Crisis of domination, 29–39, 195
Crisis of government, 24–28, 42, 300
Crisis of regime, 24–28, 42, 300
Crisis of social domination, 91, 142, 161, 300
Crónica, 328
Cúneo, Dardo, 36n
Cyert, Richard, 37n13

Dagnino Pastore, José María, 168, 179, 180n, 182–83, 215, 221, 222, 282–83
Dahl, Robert, xv, 6n, 163n
de Couto e Silva, Golbery, 164n
de Pablo, Juan Carlos, 101n33, 115, 118n, 134n, 144n1, 226n41
de Souza, Amaury, 164n
Debt, foreign, 214, 280
Deficit, fiscal, 22, 24, 41, 65n, 67, 91, 98–99, 111, 142, 160, 251, 274–76, 277; reduction of, 94, 115–16
Delich, Francisco, 135n, 159n, 262n9
Democracy, political, 1, 6, 9–10, 239, 245, 320–24; demand for, 207, 227–28; suppression of, 32–33, 63, 75, 154
Demonstrations, 47, 149, 295, 328
Devaluation. See Peso, devaluation of
Diamand, Marcelo, 37n10, 102n33
Diamandouros, Nikifouros, 164n

Díaz Alejandro, Carlos, 92n, 100n5
Díaz Colodrero, 74, 146n
Dodson, Michael, 250n
Dollar, U.S., 48–49, 114, 224, 280, 283, 284
Donghi, Tulio Halperín, 325n18
Duejo, Gerardo, 196n26
Duval, Natalia, 262n9

Economic normalization. See Normalization, economic
Economic orthodoxy, 78, 86, 115, 192–95, 204, 251; costs of, 143–44; and investors, 95–99, 126, 134–35n, 214, 223
Economic Survey, 34
Economy: control of, 95; crisis of, 15–22, 29; deterioration of, 243–44, 249; growth of, 8–10, 59, 103–20, 133, 140, 156; transnationalization of, 1, 11–15. See also Inflation; Normalization, economic
Economy Ministry, 243, 251, 319
Elections, 60, 173, 234, 252–61, 304n, 314–19; conditions for, 238–41, 248, 260; demand for, 182n, 199, 204n, 207–8, 218, 251n; and Perón, 50, 235, 243–48, 253–57, 314–19; postponement of, 146n, 152, 154, 166–67, 198, 205, 246, 249
Electoral system, 65, 75n, 201
Evers, Tilman, 136n
Exploitation rates, 128–32, 135, 286–88
Exports, 11, 12, 14, 99n, 109, 219; withholding tax on, 85, 88, 118–21, 201

Factory occupations, 44n, 48, 50, 149, 184n, 188, 218, 230, 232, 289n
Fajnzlber, Fernando, 37n9
Faletto, Enzo, 10n, 37n7
Fascism, 33n, 56, 162n, 191, 307, 313, 323
Fayt, Carlos A., 69n1
Ferrer, Aldo, 200, 206, 210–20, 223, 228, 243
Fichet, Gerard, 37n10
Filho, Luis Viana, 70n10
Fishlow, Albert, 100n5
Flichman, Guillermo, 120n
Foreign exchange, 50, 88, 93, 99, 105, 108–9, 206, 223, 276; after Cordobazo, 169
Foxley, Alejandro, 100n5
Freels, John, Jr., 36n, 114n
FREJULI, 259, 315–19
Frenkel, Roberto, 101n33, 102n34, 144n3

Frondizi, Arturo, 42–44, 47n, 49n, 50n, 52, 57n, 208n, 259, 321

Gaba, Ernesto, 144n2, 226n41
Galimberti, Rodolfo, 234n, 242n, 259n, 307n, 314n
García Lupo, Rogelio, 99n1
Gazzera, Miguel, 44n
Gelbard, José B., 35, 166n, 215n, 319
González, Norberto, 37n10
Graham-Yooll, Andrew, 250n, 263n15
Great National Accord, 232, 238–40, 246, 249n, 256, 260–61, 317; and Perón, 252, 259n, 315
Greece, 160; BA in, 164n
Grondona, Mariano, 40n
Guerrilla activity, 171–72, 185, 201n, 205, 230, 252, 260, 289, 296, 300, 327n; beginning of, 159, 165, 176–77, 184
Guerrilla organizations, 174n, 187, 233, 297, 302–5; and Perón, 240, 248–49, 322–24; and Peronism, 213, 229–31, 234n, 301, 306–11, 317—19, 321; and repression, 210, 243, 250, 292

Hellman, Ronald, 234n
Hewlett, Sylvia Ann, 7n
Hirschman, Albert O., 37n11
Hodges, Donald, 234n, 262n15
Huntington, Samuel P., 38n15

Illia, 39, 41, 42, 48; government of, 86n
Imports, 41n, 78, 99n, 109, 180, 221, 222; ban on, 249–50; duties on, 85, 101n25, 116, 126n, 201–2, 212
Industry, 8, 17–23, 34–35, 104, 106, 193, 287; productivity in, 129–30; profits for, 285–86. See also Capital
Inflation, 22, 29, 41n, 108–15, 143, 169, 292; and BA, 58–59, 65n, 91; causes of, 31, 66–67, 87, 114–15, 181, 222; control of, 46, 85, 114, 125, 133, 134, 156; effect of, 90–93, 104, 109, 213, 223, 280n; and speculation, 277, 283–86; and wages, 44, 79, 93, 250, 265, 270, 294
Investment, 20, 87, 117–18; decline in, 66, 78, 249n; domestic, 41–42, 108, 134–35, 222, 281; foreign, 22, 41, 85–86, 109, 139, 169–70, 212–14, 221, 277–79. See also Private investment; Public investment; Transnational capital

James, Daniel, 233n
Jelin, Elizabeth, 292n

Justicialist party, 256n, 259, 315–19. See also Peronism

Kaufman, Robert, 7n
Kidnappings, 243n, 296, 303–4, 328n
Kohl, James, 263n15
Krieger Vasena, Adalbert, 67, 72–73, 76, 157, 319; and devaluation, 181; and elections, 153n; program of, 83–88, 96n, 97, 139, 183, 213, 215 (see also Normalization, economic); resignation of, 130, 140, 166–68, 171, 220

La Hora del Pueblo, 207–10, 214–18, 228, 316n; and Peronism, 213, 240, 247n, 261, 312; and Lanusse, 245
La Nación, 34, 328, 329
La Opinión, 34
La Prensa, 34
La Razón, 34, 327, 328
Laclau, Ernesto, 24n, 36n2, 159n
Lamounier, Bolivar, 164n
Landi, Oscar, 24n, 36n2
Lanusse, Alejandro, 56–58, 146, 164n, 175, 186, 209n, 239, 322; and armed forces, 152, 156, 200, 318; candidacy of, 253–58; and elections, 247–61, 315n, 316–17; and Levingston, 206–8, 218; and Perón, 168, 207n, 232, 235, 242, 253, 314; and unions, 228, 250; and upper bourgeoisie, 198, 228
Lanusse government, 227–61; coup against, 244–46; goal of, 229; and economy, 264–89; political solution of, 236–41, 284, 294, 309–13, 320–22; protest during, 289–300, 302–5
Laqueur, Walter, 324n5
Lara Resende, André, 100n5
Law of Mandatory Arbitration, 65–66, 68
Law of Professional Associations, 64, 80, 83, 155, 176n, 178n, 202
Lechner, Norbert, 24n, 37n12
Levingston, Roberto M., 57, 199–200, 206, 229
Levingston government, 78, 200–207, 210–24, 236, 240; economy of, 201–2, 211–14, 221–24, 264; and nationalism, 188, 201–4, 211–21, 322; ouster of, 216–19, 238, 309, 320
Liberals, 72–79, 83, 154–58, 168, 172, 185–87, 198–200, 205, 244, 302; and economy, 95, 134–38, 163, 219, 264; and elections, 152, 236; and Lanusse, 198, 229; and Perón, 235, 242. See also Military liberals

Linck, Delfina, xiv(n), 37n9
Linz, Juan, 55, 69n6
Litt, John, 263n15
López Aufranc, Alcides, 229
López Rega, José, 234, 246n, 262n14, 311, 324
Luco, Francisco, 202, 203, 212

McLoughlin, Eduardo, 200, 203, 220
Mallon, Richard D., 37n10, 92n, 102n33, 125n, 170n
Manrique, Francisco, 200, 218, 258, 315n, 322
March, James, 37n13
Margenat, Nidia, 120n, 196n26
Martínez, Eziquiel, 258, 322
Martínez de Hoz, José A., 67n, 72, 133n, 303n
Martínez Paz, Enrique, 59–60n, 63, 67
Marxism, 148, 232, 245, 307
Metalworkers' union, 64, 66, 182, 319
Mexico, 6n, 10, 204; economy in, 14n
Military. See Armed forces
Military liberals, 54n, 56–58, 61, 63, 146, 173, 193–94; and BA, 76, 219, 228, 323; and Lanusse, 252–58, 318; and political solution, 237–38, 245
Miller, James, 262n15
Money supply, 79; expansion of, 115, 223, 250; restriction of, 87, 94, 180–83, 221, 277
Montoneros, 187, 233–34, 242n, 247n, 306–7, 311n
Moore, Barrington, 320, 325n16
Mor Roig, Arturo, 208, 227–28, 249n, 255, 259n, 321; and elections, 253n, 260, 315n
Moreno, Oscar, 159n
Moulián, Tomás, 100n5
Movement of Third World Priests, 159, 250n
Moyano Llerena, Carlos, 169n, 200–205, 220–23, 282–83

Nationalists, 61, 69, 78, 138, 228, 302; in armed forces, 54–57, 206, 318; and economy, 150–51, 204, 210–24; and Onganía, 172–73, 186–87; and political parties, 198–205. See also Levingston government
Navy, 52, 152, 200, 318
Niosi, Jorge, 36n, 127n
Normalization, economic: and agriculture, 115–16, 286; and BA, 32, 88–99, 189–91; challenges to, 45–46, 138–39, 143, 220–21; costs of, 120–27, 138–44, 160, 163, 293; end of,

184, 228, 244; and inflation, 104, 222; and investments, 147n, 211n; and orthodoxy, 96–97; profits under, 127–33; success of, 103–20, 138–44, 198, 282; and transnational capital, 126; and upper bourgeoisie, 90, 133–38, 168–69, 192, 219, 243n, 289, 302. See also Investment; Krieger Vasena; Wages and salaries
Nuñez Miñana, Horacio, 112n, 275n

O'Donnell, Guillermo, xiv(n), 28n, 36n, 37n9, 38n16, 53n, 69n1, 70n11, 100n6, 101n33, 102n34, 132n, 144n3, 164n, 196n6, 196n32, 196n33, 225n20, 262n10, 307n, 324n1, 325n17
Oil production, 50, 86n
Oliveira, Francisco de, 100n5
Onganía, government of, 59–69, 72–99, 145–63, 195, 309; and Argentine Revolution, 59–60, 74–75, 184–85; and Cordobazo, 164–68, 178–81; and economy, 85–99, 103–44; ouster of, 58, 171–73, 182–88, 197, 214, 218, 309; and paternalists, 57, 59–69; and unions, 82–87, 135–36, 148–58, 177–84; and upper bourgeoisie, 86–87, 96–99, 121, 147–49, 158, 166, 173, 264. See also Krieger Vasena; Normalization, economic; Paternalists
Onganía, Juan Carlos, 40n, 52–54, 57–76, 139, 185, 229, 233; and army, 151–52
Ongaro, Raimundo, 148–49
Oszlak, Óscar, xv, 92n

Paladino, Jorge Daniel, 153, 204n, 208, 246n, 247
Pampean bourgeoisie, 33–34, 42, 65, 127, 132–38, 141–42; and BA, 151, 183, 206, 243n; and prices, 222–23, 270–72, 283; and tax, 86n, 115–21, 134, 141
Panorama, 34
Paternalists, 59–61, 146, 167, 187, 197, 219–20, 302; and armed forces, 54–58, 138; and economy, 66–67, 74–77, 135–40, 154–57, 181–85; and Onganía, 57, 73, 173; and politics, 59, 74–76; and unions, 64–68, 80n, 83–84, 147–49, 175–84. See also Onganía, Juan Carlos
Perón, Eva, 7, 234
Perón, Juan Domingo, 68, 167–68, 240, 243, 301, 321; and elections, 247,

254, 260; and guerrillas, 240–41, 246–47, 311, 313; and Lanusse, 229–31, 252, 318; "National Revolution" of, 307, 317; and 1966 coup, 40, 62; presidency of, 323–24; presidential candidacy of, 241, 248, 256, 314–16; and unions, 82, 179

Peronism, 35, 40–53, 139–41, 148, 178, 195, 204, 207–8, 215, 229–40, 301, 323; and elections, 255–61; and Lanusse, 240–46, 253, 264; proscription of, 42–47, 51–53, 240, 257, 313, 322; radical, 153, 174, 208n, 242–48, 253, 305–8, 317–19, 323; and Radicals, 46–51, 153, 174, 208n; and unions, 42, 64n, 80, 213, 252, 288, 293

Peronist Youth, 242n, 306n, 307, 315

Peso: devaluation of, 66, 85–88, 94, 201–2, 212, 223; stability of, 114, 140, 169, 181

Pinedo, Jorge, 242n

Plan of Action. See CGT, and Plan of Action

Plunder, economy of, 21, 24, 29, 31, 89–97, 142–44, 284–89, 294

Political parties, 26–29, 44n, 56–64, 74–75, 153, 186, 201–10, 251n; and armed forces, 52–53, 173–74; and Lanusse, 227–29, 235–41, 246, 256–61, 320–21; and Peron, 315–16; proscription of, 32, 88, 154, 198–99

Popular sector, 44, 91–92, 160; exclusion of, 32, 46, 77–98, 161, 175, 191, 209, 301; and Peronism, 204, 231; political activation of, 1, 9–10, 14–15, 23, 139–42, 156, 167, 178, 184–89, 234–41, 251–52, 302–11; threat from, 25–28, 90, 162, 230. See also Pueblo; Unions

Porto, Horacio, 112n, 275n

Potash, Robert, 69n1

Poulantzas, Nicos, 37n8

Price agreements, 147, 179, 201

Price controls, 50, 66–67, 88, 183, 222–23, 228

Prices, 91–92, 132, 134, 179, 202, 206; for food, 120–21; freeze of, 114–15, 249; and wages, 270–72

Primera Plana, 34

Private investment, 22, 134–35, 143, 147n, 221–22, 249n, 277; in construction, 107, 115, 170, 281

Professionalists in armed forces, 52–57

Protest. See Factory occupations; Strikes; Student protest; Violence

Przeworski, Adam, xv, 324n1

Public investment, 41–42, 79, 104, 116–19, 222–23; in construction, 107, 281; decline of, 41, 125, 132; and economic orthodoxy, 98–99, 134–35n; in industry, 211n, 213

Pueblo, 4–10, 13, 23, 32, 56, 147, 189, 198–99, 203, 215–16, 234, 308; and armed forces, 47, 55, 172, 245; exclusion of, 189

Puiggrós, Rodolfo, 234n

Radical government, 41–52, 231; and Peronism, 46–51; violence under, 289–91

Radical party, 39, 139, 146n, 204–8, 227, 316n; and elections, 252–59, 315n, 319; and Lanusse, 239, 245, 249n, 254; and Peronism, 153, 174, 208n

Reca, Lucio, 144n2, 226n41

Redistribution of income, 99, 143, 147, 162, 207–9, 211, 219, 249n, 251

Repression, 23n, 28–29, 76, 161, 189, 201, 209, 230, 304; after Cordobazo, 165–66, 173–74, 186; of guerrillas, 250, 289, 292; and Peronism, 232; and unions, 44–48, 80n, 150, 176, 205, 293–94

Riots, 135n, 168n, 171, 232, 257

Rosario, 54, 159, 165n, 168n, 177n, 308–10

Roth, Roberto, 76n, 140n, 171n

Rouguié, Alain, 69n1

Russell, Charles, 262n15

Salimei, Jorge, 66–68, 72, 105, 282

Schenkel, James, 262n15

Schmitter, Philippe, xv, 38n16, 70n11, 164n

Schvarzer, Jorge, 133n

Selser, Gregorio, 100n1

Senén Gonzalez, Santiago, 40n, 65n, 149n

Serra, José, 100n5

Simon, Herbert, 37n13

Singer, Paulo, 100n5

62 Organizaciones de Pie, 68, 79n, 178, 179n, 182, 318n. See also Vandorists

Skidmore, Thomas, 100n5

Smith, William, xv(n)

Socialism, national, 307, 311

Socialist party, 208n

Solano Lima, Vicente, 315–19

Sourrouille, Juan V., 37n9, 37n10, 92n, 102n33, 125n, 144n4, 144n5, 170n

Speculation, financial, 20–21, 49, 91, 138, 143, 170, 249–50, 277, 283–86

SRA (Sociedad Rural Argentina), 34–35, 86n, 154n, 328
Stepan, Alfred, xv, 70n10, 225n12
Strike, right to, 135
Strikes, 44–50, 60–65, 135, 149, 156, 184, 201n, 212–13, 218, 250, 289–95, 305; in Brazil, 174n; dismissal for, 80, 81n; general, 159, 178, 188, 205, 211n, wildcat, 179, 230
Student protest, 67, 156–59, 174n, 184, 233, 250n

Tarragó, Trinidad Martínez, 37n9
Tax: on corporations, 86; revenues from, 98–99, 116–17, 275–76; withholding, 85, 88, 115–21, 134, 141, 182, 201
Textile workers' union, 64–66, 81, 150n
Theology of Liberation, 148, 159
TNC subsidiaries, 11–14, 36; and Krieger Vasena, 72–73; U.S.-based, 128, 130–31
TNCs (transnational corporations), 11, 214, 216; after Cordobazo, 170n; protest against, 159; subsidiaries of, 11–14, 36, 72–73, 128–31
Torre, Juan Carlos, 262n9, 292n, 304n
Transnational capital, 7, 9–14, 33, 41, 56, 134, 143, 198, 212, 219–20; after Cordobazo, 222; and military liberals, 61, 76, 78; and normalization program, 86–99, 106, 110, 126–27, 135, 139, 160, 180–81, 192; and Radical government, 49–50
Tucumán, 50, 205n
Turner, Frederick, 136n, 254n, 308n, 309, 313n

UIA (Unión Industrial Argentina), 33–35, 63n, 64n, 65n, 126n, 154n, 177n, 180n, 196n19, 212, 228n, 249n, 328
Unemployment, 157, 179
Union leaders: and Cámpora, 315, 323; and elections, 218, 235–36; and 1966 coup, 40n, 49n, 62, 68, 80n, 184, 294, 321; and Perón, 45, 50; Peronist, 241n, 250, 301, 314n, 317; and protest, 171, 178
Unions, 125–27, 166, 209; and collective bargaining, 154; defeat of, 79–85, 87, 292; and economic normalization, 45; funds of, 47, 80, 201–2, 250n, 257n; intervened, 81, 84, 85n, 149; and Lanusse, 229, 240–44; "legal personality" of, 80–82; and Levingston, 205; local, 291–92; national, 184, 202; and nationalism, 139, 199, 202,

205, 220; and Onganía's government, 64–66, 82–87, 135–36, 177–84; participationists in, 84–85, 148–58, 166, 175, 179, 185n, 213, 231; and paternalists, 64, 75–76, 135–40, 147–48, 177–84, 219; and Perón, 45, 68, 168, 231; and Peronism, 42–43, 153, 195, 235, 311–12; and protest, 44–48, 171, 178, 205, 212, 293; public employees', 63, 66, 68; and Radical government, 47–51; and violence, 172, 305. See also CGT; Strikes
United States, 50n, 66, 128, 130–31; aid from, 87; and Lanusse, 229
Universities, 39, 158–59, 174n, 304; intervention of, 62–63. See also Student protest
Upper bourgeoisie, 14, 31–35; and armed forces, 56, 165, 173, 237, 319; and democracy, 320; and economic orthodoxy, 86, 98–99; and Lanusse, 186, 228, 239–46; and Levingston government, 198–219; and normalization, 87, 96, 114n, 121, 130–33, 163, 190–92; and Onganía government, 61–68, 150–63, 175–80; and Perón, 242; and Peronism, 312–13; and price controls, 249–50; and repression, 80n, 166; and unions, 83, 85, 147–58, 176
Uruguay, 8–10, 22, 89, 134; BA in, xiii, 6, 27–28, 89, 160, 161

Vandor, Augusto, 68, 165n, 172n, 177n, 178, 243n
Vandorists, 44n, 68, 148–57, 166, 182, 292, 319; and CGT, 84, 213, 231; and strikes, 80n, 82, 179
Vergara, Pilar, 100n5
Villavicencia, Agapito, 115n
Villegas, Osiris, 70n15
Violence, 64, 167, 171–72, 264, 289–90, 295–300, 302–7, 313, 320, 323–24; and Lanusse government, 188, 304; and Levingston government, 201n; and Perón, 314n, 318n. See also Assassinations; Cordobazo; Guerrilla activity; Riots; Strikes
von Dellinger, Carlos, 37n9

Wage, minimum, 211n, 265, 268; and prices, 272
Wages and salaries, 67, 113, 128–30, 157, 265–72; control of, 50, 79, 92–94, 212n, 265; demands, 220–22, 250–51, 305; freeze on, 86–87, 114–15, 120, 154, 179, 201–2; increases

in, 89, 93, 130–32, 140, 156–57, 177–79, 182n, 205–6, 221–24, 228, 289; reductions in, 87, 101, 114, 129–36, 147, 277–78

Weffort, Francisco, xv, 7n, 37n6

Weinert, Richard, 7n

Wilkins, Myra, 37n9

Work stoppages, 50n, 65, 68, 250, 291, 327

Working class, 3, 48, 65, 135, 184; emergence of, 23; and Peronism, 311; and protest, 292, 308–9. *See also* Popular sector; Unions

Compositor: Huron Valley Graphics
Text: 10/13 Sabon
Display: Sabon
Printer: Edwards Brothers
Binder: Edwards Brothers